Governing the Corporation

Regulation and Corporate Governance in an Age of Scandal and Global Markets

Edited by

Justin O'Brien

John Wiley & Sons, Ltd

Other Wiley Editorial Offices

John Wiley & Sons Inc., 111 River Street, Hoboken, NJ 07030, USA

Jossey-Bass, 989 Market Street, San Francisco, CA 94103-1741, USA

Wiley-VCH Verlag GmbH, Boschstr. 12, D-69469 Weinheim, Germany

John Wiley & Sons Australia Ltd, 42 McDougall Street, Milton, Queensland 4064, Australia

John Wiley & Sons (Asia) Pte Ltd, 2 Clementi Loop #02-01, Jin Xing Distripark, Singapore 129809

John Wiley & Sons Canada Ltd, 22 Worcester Road, Etobicoke, Ontario, Canada M9W 1L1

Wiley also publishes its books in a variety of electronic formats. Some content that appears in
print may not be available in electronic books.

Library of Congress Cataloging-in-Publication Data

Governing the corporation : regulation and corporate governance in an age of scandal and global
    markets / edited by Justin O'Brien.
        p.   cm.
    Includes bibliographical references and index.
    ISBN-13 978-0-470-01506-3 (cloth : alk. paper)
    ISBN-10 0-470-01506-3 (cloth : alk. paper)
    1. Corporate governance—Law and legislation.   2. Corporations—Accounting—Law and
legislation.   3. Corporations—Corrupt practices.   4. Corporate governance.   I. O'Brien, Justin.
    K1327.G68 2005
    346′.0662—dc22
                                                                                  2005010795

British Library Cataloguing in Publication Data

A catalogue record for this book is available from the British Library

ISBN 13 978-0-470-01506-3 (HB)
ISBN 10 0-470-01506-3 (HB)

Typeset in 11/13pt Goudy by Integra Software Services Pvt. Ltd, Pondicherry, India
Printed and bound in Great Britain by TJ International Ltd, Padstow, Cornwall, UK
This book is printed on acid-free paper responsibly manufactured from sustainable forestry
in which at least two trees are planted for each one used for paper production.

Contents

List of Contributors

Paul Appleby is Director of the Office of the Director of Corporate Enforcement, Dublin.

Neill Buck is a director and managing partner of Neil Buck & Associates Pty Limited, Sydney.

Jeremy P. Carver is Head of International Law at Clifford Chance, London.

J. Patrick Dobel is Professor of Public Affairs at the Evans School of Public Affairs, University of Washington, Seattle.

George Gilligan is Logan Senior Research Fellow in the Department of Business Law and Taxation, Faculty of Business and Economics, Monash University, Clayton, Australia.

Nicholas M. Hodson is Director of Investigative & Dispute Services, Ernst & Young LLP, Toronto.

Irene Lynch-Fannon is Professor of Law at University College Cork.

Doreen McBarnet is Professor of Socio-Legal Studies at the Centre for Socio-Legal Studies, University of Oxford.

Dermot McCann is a Senior Lecturer in Politics in the Department of Law, Governance and International Relations, London Metropolitan University.

William J. McDonough is Chairman of the Public Company Accounting Oversight Board, Washington DC.

Andrea Melis is a Lecturer in Business at the Faculty of Economics, University of Cagliari.

Giovanni Melis is Professor of Accounting at the Faculty of Economics, University of Cagliari.

Justin O'Brien is Director of the Corporate Governance Programme at the School of Law, Queen's University, Belfast.

Alexander A. Schaub is Director General, Internal Market at the European Commission, Brussels.

Laureen Snider is Professor of Sociology at Queen's University, Kingston, Ontario.

David M. Walker is Comptroller General of the United States and Head of the Government Accountability Office, Washington DC.

Lisa Whitehouse is Senior Lecturer in Law at the University of Hull.

Acknowledgements

This volume demonstrates that the crisis in the probity of the corporate form does not have a geographical patent. Malfeasance (a criminal act) and misfeasance (an ethically challenged but technically legal transaction) on the scale witnessed in global capital markets provide compelling evidence to discount the parcelling of blame to corrupted actors alone. The intertwined malaise necessitates that we place equal attention on the governance of the structures in and through which individual corporate and institutional actors operate. To be effective this process requires breaking out of the self-imposed confines of traditional academic silos. Each perspective, while partially illuminating, fails to capture how the concept of governance impacts on the state's capacity to enforce its will on corporate power. How to govern the corporation has become too important and too complex an issue for a single disciplinary focus to adequately frame.

This belief underpinned the international colloquium organised by the Institute of Governance, Public Policy and Social Research at Queen's University, Belfast, in September 2004, from which this collection draws. Centred on evaluating the praxis between social science theory and corporate reality, the gathering was designed to act as a stimulus for the recalibration of public policy towards financial market regulation. The aim was to provide a more granular understanding of the dynamics through which corporate governance and regulatory oversight is politically constructed in response to the contingent nexus of internal and external influences on global markets.

The papers from practitioners, policymakers and academics led to robust and important arguments within and between particular disciplines over the nature of the malaise and the efficacy of proposed solutions. The introduction of critical perspectives from criminology, socio-legal studies, ethics and political science alongside the traditional disciplinary strengths of corporate and securities law and economics allow for a more holistic approach to one of the defining issues of the modern age. The selection included here gives a snapshot of both the intellectual energy and fresh insights that emerge from engaging in such rich dialogical exchange.

I am grateful to the management team at the Institute for their unstinting support in the development of the corporate governance research programme. The Director, Professor Elizabeth Meehan, and Deputy Director, Dr John Barry, provided the financial resources to stage the event and were at hand to provide academic guidance.

My colleagues at the Institute, Dr Ciaran O'Kelly and Ms Bronagh Hinds, provided exceptional support in coordinating the management of the colloquium in conjunction with the office manager, Barbara de Bruin, and event administrator, Catherine Madden. They were ably assisted by a team of doctoral candidates who, like more established academics and staff, freely gave their time to make the event such a success. Professor Istemi Demirag chaired a number of sessions and worked the room with consummate ease. Other session chairs, including Professor Sally Simpson of the University of Maryland, Professor Christopher Napier of the University of Southampton and Professor Michael Moran, provided key insights that helped to frame a series of research questions on accountability and governance in the private sector that extend far beyond the confines of one particular gathering.

Through events such as the colloquium and the related LLM in Corporate Governance and Public Policy, which I direct, Queen's has established an international reputation in this field. The senior management team at the School of Law recognises clearly the strategic importance of linking together pioneering research with dissemination to students and the wider community. The late Professor Steven Livingstone was a key catalyst for this programme. The Head of School, Professor John Morison, and my colleague on the corporate governance programme, Professor Sally Wheeler, have ensured that this vision has been translated into reality. They have been enormously helpful in transforming the *Zeitgeist* into innovative teaching and research agendas.

I have had the added advantage of an exceptional sparring partner in the form of Professor Mel Dubnick, who has taught me more than he realises about both the intricacies of American governance and the means to map its regulatory landscape. After formative years spent trying to persuade me that accountancy was interesting, my close friend Michael Scallon was invaluable in helping to understand the dynamics of the corporation. In extended conversations on both sides of the Atlantic, Nick Hodson demonstrated how to reach the moral core of the audit process. At Wiley, Rachael Wilkie and Chris Swain handled this project with the quiet professionalism that has become their trademark. At the later stages, the project editors, Vivienne Wickham and Samantha Hartley, accepted the inevitable revisions with unerring good grace.

My family provided a secure and stable environment in which to piece together the final form of this book. My wife Darina and children Elise, Jack and Justin were resigned to yet another absence and gave me the space to write. I am enormously thankful to them.

Finally, I would like to dedicate this book to the memory of my late parents, Jack and Peggy, who would be delighted to see their son return to the academy.

Justin O'Brien
School of Law
Queen's University, Belfast
June 2005

1

Governing the Corporation: Regulation and Corporate Governance in an Age of Scandal and Global Markets

Justin O'Brien

A vibrant well-administrated corporate sector is vital for economic development, social and political cohesion and access to international capital. In the aftermath of global corporate scandal, governance and regulatory reform can provide demonstrable substantive financial advantage while serving market and the wider public interest by restoring confidence. Equally, flawed structural changes can, at best, exert onerous costs and, at worst, legitimise conflicts of interest. Behind the illusion of fundamental change control mechanisms may be devoid of substance. This, in turn, can lead to a suboptimal allocation of resources in the fight against corporate malfeasance and misfeasance, its more problematic ethical variant.

For regulators, policymakers and academics alike, the critical question is how to assuage public concern while protecting the market from the deleterious effects of panic. Always a difficult balancing act, managing that process has become even more problematic with the deepening securitisation of the global economy (Braithwaite and Drahos 2000). The central corporate and public policy imperative is to ascertain whether an emergent global financial architecture capable of intersecting with national regulatory regimes will result in normatively improved governance structures or merely facilitate the global export of the pathological gaming that informed the operation of US capital markets on the cusp of the millennium.

While convergence is not necessarily path-dependent, changing US practice makes the transformation of global regulatory practice inevitable. The remarkable leverage gained by the regulatory model advanced by Washington is positively related not only to the country's geopolitical hegemony but also to the depth and liquidity of its capital markets. This further enhances the capacity of institutional actors working with and through the Securities and Exchange Commission and other regulatory bodies such as the Public Company Accounting Oversight Board to influence the promulgation of globally applicable standards. The provisions required for US listing act as the baseline for global capital markets, influencing not only international capital flows but the structures of national regulatory regimes.

Just as important as the capacity to create regulatory instruments is the ability to manage their enforcement. The form that enforcement takes is determined by the relative power of diverse actors within the corporate governance and regulatory equation. Law is primarily a social construct (Stryker 1994). How it is interpreted and applied depends on the clarity of the initial legislation and the degree to which its provisions are accepted by key players with separate and discrete access to policy-makers. The capacity to generate a superficially rational discourse based on the institutionalisation of technical compliance, fostered by the noise of contestation that drives media discourse, can place limits on subsequent juridical adjudication (Strine 2002). Policy legitimacy, therefore, owes its origins not simply to economic rationality but the ideational capacity to create and sustain assumptions of what constitutes the limits of acceptable behaviour in the corporate world.

While the 'state', manifested in institutional form by organisations such as the Securities and Exchange Commission, retains the residual power to regulate the markets, the form and function of that oversight are dependent on wider strategic, political and financial considerations. As the battles over the internal reporting provisions of the stringent Sarbanes-Oxley legislation on corporate liability demonstrate (Romano 2004), the legitimacy of corporate governance and regulatory reform in the United States itself remains exceptionally contested. Despite ostensible resolve, there is a profound danger that the creative interpretation of codified limits will lead to a subversion of publicly stated policy imperatives.

Underpinning all policy innovation governing financial regulation is the need to enhance transparency and accountability within corporations and the markets in which they operate. Galbraith (2004, 44) has noted recently that we must come to terms with 'the basic fact of the twenty-first century – a corporate system based on the unrestrained power of self-enrichment'. The fact that the fashionable demimonde (Bakan 2004; Klein 2000) has recruited an economist of Galbraith's stature could demonstrate either the contrariness of old age or a growing appreciation of the critical nature of the problem. While many of the contributors to this volume concur with Galbraith's bleak assessment of contemporary reality, the cynicism is displaced by proffering credible ways to critically examine and decon- struct the determinants of public policy.

The exploration by George Gilligan of how particular regulatory approaches are given global traction provides a talismanic case study of this dynamic in action. He does not doubt that cooperation can have profound normative benefit but calls for a greater understanding and appreciation of the social and political construction of what is regarded as legitimate. For Gilligan, legitimacy is an 'elastic' essentially ideological concept. Its exact focus is determined by the contingent capacity of state and institutional actors to alter the prism. Gilligan's multi-lateral framework allows us to gauge 'how gatekeepers emerge, operate, and in particular, adapt their strategies and structures, but also can act as a window on some of the key political determinants in contemporary governance praxis'.

Investigating the scandals unleashed by the collapse of Enron and WorldCom bears witness to the efficacy of this approach. In the context of a catastrophic implosion of confidence at a critical stage in the electoral cycle, something clearly had to be done, or, just as importantly, be seen to be done. The rapidity of the American political, regulatory and judicial response, linked directly and solely to domestic factors, has had profound global consequences. These are arguably as far reaching as the original ideological imperatives that helped to denigrate oversight in the first place. In fact, they are potentially even more destabilising in the longer term precisely because the reassuring balm of codification indicates that corporate governance reform has been effective.

Given the pressing nature of the problem it is ironic how little reflection on normative democratic theory is reflected in the academic study of corporate governance and financial regulation (cf. Polanyi 1944; Dobel 1999; Shapiro 2003). How power impacts on the construction and recalibration of public policy is often seen as tangential to a field that has become mired in questions of technical procedure. The malaise has reached such crisis proportions that this myopia is unsustainable. It is in the self-interest of the corporate form itself to resile from the exercise of what is perceived to be unaccountable and uncontrolled power. Yet, there is no evidence that this is happening. Noting that reformers faced an 'uphill fight', the chairman of the Securities and Exchange Commission, William Donaldson, pointedly chose a meeting of the industry-funded US Conference Board to launch a coruscating attack on the dangers of continued sharp practice.

> This erosion of trust in business is a serious and worrying development, and there's no guarantee the problem will automatically get resolved. While regulators such as the SEC can enact bright, red-line rules about what is and is not permissible behaviour, we know from the course of history that human nature will push aggressive managers and organizations to continue to test new laws. Some managers will pursue questionable activity right up to technical conformity with the letter of the law, and some will step over the red line either directly or with crafty schemes and modern financial technology that facilitates deception. The SEC and others like us can set the rules and define independence – but legal definitions can only go so far. And our free market, democratic system will gradually erode, and inevitably suffer grievous harm, if remedial efforts are not undertaken and endorsed by a broad cross-section of our business and financial communities. (Donaldson 2004)[1]

The chapters in this volume have been specifically commissioned to address why structural and systemic corporate governance and regulation problems in global markets remain intractable issues. In so doing, they amplify, in theoretical terms, the practical concerns raised by the SEC chairman. The central arguments are encapsulated in Lisa Whitehouse's assertion that 'academics and politicians alike appear to have lost sight of or have refused to acknowledge the fundamental threat to democracy posed by corporate power'. The capacity of the corporation, acting as a private entity, to subvert democratic norms occurs in myriad, often unaccountable ways. These range from the distortion caused to the deliberative process through inordinate financing of political systems to contempt from juridical norms by calculating the benefits of recidivism, a point highlighted here by the criminologist Laureen Snider.

The global crisis is a direct result of the triangulated tension between rhetorical mission statements at both corporate and political levels, corporate disregard for these aspirations and the limitations of statute or regulatory instrument to modify behaviour. Despite the ideational certainty of enfranchised self-regulation of the financial markets through 'associational governance' (Streeck and Schmitter 1985), its repeated failure threatens a profound legitimacy crisis. Franchising authority to associations, whose primary interest is to define, organise, secure and advance the agendas of their most vocal and influential members without outside policing capacity, creates an intractable conflict of interest. Far from offering normative improvements in policymaking, the putative paradigm identified by Streeck and Schmitter magnifies the risk of state capture through inertia rather than regulatory empire building.

This dynamic was a major contributing factor to the scandals in the United States. Professional associations – accountants, lawyers, corporate directors – acting as political groupings, emphasised the wider benefits accruing to society from liberalising still further the machinations of the market system without due cognisance of the need to buttress the regulatory architecture. Technical compliance with regulatory instruments agreed after consultation but wholesale derogation in spirit overwhelmed the system. The resulting strain was unsupportable, paving the way for structural implosion, a point made forcefully by J. Patrick Dobel with his devastating use of the 'perfect storm' analogy. This meteorological metaphor is usually favoured by business leaders to obviate direct causal responsibility (O'Brien 2003, 63–64). From the perspective outlined by Dobel, the sustained failure by business leaders to take direct responsibility for how their emasculation of oversight contributed to the crisis means that regulatory gaming remains unresolved. The essentially subservient position accorded to the state through market self-governance is by no means confined to the eastern seaboard of the Atlantic. Some critics suggest this is the defining aspect of globalisation. Both states and state institutions 'are increasingly transformed into agents of transnational neoliberalism... States and state actors may pursue ostensibly distinct strategies and use different tactics; however, these constitute not so much competing national models as different roads to neoliberal globalisation' (Cerny 2002, 202–203). The analysis of corporate governance reform in the United Kingdom and Germany carried out by Dermot McCann for this volume demonstrates how this dynamic operates across two countries within the European Union. In both, he concludes, 'economic change generates the impetus for reform and politics is concerned with its accommodation'.

The politics of regulation tends, ultimately, to be the politics of symbolism (Edelman 1964), with reassurance replacing tangible and decisive behaviour-modification (Hood *et al.* 2004). The reforms only tangentially address the root cause of the malaise: gatekeeper failure, excessive executive compensation and the inability of a regulatory architecture designed in the 1930s to support the much more complex financial structure erected using the mortar of securitisation. These failings are partially occluded by the propensity to concentrate on form over substance, a response which is intricately linked to elite preferences over the governance of the market system as a whole (Lindblom 2001, 248–250).

If corruption thrives in situations where motive and opportunity exceed the probability of getting caught, the global market control failure arose as a consequence of an application of a cost–benefit calculus based on the rationality of substantive recidivism. Viewed from this vantage point, critical design defects in the two main regulatory strategies adopted to combat the rising tide of scandal become immediately apparent.

The first approach, primarily associated with the United States, offers a solution based on greater legislative and regulatory codification. The centrepiece was the passage of the Public Company Accounting Reform and Investor Protection Act 2002, or Sarbanes-Oxley. It serves four interlinked purposes. It creates new structures to regulate the audit process and the profession; offers greater protection for whistleblowers; increases the responsibilities and criminal liabilities of corporate boards; and enhances the authority of the SEC to police the market. As such, Sarbanes-Oxley imposes new restrictions on the capacity of corporations seeking to raise finance on US capital markets. To secure access to the liquidity offered on the primary exchanges all corporations, regardless of domicile, must follow the more restrictive provisions of the Act. They must also follow stricter listing requirements mandated by the primary exchanges under the guidance of a more assertive SEC.

The fact that the US system was overrun despite already having one of the most codified securities markets in the world, with a plethora of interlocking federal, state and self-regulating organisations, suggests the limitations of a transactional approach (Partnoy 2002). More ominously, proscription could, in fact, prove counterproductive. Reordering the realms of acceptability by virtue of compliance with statute serves only to reconfigure the board. It fails to change ethical imperatives either inside the corporation or, more seriously, within the professions, which retain an emasculated conception of what fiduciary duty entails, themes developed by the contributions by McBarnet and Dobel to this volume.

As Laureen Snider points out in her perceptive analysis of recidivism,

> state reluctance to hold capital to account in the past has produced a series of regulatory cycles, each beginning with a high-profile event – a major bridge collapse or ferry accident, a series of frauds, massive corporate bankruptcies. The event is typically followed by volumes of lofty rhetoric from various politicians and officials, and eventually by draft legislation. After a series of revisions, new laws are passed. They are usually much weaker than originally promised, and in some cases totally unenforceable.

Juridical and regulatory activism can be given further populist traction by skilful media manipulation, attenuating the public impression that decisive action has been taken while leaving intact the structural problems that gave rise to the initial crisis.

The obvious discomfiture of previously lionized executives now paraded in handcuffs is a public demonstration of the enforcement myth (Sparrow 2000) that no one is above the equal application of the law. Delve beneath the surface-level analysis of the mainstream media and more difficult issues emerge. In large part, the executives are not being tried on substantive issues but the more prosaic and easier to prosecute charges of lying to or obstructing federal investigators (O'Brien 2004a). Indicative here are the trials of Frank Quattrone, former chief technology banker at Credit Suisse First Boston, and Martha Stewart, chief executive of her eponymous corporation. While the Quattrone cases (the first ended in a mistrial) highlighted significant corruption in the awarding of lucrative initial public offerings, this key issue was not on the indictment and receded from public view.[2]

Stewart's tenure as a director of the New York Stock Exchange and chief executive of Living Omnimedia came to a premature end as a result of a personal stock transaction in a friend's pharmaceutical company the day before the Federal Drug Administration refused to license one of its key products. Despite a media discourse that initially focused on allegations of insider trading, this lapse was not on the indictment. Stewart played the media very effectively, choosing to appeal the guilty verdict but report to prison in the interim. From a business perspective it was a shrewd calculation. It provided personal closure and saved her corporation from languishing through the uncertainty associated with the temporary freedom accorded to a criminal founder. Since reporting to jail, her stock worth has tripled in value. Tapping into the American *Zeitgeist* of personal renewal and redemption through acceptance of responsibility and punishment, Stewart was released from prison in March 2005. Unlike most convicts, Stewart was released late at night and brought by a convoy to a waiting executive jet. A message posted on her website proclaimed that the experience was

> life changing and life affirming. Someday, I hope to have the chance to talk more about all that has happened, the extraordinary people I have met here and all that I have learned. I can tell you now that I feel very fortunate to have had a family that nurtured me, the advantage of an excellent education, and the opportunity to pursue the American dream. You can be sure that I will never forget the friends that I met here, all that they have done to help me over these five months, their children, and the stories they have told me. (www.marthastewart.com)[3]

It tapped into a journalistic narrative that had been refashioned to brand the demigod of home design as a paragon of restored virtue.

The Stewart case is far from unique. Henry Blodget, the internet analyst who was barred from the securities industry for life as a consequence of his manipulation of research reports following the New York Attorney General's investigation of systemic conflicts of interest in 2002, surfaced again during the Stewart trial as a media commentator. Sanford Weill, the chief executive of Citigroup was nominated to serve on the board of the New York Stock Exchange in 2003, despite presiding over a corporation that was and remains mired in controversy over its role in the financial scandals. His withdrawal from consideration came only after protests from state regulators (O'Brien 2003).[4]

As prosecutors in New York found to their chagrin in the defenestration of Dennis Kozlowski, former chief executive of Tyco, the conflation of malfeasance with misfeasance carries the risk of blowback. After a six-month trial in 2004, the jury failed to reach a verdict and the judge declared a mistrial. Corporately approved but morally questionable ostentation may be a rhetorical weapon of choice but offers little chance of penetrating the protective shield of creative compliance in a judicial court. While this book was going to press, the New York District Attorney recalibrated the case against Kozlowski, with the detail of obscene spending sprees shorn from the indictment, if not the popular record. Kozlowski still maintained that this was a politically motivated prosecution and that his actions were approved by the board, an interpretation rejected by the second jury which convicted him and his chief financial officer in June 2005. Bernie Ebbers, the disgraced chief executive of WorldCom charged with orchestrating the largest accounting fraud in history, maintained that he was the victim of unscrupulous underlings. This defence was treated with derision by the prosecution in its closing arguments to the jury: 'You have been fed the "aw shucks, I'm not sophisticated" defence. It insults your intelligence that Ebbers could have built this company up from nothing in 10 years and still be clueless about its financial performance' (*New York Times*, 4 March 2005). The jury agreed, convicting him on all charges. A similar defence is likely to be used by Ken Lay, however, when the former chairman of Enron goes on trial in Texas. For epicures of crime, greed and hubris, across 2006 there are no better venues than the federal and state courthouses of Manhattan and Houston. There is, however, a gaping hole in the cast assembled for the reality version of a revived morality play. Like Banquo's ghost, the system itself is missing from the proceedings.

As Doreen McBarnet notes perceptively, it is essential that the true lessons of Enron be internalised. She makes the point that the corporation may have been economical with the truth but that 'it is arguable that much of Enron's off-balance sheet activity did not breach the rules . . . This is not to defend Enron. On the contrary it is merely to refine the charges.' McBarnet's analysis provides a much needed corrective to the hysteria surrounding the actions of the corporation as a unique malevolent force. It repositions critical questioning to the degree of responsibility that should be shouldered by systemic actors: complicit investment bankers and corporate lawyers willing to provide 'perfectly legal' letters of comfort. Corporations are not mandated to disclose how many legal or investment houses it had to scour before sourcing the requisite letter. McBarnet concludes that 'if change is to come, it is not just the law we need to address but the attitude towards law assumed by those subject to it, and the pervasive culture that fosters it'. She suggests that changing that mindset requires institutionalising an ethical component in strategic decision-making.

It is precisely this issue that animates those proponents of the second approach to corporate governance reform. Centred on the articulation of general guidelines of best practice, it leaves considerable discretion to corporations to operationalise the principles according to specific circumstances. These principles have, however, not remained constant over time. Indeed, the history of corporate governance reform in the UK, long recognised as a 'thought-leader' in industry-driven reform (Solomon and Solomon 2004), encapsulates the danger. Here, the single most important causal factor facilitating reform has been the attempt by associational groups to stave off external oversight (Moran 2003; McCann, this volume). This, in itself, of course, represents proto-formalisation. It also indicates that a reliance on vague and unenforceable statements of intent is an insufficient defence against regulatory gaming. Creative interpretation becomes the currency of choice for legal minds enriched when corporations grapple with ethics within a business context.

Despite outward appearances, therefore, neither policy response offers adequate protection from a rapacious management augmented by professional hired guns and faced only by somnambulant boards, now pressed into service at the new frontline in the war against corporate malefaction. Even if the European project can ensure the maintenance and enforcement capabilities of wider principles of corporate governance, it still has to deal with the problems caused by the major theoretical shortcomings associated with the application of the principal–agent paradigm. If diffuse ownership weakens the power of 'principals' the reality of organisational forms in both 'insider' and 'outsider' models of corporate control weakens the exculpatory guilt of management as 'agents'. This occurs precisely because of the existence of 'double' or 'multiple' agency relationships within divisions of the corporation and between the corporation and networked partnerships. This makes it difficult to ascertain the identity of the principal and complicates the search for effective accountability and control systems. Hierarchical organisational forms have been rendered outdated by the complexity of major corporations and the markets in which they operate. In addition, hierarchy suffers from its own shortfalls because of the propensity of subordinates to filter out bad information. A reliance on a hierarchical board without the institutionalisation of cultural restraint serves only a symbolic purpose.

The soap-operatic scheming for the control of Hollinger across the United States and Canada (O'Brien 2004b) or the implosion of the Italian diary-foods conglomerate Parmalat (Melis and Melis, this volume) following alarming failures of due diligence in the placing of corporate bonds in New York, and the banking scandals in the Irish Republic

(Appleby, this volume) make abundantly clear that the difficulties of enforceable restraint cut across regulatory forms. As Melis and Melis argue, it is unsustainable to blame the excesses within Parmalat on the egregious behaviour of the controlling Tanzi family. The collapse of the firm should be viewed as a talismanic example of systemic corporate governance failure that occurred as a result of regulatory gaming and deliberate myopia among those who ostensibly hold a residual fiduciary responsibility for upholding the integrity of the market.

This highlights one of the most serious design flaws. Both codification and more granular articulation of general principles are predicated on the introduction of control systems that limit opportunity. Neither solution deals in a systematic manner with the twin problems of motivation and rationalisation, arguably much more problematic and central concerns. As a result, misfeasance continues to be rationalised as part of acceptable rules of the game across both main regulatory types. The pressure to meet financial metrics for personal (stock option) or corporate gain (avoiding analytic displeasure) continues to provide motivation for misfeasance, the kind of sharp practice that tips all too often into malfeasance.

This concern forms a strong supporting argument in the review of the design blueprint conducted here by Comptroller General of the United States, David Walker. As head of the Government Accountability Office, Walker is ideally placed to map the changed regulatory environment. A former partner with Arthur Andersen, Walker argues that codification will not in itself provide a panacea unless it is linked directly to improvements in personal ethics and integrity. He accepts that while the fulcrum for the fundamental shift required must start with the board, the centre of gravity must extend outwards to encompass all those involved in state or quasi-state fiduciary oversight if stability is to be vouchsafed.

The moral dangers of the critical gaming these institutional actors engage in are articulated with great passion by William McDonough, Chairman of the Public Company Accounting Oversight Board. For McDonough the problems stem from the fact that business leaders have lost the navigational aid of a 'moral compass'. He condemns 'obscene' levels of compensation linked to the misguided 'drive for ever-increasing and fully predictable quarterly profits'. These are strong words for a former chairman of the Federal Reserve Bank of New York. The short-term tactical meeting of Wall Street metrics in markets defined by diffuse ownership, a growing preponderance of hedge funds over traditional corporations and hyper-competition in the provision of professional services intensify the moral hazard. They progressively weaken integrity and contribute to 'the corrosion of character' (Sennett 1999) that is symptomatic of the corporate age.

Recent survey evidence suggests that the integration of an ethical component in strategic decision-making is now an overwhelming corporate priority (O'Brien 2005). So too, however, is the determination by corporate leaders to repeal or dilute external oversight, based on the argument that governance reform has become too expensive, with regulators too aggressive, emboldened by unrealistic expectations that risk can be legislated out of existence. As the rhetoric takes on ever shriller tones, regulators are feeling the pressure.

Now that Congress has acted and passed what, on paper, amounts to the most sweeping securities reform since the 1930s, the media and political spotlight has moved on, leaving the negotiation of details to technical experts under constant but subtle pressure to conform to industry norms. Building slowly but unmistakably, the underlying message is that quiescence with what are perceived to be inappropriate and unwarranted interferences in the private affairs of corporate citizens is time-limited. The pessimism of the Donaldson speech cited above is indicative of how little corporate America has internalised the lessons of the recent past. To a certain extent the regulators have only themselves to blame.

The governance changes introduced since the collapse of Enron have failed to deliver on their stated objectives precisely because of an inordinate emphasis on the form of rules rather than their underlying function. This emasculated conception of governance pre-ordains future ethical lapses while offering intellectual ammunition for the critics of external oversight that the reforms introduced are merely a charter for job creation in the legal and accounting profession (Romano 2004). It is therefore imperative that the limitation of the corporate governance paradigm as presently construed is investigated and the function of regulation interrogated.

Corporate governance centres primarily on the 'direction and control' of corporations (OECD 2004). The range and responsibilities of the actors involved in that process, however, depend on the wider national socio-legal environment in which the corporation is domiciled or its shares primarily traded. They can extend beyond a narrow legalistic form to encompass not just conventional corporate practice but also implicit and explicit obligations to employees and other stakeholders.

The debate on the normative limits of corporate governance inquiry has, however, been heavily influenced by Anglo-American terms of reference. This concentrates solely on the tripartite relationship between the board, management and the shareholders and suggests that the governance of a corporation is an essentially private matter. Even when that relationship is extended to encompass the interests of stakeholders – including employees; the communities in which it operates (actualised through corporate social responsibility programmes); or wider society – there is a privileging of rights and concomitant ordering of legal priorities. The extent that critical perspectives are given voice and status depends not just on legal statute but the relative strength of ideational concepts that are given legitimacy through national, supra-regional and international organisations.

As Lynch-Fannon points out, given the centrality of the corporation and corporate power in today's world, the regulation of corporate governance profoundly influences the nature of society. She criticises the propensity of academic scholarship in the United States to buttress a hegemonic conception of the corporation as a private entity. This, she argues, privileges 'managerial prerogative and present[s] very little demands in terms of managerial and corporate accountability'. The inordinate strength of individual private rights is contrasted with what she terms the more 'communitarian understanding of corporate function' in the European Union, outside of the United Kingdom and (to a more limited extent) the Republic of Ireland.

The European model, she argues, is predicated on an acute understanding of the corporation as a social entity, a formulation that more closely corresponds with Asian conceptions of corporate responsibility to the society in which it is nested. She cites how workers' rights to be consulted in all major strategic decisions are enshrined through the operation of a two tier board in Germany. As such the role of the corporation in society is much more broadly defined than in the United Kingdom and the United States, where much of the debate on the efficacy of proposed theoretical and practical measures to improve corporate governance design originates.

The forces of globalisation place inordinate strain on the capacity of states or even regional groupings to uphold differentiated responses because of the power of epistemic communities. As the political economist Philip Cerny (2002, 195) has pointed out, 'the state is being cut across by multilayered networks of influence, interests and decision-making and enmeshed in more and more complex and hybrid webs of governance'. The analysis provided by Dermot McCann of corporate governance reform in Germany confirms this dynamic. He argues that 'the objective of enhancing shareholder value is much more central to management thinking than has been the case heretofore'. Likewise, the OECD Principles on Corporate Governance (OECD 2004) make it abundantly clear that the protection of shareholder interest is a pre-eminent concern across both traditions. This has the effect of limiting governance to a procedural tool designed to curtail management.

The growing power of equity markets and the related securitisation of the global economy, therefore, place considerable strain on corporate diversity, a point tacitly accepted by Alexander Schaub, the Director of Internal Markets at the European Commission. For Schaub,

> convergence matters both for investors and for issuers. Investors must be certain to benefit from the same level of protection no matter whether they invest in the EU or in the US. Companies need a level playing field with their competitors. Convergence contributes to restoring confidence and building trust in our markets.

Acknowledging the competing dynamics of suspicion towards European integration, Schaub offers a sticking plaster solution that is based on being firm on the principles underpinning corporate governance, but flexible in their application. Whether this will prove sufficient to stem the deleterious effects of amoral behaviour on the capital markets remains very much an open question.

The economic benefit of integrity and the need to anchor business practices and governance within a framework capable of overriding systemic gaming informs the debate carried out by regulators and academics alike in this volume. As David Walker points out, 'restoring public trust and confidence over the long-term will require continuous and concerted actions by various parties to overcome past systemic weaknesses in corporate governance, accountability and related systems'. This requires a fundamental overhaul of corporate governance struc-tures based on the integration of transparency, accountability and integrity through leadership and innovation. This is certainly an ambitious course of action. It suggests that while ethics cannot be legislated for, society can ensure that the markets are adequately governed. The question is whether this can be achieved within the largely unchal-lenged ideational paradigm that makes self-regulation (outside of the auditing profession) both an operational and strategic imperative.

Both the Comptroller General and William McDonough, chair of the Public Company Accounting Oversight Board, argue that it can. Positive change, in their opinion, can be achieved through a calibration of incentive structures and the inculcation of an ethical tone that has the potential to seep down and infuse decision-making across the organisation. Other senior policymakers in the United States call for a much more radical surgery to eradicate the cancer of malfeasance. Chief among them is the New York Attorney General, Eliot Spitzer, the focus of the substantive chapter by O'Brien in this volume.

With a powerbase serendipitously located at the intersection of economic and political governance against the backdrop of the pre-eminent global financial capital, Spitzer has skilfully maximised his leverage to act as a successful if controversial policy entrepreneur. The US Chamber of Commerce has been particularly vociferous in its opposition, accusing the New York Attorney General of acting as 'judge, jury and executioner'. The Chamber has also lodged a 'friend of the court' brief in a case involving a challenge to the 'fair disclosure' rules established by the SEC. Stating that the disclosure restrictions amounted to a threat to a 'free, robust, order and democratic society', the brief continues:

> Regulation F[air] D[isclosure] requires corporate executives either to share their material business information with no one, so as to avoid triggering the disclosure requirement, or to share it with everyone. The former result chills protected expression; the latter mandates unwanted speech. In either case, Regulation FD impermissibly violates corporate executives' right to freedom of association and expression. (*New York Times* 4 March 2005)

Spitzer's importance rests on the fact that the competing dynamics of federalism has provided an important check on the capacity of industry to cow the main federal regulatory agencies. As O'Brien demonstrates, there is considerable merit in Spitzer's criticism of the initial startled inaction of the Securities and Exchange Commission and the gross negligence displayed by the New York Stock Exchange under the tenure of the now disgraced Dick Grasso, which is now subject to state court adjudication. While the methods deployed to position the office of State Attorney General as a key manufacturer of federal market regulation have indeed been controversial, regulators and business alike are aware that the systemic defects revealed as a consequence necessitate change, if only to limit the interference of a State Attorney General in need of press coverage to fund his recently announced 2006 gubernatorial campaign. As William Donaldson proclaimed in a recent speech in London, passivity is simply no longer an option.

> The overwhelming majority of investors – regardless of their nationality and regardless of where they are investing – demand honesty and integrity. They demand that boards of directors take their fiduciary duties seriously. They demand that companies have the internal controls they need in order to ensure the accuracy of their financial disclosures. And when there is fraud or where securities laws or regulations are violated, investors rightly expect regulatory authorities to aggressively pursue enforcement action. (Donaldson 2005)

Corporate failure and fraud are, of course, constant variables in business life. By its very nature fraud is designed to remain undetected. In order to deal with a corporate system that is, as senior investment bankers in New York have privately confided to this author, 'hopelessly corrupt' (O'Brien 2003), the investigative process needs significant redesign. Despite the reforms mandated by Sarbanes-Oxley the financial reporting model remains wedded to certification and verification based on albeit weakened presumptions of management good faith.

Nick Hodson, taking up the challenge laid down by Walker for the design of effective control mechanisms, makes clear that the audit process itself needs to be subjected to a fundamental cultural and conceptual shift. The differing skills of the forensic investigator and the auditor are nicely illustrated with his metaphorical use of the difficulties of finding the proverbial 'needle in a haystack'. Faced with this dilemma the

> audit experience would lead to sampling the hay to support the conclusion that the hay was what it purported to be, within sampling precision and confidence measures. Investigative experience would lead to renting a metal detector. The difference is that the focus has shifted from the hay to the needles and knowing what needles look like is crucial to the effectiveness of the investigation.

While supportive of the creation of the PCAOB, Hodson raises concerns about the failure to render explicit ownership of risk management processes. He calls for clarifications that 'might include the express articulation of the audit committee's responsibility relating to the risk of collusive subversion of financial reporting controls by senior management'. This is an essential prerequisite because in their absence, accountability is also missing, a situation that is usually a predicate for fraud. Hodson places responsibility for this state of affairs on the failure to integrate ethics programmes into strategic management, a failing also highlighted by Whitehouse, McBarnet and Dobel.

The academic community has also a role to play in redesign but only in context of a rejection of the intellectual ghettoisation. As noted above, the academic literature, heavily influenced by the law and economics tradition, tends to limit the discussion of governance to technical questions of procedure. In this context, ethics and corporate social responsibility (CSR) programmes are usually seen as voluntary compacts designed to advance strategic objectives by presenting the corporation as responsible. Under the terms of the current paradigm the fact that a company has a restricted view of its roles and responsibilities towards wider society does not in itself equate to poor corporate governance. CSR offers a way out of this barren legalism. For Whitehouse the critical advantage of CSR rests on the fact that while it accepts the creative force of individualism, capital and markets, it does not accord them pre-eminence. For the CSR movement to be translated into an effective policing mechanism, it needs to accept that the focus of corporate citizenship must be narrowed to 'how the exercise of public power can be legitimated so as to ensure that all values associated with a liberal-democracy are protected'.

Ironically, Sarbanes-Oxley offers two interlinked mechanisms to achieve this aim. Copies of corporate ethics programmes must be deposited with the SEC and any derogation from their provisions reported. Introduced to stop the egregious activities sanctioned through board authorised derogation, the reform is potentially one of the most important, if underreported, internal control mechanisms. It allows not only a benchmark on which to gauge strategic decision-making. Its power as a restraining agent, however, would be exponentially increased if regulators sought to ensure that the ethics programme itself became part of the internal control systems mandated by the controversial section 404 of the Act. At a stroke, this has the potential to move ethics to the centre of the enforcement agenda.

Of course this is easier said than done. Just how difficult it is to break the culture of technical compliance is proved by the decision by Citigroup, the largest financial services conglomerate in the world, to reconfigure its internal code of ethics and announce the appointment of a Director of Ethics (O'Brien 2005). Announced with considerable fanfare, the code of conduct highlights three key corporate aspirations. Citigroup strives to be a company with the highest standards of ethical conduct; an organisation that people can trust; and dedicated to community service. Within the conglomerate, the code establishes codified limits of acceptable behaviour, offers guidance to concerned employees, provides hotlines, and emphasises the need for both professional integrity and personal responsibility. Rooted in a cultural framework that emphasises the importance of compliance, it serves to demonstrate to employees and regulators that credible risk management structures have been put in place. In large respect, the code is a paragon of industry best practice.

To be effective, however, a code of ethics requires what Schwartz (2002, 40) terms 'penetration' across 'policies, processes, programs, structures, systems, and objectives'. In order to assess the efficacy of the Citigroup approach, it is therefore imperative to distinguish between 'form', 'implementation' and 'administration', both in terms of design and ultimate purpose.

Within the code of conduct, Citigroup argues that structured finance products, similar to those which help facilitate the earnings management practised by Enron, must be handled carefully:

> Each of our clients must commit to disclose promptly to the public the net effect of any financing transaction proposed to be executed by Citigroup that is material to the client and not intended to be accounted for as debt in the client's financial statements. If a client does not commit to make the disclosures required by our policy, Citigroup will not execute the covered transaction. (Citigroup 2004, 18)

Arguably, this formulation, designed to separate cause and effect, can be justified on the grounds that malfeasance by a third party should not be used to tar the reputation of a service provider of a service that is technically compliant with legislation. It also, however, transfers responsibility outside the corporation, absolving the financial designers of misfeasance or moral side-restraints by situating the creative accounting of structured finance within acceptable rules of the game and externalising the material and moral costs of non- or creative compliance. Within this narrow prism, the deception is not in the design of an aggressive and, if misapplied, potentially fraudulent instrument, but rather its inappropriate application. Within Citigroup, corporate ethics are placed within a libertarian normative context. In short, ethics, if applied at all, can only be justified if it adds to the bottom line (O'Brien 2005).

While demonstrating the limitations of ethics in a business context as presently construed, the Citigroup case presents an opportunity for the kind of innovative proactive policing that is required if cultural change is to be institutionalised. Regulators and campaigners (including institutional investors) can now under Sarbanes-Oxley highlight the dichotomy between appearance and reality in terms of a corporation's actual activities and their impact on wider society in order to test empirically claims of responsible behaviour.

Compliance programmes, if properly enforced, have the potential to minimise the risk of corporate corruption. They act as early warning systems: guarding against catastrophic damage to corporate reputation and providing the market with confidence that effective risk management systems are in place. If allowed to degenerate into 'box-ticking' within the corporation, governance advances into the same cul-de-sac that has already deprived the wider business ethics and corporate social responsibility (CSR) movements of the necessary traction to move beyond adroit public relations. As Buck makes clear, effective corporate governance necessitates a modification of cultural norms.

For corporate governance and related regulatory oversight to be effective in an age of global markets, the overriding policy imperative is to institutionalise an ethical framework that is capable of transcending technical compliance (O'Brien 2005). A functioning ethical framework systematises and rationalises corporate thinking within a normalised rule structure. It offers a template to deal with all situations or moral hazards arising from excessive discretion. To be effective it must be situated within a matrix that gives due cognisance to the competing imperatives of culture, law, ethics and accountability. It must be underpinned by the concepts of trust and integrity. In other words it is only through the inculcation of values into the determination of value that the corporate system can be effectively brought to account.

Notes

1. Donaldson subsequently increased the geographical range of the miscreants to a global basis in a speech to the London School of Economics in January 2005. Citing deficiencies in Ahold (Netherlands), Parmalat (Italy) and Vivendi (France), the chair of the SEC claimed: 'Related to these disclosures of gross corporate malfeasance, there was also a more widespread erosion of standards throughout our markets, with questionable practices becoming accepted and ethical corners being cut on a too frequent basis. The net effect has been to undermine the faith investors have in the integrity of the world's capital markets' (Donaldson 2005). Full text of the speech is available at http://www.sec.gov/news/speech/spch012505whd.htm
2. The issue remains central to SEC enforcement activity. On 25 May 2005, Morgan Stanley and Goldman Sachs agreed to fines of $40 m each to settle SEC actions relating to allocation of stock to institutional clients in 1999 and 2000 at the height of the technology bubble. Steve Cutler, the Director of Enforcement, claimed the settlement demonstrated the 'Commission's resolve to ensure the integrity of the IPO markets by prohibiting conduct that could artificially stimulate demand [Goldman Sachs] or higher prices in the aftermarket [Morgan Stanley] – whether or not there is a manipulative effect'. See http://www.sec.gov/news/press/2005–10.htm
3. http://www.marthastewart.com/page.jhtml;jsessionid=UFEQ3CQDKYGAD WCKUUXCGWWYJKSS0JO0?type=learn-cat&id=cat19737 &rsc=sc22020
4. Indicative too of Citigroup's relative power is the continued failure of the Department of Justice to launch criminal proceedings against it for its role in facilitating Enron's deception through Special Purpose Vehicles, despite securing substantive interference in the internal governance of Merrill Lynch for precisely the same charges (O'Brien 2005).

2

Restoring Trust After Recent Accountability Failures

David M. Walker

Introduction

Major corporate accountability failures in recent years have led to bankruptcies and restatements of financial statements that harmed thousands of shareholders, employee pensioners, and other stakeholders. These failures also created a crisis of investor confidence and resulted in billions of dollars in capital vanishing from the stock market. At the same time, the accounting and auditing profession was also tarnished by these scandals as the trust and confidence in the integrity of the financial reporting and auditing processes took a big hit.

These scandals damaged the public's trust and confidence not only in accountants and auditors but also in other key players and market participants, including regulators, investment analysts, money managers, investment bankers, chief executive officers of major corporations, boards of directors, and others. For example, regulatory systems were ill-prepared to detect and correct serious weaknesses that had developed in the accountability process. Corporate officers and various professionals worked to achieve certain financial reporting results that were arguably acceptable but not appropriate. Many auditors came under pressure by corporate management to accept aggressive accounting policies, which at times they did not effectively resist. In many cases, the client's governance structure (for example, the audit committee's role) was not adequate to ensure that the most appropriate financial reporting was achieved, given the individual facts and circumstances. In too many cases, the result was audited financial statements that inappropriately accelerated revenues, deferred expenses, artificially smoothed earnings, and increased earnings per share. At the same time, it is important to remember that most auditors maintained their professional integrity by not yielding to these pressures.

Unfortunately, these accountability failures were not isolated instances. Many were the result of significant structural weaknesses in institutional corporate governance and accountability models combined with a lack of personal ethics and integrity. Forces that led to the corporate scandals and audit failures included:

- ineffective governance systems;
- ineffective regulation and oversight of the accounting profession;
- inadequate accounting and auditing standards;
- inadequate attest and assurance procedures;
- financial managers who, along with their legal and financial advisors, worked to achieve certain reporting results, rather than report the facts;
- inappropriate and unreasonable executive compensation arrangements;
- confusion over who the auditors worked for;
- auditors' services to clients that impaired independence; and
- auditors and financial professionals who did what was minimally required and fought tighter standards.

Other factors were simple greed by corporate executives and inadequate oversight and accountability actions by boards of directors.

Accountability Failures Lead to Major Reforms

In response to these accountability failures, major reforms have been implemented in the United States and in other countries. In the United States, the Sarbanes-Oxley Act of 2002 represents the most sweeping reforms to United States securities law since the Securities Act of 1934. This far-reaching legislation is intended to protect investors and the public interest through reforms in corporate governance, changes in the relationship between the auditor and client, improved auditor independence, additional management responsibilities for and auditor reporting on the effectiveness of internal control, and enhanced oversight and regulation for auditors of publicly traded companies through creation of the Public Company Accounting Oversight Board (PCAOB).

The Act required that the PCAOB develop a continuous programme of auditor oversight 'in order to protect the interests of investors and further the public interest in the preparation of informative, accurate and independent audit reports for companies the securities of which are sold to, and held by and for, public investors.' (Sarbanes-Oxley, section 101).

To carry out this charge, the Act gives the Board significant powers, including the authority to:

- register public accounting firms that prepare or participate in the preparation of audit reports for issuers;
- inspect registered public accounting firms;
- conduct investigations and disciplinary proceedings concerning, and impose appropriate sanctions upon, registered public accounting firms and associated persons of such firms;
- enforce compliance by registered public accounting firms and their associated persons with the Act, the Board's rules, professional standards, and the securities laws relating to the preparation and issuance of audit reports and the obligations and liabilities of accountants; and
- establish auditing, quality control, ethics, independence, and other standards relating to the preparation of audit reports for US issuers (Sarbanes-Oxley, section 101).

Section 404 of the Act also requires that management assess the effectiveness of the company's internal control over financial reporting and report on that assessment at the close of its fiscal year. Furthermore, the Act requires a company's external auditor to attest to and report on the assessment made by management (Sarbanes-Oxley, section 404). In March 2004, the PCAOB approved its *Auditing Standard No. 2, An Audit of Internal Control Over Financial Reporting Performed in Conjunction with an Audit of Financial Statements*. The Securities and Exchange Commission (SEC) approved this standard in June 2004.

The Act's requirements on internal control reporting represent a significant change in both management's reporting responsibilities and the scope and nature of the responsibilities of the independent auditor. As a result of these requirements, management must evaluate the effectiveness of internal control over financial reporting and support its evaluation with documentation, and auditors must evaluate and test a company's internal control in greater depth as part of the financial statement audit. The overall goal of these new requirements is to strengthen internal control over financial reporting, provide more reliable financial reporting to investors, and renew investor confidence in the US capital markets.

These efforts are yielding results. Since the passage of Sarbanes-Oxley, public trust and confidence in the capital markets have increased and many aspects of corporate governance have been modified. Needed changes in auditor relationships with clients have taken place as a result of more active and effective audit committees. In addition, chief executive officers (CEOs) and chief financial officers (CFOs) are increasing their attention to key governance, internal control, and financial reporting issues. New internal control requirements, while not without cost, are adding value for many companies. The PCAOB's inspections of audit firms are finding areas where audit quality can be significantly improved. Finally, many entities not covered by the Act have voluntarily implemented similar practices.

At the same time, it is important to acknowledge that Sarbanes-Oxley was a significant, complex, and controversial piece of legislation, as illustrated by the diverse aspects of reform it encompassed. Many companies are encountering challenges in implementing Sarbanes-Oxley. For example, some companies are finding the internal control requirements to be more difficult and costly to implement than expected or are struggling with the implementation timeframes. In addition, Board members and audit committees have seen their roles and workloads greatly expand.

The reforms in the United States have also affected other countries. About 1400 non-US issuers have their securities registered to trade in US markets and must file audited financial statements with the SEC. Most of these companies are audited by accounting firms based in their home countries. The non-US auditing firms and corporations have expressed concerns about potential conflicts between US and home-country laws and regulations and administrative burdens in trying to meet requirements of both US and home-country regulators. In addition, concerns have been raised that inspections by US regulators may result in dual oversight. Some corporations and their auditors have said that implementation timeframes will prove difficult. Finally, non-US issuers have said that SEC delisting requirements make it difficult to withdraw from US exchanges, and, therefore, withdrawal from US exchanges is often not a practical option.

Significant progress has been made in addressing the concerns of non-US issuers and their auditors. The PCAOB is engaged in an ongoing dialogue with other international regulators to improve auditor oversight and, where possible, to minimise inconsistencies and duplicative regulation. For example, constructive discussions have taken place between the PCAOB and the European Commission, various European countries, Canada, Australia, Japan, and others. The Board has also begun several initiatives based in large part on the ideas developed in this dialogue. These initiatives include adopting certain accommodations in the US registration system to the Board's oversight of non-US firms that take advantage of the assistance and expertise of local regulators. The PCAOB has recognised home-country laws and regulations in tailoring requirements for non-US corporations and auditors. It has also made accommodations for auditing firms, such as extending deadlines and providing registration flexibility. It has made similar accommodations for corporations, such as allowing them interim reporting on the basis of home country rules, identifying alternatives for satisfying audit committee requirements, extending compliance deadlines for internal control reporting and other requirements, and working toward harmonised international financial reporting standards.

In the same way that the US Congress acted to restore public confidence in the US markets, the European Commission has taken important steps to help restore confidence in European markets. The European Commission's landmark legislative proposal contains requirements similar to Sarbanes-Oxley for corporate governance and auditing. The European Commission is also actively working to develop a common oversight approach for the European Union's financial services market.

Recent Reforms Will Carry into the Future

It will take some time before we realise the full benefits of the recent reforms. In the interim, it is important that we continue to review and evaluate the effectiveness of the reforms as they are being implemented and after a full implementation cycle. The following three elements are key to these efforts:

- Regulators, boards, public interest organisations, and accountability organisations must continue to closely oversee corporate management, auditors, and others to ensure that reforms are being implemented as designed and applicable laws and regulations are being complied with.
- These groups must provide insight by continuing to evaluate and identify policies that work and those that do not. This involves sharing best practices and benchmarking information and identifying areas where adjustments are needed.
- These groups must use foresight to identify key trends and emerging challenges before they reach crisis proportions and act on them to maximise value and minimise risk.

Current reforms are well under way, but many challenges lie ahead. Moreover, although the current reforms deal specifically with publicly traded companies, we must also consider the implications and applicability of similar reforms, as appropriate, for government, closely held companies, and not-for-profit entities.

Addressing Challenges in Corporate Governance, Auditing, and Financial Reporting

One of the most critical accountability elements that needs to be addressed in the future is the overall governance model for public companies. The current US corporate governance model for public companies proved inadequate to protect the interests of shareholders and other key stakeholders.

To ensure that the recent accountability failures are not repeated, we need to answer the following questions: Where were the boards of directors? Where were the audit committees? What was the role of top corporate management in these business breakdowns? What was the involvement of other key players? These and other questions are worth exploring to determine what changes are needed to minimise the possibility that these types of events will occur in the future.

The Role of the Board

Boards need to play at least three roles. First, they should provide strategic advice to management in order to help maximise shareholder value over the long term. Second, they need to help manage risk, including those related to actions that might enhance value or provide benefits in the short term at the expense of mortgaging the future. Risk management must also consider the interests of key stakeholder groups, such as employees, customers, and the communities in which the company operates. Third, boards have a clear responsibility to hold management accountable for results both in the short term and the long term, with proper balance.

Board member qualifications are more than a matter of education and experience; they are also a matter of personal attributes, of which courage and integrity are critical. Building a strong and effective board of directors begins with placing the right people on the board – individuals who are independent, knowledgeable, and ethical and whose integrity is unquestionable. Board independence does not require the elimination of all inside directors, but it would seem to call for ensuring a super-majority of board members who are truly independent both in fact and in appearance.

Another key consideration is whether it is appropriate for the CEO to serve as chairman of the board of directors. Under modern governance theory, the board works for the shareholders and the CEO works for the board. But how can this be if the CEO also serves as chairman of the board? At many major public companies, this is the case. The person who is both chairman and CEO has tremendous control over the direction of the company, the role of the board, the composition of the board, as well as the board's agenda and activities. All too frequently, such individuals have significant influence over who is asked to join the board and who is asked to leave it. Boards are often composed primarily of internal management officials, high-level executives from other companies, and major service providers to and customers of the company. Although all these individuals have valuable experience and perspective to bring to the table, they are not always well positioned to address all of the key roles and responsibilities of an independent board.

In order to fulfil its responsibility of effectively overseeing management, the board must thoroughly understand the company, its business model and related risks, corporate culture, and the various stakeholder interests the board represents. The board has a responsibility to educate itself through the use of external advisors and other independent parties and not rely solely on information provided by management. This puts the board in a better position to ask difficult questions and probe issues, provide input on strategy, assess and manage risk, and hold management accountable. The timeframes for consideration of management strategy and actions must be made very clear, as creating value is a long-term, not a short-term, process. Most investors are not looking for quick-profit schemes that endanger the long-term prospects of the company.

In addition to its responsibility to oversee management, the board also has a responsibility to shareholders and other stakeholders of the company, including employees, creditors, and the public. Boards need to identify their constituencies and stakeholders and act to consider those interests, as appropriate. Finally, board members must remember that, ultimately, they represent the interests of the shareholders. We have become a nation of investors, and boards need to be mindful that more and more shareholders today are institutional investors, such as pension plans and mutual funds, which are acting as fiduciaries for others.

To help restore investor confidence, it is important to continue working to establish more effective boards of directors and to clearly define and, in some cases, redefine the roles and responsibilities of the board of directors. Board members have a fiduciary responsibility to the shareholders they represent. They must do their best to do the right thing and not breach their fiduciary duties through either commission or omission.

The Role of the Audit Committee

Another important component of the corporate governance system is the audit committee. In enacting Sarbanes-Oxley in the United States, US lawmakers recognised the tremendous value of audit committees. The Act directs the SEC to adopt a new rule to direct the national securities exchanges and national securities associations to prohibit the listing of any security of an issuer that fails to comply with the Act's audit committee requirements. The requirements state that these organisations will be prohibited from listing any security of an issuer that does not comply with the following standards:

- Each member of the audit committee of the issuer must be independent according to specified criteria.
- The audit committee of each issuer must be directly responsible for the appointment, compensation, retention, and oversight of the work of any registered public accounting firm engaged for the purpose of preparing or issuing an audit report or performing other audit, review, or attest services for the issuer, and each such registered public accounting firm must report directly to the audit committee.
- Each audit committee must establish procedures for the receipt, retention, and treatment of complaints regarding accounting, internal accounting controls, or auditing matters, including procedures for the confidential, anonymous submission by employees of the issuer of concerns regarding questionable accounting or auditing matters.
- Each audit committee must have the authority to engage independent counsel and other advisors, as it determines necessary to carry out its duties.
- Each issuer must provide appropriate funding for the audit committee.

Audit committees should not only oversee both internal and external auditors, but also actively seek to understand issues related to the complexity of the business, and, when appropriate, challenge management through discussion of choices regarding complex accounting, financial reporting, auditing, and accountability issues. In that respect, the role of the audit committee, which in some cases has not been very active or effective in its oversight of management's financial reporting and the audit process, is evolving to include not only oversight of the financial statement preparation and audit processes, but also other aspects of financial reporting, such as releases on earnings expectations and quarterly financial reports. Audit committees are also becoming involved in a range of other risk management and accountability related activities, such as activities and results assessment associated with corporate 'whistleblower lines'. Concerns have been raised, however, over whether audit committee members are focusing on procedural matters more to protect themselves from liability rather than to improve their effectiveness as a committee.

The ongoing support of the board of directors is critical to the effectiveness of the audit committee. The board of directors is responsible

for ensuring that audit committee members are independent, finan-
cially literate, have sufficient information and interaction with
management, and have the personal attributes needed to serve as
effective audit committee members. These attributes include a general
understanding of the company's major economic, operating, and
financial risks; a broad awareness of the interrelationship of the
company's operations and its financial reporting; and an understanding of the differences between the oversight responsibilities of
the committee and the decision-making responsibilities of management.
Audit committee members must also be able to formulate and ask
probing questions about the company's financial reporting and
accountability processes. In fact, members of the audit committee and
the board, in their oversight function, should have the ability to
challenge the CEO when necessary.

One of the significant aspects of Sarbanes-Oxley is the relationship
the Act establishes between the auditor and audit committee by
providing the audit committee with the responsibility for overseeing
the audit rather than management. Historically, the auditor communication with audit committees has been viewed as variable. Auditors
should be able to speak freely, openly, and honestly with audit
committees on the risks facing a company, the appropriateness of a
company's accounting policies, and the quality of related company
personnel. Audit committees should ask probing questions of the auditors and ensure that the auditors have the resources, both in number
and expertise, to adequately perform the audit. Working together,
audit committees and auditors can become good safeguards for investors.

The Role of Management

Corporate leadership must set the appropriate 'tone at the top' and
take steps to help ensure that the corporate culture includes commitment to a set of principles and values that promote honesty, integrity,
transparency, and accountability. In this regard, top management must
help to ensure that this effort begins in the executive suite and reaches
throughout the organisation.

CEOs must remember that they are stewards, not owners, of the
company and that they are responsible for hiring the right kinds of
people with the right skills and values, creating and demanding

accountability throughout the organisation, and ensuring that values are an integral part of the workplace. Employees should understand the role and function of the organisation and how their jobs fit into that mission, how decisions are made, how decisions should be executed, and where to go if they believe that illegal or inappropriate acts have occurred. CEOs must also remember that as stewards, their job is not just to focus on short-term results but to leave the company better off and better positioned for the future when they pass the baton to their successor.

Sarbanes-Oxley reinforces the role of management as stewards of the stockholders' interest. In enacting Sarbanes-Oxley, lawmakers recognised the important role of management in providing assurance over reliable financial reporting. Section 404 of the Act requires management to take responsibility for, and assess the effectiveness of, internal controls for financial reporting. Also, section 302 makes corporate officers liable for the accuracy of information presented in financial statements, while section 409 requires companies to provide timely reports to investors, the SEC, and other involved parties on material events. Although the CEO and CFO are ultimately responsible for the accuracy and certification of financial statements, the process of certification will involve employees throughout the organisation who play a role in the internal control system and in generating data and transactions that ultimately are reported as part of the financial statement.

Transforming the Financial Reporting Model

The current financial reporting model needs to provide more useful and timely information on a company's results. The current model has value but fails to meet the broader range of information needs of investors who want more forward-looking information and data that reflect a company's overall performance, risk profile, and expectations for future performance. In addition, in the current financial reporting model, financial statement disclosures are often extensive and difficult to understand.

Another significant issue related to the current financial reporting model is that users often believe that the reported figures are highly exact and precise. This assumption results in the expectation gap that often exists between what an audit is and what users expect when auditors issue their opinion on the financial statements. Users often have the impression of precision where it may not be warranted. According to the American Assembly's *Future of the Accounting Profession*:

> The reality is that producing and auditing a complete set of financial statements in our increasingly complex global economy is now more of an art than a science, and one that must be, by definition, reliant on judgments that flow from experience and a sophisticated understanding of business and accounting. This, however, goes unrecognized all too often. Rather, investors and others who continue to rely on audited statements to give them a degree of certainty, have been disappointed – and have demanded redress. (American Assembly 2003)

We need to continue the dialogue on business reporting and ask some key questions. For example, what should be disclosed, what is the purpose of financial statements, and how useful are they? How are analysts and others using financial statements? Are they using financial statements in their evaluation of stocks and, if so, what information in the financial statements are they using and what additional information would assist them in analysing stock?

Modernised financial reporting should provide meaningful information that is useful, timely, and relevant. This information includes:

- generic provisions common to all entities to provide a fundamental understanding of financial position and results of operations;
- industry information that would help users compare and evaluate companies' performance within a specific industry; and
- entity-specific information, such as non-financial indicators that can help give users of those financial statements greater insight into a company's past performance and future prospects.

Financial reporting should also recognise the difference between certain types of financial and other information, such as historical cost, readily marketable assets, non-readily marketable assets, projection information, and performance information.

Efforts to transform the financial reporting model should seek to improve transparency, reliability, and accountability in companies' financial reporting and generate information that more effectively meets the needs of investors, analysts, and other users.

The Future Audit Reporting Model

We also need to review the audit reporting model to determine how to provide clearer information about the auditor's conclusions, expanded discussion about the levels of estimation and judgements used in both the financial reporting and audit processes, and any additional information that the auditor believes should be emphasised or disclosed.

Specifically, we need to look at the wording of the auditor's report to help ensure that it meaningfully communicates to users the process used by auditors in reaching a judgement about the 'fairness' of the overall presentation of the financial statements. Critical auditor considerations include: (1) management's selection and application of accounting principles, including the reasonableness of estimates; (2) the adequacy of disclosures; and (3) whether literal compliance with GAAP results in financial statements that may be misleading. The auditor's judgements on these matters necessarily involve both qualitative and quantitative factors and the concepts of materiality and consistency and may include other considerations. These critical judgements are not adequately described in the current audit report. As a result, some modification may be in order – namely, how best to make it clear that the financial statements are not just prepared in accordance with generally accepted accounting principles (for example, those promulgated by the Financial Accounting Standards Board, International Federation of Accountants, Governmental Accounting Standards Board, and Federal Accounting Standards Advisory Board) but that they also fairly present the financial condition of the reporting entity. Changing the auditor's report would also likely cause changes in the behaviour of auditors based on what is articulated in the report that is issued and signed by the auditor.

Another area where the audit-reporting model needs to be reviewed is whether additional explanation should be included to more adequately describe the nature of the information included in the financial statements and disclosures. The audit-reporting model currently does not reflect the fact that the financial statements and disclosures contain different types of information with differing degrees of certainty. Specifically, we need to look at whether the current wording of the auditor's report adequately conveys the concept that the financial statements and disclosures include a series of judgements and estimates, as does the audit process itself.

Finally, although current standards allow auditors to emphasise matters regarding the financial statements, such disclosure is not required and is not commonly done in practice. We need to change either the standards and/or auditor behaviour so that auditors include important information in the audit report that would assist users in understanding the entity's current financial condition and related risks. For instance, it may be appropriate for auditors to include information that results from the auditor's overall analysis of the financial statements, including matters related to risk, potential contingencies, valuation of assets and liabilities, etc. In this regard, auditors need to consider inserting an emphasis paragraph in their audit reports where the entity has a "broken business model" even though it may not deserve a "going concern qualification."

Ultimately, the goal should be global convergence in major accounting and audit matters, such as reporting models, audit models, and accounting and auditing standards. Although the major stakeholders are still wrestling with the meaning of convergence and what it would encompass, we must continue to coordinate US and international efforts to achieve consistency in core issues with global implications.

US Joint Auditing Standards Coordinating Forum

In 2003, GAO worked to establish the US Joint Auditing Standards Coordinating Forum as a mechanism to coordinate and modernise the auditing standards process among the various bodies responsible for setting auditing standards that apply to different entities in the United States, including governmental agencies and departments, publicly traded and privately held companies, and not-for-profit organisations. The heads of the three US auditing standards-setting bodies – the PCAOB, the Auditing Standards Board of the American Institute of Certified Public Accountants, and myself as Comptroller General of the United States and head of the US Government Accountability Office (GAO) – meet several times a year. The goal of the forum is to coordinate priorities and standards-setting agendas among the three groups in order to:

- maximise complementary standards-setting agendas;
- minimise duplicative or competing efforts;

- identify any significant gaps not being addressed by the standards setters;
- ensure consistency, where appropriate, in core auditing standards in the United States;
- develop strategies for overcoming challenges and avoid unintended barriers to movement between the sectors;
- modernise the accounting profession in the United States; and
- explore opportunities for international coordination.

Members view the forum as an opportunity to work together on issues of mutual concern. The forum's efforts are already getting results. In the United States, we are seeing greater cooperation and coordination on reforms; the development of new standards; and dialog on important emerging challenges, including harmonisation between US and international standards. With a commitment to advancing the clarity, integrity, and consistency of auditing standards, the US Joint Auditing Standards Coordinating Forum will continue to further its overarching goals of accountability in the public interest.

Consolidation of Public Accounting Firms

There are hundreds of public accounting firms that audit public companies in the United States. However, a small number of very large firms have traditionally provided audit and attest services for the majority of public companies, particularly large national and multi-national companies. The number of firms widely considered capable of providing audit services to large national and multinational companies decreased from eight ('the Big 8') in the 1980s to four ('the Big 4') today. The reduction was the result of mergers involving six of the top eight firms since the late 1980s and the abrupt dissolution of Arthur Andersen LLP (Andersen) in 2002. The Big 4 firms are substantially larger than the other US or international accounting firms, each with thousands of partners, tens of thousands of employees, offices located around the world, and annual revenues in the billions of dollars. In 2003 we reported (GAO-03-864 2003) that these four firms currently audit over 78% of all US public companies and 99% of public company annual sales. Internationally, the Big 4 dominate the market for audit services.

Big 8 mergers and Andersen's sudden dissolution prompted heightened concerns about concentration among the largest accounting firms and the potential effect on competition and various other factors. As a result, Congress mandated in Sarbanes-Oxley that we study these issues.

Our work found that the largest firms have the potential for significant market power following mergers among the largest firms and the dissolution of Arthur Andersen. Although GAO found no evidence of impaired competition to date, the significant changes that have occurred in the profession may have implications for competition and public company choice, especially in certain industries, in the future.

Existing research on audit fees did not conclusively identify a direct correlation with consolidation. GAO found that fees have started to increase, and most experts expect the trend to continue as the audit environment responds to recent and ongoing changes in the audit market. Research on quality and independence did not link audit quality and auditor independence to consolidation and generally was inconclusive. Likewise, GAO was unable to draw clear linkages between consolidation and capital formation but did observe potential impacts for some smaller companies seeking to raise capital.

However, given the unprecedented changes occurring in the audit market, GAO observes that past behaviour may not be indicative of future behaviour, and these potential implications may warrant additional study in the future, including preventing further consolidation and maintaining competition.

Finally, GAO found that smaller accounting firms faced significant barriers to entry – including lack of staff, industry and technical expertise, capital formation, global reach, and reputation – into the large public company audit market. As a result, market forces are not likely to result in the expansion of the current Big 4. Furthermore, certain factors and conditions could cause a further reduction in the number of major accounting firms.

Mandatory Audit Firm Rotation

Another issue considered in the congressional hearings that preceded Sarbanes-Oxley was mandatory audit firm rotation. Mandatory audit firm rotation (setting a limit on the period of years a public accounting firm may audit a particular company's financial statements) was considered as a reform to enhance auditor independence and audit quality in those hearings, but it was not included in the Act. Congress decided that mandatory audit firm rotation needed further consideration and required GAO to study the potential effects of requiring rotation of the public accounting firms that audit public companies registered with the SEC.

In two reports (GAO-04-216, 2003 and GAO-04-217, 2004) on this issue, GAO noted that the arguments for and against mandatory audit firm rotation centred on whether the independence of a public accounting firm auditing a company's financial statements is adversely affected by a firm's long-term relationship with the client and the desire to retain the client. Concerns about the potential effects of mandatory audit firm rotation include whether its intended benefits would outweigh the costs and the loss of company-specific knowledge gained by an audit firm through years of experience auditing the client. In addition, questions exist about whether Sarbanes-Oxley requirements for reform will accomplish the intended benefits of mandatory audit firm rotation.

Regarding auditor independence and audit quality issues, we found the following at that the largest accounting firms and Fortune 1000 public companies:

- The average length of the auditor of record's tenure, which proponents of mandatory audit firm rotation believe increases the risk that auditor independence and ultimately audit quality may be adversely affected, was about 22 years for Fortune 1000 public companies.
- About 79% of the largest accounting firms and Fortune 1000 public companies believe that changing audit firms increases the risk of an audit failure in the early years of the audit as the new auditor acquires the necessary knowledge of the company's operations, systems, and financial reporting practices and therefore may fail to detect a material financial reporting issue.
- Most of the largest accounting firms and Fortune 1000 public companies believe that mandatory audit firm rotation would not have much effect on the pressures faced by the audit engagement partner in appropriately dealing with material financial reporting issues.

- About 59% of the largest accounting firms reported they would likely move their most knowledgeable and experienced audit staff as the end of the firm's tenure approached under mandatory audit firm rotation to attract or retain other clients, which they acknowledged would increase the risk of an audit failure.

Regarding audit costs, our survey results show that the largest accounting firms and Fortune 1000 public companies expect that mandatory audit firm rotation would lead to more costly audits.

- Nearly all of the largest accounting firms estimated that initial year audit costs under mandatory audit firm rotation would increase by more than 20% over subsequent year costs to acquire the necessary knowledge of the public company, and most of the largest accounting firms estimated their marketing costs would also increase by at least 1% or more, which would be passed on to the public companies.
- Most Fortune 1000 public companies estimated that under mandatory audit firm rotation, they would incur auditor selection costs and additional auditor support costs totalling at least 17% or higher as a percentage of initial year audit fees.

Our check of audit fees and total company operating expenses reported by a selection of large and small public companies in 23 industries for the most recent fiscal year available found that for the large public companies selected, average audit fees represented approximately 0.04% of company operating expenses and, for the small public companies selected, average audit fees represented approximately 0.08% of company operating expenses. Based on estimates of possible increased audit-related costs from survey responses from the largest accounting firms and Fortune 1000 public companies, mandatory audit firm rotation could increase these audit-related costs from 43% to 128% of the recurring annual audit fees. This illustration is intended only to provide some insight into how, based on the largest accounting firms' and Fortune 1000 public companies' responses, mandatory audit firm rotation may affect the initial year audit-related costs public companies may incur and is not intended to be representative.

In our study on the consolidation of public accounting firms, we found that the number of public accounting firms providing audit services to public companies is highly concentrated. Many Fortune 1000 public companies reported that they will only use a Big 4 firm for a variety of reasons, including the capability of the firms to provide them audit services and the expectations of the capital markets that they will use Big 4 firms.

Mandatory audit firm rotation would further decrease their choices for an auditor of record, and Sarbanes-Oxley's auditor independence requirements concerning prohibited non-audit services may also further limit the public companies' choices for an auditor of record. The largest accounting firms expected that public companies in specialised industries, which in some industries currently have more limited choices for an auditor of record than other public companies, could be more affected by mandatory audit firm rotation than other public companies.

GAO believes that mandatory audit firm rotation may not be the most efficient way to enhance auditor independence and audit quality given the additional financial costs, the loss of institutional knowledge of a public company's previous auditor of record, and the current reforms being implemented. The potential benefits of mandatory audit firm rotation are harder to predict and quantify, but GAO is fairly certain that there will be additional costs. In addition, the current reforms being implemented may also provide some of the intended benefits of mandatory audit firm rotation. In that respect, mandatory audit firm rotation is not a panacea that totally removes the pressures on the auditors in appropriately resolving financial reporting issues that may materially affect the public companies' financial statements. These inherent pressures are likely to continue even if the term of the auditor is limited under any mandatory rotation process. Furthermore, most public companies will only use the Big 4 firms for audit services. Given this preference, these public companies may only have one or two real choices for auditor of record under any mandatory rotation system given the importance of industry expertise and Sarbanes-Oxley's auditor independence requirements. However, over time a mandatory audit firm rotation requirement may result in more firms transitioning into additional industry sectors if the market for such audits has sufficient profit margins.

It will take at least several years for the SEC and the PCAOB to gain sufficient experience with the effectiveness of Sarbanes-Oxley in order to adequately evaluate whether further enhancements or revisions, including mandatory audit firm rotation, may be needed to further protect the public interest and to restore investor confidence. The current environment has greatly increased the pressures on public company management and auditors regarding honest, fair, and complete financial reporting, but it is uncertain if the current climate will be sustained over the long term. Rigorous enforcement of the Act's requirements will undoubtedly be critical to its effectiveness. GAO therefore believes that the most prudent course of action at this time is for the SEC and the PCAOB to monitor and evaluate the effectiveness of existing requirements for enhancing auditor independence and audit quality.

GAO's Work to Improve and Modernise Accountability

One of GAO's major goals over the next few years is to lead by example in the effort to modernise and transform the accountability profession, both in government and the private sector. As part of these efforts, in 2002, we issued significant changes to the auditor independence requirements under Government Auditing Standards. First issued by GAO in 1972 and commonly referred to as the 'Yellow Book', these standards cover federal entities and organisations receiving federal funds and many state and local government entities. Various laws require compliance with the Comptroller General's auditing standards in connection with audits of federal entities and funds. Furthermore, many state, local, and national governments, along with other entities, both domestic and international, have voluntarily adopted these standards.

Although the new independence standard deals with a range of auditor independence issues, the most significant change relates to non-audit, or consulting, services. Auditors have the capability of performing a range of services for their clients. However, in some circumstances it is not appropriate for them to perform both audit and certain non-audit services for the same client. In these circumstances, the auditor and/or the client will have to choose which of these services the auditor will provide. The standard uses a principles-based approach supplemented with certain safeguards. The new independence standard for non-audit services is based on two overarching principles.

- Auditors should not perform management functions or make management decisions.
- Auditors should not audit their own work or provide non-audit services in situations where the amounts or services involved are significant/material to the subject matter of the audit.

For non-audit services that do not violate the above principles, certain supplemental safeguards also need to be met. For example: (1) personnel who perform non-audit services would be precluded from performing any related audit work; (2) the auditor's work could not be reduced beyond the level that would be appropriate if the non-audit work were performed by another, unrelated party; and (3) certain other documentation and quality assurance requirements must be met.

The new standard expressly prohibits auditors from providing certain bookkeeping/recordkeeping services and limits payroll processing and other services that would generally be considered management functions. At the same time, the standard recognises that auditors can provide routine advice and answer technical questions without violating these two principles. The standard also provides examples of how various services would be treated under the new standards.

Protecting the public interest and ensuring public confidence in the independence of auditors of government financial statements, programmes, and operations, both in form and substance, were the overriding considerations in the decision to adopt these new standards for non-audit services. The new independence standard represented an important step in enhancing the independence of external auditors and better protecting the public.

In 2003, GAO issued a new edition of Government Auditing Standards. These auditing standards provide a framework for ensuring that auditors have competence, integrity, objectivity, and independence in planning, conducting, and reporting on their work so that their work can lead to improved government accountability and oversight, decision-making, oversight and accountability.

These revised standards:

- redefine the types of audits and services covered by the standards, such as expanding the definition of performance auditing to incorporate prospective analyses and other studies and adding attestation as a separate type of audit;

- provide consistency in the field work and reporting requirements among all types of audits defined under the standards, such as clarifying that auditors are required to report findings on internal control and compliance on attestation engagements and performance audits; and
- strengthen the standards and clarify their language, emphasising professional judgement, scepticism, and integrity.

In other areas of reform, GAO continues to monitor the implementation of the major accountability reforms in Sarbanes-Oxley and to promote the important principles of those reforms that can be applied to government entities. GAO has worked with the Director of the Office of Management and Budget and the Secretary of the Treasury to redefine success in financial management as more than obtaining a clean opinion on financial statements to include accelerated financial reporting due dates and many other important improvements. In GAO's view, successful financial management also depends on having financial systems that produce timely, accurate, and useful information and have no major weaknesses in controls or compliance. Furthermore, GAO has voluntarily decided to provide opinion-level assurance on internal controls and compliance in its audit of the consolidated financial statements of the US Government and its various other audits of federal entities. GAO also advocates enhanced reporting of key federal performance and projection information.

As the leading performance and accountability organisation in the United States, GAO takes its responsibilities very seriously and strives to lead by example. We set high standards for ourselves in the conduct of GAO's work. Our agency takes a professional, objective, fact-based, non-partisan, non-ideological, fair, and balanced approach to all activities. All of GAO's work is guided by applicable professional standards and our agency's core values – accountability, integrity, and reliability.

In March and December 2002, GAO convened corporate governance and accountability forums with prominent leaders from the public, private, and not-for-profit sectors to discuss accountability failures in the private sector and what could be done to prevent them in the future. These forums provided key insights for future GAO work and other efforts to support Congress, including our analysis of the issues associated with oversight and conduct within the accounting profession before the passage of Sarbanes-Oxley.

GAO is also working closely with accountability organisations around the world, such as the International Organisation of Supreme Audit Institutions, the International Federation of Accountants, and the International Auditing and Assurance Standards Board. Coordination with international accountability organisations is critical given the increasing interdependence of the world's economy.

To promote a high level of integrity and accountability throughout the financial reporting and auditing profession, GAO has sent its experts on these topics to numerous forums and conferences of state, local, federal, and international government and private sector accountability professionals. GAO has also raised awareness and furthered understanding of current reforms and changes, their impact, and their implementation in hundreds of speeches, training, and conferences for accountability professionals at all levels across the country.

GAO plays an integral role in the deliberation process for developing auditing standards for both the government and private sector. It provides input to standards setters on key priorities that need to be addressed as well as written comments on proposals by other standards setters. GAO also responds to emerging issues and initiatives. These efforts to transform the profession have led to important dialogue and the development of new principles to help restore integrity and reliability in the profession and ensure the primacy of the public interest.

Restoring Public Trust

Restoring public trust and confidence over the long term will require continuous and concerted actions by various parties to overcome past systemic weaknesses in corporate governance, accountability, and related systems.

As damaging as the recent accountability failures have been, they have presented us with an incredible opportunity to strengthen and enhance our accountability systems, oversight mechanisms, and the performance and accountability professions. The many reforms and actions taken by legislators, regulators, accountability professionals, and others show that progress is being made on several fronts.

Restoring public trust will require every participant in the corporate reporting supply chain to embrace three essential values:

- A spirit of transparency – all participants should stop playing games with financial and performance data and full disclosure must become the norm.
- A culture of accountability – management, staff, boards, auditors, and stakeholders must ensure high quality, unbiased information to support decision-making.
- People of integrity – every participant in the process must have a commitment to individual integrity (Eccles and DiPiazza 2002).

A critical ingredient in restoring the public's trust in our capital markets and oversight systems is the reliability of the accountability professional. Members of the accountability profession have the trust of shareholders, investors, and other members of our society who rely on fact-based, accurate, and objective financial information to make decisions affecting their families and our economic system. Auditors will face many situations in which they could best serve the public exceeding the accounting and auditing standards' minimum requirements. As stewards of the public trust, members of the accountability profession must:

- put public trust before personal interests;
- recognise the difference between the floor (rules, regulations, laws, and accounting standards) and the ceiling (principles and values);
- do what is right instead of what is acceptable;
- strive for economic substance over legal form;
- be concerned with both fact and appearance regarding independence;
- use judgement rather than just complete a checklist;
- recognise that continuing improvement in today's rapidly changing world is essential; and
- remember that trust is hard to earn, but easy to lose.

As businesses and governments face an increasingly complex and interdependent world, sound governance structures and accountability systems will be critical. Accountability professionals must always be mindful of their unique responsibility as part of that governance system and lead by example to maintain the public trust and show others the way forward. To fulfil those responsibilities, accountability professionals must remember the three personal attributes essential to achieving excellence and assuring real progress: courage, integrity, and innovation.

In the final analysis, for any system to work, the people at the top need to ensure that the key participants in the system have the courage to do the right thing and the integrity to know what is right. In addition the information provided to key stakeholders must be timely and reliable, and that those providing assurances about the reliability of any financial and non-financial information must be qualified and independent both in fact and appearance. The importance of integrity cannot be overstated.

At the same time, systems should incorporate incentives to encourage people to do the right thing, adequate transparency mechanisms to provide reasonable assurance that people will do the right thing, and appropriate accountability mechanisms if people do not do the right thing. These basic principles can be applied to a broad range of professional, business, government and personal situations, including how to restore trust and confidence not only in the performance and accountability profession but also in the broader business community and the world's capital markets.

Although it is too early to predict the outcome of many of the reforms taken by legislators, regulators, accountability professionals, and others, it appears that we are headed in the right direction. If effectively implemented, analysed and adjusted as needed, these reforms should prove effective. I believe that continual dialogue and cooperation among these parties as well as sustained reform efforts will ultimately create an environment that will help our financial markets to thrive and grow. Finally, each individual in the accountability, management, governance, and oversight process needs to take personal responsibility for his or her actions; fulfil the obligations and responsibilities of their respective profession; and work diligently to restore, sustain, and expand the integrity and future of our capital markets.

This article is based on a speech Mr. Walker gave at the Institute of Governance, Public Policy, and Social Research at Queen's University in Belfast, Northern Ireland, in September 2004. Since then, the PCAOB and the SEC have taken several steps to help implement the internal control provisions of the Sarbanes-Oxley Act. For example, in March 2005, the SEC extended the section 404 compliance dates for foreign issuers and "non-accelerated filers" (filers with equity market capitalization of less than $75 million) to the first fiscal year ending on or after July 15, 2006. The SEC also established an Advisory Committe on Smaller Public Companies. In April 2005, the SEC held a roundtable discussion to obtain input for its study of the initial implementation of the internal control reporting provisions of the Sarbanes-Oxley Act. The roundtable included the PCAOB and featured a broad range of stakeholders. In May 2005, the PCAOB issued further guidance to auditors on issues raised in implementing PCAOB's Auditing Standard No. 2, which is aimed at making the audits of internal control over financial reporting more efficent and cost-effective. GAO continues to monitor the implementation of the Sarbanes-Oxley Act and provides regular input to the PCAOB, the SEC, the accounting profession, and Congress on these matters.

3

Accountability in the Age of Global Markets

William J. McDonough

Introduction

As the publication of this book demonstrates, the corporate scandals of recent years have provided much fodder for academic research and debate. It is my hope that such research, along with robust discussions in university classrooms and other forums, may encourage the development of a new generation of business leaders – leaders, needless to say, who would take a higher road than the one we have seen used in recent years.

More than three years have passed since Enron became the first in a series of scandalous business failures. The fact that regulators, lawmakers and investors believe there is still much work to be done says much about how deeply public confidence has been undermined as a result of corporate misdeeds. Sadly, I have not seen the private sector dignifying itself by a heroic response to the crisis in confidence. Some companies are doing the right thing, and some business groups are saying the right things. Vastly more needs to be done.

Free and open markets are the foundation of democratic nations and their citizens. Such markets are the ultimate reflections of democracy: citizens and institutions can weigh for themselves the value of an investment and decide for themselves how much of their future well-being to stake to that investment. And the companies that wish to tap the public markets must campaign for the public trust and convince the investors, as voters must be convinced, that investment in those companies is worth the risk. It is the job of regulators, government officials and business leaders to ensure that the marketplace for these investor-voters is open, efficient, transparent and, above all, fair.

At no time in the history of the world has this duty been more important than now. International business and finance is not a theory, it is a reality. Many shared what appeared to be the good times of the 1990s, and many have shared the bad times brought on by the corporate failures of the last three years. I recognise that, despite the interdependence of economies across the globe, the political jurisdictions are still those of the nation-states. For regulators, the challenge is to minimise the burdens of duplicative regulation at the same time that they fulfil their obligations to the investors and the public to close the gaps that the limitations of local regulation can foster.

Let me describe the response in the United States to the corporate failures. Keep in mind that more than half of all households in the United States are invested in some way in the US stock markets. When the stock markets fell in response to the corporate failures, those households lost money and in many cases the ability to retire from work. Those investors are also voters, and when voters demand change, the US Congress listens. Congress responded to the corporate failures with the Sarbanes-Oxley Act of 2002.

The Act was radical in the actions it prescribed – and those it proscribed – for the participants in US securities markets. Yet it passed the US Senate unanimously. More significantly, it was approved in a Republican-led House of Representatives with only three 'no' votes, and it was signed into law by a Republican President. How could that have happened? I believe it happened because in the course of the 1990s, many American business leaders got confused and their moral compasses stopped working.

Ten years ago, even five years ago, the US market economy was the model for and the envy of the world. The marvellous flexibility of our economy, our conviction that 'change' is a good word, and the market's constant striving for innovation were and are factors that make our economic system one that can compete with – and, we believe, beat – any other.

It is particularly sad that such confusion took place because in other respects US businesses in the 1990s responded in a brilliant way to a very serious challenge. Global competition in the world economy became much more intense in the course of the decade, and many American companies lost pricing power. It is easy to see why a manu-facturing firm in Chicago cannot increase prices if it has to compete with firms in Mexico, China, India and other countries with dramatically lower labour costs. But service firms discovered that they had the same problem. A US firm could not raise prices for, say, a call centre in New Jersey if it was competing with call centres in New Delhi. Only very local services, such as health care and legal services, have been immune from this global pressure to reduce prices.

At the same time, the tight labour market that existed in the United States in the 1990s made it even more difficult for US companies to reduce prices. The only way to avoid funding the wage increases by reducing profits is to improve labour productivity, the output per unit of labour input.

Labour productivity increased on average about 1.5% per year from 1973 to 1995, which meant that the economy could grow only slowly without putting strong pressure on resources and forcing inflation. One of the major tenets of post-World War II economic theory is that there is what I call a speed limit on the economy. That speed limit is the sum of labour force participation growth, about 1% per year, and labour force productivity. So the speed limit from 1973 to 1995 was 2.5%.

A different but related tenet is the relationship between unemployment and inflation, known as the non-accelerating inflation rate of unemployment, or NAIRU. Most economists agreed that the NAIRU was 6%. An unemployment rate below that would bring inflation. And yet in 1996 and later, the economy was growing at well above 2.5% and unemployment kept heading down, eventually below 4%. Not even paranoid central bankers could see inflation anywhere. US businesses, lacking pricing power and facing rising wages, solved part of their problem by investing in information technology to help them run their businesses more efficiently. Investing in IT was just the beginning. The way of doing business also had to change.

Retail trade is an obvious example. At checkout in a modern store, a bar code tells the clerk what each item costs and what the total bill is. More importantly, the same information system updates the inventory records and the order book when the inventory hits a level indicating it is time to order. What is saved, compared to an earlier era, is that there is no need for clerks with pencils to keep inventory records; no need for sizeable warehouses, thanks to the model of the Japanese just-in-time delivery system previously used only in manufacturing; and there is a saving on the cost of financing now unneeded inventories.

This was a brilliant response by business executives throughout the United States. These and similar systems not only financed higher wages for those working, but increased profits substantially. Productivity at the national level averaged 2.5% from 1996 to 2000 and over 5% since then.

Business leaders deserved credit for their response. But that credit may have helped confuse them. Pundits told them it was a new economic era, and the excitement went to people's heads in a variety of ways. Two things stand out: executive compensation and the drive for ever increasing and fully predictable quarterly profits.

In 1980, the average chief executive officer of a large company made 40 times more than the average employee in his or her firm. That multiple could be presumed to make sense because of the extra preparation, the risk-taking ability and the leadership skills that are necessary for CEOs.

By 2000, the multiple of the average CEO's pay over that of the average worker in the firm had risen to at least 400 times. This means that, in the course of 20 years, the multiple of CEO pay went up by a factor of 10. There is no economic theory, however far-fetched, that can justify that increase. I believe it is also grotesquely immoral. I knew a lot of CEOs in 1980, and I can assure you that the CEOs of 2000 were not 10 times better than their predecessors – if better at all. The most famous US banker and probably the most highly respected in that earlier era was Walter Wriston of Citibank. Walter never made as much as $1 million in any year in his entire career.

Now let's look at earnings performance. During the 1990s, there developed a theme in corporate America of predicting quarterly earnings, something accomplished by the people in the financial management of public companies guiding allegedly independent investment analysts to a consensus on how much the company would make in the next quarter. That morphed into a string of predictions of ever rising quarterly profits. Now from time to time the profits of a few companies may grow steadily, but the notion that profit growth would go on indefinitely for lots of companies requires that we forget that there is a business cycle, a profit cycle and the law of gravity.

In this time of confusion, if a company made its forecast, the genius CEO – the one earning 400 times the employees' income – was truly a genius. If the forecast was missed by underperforming, the genius was a fool and his or her tenure was questioned by the pundits of the investment banking community and the financial press. What was really going on, in many cases, was that companies were cooking the books, with the help of outsiders such as lawyers, investment bankers, commercial bankers, accountants, and auditors.

The American people – that wise body politic that in times of national crisis has picked such great presidents as Lincoln, Teddy Roosevelt, Franklin Roosevelt and Harry Truman – were noticing the steady but implausible increases in executive pay and quarterly earnings, and they didn't like it. But until the middle of 2000, everybody was enjoying the longest economic expansion in American history, and the public did not react. However, when the tech bubble broke in the second quarter of 2000 and the large market correction began and continued, the half of American households invested in the stock market began to notice that their retirement plans and mutual funds were losing value. They were getting unhappy, but they were not sure who to blame.

The scandals taught them who to blame: corporate executives. Enron was not only managed by people of questionable integrity – the CFO has been sentenced to 10 years in prison – but people of such shocking selfishness that they sold their stock on insider information at the same time their employee stock plans were frozen. Lest anybody think it was just Enron and WorldCom, financial implosions were happening with sufficient rapidity to make the American people very, very angry. Congress responded with the Sarbanes-Oxley Act of 2002, and it was signed by a President who called it the most important securities legislation since 1934, when Franklin Roosevelt occupied the White House.

At the heart of the Sarbanes-Oxley Act is the intent of Congress and the President to force the private sector to clean itself up and behave in a way that the public can both trust and respect. It is important to note that Congress directed the law at public companies – those that seek to raise capital in US markets. In the United States, the Sarbanes-Oxley Act directly affects as many as 15 000 US public companies. Those companies are headquartered in the United States, but they often have significant operations in other countries as well.

From outside the United States, the securities of about 1200 public companies trade in US securities markets, and so those companies must also follow many of the requirements of the Act. Indeed, the flag of a multinational company can change very quickly with a merger or significant acquisition, and with such changes companies can find themselves subject to different regulatory structures just as quickly.

As we saw with Royal Ahold, Parmalat and others, no borders and no oceans could contain the tidal wave of losses and uncertainty brought about by business failures. In the same way that the US Congress took steps to restore the public's confidence in our markets, EC Commissioner Frits Bolkestein and his staff took important steps to help restore confidence in European markets.

It was no accident that my first trip outside the United States as chairman of the Public Company Accounting Oversight Board was to Brussels in September 2003. To say that Europe is the United States' most important strategic ally and economic partner is simply an understatement.

I personally have always been an ardent supporter of a strong and unified Europe. As a central banker and chairman of the Basel Committee, I championed the adoption of the euro and the creation of the European Central Bank. So, it makes sense that, as chairman of the PCAOB, I came first to the European Commission to start the dialogue concerning our mutual interests. I wanted to assure those who are regulators, accountants and investors here in Europe that we in the United States recognise the huge – and hugely important – steps involved in building new safeguards for their public markets and that we support their efforts to build those safeguards in a manner that will allow us together to protect our global markets.

Reformers in Europe will undoubtedly encounter opposition, particularly that rooted in fear of what some call overregulation, or the fear that regulation will squelch the economic rewards of the risk-taking we encourage in the business world. I have urged our colleagues in Europe to stay the course. In the United States, we have heard concern over whether the reforms in our new law could slow economic growth. I offer the same answer to all business leaders: nobody ever made a company, or an auditing firm, or any other endeavour, great by playing defence. Organisations are made great by great leaders, who will continue to take deliberate risk. I think any concern that such leaders have about the implementation of the Sarbanes-Oxley Act is marginal.

The investing public in both the United States and in Europe expressed their mistrust of the private sector. Having spent half my life in the private sector, I find that disappointing. Therefore, I regularly call upon the leaders of the private sector in the United States to show the courage to do everything possible to run their organisations better not just in a business sense, but in a business ethics sense, and in a moral sense, to restore the public's confidence.

Failures in financial reporting were among the specific concerns addressed by Congress in the Sarbanes-Oxley Act. The reliability of a company's statements of its financial condition and results of operations – statements depended on by shareholders, management, directors, regulators, lenders and investors – is the cornerstone of our financial markets. More specifically, Congress found that the system of checks and balances that was supposed to vouchsafe those financial reports was badly broken. In this system are directors, members of audit committees, management and, of course, external auditors. The Act prescribed specific steps to address specific failures and codify the responsibilities of corporate executives, corporate directors, lawyers and accountants.

The merits, benefits, cost and wisdom of each of the prescriptions can and will fuel debate. But the context for the passage of the Sarbanes-Oxley Act, and the President's signing it into law on 30 July 2002, cannot be ignored: corporate leaders and advisors failed. People lost their livelihoods and their life savings. The faith of America and the world in US markets was shaken to the core. The US Congress singled out the auditors of public companies for a new regime of external and independent oversight. Again, the wisdom and the effects of this special attention can be debated, but these two points are indisputable. First, the law is intended to improve the financial reporting of companies that wish to participate in the US securities markets. Second, it is the law. It must be obeyed by all actors in the US capital markets.

For auditors, the changes brought about by this law are a cataclysmic shift in how they do their jobs. For decades, the accounting profession was self-regulating, both in setting standards for audits and in overseeing the application of those standards. Congress and President Bush believed that the self-regulatory system was no longer working, so the Public Company Accounting Oversight Board was created.

Before Sarbanes-Oxley created the PCAOB, auditors of public companies wrote their own standards and regulated their own adherence to those standards. The Securities and Exchange Commission had the power to prescribe the kinds of financial statements and other disclosures public companies should file. The SEC also had the power to limit an auditor's ability to practise before the Commission if an auditor failed to live up to professional standards or violated the federal securities law. But Congress and the President decided that more was needed.

Sarbanes-Oxley established the PCAOB as an independent, private-sector regulator. Our mission is to oversee the auditors of public companies in order to protect the interests of investors and further the public interest in the preparation of informative, fair, and independent audit reports. In other words, we are in business to hold auditors accountable for their work. All five Board members are appointed by the SEC. The Sarbanes-Oxley Act requires that the Board members take on their duties as full-time jobs. The Act also spells out that the Board members serve staggered, five-year terms, and that two members be certified public accountants.

The PCAOB's budget and rules, including the auditing standards developed by the Board and its staff, must be approved by the SEC. But the PCAOB is neither a government-sponsored nor a taxpayer-funded enterprise. Once a year, the PCAOB submits its budget to the SEC for approval, after which the Sarbanes-Oxley Act requires public companies to pay a pro rata share of that budget based on relative market capitalisation. Congress carefully prescribed that funding system to keep the PCAOB independent both of financing by accounting firms and of the political pressures that can come to bear on regulatory bodies that rely on federal appropriations.

About 8800 public companies and mutual funds, including non-US companies that trade in US markets, paid fees to support our 2004 budget of $103 million. The support fees are not the only connection between the PCAOB and public companies. Even though the Board's direct oversight is limited to the auditors of publicly traded companies, the companies may encounter the PCAOB as a result of its work as inspectors and as standards setters. The PCAOB is going about that mission by fulfilling the four key tasks set out for the Board in the Sarbanes-Oxley Act: registration, inspection, enforcement and standards setting.

Registration

Under Sarbanes-Oxley and the Board's rules, any accounting firm that audits a company whose securities trade in US markets – or plays a substantial role in those audits – must be registered with the PCAOB to continue doing that work. The SEC will not allow a public company to submit a financial statement that is audited by an accounting firm that is not registered with the PCAOB.

The PCAOB built its online registration system from scratch – and in time to meet the statutory deadline for US firms to be registered as of 22 October 2003. By that deadline, 598 accounting firms were registered with the Board. By the end of 2004, almost 1400 accounting firms were registered with the Board. Before any firm is registered with the PCAOB, the Board and staff confirm that the firm is licensed and in good standing with its local authority. Our registration staff works with many non-US regulators for assistance on licensure issues.

About two-thirds of the registered firms are based in the United States, but the Act applies to the auditors of any company whose securities trade in US markets. It is not surprising that more than 500 non-US accounting firms were registered with the PCAOB by the end of 2004. Many US companies have significant operations abroad, and their operations are also typically audited by non-US registered firms.

As I mentioned, registration is a prerequisite for accounting firms to continue their work as auditors of public companies. It is also the foundation, established in the Sarbanes-Oxley Act, for the PCAOB to perform its important functions of inspection and enforcement.

Inspections

The PCAOB is now in the second year of the regular inspections that are called for in the Sarbanes-Oxley Act. The Act specifies that regular inspections will occur every year for firms with more than 100 audit clients. There are eight such firms in the United States and one in Canada. Firms with one to 100 audit clients will be inspected once every three years. And when the Board thinks circumstances warrant, the Act authorises us to order a special inspection, regardless of timing. Needless to say, the largest single group of employees at the PCAOB is in its inspections division – all of them highly experienced auditors. They are based in our headquarters office in Washington, as well as New York and six other regional offices in the United States to make it easier for them to reach the regional offices of the registered accounting firms.

The Board's inspections take up the basic task that had been the province of the profession's peer review system in the United States, but the inspections go much further than peer review ever did. Under the peer review system, reviewers focused on technical compliance with professional accounting and auditing standards and, on the basis of that review, opined on overall quality control.

At the PCAOB, we begin by looking at the business context in which audits are performed. We focus on the influences – both good and bad – on firm practices. These include firm culture and the relationships between a firm's audit practice and its other practices and between engagement personnel in field and affiliate offices and a firm's national office. By doing so, we believe that we will gain a much better appreciation for the practices and problems that led to the most serious financial reporting and auditing failures of the last few years.

When they go to an accounting firm, PCAOB inspectors are looking for the compliance required in the Sarbanes-Oxley Act, that is, compliance with the Act, the rules of the Board and the SEC, and professional standards. The Board has given considerable thought to how our oversight programme should operate *vis-à-vis* non-US firms that audit or play a substantial role in auditing US public companies. We had several in-depth discussions with Commissioner Bolkestein, EC Director General Alexander Schaub, the staff of the Internal Market Directorate, and others involved in regulating financial reporting and auditing in Europe. On the basis of those discussions, we published, in October 2003, a briefing paper that described a framework for oversight that depends, to the maximum extent possible, on cooperation among regulators.

In June 2004, the Board adopted rules for oversight of non-US firms that implement this framework. The rules permit varying degrees of reliance on a firm's home-country system of external quality assurance inspections. That reliance is based on a sliding scale, in much the same way that an auditor decides on how much he or she may rely on the work of others in assessing the financial statements of a company. The more independent and rigorous the local system of oversight, the higher the reliance on that system can be. The PCAOB hopes to be able to rely to a great extent on the inspection work of other regulators, and it is in that regard that the Board welcomes the establishment of new, independent oversight systems outside the United States.

The Board's reliance will necessarily depend upon whether it is able to reach arrangements among regulators concerning inspection work programmes for non-US firms scheduled for inspection. Among other things, an inspection work programme will identify appropriate procedures to test a firm's quality control system and to confirm that quality control is effective by sampling engagements.

While I've been talking about the assistance of non-US regulators in the oversight of firms registered with the PCAOB, true cooperation is obviously a two-way street. The Board has repeatedly stated its willingness to assist non-US regulators in their oversight of US accounting firms, to the greatest extent permitted by law. What the PCAOB is looking for inside accounting firms is a quality control system that, through good governance and other means, establishes and reinforces a commitment to the highest quality auditing. PCAOB inspectors look for the 'tone at the top' of the firm. Do the managing partner and the audit team leader understand what is demanded of the accounting firm in this new era of regulation and oversight? Do they understand the standards for audits, and, just as important, do they understand why those standards are in place? Do the managers lead by example, demonstrating every day the value of those standards?

The Board and its inspectors want to know if the message of 'doing the right thing' is reaching the rank and file in the firms. Our inspectors talk to the managers, but they also talk to the least experienced members of the audit teams to find out if the message is reaching them. The inspectors look at how often and how well the message is delivered.

PCAOB inspectors look at the firms' systems for compensation and promotion. Are the best auditors rewarded for being the best auditors, or are they rewarded for something else? The inspectors look at how clients are selected and how they are let go. PCAOB inspectors will look at audits as well. They identify and examine the audits that carry the most risk, and we sample what should be simpler, more routine audits. As part of the examination of specific companies' audits, the inspectors interview the chairs of the audit committees at those companies to find out how well the auditor is communicating with the audit committee, which is now responsible to shareholders for hiring and firing the auditor. PCAOB inspectors also want to know if and why audit partners are transferred from one engagement to another. Accounting firms and corporate management should be on notice that the PCAOB takes a dim view of the so-called 'partner switching' that has been known to occur when managers believe an audit partner is being too tough.

Even before they were registered, the Big 4 accounting firms – Deloitte & Touche, Ernst & Young, KPMG, and PricewaterhouseCoopers – showed commitment to the success of Sarbanes-Oxley's reforms by allowing PCAOB inspectors on their premises in 2003 for limited procedures. The inspectors went into the national and regional offices of the Big 4 in the United States, looking for the compliance I described and, in each firm, examining selected portions of a minimum of 16 audit engagements.

The inspectors identified significant audit and accounting issues that were missed by the firms and identified concerns about significant aspects of each firm's quality control systems. Nevertheless, nothing that the inspectors found in the limited procedures undermined the Board's belief that these firms are capable of the highest quality auditing. The Board published the public reports of the limited inspections in late August 2004. The reports summarise the inspectors' findings, and they give clues to how the work of the PCAOB intersects with publicly traded companies.

More specifically, the reports spell out that in the course of examining individual audits, our inspectors identified possible departures from Generally Accepted Accounting Principles in companies' financial statements. When that happens, we encourage the accounting firm to consider the issue and review it with the company and its audit committee. In appropriate circumstances, the Board may also report that information to the SEC, which has ultimate authority for determining a company's compliance with GAAP.

The Board's reports do not identify the companies whose audits have been examined. The reports describe the inspectors' observations about apparent failures or deficiencies in individual audits, but the reports do not identify the clients involved.

The inspectors' discussions with the accounting firms about deficiencies started a process that resulted in some companies restating their financial statements as a result of questions raised by PCAOB inspectors. That may continue to happen as the Board proceeds with its inspections. But the Board is firm in its belief that it is plainly in the public interest that errors caught in our inspections be corrected, where appropriate, through restatements.

When PCAOB inspectors find potential errors, their first step is to present the potential error to the auditor in the form of a comment. Although the auditor may be – and in many cases ought to be – talking with the issuer about the potential auditing or accounting error the inspectors have identified, the inspection processes do not involve our addressing the matter directly with the issuer.

Some errors are resolved at this stage in the process, either by the firm conducting additional audit work, by the firm working with the issuer to determine whether a restatement is necessary, or otherwise. In appropriate cases where an error has caused financial statements not to be presented fairly in accordance with GAAP, and the error goes uncorrected, the Board will take all necessary steps to bring the error to the attention of the people responsible for seeing that it is addressed. In many cases, this means the Board will refer the matter to the SEC to follow up with the issuer.

The Board will address many of the auditing problems identified during our inspections through a combination of supervision through the inspection process and standards setting. Situations will inevitably arise in which those tools are inadequate, however.

Enforcement

When the Board finds serious violations of PCAOB standards or the securities laws by auditors under the Board's jurisdiction, we will use our authority under the Act to investigate and, as appropriate, to seek disciplinary sanctions.

The authority to investigate includes authority to seek relevant documents and testimony from auditors and others, including the firms' clients. Because audit failures typically have an impact on the reliability of the financial statements, PCAOB investigations may often be a component of a larger investigation of the financial reporting itself and management's role in that reporting. The Board therefore expects to work very closely with the SEC in such cases.

The Board's inspections and enforcement activities will also provide robust empirical and anecdotal evidence that will enable those developing auditing standards – our Board members and staff – to set priorities and to identify needs to develop or amend standards.

Standards setting

The Board has already embarked on an aggressive agenda that is aimed at strengthening auditing standards in areas that were of particular concern to the Congress, as expressed in the Act, and in areas that the Board identified internally through inspections or externally through outreach to investors, auditors, regulators, managers, academics and others.

First, as required by the Act, the Board adopted interim auditing standards – the body of auditing standards that had been developed by the profession, through the American Institute of Certified Public Accountants. At the same time, the Board announced that it would review all of the interim standards and would determine whether they should be modified, repealed, or made permanent. This will, of course, be a long-term project.

Second, the Board developed and adopted three new standards – on references to PCAOB standards in audit reports, on auditing internal control over financial reporting, and on audit documentation. As a result of these standards, audit reports on public company financial statements will now say that the audit was conducted in accordance with the standards of the PCAOB where it previously referred to Generally Accepted Auditing Standards. In the standard for auditors' documentation of their work on audits, the PCAOB ask that an auditor's work papers be sufficient to enable another auditor, such as one of the Board's inspectors, to understand the work the auditor performed and the evidence that was obtained to support the auditor's report.

Finally, the Board's auditing standard on internal control implemented a significant requirement of Sarbanes-Oxley. Section 404 of the Act directed the SEC to set out the rules for management's assessment of internal control, but 404 directed the PCAOB to set out the standards for auditors to follow when they attest to management's assessment.

The Board did that through our Auditing Standard No. 2. Under AS 2, auditors must examine in detail and report on whether a company's internal control over financial reporting is designed and operating effectively. The examination of internal control helps the auditor better plan and conduct the audit of the financial statements and determine whether those statements are fairly presented. In this way, the integrated audit helps to achieve the Congress's intention to improve the quality and integrity of both corporate controls over financial reporting and of independent financial statement audits. The Board has told the accountants that they must restore the faith of the investing public in their profession and that will be done sooner and better if they run their firms in a way aimed at just that: restoring public confidence.

My impression as of now is that the accountants are taking exactly that approach and opting to see the Public Company Accounting

Oversight Board as a catalyst for restoring investor confidence. That, if I am right, is a very wise choice. Wise choices are what all of us should be considering at this time, whether we are in the public or private sector. Whatever our calling, we must ask ourselves: does the tone at the top of my organisation – does my tone in my daily dealings with those who are less successful, less fortunate – reflect my recognition of my role in promoting the greater good?

Those of us who are successful should realise that good luck, and not just our own efforts, got us here. I believe that we owe to those less fortunate than us the opportunities they need to be successful. So the investment in and belief in our peoples is the moral obligation and responsibility of all of us who have the opportunity to lead. No country should be complacent about good leadership. We all have to do better.

In a world in which modern communications make people much more aware of the lives enjoyed by people of other countries than ever before, individuals in government and in leadership positions are dependent more than ever on the goodwill of the people. The way in which the people express their goodwill depends on the history, the culture, and the desires of the people of a given country. But anyone who thinks that the people do not have a view and will not express it if they become unhappy enough is living in the past, not the present. The best way for the leaders in any endeavour to maintain and deserve the support of the people is to give them the opportunity to share fully in that leadership, or at least to believe that their children can and will.

In short, the best way to achieve and maintain the support of the people is to deserve it by the way we work and live and behave. What's at stake for all of us is the trust of the people in our markets and the companies that drive our economies. I challenge our leaders in business and government to find and take every opportunity to restore that trust.

4

European Responses to Corporate Governance Challenges

Alexander A. Schaub

Introduction

Books such as this, gathering so many leading academics, practitioners and regulators, from both Europe and other parts of the world, contribute to broadening our horizons and converging our thinking on these crucial corporate governance issues. The growing interdependency of world economies, especially between the EU and the US, makes such dialogue a necessity, not an option. Interdependency will grow, not shrink. Our capital markets are integrating, not fragmenting. Strong transatlantic cooperation is vital to restore investors' confidence in the way companies are run and governed. If our capital markets cannot regain confidence, there will be very serious consequences on the financing of companies because the cost of capital will increase, and also on pensioners who enjoy smaller, more fragile, incomes. So corporate governance is not a fashion – it is an imperative. Standards have got to improve.

The Importance of Corporate Governance for the Economy

The fact that corporate governance is now at the heart of the political agenda is not simply a response to the recent wave of scandals in the US and in Europe. A sound corporate governance framework is a key condition for liquid capital markets to function well. It is a key component of businesses, competitiveness and efficiency. Corporate governance is about building trust and confidence in corporations and markets by enhancing transparency and ensuring the fairness and account-ability of corporations towards shareholders and other stakeholders. It is a prerequisite to the integrity and credibility of individual companies, financial institutions, stock exchanges and indeed the entire market economy.

Corporate governance, therefore, is not an aim in itself. The trust and confidence which it seeks to promote is crucial in attracting investment, supporting corporate development and fostering long-term economic growth. In today's largely integrating markets, failure to address corporate governance and deal with the regulatory issues associated with it will have strong repercussions on global financial markets and may jeopardise financial stability.

The recent scandals, nonetheless, prompt us to consider all the tools in our possession to minimise the future risk of corporate malpractice. Strengthening the internal controls of corporations, restoring the credibility of external audit and promoting fair and reliable accounting will contribute significantly to reducing this risk. Information disclosed by issuers and companies must be clear, complete and fair. It must also be disclosed on time. Improving disclosure to enhance transparency is, there-fore, crucial. No issuer must be allowed to disclose misleading information.

The European Commission has taken significant steps in this direction.

The Prospectus Directive[1] harmonises the content of prospectuses in the EU. It gives national authorities extensive supervisory powers in this respect, not least the power to prohibit public offers when the provisions of the directives are not complied with.

Issuers should also systematically disclose non-public price-sensitive information to the market. The Market Abuse Directive[2] sets clear standards for the prompt and fair disclosure of this information.

Furthermore, complex shareholding structures and the recourse to off-balance sheet arrangements should be systematically disclosed. The Commission proposed a directive amending the fourth and seventh company law directives. The proposed amendments aim at imposing specific disclosure requirements with regard to off-balance sheet arrange-ments, covering Special Purpose Vehicles. The same proposal extends the requirement to disclose related party transactions to non-listed companies.

However, efficient risk mitigation requires that other complementary aspects are also taken into account, covering also taxation and law enforcement, with a strong emphasis on international cooperation. In a communication on preventing and combating corporate and financial malpractice adopted in September 2004,[3] the Commission outlined such a global strategy to reinforce the four lines of defence against such malpractice, namely internal controls in the company (mainly through board members), independent audit, supervision and oversight, and law enforcement. This strategy covers not only financial services; it extends to justice and home affairs and tax policy.

The above-mentioned instruments form part of the global framework set up at EU level to enhance the financial transparency of companies, as a key ingredient to healthy financial markets and sound corporate governance. The EU's approach to corporate governance, however, pursues other lines of action. Weaknesses which have been identified in the past, notably with regard to the internal and external controls of companies, must be consistently addressed.

The EU Corporate Governance Framework – Summary Presentation of Main Axes

The European Commission has devised a corporate governance framework which relies on four pillars:

- enhancing transparency on EU capital and securities markets;
- encouraging trustworthy and competent financial intermediaries and proper supervision of financial institutions;
- developing sound mechanisms for internal controls, including real shareholder control; and
- ensuring effective external controls by auditors.

Our main trading partners have chosen a similar approach and share the same objective of enhancing transparency and strengthening the balance of powers within corporations to restore investors' confidence in corporations and in the financial markets.

Three Common Challenges

Recent scandals have highlighted that there are common challenges, which both the US and the EU must address, as a matter of urgency. The main three challenges are, first, to improve the integrity and accountability of board members and enhance shareholders' rights; second, restore the credibility of the audit function; and, last, ensure that accounts give a fair and reliable view of companies' performance.

First Common Challenge: Improve the Integrity and Accountability of Board Members and Enhance Shareholders Rights

The first major common challenge is to improve the integrity and accountability of board members and enhance shareholders' rights.

There is no need to describe the key role which companies' boards play in the governance of companies. Boards must understandably have an in-depth knowledge of the company and act in its best interests. At the same time, they must demonstrate the required independence to oversee management and deal satisfactorily with conflicts of interests, such as remuneration matters. Lastly, and most importantly, they must have proper regard to the shareholders. In listed companies, with dispersed ownership, special consideration is to be given to independent directors. Between often uninformed shareholders and fully informed managers, independent board members have a crucial role to play in overseeing management and dealing with situations which involve conflicts of interests. Fostering the competence and active role of independent directors in these respects will contribute significantly to restore confidence in financial markets. But it is crucial we do not create conditions in which good, competent, professional people, people of honest stock, are afraid to take on such responsibilities because of the fear of excessive liability.

Boards are accountable to shareholders. Shareholders must be given the adequate means to question the boards of the companies they invest in and control the way companies are run. They must be given adequate means to this end.

The Commission has taken a series of initiatives both to increase the integrity and accountability of companies' boards and to enhance shareholders' rights.

The Commission adopted a non-binding recommendation on the role of non-executive or supervisory directors on the board committees of listed companies.[4] This recommendation insists on the necessary balance of executive and non-executive directors in the administrative, managerial and supervisory bodies of listed companies, to avoid that an individual or a small group of individuals dominates decision-making. Boards should be organised in a way that enables a sufficient number of independent non-executive or supervisory directors to play an effective role in defining and dealing with potential conflicts of interest. To this end, the recommendation defines minimum standards for the creation, composition and role of the nomination, remuneration and audit committees of the board committees. The recommendation also lists criteria regarding the qualifications, commitment and independence of directors. As regards independence, a director should not be considered to be 'independent' if he/she is not free from any business, family or other relationship with the company, its controlling shareholder or the company's management. It is also important that companies clearly indicate upon the appointment of any board member whether they consider him/her as independent.

The Commission adopted another non-binding recommendation on directors' remuneration in listed companies.[5] Directors' remuneration is a key area where the risk of conflicts of interests is particularly high and where board accountability must be ensured. Managers should not be able to decide on their own pay. The recommendation, therefore, invites members states to adopt a number of measures ensuring that shareholders are provided adequate information with regard to the remuneration policy and individual pay packages. Companies should publish an annual remuneration policy statement, in which they disclose not only their remuneration policy in the previous year but also details of the breakdown between fixed and variable remuneration, the eligibility criteria for bonuses and non-cash benefits, and their contract policy. Furthermore, companies should disclose detailed information on the pay packages of individual directors, including other cash and non-cash benefits. Proper accountability also means that shareholders should also be given the opportunity to express their view on remuneration policies and approve share option schemes, which are often costly for companies. The recommendation, therefore, provides that the remuneration policy should be a compulsory item at the annual general meeting, thus affording shareholders the opportunity to discuss and vote, though this vote may be of a mere advisory nature. As regards variable remuneration schemes under which directors are paid in shares, options, or granted any right to acquire shares, the recommendation provides that these, and any significant change to them, should be subject to the prior approval of the general meeting. Such approval, which would concern the remuneration system and not the individual packages of directors, would give shareholders much needed oversight over schemes which, in many instances, entail heavy costs on the part of companies.

The Commission also proposed key revisions to the so-called 'accounting directives',[6] with a view to enhance the transparency and confidence in annual reports and accounts.

The accountability of the board for the financial information released by the company should be clearly established. This proposal, therefore, confirms the collective responsibility of the supervisory, administrative and management boards for both financial and key non-financial statements, but leaves Member States free to introduce sanctions to underpin this responsibility. Collective responsibility also does not stop Member States from imposing individual responsibility and/or any criminal liability on board members.

In addition, the proposal imposes the publication by listed EU companies of an annual corporate governance statement which describes the company's corporate governance practices. The corporate governance statement indicates the corporate governance code to which the company is subject, describes the extent to which this code is complied with and, where this is the case, explains the extent of, and the reasons for, any non-compliance. The corporate governance statement further gives information about shareholders' meetings, and the composition and operation of the board and its committees. The corporate governance statement embodies the 'comply or explain' principle, which is the cornerstone of the EU corporate governance framework.

The proposal contains two additional measures which further enhance the transparency of accounts. The first measure relates to Special Purpose Vehicles. Recent scandals have highlighted the fact that such entities often are not captured in the balance sheet. We believe that all off-balance sheet arrangements and their financial impact must be disclosed if they can be material for an investor's assessment of a company's financial position. This is in line with the overarching principle that financial statements must present a true and fair view of a company's financial situation. Accordingly, the

Commission proposes that additional specific information on material off-balance sheet arrangements be disclosed in the notes to the annual and consolidated accounts. The second measure increases the disclosure requirements with regard to related party transactions in unlisted companies by introducing disclosure requirements akin to those contained in IAS 24 with some variation to avoid undue burdens on companies which generally are of more limited size.

The Commission is also looking into legislative measures geared at strengthening shareholders' rights, in particular with regard to the general meeting and cross-border voting. Sound governance requires that shareholders be given adequate means to express their views, participate in debates and exercise due control. In a Single European Market, this means that shareholders should enjoy the same rights regardless of whether they reside or hold an account in the country of the issuer. In cross-border situations, however, the investor's investment is channelled via a chain of financial intermediaries, with the result that it is often not the investor, but an intermediary, who is registered or acknowledged as a shareholder. As a result, cross-border investors, who have paid for their shares exactly as any other shareholder, are often deprived of the right to vote. In addition, the variety of national rules with regard to participation in the general meeting, local constraints on proxy voting, constraints on the right to ask questions and place items on the agenda or table resolutions are further obstacles to the exercise of shareholders' rights on a cross-border basis. The use of electronic means would help bridge the distance, enable direct communication and should, therefore, be encouraged. Two public consultations were launched in September 2004 and May 2005,[7] which could pave the way to a directive laying down minimum standards for shareholders' rights in listed EU companies and abolishing the main obstacles to the cross-border exercise of shareholders' rights.

Lastly, on a slightly different note, the Commission, as announced in our Action Plan, set up the European Corporate Governance Forum.[8] This Forum, which is chaired by the Commission, comprises a limited number of outstanding high-level representatives from various backgrounds. The Forum, which held its first meeting on 20 January 2005, will be convened about twice a year, and should contribute to encourage the coordination and convergence of national corporate governance codes. Coordination should not only extend to the designing of national corporate governance codes but also to the procedures existing in member states to monitor and enforce compliance and disclosure. The Forum will offer significant added value in facilitating dialogue among representatives from all over Europe and from interested parties. It will also play an important role in spreading best practice.

Second Common Challenge: Restore the Credibility of the Audit Function

The second common challenge I mentioned is the need to restore credibility in an effective external control mechanism. The most prominent external control mechanism is control by the public authorities. Effective financial market regulation actually relies on independent audit and the required disclosure to the supervisory bodies. Recent financial scandals, however, have happened in front of the eyes of the companies' auditors. In some instances, only months before, auditors had still given their certification of the financial statements of the company without any qualification. Parmalat had annual losses of between €350 and €450 million between the mid-1990s and 2001. Yet its accounts showed positive earnings. How was this possible? Recent years have seen independent auditors entering into commercial activities that risked compromising the independence and objectivity that shareholders and investors expect from them. Concerns have been expressed about the consistency between these commercial incentives and the interests of the shareholders.

Urgent action was required to restore the credibility of external audits. This led the European Commission to adopt the proposal for a directive to modernise the statutory audit within the European Union.[9] This proposal notably seeks to improve and harmonise audit quality in the EU. It contains a series of measures that contribute to improving audit quality. But, equally important, these measures should be perceived by investors and the markets as doing so, which is crucial for restoring the confidence in the audit function.

Some of the most important elements of the proposal are:

1. The Commission considers that the traditional self-regulation of the audit profession no longer gives investors enough comfort. It

therefore proposes that Member States organise an effective system of public oversight for all statutory auditors and audit firms. The proposal defines functional criteria to ensure fully independent, transparent and knowledgeable oversight by Member State authorities. But also, there must be strong ties between the oversight structure in the EU and third country oversight structures, such as the PCAOB. We are in the same boat – we must work together, and we can *learn* from each other. The key issue here is to be sure that the supervisory structures we have in the EU are able to deliver and implement the requirements of the directives to achieve integration. Before thinking of alternative future structures, we should first analyse whether the EU regulatory networks are working to their maximum efficiency. Whether there are any gaps and – if so – how these can be filled most effectively. So we must move step by step in an open discussion, bringing all Member States and, of course, the European Parliament and market participants along in the process.

2. The requirement for a system of independent external quality review is not only important to detect and correct, but also important to prevent, poor audit quality. But this may not be enough. Ensuring high quality audits in all parts of an audit firm's network can only be achieved if adequate internal quality controls to supplement the external quality assurance are in place. Top class education and training of employees is equally essential in an environment where standards change rapidly and transactions become ever more complex. High ethical standards will raise investors' confidence in the audit profession and I see ethics closely linked to the corporate spirit of management.

3. The proposed use of International Standards on Auditing (ISAs) will lead to fully harmonised audits within the EU. However, the Commission will still have to endorse ISAs which it can only if they have been prepared with a proper due process, transparency and proper oversight.

This leads to an issue which is currently high on the agenda: democratic governance and political accountability of international standards setters. For instance the political accountability of various standards setting bodies, e.g. the International Accounting Standards Board (IASB) and the International Auditing and Assurance Standards Board (IAASB). Governance, financing and the accountability of international standards setters is becoming a subject in the public debate, not only in the European Parliament, but also in national parliaments. If we go back to 2002, the European Union opted for international and not for European accounting standards. About 8000 listed European companies are starting now to prepare their financial statements using International Accounting Standards (IAS) for their 2005 accounts. The Commission remains fully committed to this agenda. But for the more general question of governance of international standards setters, the Commission is working hard to influence the reform process under way within the International Accounting Standards Board (IASB) and is looking very carefully at the arrangements proposed for the International Auditing and Assurance Standards Board (IAASB). In considering this issue we must not lose sight of our overall goal, namely the adoption of international standards which will make it easier for companies to list in the EU and elsewhere across the globe.

There are three key points:

First, that representation within the international standards setter and within a public oversight body should correspond more appropriately to jurisdictions that directly apply the standards.

Second, that effective oversight bodies which approve the work programme of an international standards setter should be in place. If the oversight is effective management of the organisation will improve and confidence will grow.

Third, the funding system; the standards setters are currently sponsored by voluntary contributions from contributors ranging from central banks to listed companies, which raises potential issues of conflict of interest. We will favour all initiatives attempting to solve this issue.

4. In the light of the general confidence crisis, the Commission considers that auditor independence, because it is a vital vehicle for ensuring objective auditors' reports, has to be carefully considered. The Commission proposal makes broad reference to the Commission Recommendation[10] of 2002 on the independence of statutory auditors. We have observed since we issued our proposal spectacular exchanges of views among Member States. A main issue here is provision of non-audit services. One part of the Member States would have preferred, immediately, to prohibit provision of non-audit services whereas others support self-assessment combined with safeguards. We expect that the text will reflect a fair balance of the two approaches. In addition,

with our proposal audit committees should be made compulsory. This would strengthen the independent monitoring of the financial reporting process and help to prevent any undue influence by the executive management.

5. We also have *mandatory rotation* to ensure independence. I think this part of the directive will enhance auditor independence. The rotation of the audit partner or the audit firm should also be made mandatory to further contribute to avoiding conflicts of interest. Member States would have the option of requiring either a change of key audit partners dealing with an audited company while the audit company would keep the work, or a change of the audit firm itself every seven years.

Recent corporate scandals have emphasised the strong need for internationally consistent oversight over audit firms. In this context, the European Commission proposed a framework for cooperation between relevant authorities of third countries. The Commission developed this approach in intense and close cooperation with the US Public Company Accounting Oversight Board (PCAOB). The PCAOB has issued a rule on oversight of non-US audit firms which is the counterpart to our proposal. I believe that this innovative cooperative work-sharing approach is the only sound way to deal with the regulatory challenges of globally operating audit firms. I would like to pay tribute to the outstanding leadership of Bill McDonough on the US side, who helped to make this possible. We have not, and cannot, resolve all the conflicts of law, but we have minimised them – and set up fair cooperative procedures to ensure that we can avoid them.

Third Challenge: Fair Presentation of the Company Through Sound and Reliable Accounting

The third and final challenge is to ensure a high level of 'truth and fairness' of the financial statements. Financial statements give a true and fair view of the company position in a way which is clear and transparent to all stakeholders. To this end, the decision to require publicly traded companies to apply International Accounting Standards (IAS)[11] for the preparation of their consolidated financial statements is a major decision. It enhances significantly transparency by making

European company consolidated accounts comparable, thus helping to build confidence in the markets. Since the beginning of 2005 they are applicable to all listed companies providing a platform for efficient cross-border investment. By and large, IAS are based on principles. Therefore, IAS should be more easily adaptable to financial innovation than more rule-based standards such as US GAAP. We have now adopted all existing IAS except certain provisions of IAS 39 where we – in agreement with most member states and the European Parliament – considered that they require further revision in 2005.

To be more specific, there were two carve-outs:

- The carve-out of the full fair value option (FVO). The full and unlimited FVO was opposed as it could introduce spurious volatility into bank accounts. In particular, the FVO would allow banks to use deteriorations in their own credit worthiness to increase their own accounting profits ('the own credit risk problem').
- The carve-out of certain hedge accounting provisions reflects criticism by the majority of European banks, which argued that IAS 39 in its current form would force them into disproportionate and costly changes both to their asset/liability management and to their accounting systems and would produce unwarranted volatility.

The carve-outs were not optimal or a desired solution. However, under the IAS regulation the Commission cannot rewrite IAS. Hence, we could not propose a modified standard to solve the problems for banks and insurers. In November 2004, the best the Commission could do was to propose endorsing the existing IAS 39 standard with the two carve-outs. We want to underline, however, that the two 'carve-outs' are temporary and exceptional. The Commission expects the IASB to work together with the interested parties to remedy the outstanding problems quickly. We are pleased to notice the steady progress on both issues. In particular, a solution for the fair value option now seems within reach.

A common IAS platform for Europe is an important step, but it is not sufficient. We need to go further and work towards a global consensus on the key prerequisites for a fair presentation of the company in order to limit inconsistencies and confusion. There are two ways to achieve this. While the convergence of accounting standards towards a global set of standards remains the long-term objective, a short-term solution by accepting standards as equivalent should be the way forward. Let me add that convergence and equivalence require technical examinations of what is in the interest of our investors.

The EU has already given the Committee of the European Securities Regulators (CESR) a specific mandate to provide a technical advice on the equivalence between certain third country GAAP (i.e. US GAAP, Canadian GAAP and Japanese GAAP) and IAS/IFRS.[12] The mandate sets the deadline for CESR's technical advice on 30 June 2005. To tackle this mandate, in February 2005 CESR finalised its concept paper clarifying the meaning of equivalence and the goalposts to be used for the technical assessment of the equivalence. The concept paper also outlines the possible remedies in the case that the third country GAAP is not considered fully equivalent with the IAS/IFRS. The second step for CESR is to conduct the technical assessment of equivalence under the EC mandate, in line with the mandate and the principles set out in the concept paper.

Ultimately, the EU and the US will have to cooperate on recognising the equivalence of each set of standards. The recent roadmap agreed between Commissioner McCreevy and SEC Chairman, William Donaldson, represents an important breakthrough and sets a date as early as 2007, but no later than 2009, for a possible SEC decision on the equivalence of IAS.[13] An early date is preferable as the cost savings of avoiding US GAAP reconciliation for EU issuers with US listings are substantial and IAS–US accounting equivalence has been identified as a priority at the political level (EU–US Dialogue) and by the TABD (Trans-Atlantic Business Dialogue).

The European Approach

While the EU and the US face identical key challenges and share broadly the similar objectives of investor protection and restoring the confidence in the capital markets, differences in culture and lawmaking exist. The EU's approach, therefore, is somewhat different to the approach chosen by the US in the Sarbanes-Oxley Act. The Sarbanes-Oxley Act reflects a rule-based approach, which introduces detailed rules of corporate governance. The EU's corporate governance approach is a bottom-up, principle-based approach, with the 'comply or explain' principle as its cornerstone. Concepts such as subsidiarity, proportionality, mutual recognition and home-country control are common language in an EU regulatory environment but somewhat alien in a US environment. Given the cultural diversity and the diversity of business traditions in the EU, a 'one-size-fits-all' approach would be counter-productive and strongly rejected by market participants. As high-lighted by the Commission in its Action Plan on Corporate Governance,[14] the EU's regulatory approach on corporate governance is to be firm on the principles but flexible on their application. Our action concentrates on priorities and is subject to proper due process and consultation. For this reason, we specifically cover cross-border issues where Community action appears to be the only way to achieve an objective. In order to reduce legal uncertainties due to the differences between the national regulations, a minimum degree of harmon-isation is sometimes necessary. Our approach, as described in our Action Plan, distinguishes between measures for which legislative intervention is required and others for which non-binding recommen-dations are regarded as sufficient. Legislation is limited to areas where legal obstacles need to be overcome.

The Need for Strong Cooperation between the EU and the US

As already mentioned, the strong interdependency of EU and US economies calls for strong cooperation in the field of corporate governance, notably given the differences in approach which I have highlighted. Together, the EU and the US account for more than half of the world economy and some 90% of the world capital markets (about $50 trillion). Whatever is done on one side of the Atlantic ripples across to the other. Cooperation in the field of corporate governance is not only beneficial to the EU and the US, it is a necessity. And in everyone's interest. Failure to deal with the regulatory issues associated with corporate governance would expose global financial markets to major adverse impacts. A cooperative approach with the US has proven to work well in the past, as evidenced by the resolution with the PCAOB of problems of audit firm registration and oversight in the US. This cooperation should evolve towards an *ex-ante* cooper-ation and convergence to prevent *ex-post* conflicts from emerging. We have to intensify our efforts in the future. And my clear conviction is that both sides are ready to do so.

Convergence matters both for investors and for issuers. Investors must be certain to benefit from the same level of protection no matter whether they invest in the EU or in the US. Companies need a level playing field with their competitors. Convergence contributes to restoring confidence and building trust in our markets.

Conclusion

The determination with which corporate governance is being addressed worldwide, and notably in the EU and in the US, highlights its importance. In this context, dialogue is key, between the public authorities within the EU and across the Atlantic, of course, but also involving other stakeholders and interested parties. And this extraordinary conference offers the best illustration of what I mean. The end result should be a carefully balanced framework which takes full account of the global activity of market players, and which boosts their efficiency while affording sufficient protection to stakeholders with higher-level standards all round.

Notes

1. Directive 2003/71/EC of 4 November 2003 on the prospectus to be published when securities are offered to the public or admitted to trading and amending Directive 2001/34/EC, OJ 31.12.2003, L 345/64.
2. Directive 2004/39/EC of 28 January 2003 on insider dealing and market manipulation (market abuse), OJ 12.04.2003, L96/16.
3. Communication from the Commission to the Council and the European Parliament on Preventing and Combating Corporate and Financial Malpractice (COM) 2004 211 final – http://europa.eu.int/comm/internal_market/company/financial-crime/index_en.htm#malpractice
4. Commission recommendation on the role of non-executive or supervisory directors and on the committees of the (supervisory) board – http://www.europa.eu.int/comm/internal_market/company/independence/index_en.htm
5. Commission recommendation on fostering an appropriate regime for the remuneration of directors of listed companies – http://www.europa.eu.int/comm/internal_market/company/directors-remun/index_en.htm

6. Proposal for a directive of the Council and the European Parliament amending Council Directives 78/660/EEC and 83/349/EEC concerning the annual accounts of certain types of companies and consolidated accounts – http://europa.eu.int/comm/internal_market/company/board/index_en.htm

7. http://europa.eu.int/comm/internal_market/company/shareholders/index_en.htm

8. http://europa.eu.int/comm/internal_market/company/ecgforum/index_en.htm

9. Proposal for a directive on statutory audit of annual accounts and consolidated accounts and amending Council Directives 78/660/EEC and 83/349/EEC.

10. Commission Recommendation of 16 May 2002 – Statutory Auditors' Independence in the EU: A Set of Fundamental Principles C(2002) 1873. OJ L 191, 19/07/2002, p. 22 – http://europa.eu.int/comm/internal_market/auditing/officialdocs_en.htm

11. http://europa.eu.int/comm/internal_market/accounting/ias_en.htm

12. http://europa.eu.int/comm/internal_market/securities/docs/cesr/final-mandate-ias-equivalence_en.pdf

13. Commission Press Release IP/05/469, 22 April 2005.

14. http://europa.eu.int/eur-lex/en/com/cnc/2003/com2003_0284en01.pdf

5

Economic Globalisation and National Corporate Governance Reform

Dermot McCann

Introduction

The convergent reform of national regulatory systems is a frequently anticipated consequence of the impact of economic globalisation on national economies. It is argued that open economic borders unleash global market forces to operate across and within nation-states. This easing of international exchange 'heightens the transmission of world economic trends to domestic political economies' (Frieden and Rogowski 1996, 32). As firms and countries compete, 'they are driven towards the most efficient modalities of economic activity' (Gourevitch 2003a, 316). The desire for individual survival induces a collective pursuit of 'best practice'. Currently, best practice in economic and regulatory behaviour is widely perceived as Anglo-American practice.

In respect of corporate governance specifically, the process of globalisation has been linked with the growing dominance of the shareholder-oriented model. In a clear statement of this position, Hansmann and Kraakman argue that, 'as a consequence of both logic and experience, there is a convergence of view that the best way to [maximise aggregate welfare] is to make corporate managers strongly accountable to shareholder interests and, at least in direct terms, only to those interests' (Hansmann and Kraakman 2002, 58). The model holds that other corporate constituencies, such as creditors, employees, suppliers and customers, should have their interests protected by contractual means rather than through participation in corporate governance. Non-controlling shareholders should receive strong protection from exploitation by controlling shareholders. Finally, it is argued that the 'principal measure of the interest of the publicly traded corporation's shareholders is the market value of their shares in the firm' (Hansmann and Kraakman 2002, 58). Mechanisms such as cross-shareholding alliances, group pyramiding arrangements, employee board representation rights, opaque accountancy practices etc., that privilege insider shareholder and other stakeholder groups to the detriment of outsiders and that inhibit the development of an effective market for corporate control, need to be restricted.

The perceived growing influence of this 'standard model' of corporate governance across the world is portrayed as being partly the product of 'the widespread acceptance of a shareholder-centred ideology of corporate law among international business, government and legal elites' (Hansmann and Kraakman 2002, 56). However, the greatest impetus for the triumph of these ideas is said to derive from the related 'inter-nationalisation of both product and financial markets [that] has brought individual firms from jurisdictions adhering to different models into direct competition' (Hansmann and Kraakman 2002, 66). Firms operating under national regimes that apply a shareholder-oriented model can be expected to have important competitive advantages over firms adhering more closely to other models. These include access to equity capital at lower costs (including start-up capital), more aggressive development of new product lines, stronger incentives to reorganise along lines that are managerially coherent, and more rapid abandonment of inefficient investments. The comparative quality of law and regulation has become a major competitive factor. National systems that do not conform to the standard model will inevitably be constrained by relative economic failure to embrace it. Ultimately, the dynamics of market competition between firms and states will effect a transformation of regulatory practice.

Such analyses, which can be broadly termed 'competitive efficiency' perspectives, have the merit of clarity and confidence in their reasoning and predictions. They anticipate that economic globalisa-tion will inevitably and inexorably induce convergence in national regulatory practice as a by-product of market competitive dynamics. However, as a model of linkage between economic globalisation and national reform they can never be more than partial. Typically their analysis of the implications of global economic change for the economic interests of firms and states is not matched by an analysis of the rather different dynamics of national public policymaking. Too often it is assumed that politics will inevitably accommodate the functional requirements of the economic system and produce policy change. This is an unsatisfactory perspective. It is implausible to suggest that systemic need (even if such could be established) will generate the requisite policy response. To understand the source of specific legal and regulatory changes, it is necessary to address questions of political agency. Who acts and why?[1] In what ways and through which mechanisms do globalisation pressures feed into and shape the actions of individuals and groups? To what extent are the nature and consequences of this political mobilisation affected by the particular structure of a political system and the opportunities it affords reformers to influence policy? In short, the analysis of the pressures generated by economic globalisation must be accompanied by an analysis of how such pressures are translated into public policy. What is required is a model of linkage between economic globalisation and domestic regulatory change that addresses the economic and political processes involved and the nature of the connection between them.

The need for such explanatory models is well recognised in the general political economy literature on globalisation. The purpose of this chapter is to outline two of the most influential approaches that have emerged in recent years and assess their relative plausibility in explaining the specific issue of corporate governance reform. The basis for this assessment will be provided by two brief case studies of reform in Britain and Germany. Possessed of markedly different systems of corporate governance, both countries have introduced major change in the last decade or so. To what extent do these explanatory perspectives offer a convincing insight into the causal dynamics of these developments?

The next section will outline the central analytical claims of the two explanatory perspectives. This will be followed by a brief sketch of the nature of the reforms in Britain and Germany. The concluding section will then evaluate the relative explanatory merits of the two perspectives in the light of the politics of reform in Britain and Germany.

Perspectives on Linkage and Convergence

Explanations of the relationship between global economic change and national regulatory reform have been dominated in recent years by two broad competing perspectives. The first, which can be termed the interest-based or 'corporate pluralist' approach, seeks to supplement the economic insight of the competitive efficiency model with a related analysis of the nature and sources of political agency that economic processes generate. The second approach falls under the rubric of national production systems or 'varieties of capitalism' analysis. This rejects the universalist economics of the competitive efficiency analysis, instead attributing a decisive weight to the economic institutional particularities of specific national production systems in explaining responses to globalisation.

Corporate Pluralism

This perspective starts with the basic contention that economic globalisation will have a differential impact on the interests of economic actors. Though the nature of the impact anticipated is sensitive to the underlying economic model employed, the thesis at its most basic is that the process of globalisation benefits those who export and those who consume imports while hurting those who compete with imports (Frieden and Rogowski 1996, 29–30). It is this fundamental division of economic experience and opportunity that feeds into and structures the process of public policy reform. It is anticipated that those who see significant potential benefit from globalisation will have an incentive to defect from established systems and practices that inhibit market liberalisation, and to mobilise politically to press for reform. The presumption is that as economic globalisation unfolds, the proportion of the economy that will benefit from liberalisation will expand and the number of economic actors with an incentive to defect will grow.

The political analysis offered by corporate pluralism has two variants. In the simple version, the expectation of a growing business constituency for reform is linked to a pluralist model of politics. Governments respond to lobbying power. The tipping point between policy continuity and significant change will come when the potential beneficiaries outweigh the likely losers from reform. In the case of corporate governance specifically, demands for reform can be anticipated from a range of actors, both investors and creditor firms, that seek the freedom to exploit the new competitive opportunities opened up by globalisation. Hansmann and Kraakman speak of an emerging shareholding class 'as a broad and powerful interest group in both political and corporate affairs across jurisdictions' (Hansmann and Kraakman 2002, 66). In relation to minority shareholder rights, Shinn outlines a model of linkage that identifies blockholders as having an incentive to supply enhanced minority protection, both directly and through lobbying for regulatory reform, in order to attract higher valuations by foreign investors (Shinn 2001). Resistance to reform may be expected to come from groups that are sheltered from competition by existing regulations and are anxious to protect their advantageous 'rents'. Globalisation will inevitably empower the former and undermine the latter until reform is triggered.

A more widely adopted 'political institutionalist' version of corporate pluralism modifies the assumption that the reformist lobby, working with the grain of global economic change, will necessarily succeed fully and speedily in achieving the desired reforms. Instead, it emphasises the importance of political institutions in facilitating or inhibiting reform.[2] Depending on the institutional properties of a given political system, reform may be more or less attainable. In consensual political systems, typically marked by decentralised power and multi-party coalition government, there are multiple 'veto points'. The opportunities to resist, dilute or redirect reforms may be considerable, irrespective of the extent of the clamour for reform induced by globalisation. In majoritarian systems, in contrast, where power is centralised and the impact of a small shift in votes on government composition may be considerable, radical reform may be a far more feasible option (Gourevitch 2003a, 319). In short, the demand for change generated by economic globalisation is refracted by the specific political institutional features of a given system. While corporate governance convergence rather than continuity across states is anticipated, the degree and timing of reform will vary greatly, depending on the extent of the opportunity a political system affords vested interests to inhibit the economically rational demand of business interests for an adjustment of policy.

The 'Varieties of Capitalism' Approach

The national production systems or 'varieties of capitalism' perspective offers a radically different analysis of the process through which globalisation pressures are politicised and, ultimately, translated into concrete policy reform outcomes (Hall and Soskice 2001). In contrast to the neo-classical assumptions that inform the corporate pluralist perspective, it is argued that the response of states to globalisation will be shaped by the prevailing pattern of socio-economic institutions that underpin the national economy. National capitalisms are unique systems, composed of a multitude of economic actors who are deeply implicated in, and committed to, its specific institutionalised pattern of organisation and behaviour and who calculate their interests and action in accordance with its particular logic. In the case of Liberal Market Economies (LMEs), this pattern is considered to be highly compatible with the logic and requirements of globalisation. In contrast, in Coordinated Market Economies (CMEs) the 'fit' with globalisation is much more problematic. The institutional structure of such systems has encouraged the investment in industry-specific assets by both capital and labour. As workers, managers, investors of capital, professionals and other actors make such investments, 'their interests and preferences are altered' (Gourevitch 2003b, 1855). In Germany, for example, both employers and workers have invested enormous time and expense in the acquisition of highly specific industry skills that underpin firms' competitive strategies. The overriding concern of both parties to protect these investments often leads them to seek to safeguard rather than transform the integrity of the national model in the face of globalisation pressures. The nature of a state's response to such pressures will be largely determined by the nature of its socio-economic institutional character.

The political analysis offered by the varieties of capitalism approach is underpinned by its perception of a fundamental complementarity between economic and political institutions. The product of historical co-evolution, this complementarity, it is argued, ensures mutuality in the politics and economics of adjustment. Different types of political system facilitate and sustain different patterns of socio-economic institutions. The investment by employers and workers in specific assets that is typical of CMEs is only feasible where political institutions inhibit rapid policy change – namely consensual political systems with decentralised patterns of power and multiple veto points. In contrast, the reliance on markets and hierarchies to coordinate economic activity that is typical of LMEs is better adapted to the greater political and policy volatility characteristic of majoritarian political systems (Wood 2001). The integrity of these political and economic institutional systems determines the pattern of response to globalisation pressures. Politics will accommodate the reforms that are economically demanded. These demands will be essentially conservative as path dependence exercises an overwhelming influence on the interests of economic actors.

Case Studies

In order to provide a basis for the evaluation of the relative plausibility of these two perspectives, this section will outline and assess the recent developments in corporate governance, particularly in respect of enhancing shareholder protection, in two emblematic cases. Britain is typically offered as a prime exemplar of a liberal market economy while Germany is widely viewed as the quintessential coordinated market economy. What has been the nature, extent and dynamic of reform in these two contrasting countries?

Britain

Corporate governance reform has been on the political agenda in Britain for over a decade and important changes have been introduced. Between 1992 and 2003, the Cadbury, Greenbury and Hampel reports, and the more recent Company Law Review process and the Higgs report initiated by the Labour government, have generated a range of new codes and practices. Collectively, these have had a very significant impact on the structure and operation of corporate governance in Britain. All of them have been fully consonant with the central tenets of the shareholder-oriented model.

The purpose of reform has been to create a system of governance that would offer a high standard of investor protection and enhance the standing of firms listed on the Stock Exchange (Cheffins 2000, 21). The core belief guiding the reformers has been, as the Hampel report expressed it, the need to facilitate 'the single overriding objective shared by all listed companies, whatever their size or type of business, [that] is the preservation and the greatest possible enhancement over time of their shareholders' investments'.[3] The key strategy was to align more closely management behaviour with shareholder interest. In furtherance of this objective, for example, non-executive directives have been attributed a far greater importance as monitors of management practice, and the question of their independence has been the subject of much closer scrutiny (Cadbury, Hampel, Higgs). There has been a considerable evolution of practice in relation to the separation of the roles of board chairman and chief executive (Cadbury). Moreover, efforts have been made to ensure that executive pay is more closely linked to fluctuations in shareholder returns (Greenbury, Hampel). Most recently, great emphasis has been placed on the role of institutional investors in effectively monitoring and, when necessary, sanctioning poor management performance. The cumulative effect of these changes is that 'from a historical perspective, the extent of shareholders' pre-eminence achieved in the 1980s and 1990s, far from being a normal state of affairs, is an anomaly' (Armour *et al.* 2003, 532).

This pattern of change was not inevitable. The system of corporate governance had been the subject of intense debate in the late 1980s and throughout the 1990s and more radical reforms had been widely canvassed. Will Hutton's *The State We're In* became a bestseller and for a time the virtues of a broader stakeholder model of governance appeared even to have drawn the support of Tony Blair. In 1996, in a period when the Labour opposition was in search of a 'big idea' that would help propel them to power, the future Prime Minister endorsed the concept of stakeholding as a means to improve the governance and performance of British business. He offered a vision of the company 'as a community or partnership in which each employee has a stake, and where a company's responsibilities are clearly delineated'.[4] Yet, the impact of all of this analysis and debate on the practice of reform appears to have been marginal. Blair quickly backed away from the radical edge of the stakeholding concept. Of the various reform committees and investigations, only the Company Law Review seriously addressed alternatives to the shareholder model, assessing the possible merits of a 'pluralist' approach that would commit directors to advance the interests of a broad range of groups in addition to shareholders. However, ultimately it opted to support an 'enlightened shareholder' stance that did not significantly alter the status quo position (Armour *et al.* 2003, 536–538).

The explanation of this pattern of significant but conservative incremental reform partly lies in the origins of the reform committees. In particular, the Cadbury Committee, whose perceived success exercised a strong conditioning influence over all subsequent reform initiatives, was a response to a series of spectacular corporate failures in the early

1990s.[5] These were the product of a mixture of poor management and illegal practice that threatened to bring the entire system of corporate monitoring into disrepute. The overriding concern was to shore up investor confidence in the system and it was the judgement of both government and committee members that this was not going to be aided by the introduction of radical departures of principle. The reform imperative was essentially defensive/adaptive.

The direction of reform is also explicable in terms of the process by which problems were investigated and solutions promulgated. Most basically, the membership of the key committees was drawn from a narrow constituency. The Cadbury Committee had 12 full members. Two were businessmen, two were drawn from the major general business lobby groups (the Confederation of British Industry and the Institute of Directors), two were representative of the financial sector, two were drawn from the professions (law and accounting), one was the chairman of the London Stock Exchange and one was an academic accountant. None of the committees had any labour or consumer representation. Reform was left to the professionals and, in large measure, the professions. Moreover, the advent of the Labour government did not alter this characteristic, with neither trade union nor consumer rights lobbyists gaining membership of the Company Law Review Steering Group. Despite occasional threats to the contrary, successive governments encouraged the operators of the system to devise, implement and police their own reforms.

However, it would be a mistake to conclude that the conduct and outcome of the reform process was a simple manifestation of 'business power'. The pattern of support and influence within business was quite complex. Jones and Pollitt (2002), for example, have concluded that the 'corporates' (those companies whose governance was the object of reform) were reluctant participants in the process. In respect of the Cadbury Committee, they did not engage with its creation or delibera-tion to any significant extent. Evidence of serious involvement by their representatives only followed the publication of the interim report though, from that moment on, the trenchant criticisms made by both the CBI and the IOD in respect of the role of non-executives appear to have had some impact.[6] Jones and Pollitt have concluded that financial stakeholders had much less influence on the process and content of the enquiries than might have been expected, given that the protection of their interests was one of the principal objectives of the reforms. In relation to the crucial Cadbury Committee, for example, financial stakeholders do not appear to have exercised any influence over its terms of reference and only a moderate influence over its deliberations (Jones and Pollitt 2002, 21). Rather, at every stage, it was the professional representatives, lawyers and accountants, who were most fully engaged and most effective in shaping the content of reform proposals.

That reform took the path that it did, and that the mechanisms of its formulation and implementation took the form that they did, was greatly facilitated by the attitude and ambition of successive governments. The Conservatives were instrumental in initiating reform but they were motivated by a desire to rescue rather than trans-form the system. It is notable, for example, that while the government had a high level of interest in the initiation of the Cadbury Committee, its impact on the Committee's composition, terms of reference, deliberations, and the implementation of its proposals, was virtually non-existent (Jones and Pollitt 2002, 21). Perhaps more tellingly, when Labour came to power in 1997 its more robust rhetoric was frequently belied by a chivvying approach in practice. Thus, in rela-tion to the Company Law Review initiated by the new government, it exercised little influence over either its deliberation or its proposals. Rather than play a decisive leadership role, the government 'has grad-ually withdrawn from its direct influence as the process has progressed' (Jones and Pollitt 2002, 46). Rather than act upon the stakeholder critique as the proponents of more radical reform had hoped a Labour government might do, it made little effort to challenge the dominant influence of the shareholder-oriented model in shaping proposals. Indeed by 2003, the Secretary of State at the Department of Trade and Industry, Patricia Hodge, could equate the enhancement of share-holder rights with the social democratic goal of public empowerment: This 'is a classic example of modern social democracy in action: using the power of government not to impose solutions, but to transfer power into the hands of people, so they can drive change forward' (Hodge 2003). Where social democratic principles and the shareholder-oriented model proved incompatible, the former had to be reinterpreted and 'modernised' to achieve harmony. This practice in turn reflected a broader New Labour understanding of what was feasible and desirable in a context of globalisation. Overall, the broad thrust of corporate governance reform was towards 'the flexibility and dynamism of self-regulation and to an invocation of a neo-liberal minimal state that will not place what are perceived as unnecessary hurdles in the way of wealth creation' (Wilson 2000, 163). What was required was a refinement of the corporate governance system to ensure its more efficient functioning. What was deemed impractical and counterproductive was any attempt at its fundamental restructuring. By 2001–2002, the central thrust of government rhetoric was towards encouraging institutional investors to bear the burden of company monitoring that the shareholder-oriented model typically allotted to them. It came closest to legislative activism in 2002 when it considered legally enshrining the duty of fund managers and trustees to 'intervene in companies where it was in the interests of shareholders and beneficiaries to do so' (Williamson 2003, 525). Only a strong lobbying campaign by fund managers dissuaded the government from taking this step. By mid-decade, the range of support within business, political circles and the media in favour of maintaining and strengthening the functioning of the shareholder-oriented model appeared virtually all-embracing.

Germany

The claim that economic globalisation will induce a convergence towards the shareholder-oriented model faces a much more challenging test in the case of Germany. There, in contrast to Britain, corporations are conceived as public bodies. Directors are legally required to act in the best interests of the enterprise as a whole rather than any particular constituency within it (Jackson 2001). This conception of the firm is most clearly manifest in the system of codetermination which provides for a substantial representation of all sections of the firm on the supervisory board, with 50% of seats allotted to workers in firms that employ more than 2000 people. In addition, in comparison with Britain, securities markets are far less important sources of investment finance. Instead, banks have performed the major role in providing finance and, correspondingly, in the exercise of governance within the corporation. Partly as a consequence of this, and again in sharp contrast to Britain, firms are frequently closely held. Block-holding is common and complex cross-shareholding relations between networks of firms are pervasive. Finally, with a few spectacular recent exceptions, the market for corporate control is largely moribund.[7] Collectively, these properties have marked Germany out as a distinct model of corporate governance that offers the most coherent theoretical and practical challenge to the shareholder model. For these reasons, the nature and outcome of corporate governance reform in Germany is of particular interest.

While the full story of reform cannot be rehearsed here, a few key elements need to be acknowledged. Most basically, since the late 1990s there has been a series of significant reforms in German corporate governance. In 1998, the Control and Transparency Act (generally known as the KonTraG) was passed into law. In July 2000, important changes in capital gains tax were legislated. These were designed to facilitate the profitable unwinding of cross-shareholding networks. In 2001, new national takeover rules were agreed as a direct consequence of the dramatic and controversial blocking of the EU's 13th Directive on Takeovers in the EU Parliament in June of that year by a German-led coalition of MEPs.

Taken together, these reforms did serve to shift the German model in a more liberal direction. The KonTraG trimmed the power of the banks by restricting the use of proxy votes, strengthened the role of the supervisory board, introduced the 'one share, one vote' principle and allowed the use of share buybacks and stock options. Tellingly, the only exemption from the 'one share, one vote' principle was designed to restrict the exercise of voting rights by interfirm cross-shareholding networks. Crucially, the impact of these reforms was greatly reinforced by the changes in corporate gains tax. The attempt to limit the power of cross-shareholding arrangements was now accompanied by a strong financial incentive to unwind them. In short, as Cioffi has argued, the thrust of the legal changes was 'towards transparency, equal treatment of shareholders and curbing the rent seeking of corporate insiders' (Cioffi 2002, 25). They were intended to make German corporations attractive to, and fit recipients of, equity finance.

However, the limits of the shift towards the shareholder model must also be acknowledged. Most importantly, the principle of codetermination and the concomitant fiduciary duties of directors to protect the interests of employees as well as shareholders have not been compromised thus far. German firms are still not private organisations owned by their shareholders, in the Anglo-American sense, and maximising shareholder value is not their sole legal *raison d'être*. Moreover, reform has been neither unambiguously liberal nor wholly irreversible. Thus, for example, the impact of the KonTraG reforms in restricting the capacity of management to resist hostile takeovers was partly overturned by the new takeover rules of 2001 (Gordon 2002).

While this complex and, in some respects, contradictory pattern of corporate governance reform was partly motivated by the need to respond to a series of corporate scandals, of far greater importance in shaping events was the pervasive sense that the German economic model was struggling to cope with the intensifying competition of globalising markets. A perception of systemic crisis conditioned the approach of business and the state. Reform of financial markets with a view to improving their operational efficiency and enhancing their centrality in the German economy had already been initiated in the 1980s and early 1990s. By the mid-1990s, 'protecting shareholders and increasing the use of securitized finance had become important policy goals' (Cioffi 2002, 8). German companies began to compete to establish a capital market orientation and 'suddenly interlocking directorates, insider-oriented accounting standards and limited minority share-holder protection were inconsistent with the political goals of an emerging "competitive state"' (Beyer and Hoepner 2003, 191).

However, recognition of a general reformist orientation does not explain the often contradictory mix of measures that were implemented. Here it is necessary to look more closely at the politics of reform. Within the business community, for example, there is clear evidence that reform was considered essential by most segments. However, precisely what sort of reform should be implemented was a much more problematic issue. Ziegler has identified a 'genuine ambivalence and uncertainty among Germany's business leaders about where their interests lie' (Ziegler 2001, 216). Most sought adjustment of those aspects of the established model that were least advantageous to them, without abandoning the model completely. While many large companies began to espouse the importance of enhancing shareholder value as they invested abroad, they chose as frequently to maintain the German character of their internal organisational and management structure (e.g. Daimler Chrysler). While many top managers began to emphasise the norms of shareholder interest in the running of the company, there is little indication that they were keen to lose the freedom of action they enjoyed under the old system. While the large banks supported improved transparency in company accounts and management strategy, the strengthening of the supervisory board and a greater emphasis on shareholder value, they strongly and successfully resisted proposals to restrict the proxy voting rights that they enjoyed (Cioffi 2002, 17). Moreover, while these banks wanted to enhance the development of the Frankfurt Stock Exchange and improve their ability to develop their investment function and act globally, they also sought 'to perpet-uate their privileged ties with Germany's largest enterprises' (Ziegler 2001, 217). Finally, while some moderation of the power of labour within the firm was generally attractive, peak business associations were reluctant to undermine the more general pattern of cooperative relations with labour of which intrafirm institutions formed a part. These arrangements are pivotal to the production model of many manufacturing firms and their concern not to damage them has been apparent.

Significantly, the more radical demands of shareholder pressure groups met with disappointment. The Association of Small Share-holders (SGK) lobbied unsuccessfully for the restriction of bank power through the imposition of a limit on bank ownership of industrial firms to a maximum of 10%. The German Association for Share Ownership (DSW) sought equally unsuccessfully to restrict severely the practice of interlocking directorates (Ziegler 2001). There was a considerable business constituency for reform but its embrace of the shareholder-oriented model was partial. Liberal adjustment rather than liberal transformation appears to be the more appropriate characterisation of its ambition.

The stance of the political parties was also often ambiguous and in some cases counterintuitive. Thus, for example, while the Free Democratic Party (FDP) was consistent in advancing a liberal reformist agenda, the Social Democratic Party (SPD) was often mark-edly more in favour of liberal corporate governance reform than the centre-right Christian Democratic Party (CDU) (Hoepner 2003, 19). In the formulation of the KonTraG, for example, it was the SPD that favoured a more ambitious attack on the established networks of corporate power. While the CDU/FDP coalition steered the legisla-tion through parliament, anxious to enhance shareholder rights and thereby increase the prospective returns from the imminent privatisa-tion of Deutsche Telekom, the CDU succeeded in pruning the more radical anti-bank power measures from the proposals. While the SPD unexpectedly pushed through the corporate tax reform of 2000, with the explicit purpose of stimulating a more active market for corporate control, the CDU challenged it on the grounds of its unfairness (Hoepner 2003, 24). Edmund Stoiber, the conservative candidate for Chancellor in the 2002 election, promised to reintroduce the tax if he gained office. Though the CDU stood to the right of the SPD, its role as architect of the post-war Germany model and representative of the interests of many small and medium-sized firms made it much more wary of the liberal drift in developments (Vogel 2002, 1114; Cioffi 2000, 594). Many of the institutions that were the subject of reform were the embodiment of social market rather than social democratic socio-economic principles.

There is also evidence to suggest that the axiomatic expectation that labour and shareholder interests are inevitably in conflict has not been wholly borne out by events. Thus, for example, the strengthening of the rights of the supervisory board in the KonTraG was attractive to both shareholder and worker directors in a codetermined firm, as it tilted (admittedly only slightly) the balance of information and power away from the management board. Labour was only too well aware of the difficulties in practice of exercising genuine control over company management boards that, in many cases, denied supervisory boards the sort of detailed financial information that they required to function effectively. It may be that any losses suffered in terms of class conflict may be 'less visible compared to the gains from conflict over managerial control, which makes trade unions support capital-market-oriented corporate governance reforms more than one might expect' (Hoepner 2003, 31).

The complex nature of the interests of political parties, management and labour, and the variable coalition patterns that can prove feasible depending on the circumstances, were again manifest in the matter of the EU's 13th Directive. This proposal was designed to create a Europe-wide takeover regime and, after many years of negotiation, looked set to pass into law in 2001 with the unanimous support of the Council of Ministers. By the spring of 2001, however, it was beginning to provoke widespread opposition in Germany. The point of particular controversy was its so-called neutrality clause. This required management to remain neutral in the event of a bid but did not disbar the use of golden shares (common in Italy and France). Partly due to the reforms of the KonTraG, this would leave Germany defenceless in the face of bids from abroad without offering a reciprocal advantage to German firms seeking to buy firms in other countries. Though the directive was attractive to shareholders who could expect to profit significantly in such a regime, their lobbyists proved unable to resist the mobilisation of a broad coalition of opposition to the measure in Germany. German management feared their vulnerability to takeover, especially from abroad. German labour feared the likely reordering of company priorities that would follow a successful bid. The CDU and the SPD united in defence of 'Germany Inc.'. While their reading of the dangers may have differed, both could agree that 'unfair' Europeanisation of take-over rules threatened the integrity of the national production system. In this case, a corporate governance reform designed to entrench key aspects of the shareholder-oriented model in European law provoked a powerful national defensive reaction and was defeated in the European Parliament – if only by the casting vote of the Parliament's president (Gordon 2002, 52).

Models and Cases: A Brief Assessment

Corporate pluralism (CP) and the 'varieties of capitalism' (VofC) analysts offer sharply different perspectives on the relationship between economic globalisation and national regulatory reform. Though eschewing the confident certainties of the competitive efficiency model, CP does anticipate a process of convergence across states over time. In contrast, VofC predicts the persistence of diversity. Though recognising that conflict within the business community may be intense, CP looks to the business beneficiaries of globalisation for the motor force of reform. In contrast, VofC analysts anticipate a fundamental unity of view both within business and between national business and state elites. It is argued that a common socio-economic institutional framework generates a mutually supporting set of interests that leads to the development of a shared national strategic response to globalisation pressures. CP expects the political institutional structure to exercise a powerful independent constraint on the speed and extent to which public policy adjusts to the demands of business. In contrast, VofC analysts posit a fundamental complementarity of economic and political institutional structures that renders the political accommodation of business interests relatively unproblematic. What matters in determining the nature of corporate governance reform, in this view, are economic rather than political institutional factors.

Though far from comprehensive, the two case studies do provide a basis for a preliminary evaluation of these differing claims. In respect of the issue of convergence, it is apparent that both national systems have moved closer to the 'pure' shareholder-oriented model from very different starting points. Though already possessed of the basic institutional building blocks of the model, Britain has seen a systematic and quite self-conscious effort to implement it more fully and coherently. Possible alternative models are no longer the subject of serious consideration by policymakers. There is a broad-ranging consensus within business and the state that there is no feasible or desirable alternative to the further development of the shareholder-oriented model.

In the case of Germany, the extent of the reform has been even more striking because it is more surprising. Most observers agree that the objective of enhancing shareholder value is much more central to management thinking than has been the case heretofore. Beyer and Hoepner offer corporate governance as a prime example of what they call the disintegration of organised capitalism in Germany (Beyer and Hoepner 2003). A number of qualifications of this assessment need to be entered. Codetermination has not been seriously challenged thus far. There is evidence of concern among many elements of business that corporate governance reform should not lead to the unravelling of the entire network of business–labour cooperation that lies at the heart of German economic competitiveness. Yet, the overall assessment must be that the degree of movement towards the shareholder model accords more closely with the expectations of corporate pluralists than it does with those of VofC advocates.

However, while the path of developments may conform more closely to the expectations of corporate pluralists, an analysis of the sources of reform agency is less supportive of its claims. In particular, there is only modest support for viewing business as the primary motor force of reform initiatives. In Britain, there is little to indicate that reform was sought by the corporations themselves nor is there any evidence that financial investors, such as pension and insurance funds, actively lobbied for them. The truer cause of change was the need to buttress and refine the established system following a series of scandals and the concomitant commitment by government to a defence of the City of London's role in a globally integrating financial system. It was the failures of the established system that triggered reform rather than the pressure of business interests responding to the opportunities generated by globalisation. Serious business engagement followed change rather than initiated it.

The evidence from the German case is a little more mixed. German shareholder rights groups, in alliance with international investor institutions such as Calpers, did exercise considerable pressure for reform. The large German banks, anxious to globalise their business and move into more profitable investment banking operations, did support a greater emphasis on shareholder value norms. A range of large German firms clearly began to speak the language of shareholder rights and adopt more transparent financial accounting mechanisms. However, there is little evidence to support a claim that business was the major source of pressure for regulatory reform. The commitment to shareholders' rights most frequently manifested itself in terms of company practice (and rhetoric) rather than in a powerful lobbying campaign for regulatory reform. The enhancement of shareholder rights as often appeared as a threat to incumbent management and dominant shareholders as it did a benefit. The peak associations were often constrained by their diverse memberships to eschew radical reform policy stances. As in Britain, the impact of business interests on developments was felt more in the shaping than the initiation of reform. Moreover, as in Britain, government appears to have played a more central role in promoting reform than can be satisfactorily explained by a pluralist lobbying model.

CP and VofC offer quite contrasting views of the role of state structure in determining outcomes. For the former, the nature of political institutions may serve to facilitate or delay reform. Highly centralised states characterised by single-party governments should respond more rapidly and completely to lobbying pressure than highly decentralised states characterised by diffuse, complex and consensual policymaking structures. In contrast, VofC anticipates a fundamental compatibility between economic and political institutions that renders the introduction of necessary reform unproblematic. In adjudicating between these two different perspectives, the British case is not particularly helpful. Both models predict a relatively easy political adjustment to the need for the enhancement of the shareholder-oriented model. For CP, the centralised structures of the British state minimise the opportunities for vested interests to block necessary reform, and it can be expected that public policy responses to the pressures for change generated by globalisation will be both speedy and thorough. In practice, the experience of corporate governance reform in Britain appears to bear out many of these expectations. The mechanisms of reform effectively isolated the process from the wider political system and its attendant pressures. The adoption of the system of investigative committees, and the reliance on voluntaristic and market mechanisms of implementation, succeeded in excluding actors and interests that were not part of the existing system and broadly committed to its protection. The defeat of proponents of more radical reform was strikingly complete.

Perhaps the one surprise, from a CP perspective, was that the election of a Labour government did not materially affect reform. It might have been expected that trade union support for a more stakeholder-oriented model would have gained political purchase and had some substantial impact on the Company Law Review process in particular. Notwithstanding this caveat, however, the pattern of reform in Britain is broadly explicable when viewed through the lens of corporate pluralist analysis.

The analytical problem, however, is that the VofC perspective offers an equally plausible analysis of the British case. Britain is a liberal market economy. The shareholder-oriented model is entirely compatible with such a system. The decision to embrace such a model more fully in the face of global market pressures is entirely explicable in terms of the economic institutional structure of the British system and, correspondingly, its economic and political interests. Moreover, for VofC analysts, the behaviour of New Labour is equally unsurprising. Governments, whether of the centre-right or centre-left, will seek to protect the nation's 'comparative institutional advantage' (Hall and Soskice 2001). New Labour simply pursued the strategy that any British government would in seeking to protect the key institutional basis of the national economy's global competitive position. Corporate governance reform served to move Britain further along its developmental path and the politics of reform reflected the fundamental compatibility of both business and state interests and the country's economic and political institutions.

Germany is a more challenging case for both perspectives. As a federal system characterised by decentralised policymaking networks, coalition governments and highly consensual patterns of economic management, CP would anticipate a very slow and partial adjustment to external pressures and business lobbying. However, while some non-liberal features of its system were strongly defended, the pace of liberal corporate governance reform in the late 1990s was quite rapid. Moreover, the most important liberal reforms were overseen by a coalition of the Social Democrats and the Green Party, both of which might have been expected to be instinctively wary of liberal economic prescriptions. Perhaps most uncomfortably for corporate pluralists, when the process of reform was halted, most notably in the case of the EU's 13th Directive, this was the product of resistance from a very broadbased coalition of opposition rather than the exploitation by well-placed sectional groups of the institutional opportunities for veto.

Similarly, the unchallenged status of codetermination has been more a reflection of its deep and broad political support rather than of the difficulty of overcoming resistance to reform by entrenched minority groups in a complex political system.

For VofC, the explanatory problems in the German case are the inverse of those facing corporate pluralists. The rejection of the EU Directive and the defence of codetermination conform with its vision of national, systematically rooted interests encompassing nearly all of business, the state and (in CMEs) labour. Similarly, the CDU's wariness of the liberal turn and its desire to defend the integrity of the German economic system are entirely in accordance with its expectations. However, the role of the SPD in pushing through liberal reform presents a major explanatory problem. The defection from the national coalition of interests by the major left party in order to pursue an essentially liberal reform agenda cannot easily be accommodated within a VofC perspective. An adequate explanation of developments would require an analysis of why and when political parties and governments might choose to move 'off-path' and foster fundamental systemic reform. This is not the sort of problem that VofC perspectives either anticipate or address.

Conclusion

These two perspectives offer a very different understanding of the nature of economic globalisation and its implications for national regulatory systems. They also offer sharply contrasting analyses of the dynamics of public policy reform. It is perhaps ironic, then, that in their application to an examination of corporate governance reform in Britain and Germany, they demonstrate a common explanatory weakness. Most basically, neither offers a satisfactory explanation of the behaviour of the state in reforming policy. Too often public policy-makers were either too proactive or too innovative to conform to the expectations of corporate pluralism and VofC. While committed to offering an integrated economic and political analysis of the relationship between globalisation and national regulatory reform, it is apparent that both conceive of the state and national politics in overly passive terms. They share a view of causality in which economic change generates the impetus for reform and politics is concerned with its accommodation. The cases examined here suggest that greater consideration needs to be given to the dynamics of domestic politics and the potential for creative state strategies if a fully satisfactory model of the linkage between economic globalisation and domestic regulatory change is to be developed.

Notes

1. In this chapter the focus of attention is on the national rather than the European level. There is clear evidence that, in relation to corporate governance, it is national rather than EU politics that matter. The history of attempts to establish European-wide corporate governance regulations is littered with failure (see Lannoo 1999). The key relationship is between globalisation and the politics of national regulatory reform.
2. See, for example, Garrett and Lange (1996).
3. Committee on Corporate Governance, Final Report, London, 1998, paragraph 1.16.
4. Quoted in Williamson (2003).
5. Key examples involved Polly Peck, Robert Maxwell's MCCI and the bank BCCI.
6. See Andrew Jack, *Financial Times*, 4 December 1992.
7. These properties are closely, causally, interlinked but this need not detain us here.

6

From Workers to Global Politics: How the Way We Work Provides Answers to Corporate Governance Questions

Irene Lynch-Fannon

Introduction

The organisers of the conference generating this collection of essays made the crucial observation that the

> interdependent power relationship between the market and its key actors – the state, parties, regulators, corporations and the community of market professionals – has become one of the most pressing issues facing democratic capitalist society. As the recent waves of corporate scandal in the United States, Asia, Europe and Australia have revealed, there is a pressing need for cross-disciplinary research in which the forensic capabilities of management, accountancy, law and business are married with political science in order to maximise our understanding of modern governance.

This statement is exciting because it highlights both a fascinating question and adumbrates also the source of its resolution: first, the question is about the nature of the exercise of power in developed capitalist societies, which is largely market and capital driven, and second, the recognition that the resolution of questions we should ask about the exercise of power in society lies largely in a close examination of the corporation and its relationship to its stakeholders. Many academic colleagues are interested in relationships where power is imbalanced, the relationship, for example, between the citizen and the state, the relationship between the victim and the perpetrator of crime, the relationship between the accused and the criminal justice system, the power relationships which are abused and become the focus of human rights enquiries and so on. For many years the enormous power wielded by corporations and regulation of corporate activity through law was neither a fashionable nor profitable area of academic study.[1] So for those of us who recognised that fundamental principles of corporate law such as the doctrine of corporate personality and the principle of limited liability, created by judicial decision and statute respectively, represented a breathtaking and decisive societal choice in favour of a vigorous market-driven capitalist economy, our enthusiasm for the political context and significance of corporate law was sadly disregarded as obsessive. But these legal events, taking place in the British Isles at any rate towards the end of the nineteenth century and consolidated in the early part of the twentieth century, actually established the bedrock of our capitalist system, encouraging entrepreneurial risk-taking and shifting the costs of that risk-taking away from the corporation, its shareholders, and management to the other stakeholders, creditors, employees, customers, consumers and the state.[2] The potential for conflict thus generated has been recognised from the beginning when the limited liability company and its creation was denounced by the *Manchester Guardian* 'as the creation of "a rogue's charter"'. On the other hand a famous jurist observed in the *Columbia Law Journal* many years ago that the limited liability company may have been the greatest invention since the wheel (Fletcher 1917).[3] This balancing of the interests of risk-takers with the interests which other stakeholders have in our society was also recognised in the agenda to this conference: 'The primary function of economic regulation is to square the circle between ensuring the conditions for responsible entrepreneurial risk-taking, while ensuring that the market is conducted within ethical and equitable restraints.' So now, in the early part of the second millennium, happily, corporate governance and corporate law theory are in.

Therefore, when we speak of governance systems we must recognise that *corporate* governance will be central to our enquiry as to how modern society is shaped. Many of the principles evolved through the study of good corporate governance practice are now applied to many different governance systems and similarly study of good governance in other areas will inform how corporations are governed in the future.[4] Equally important, however, is the recognition that the regulation of corporate governance issues will profoundly influence what our societies look like given the centrality of the corporation and corporate power in today's world. Taking a comparative approach to the effect different corporate governance systems have on a distinct set of issues illustrates this argument about the centrality of corporate governance very clearly.

The Corporation

Today, many large corporations have a greater turnover than the GDP of numerous small states. The power of the modern corporation in its relationship to government or the state and in its relationship to stakeholders including shareholders is such that the corporate impact on many societal issues such as environmental destruction or preservation, development of the third world, the negotiation of labour standards both domestically and overseas, and consequent impact on quality of life is indeed misunderstood, or as President George W. Bush might say 'misunderestimated', by many. Different ideological perspectives on corporate function yield very different answers to specific governance questions. This is particularly true when one considers the understanding of the function of the corporation in its relationship to employees prevalent in the United States, compared with a European understanding of corporate function. Considering these issues by focusing in particular on the regulation of one vital relationship in the corporate governance debate, that of the corporation and its employees allows us to understand how different the understandings of what an ethical and accountable corporation should be really are on both sides of the Atlantic (Lynch-Fannon 2003). (It is important to acknowledge that the regulation of different corporate relationships, for example the corporation and the stock market or investor, or the corporation and the consumer, will yield different insights.)

In the context of corporate employees, legal strategies in both the US and the EU provide context and illustration to theoretical concepts which are the focus of much governance literature including the nature of the employment relationship as a stakeholding relationship, concepts of ownership, the role of trust in organisations and organisational theory more generally. In addition this chapter will illustrate the real impact such divergent approaches have in a practical way on ordinary employees. Previous research in the area of EU–US comparative labour market regulation (Lynch-Fannon 2003) identified that the law and economics or neo-liberal understanding of corporate function and the corporate role is particularly hegemonic among academics in the United States and particularly so when issues regarding employees as stakeholders are considered. This leads to corporate governance solutions and laws that favour managerial prerogative and present very few demands in terms of managerial and corporate accountability. This is in contrast to the European understanding of the role of the corporation as expressed through the policies and laws of the European Union, laws that emerge from a different, more communitarian understanding of corporate function.

This theoretical analysis of corporate function and corporate law theory is not as strongly pursued in relation to other areas and other stakeholder relationships, for example in relation to the corporation's relationship to consumers or to the environment. It becomes apparent that as one examines how these transatlantic differences have come about there are no easy answers to our understanding of corporate function, how differences exist and what the consequences are: 'the institutions and objectives of corporate governance cannot be explained simply by reference to stylised economic interactions, but must instead be examined in the light of the social and political contexts and different forms of market system within which they have developed' (Parkinson 2003).

The Corporation as Employer

Corporate law theory in the United States is therefore largely rooted in law and economics scholarship (Coase 1937; Alchian and Demsetz 1972) and the central tenet of this still predominant view of the corporation is that the corporation is a private entity, which should be free to pursue its own goals. Simply put these are described by the law and economics scholars as the minimisation of transaction costs and the pursuit of efficiency (a many headed monster as it turns out or if the reader prefers, a complex goal if ever there was one) (Kelman 1979; Lynch-Fannon 2004).[5] Specifically the law and economics school of thought proposes that the employee is similarly placed to a consumer (Alchian and Demsetz 1972), in a position to shop around and bargain for the best deals when it comes to leave and other similar benefits. For the law and economics scholar both the corporation and the prospective or existing employee are viewed as rational maximisers, in a position to find an equilibrium through contract in an unregulated environment.

Both these propositions seem intuitively problematic as they are for many US corporate law theorists who have presented alternative views of the role and obligations of the corporation. For example, many of the Progressive Corporate Law Scholars (Mitchell 1993, 1995, 2001a, 2002; Green 1993; Millon 1993, 2002) have tried to construct a clear communitarian view of the corporation. Their understanding of the issues surrounding the exercise of corporate power and wealth are more in tune with the European response to these issues[6] (Green 1993; Lynch-Fannon 2003). As a legal comparativist Allen (1993) clearly and eloquently outlined the issues, identifying two schools of thought regarding the role of the corporation.

The first school of thought is the liberal–utilitarian model grounded in the work of Hobbes, Locke and Smith and shaped by the work of Bentham and Mill. Allen states that under this model 'the law creating and protecting property rights and the law enforcing contracts is the law of greatest importance to our welfare. The legal value of the highest rank in this classical liberal view is...human liberty, and the greatest evil is oppression by the State' (Allen 1993). He then describes the evolution of the law and economics analysis of corporations beginning with Coase, through Alchian and Demsetz and on to Easterbrook and Fischel in their work *The Economic Structure of Corporations*: 'The dominant legal academic view does not describe the corporation as a social institution. Rather the corporation is seen as the market writ small' (Allen 1993). This has led to the nexus of contracts paradigm.

The second school of thought described by Allen is the social model grounded 'in the dominant concepts of continental Europe and a yet earlier age' (Allen 1993). Allen refers to Durkheim as a philosophical influence.

This alternative paradigm describes the world as populated not by altru-
istic rational maximizers, but by persons of limited rationality who lead
lives embedded in the social context, in a community... Those holding
this perspective are more willing to regulate and define the legal institutions of property and contract in service of social values. The pragmatic
or managerialist view can be loosely categorized as part of this school.
(Allen 1993)

Allen points out that the liberal–utilitarian model is not necessarily
'conservative' or 'right'. This model has both a (classical liberal) right
of centre school and a left of centre (left liberal) school. The social
model also has a left (communitarian) and right (moral majority). In
concluding he states that:

In the United States the liberal utilitarian account of and prescription
for corporate law is the dominant legal academic model and will remain
so for some time. The coherence and power of the economic
model... have for many an all but irresistible appeal. Moreover, in our
pluralistic society, it may be especially difficult to formulate any alternative comprehensive theory of corporations that takes its animating
power from a conception of human connectedness and responsibility.
(Allen 1993)

The European Corporation

Allen's observations resonated at the time with documents emanating
from the European Commission describing the foundations and future
directions of the European Social Policy dealing specifically with
issues concerning employee welfare and also with related matters
concerning social security issues. These documents not only outlined
policy but they also served to provide a foundation for subsequent
substantive legislation. In 1993 and 1994 respectively, a Green Paper
entitled 'European Social Policy: Options for the Union' (hereinafter
referred to as the Green Paper) and a subsequent White Paper entitled
'European Social Policy: A Way Forward for the Union' (hereinafter
referred to as the White Paper) were published in conjunction with a
further White Paper on 'Growth, Competitiveness and Employment'.
    These documents clearly outlined the Commission and Council's
commitment to social goals while striving for competitiveness and

economic growth and also importantly from the corporate governance perspective clearly identified the role of the corporation in achieving these goals:

> The premise at the heart of this Green Paper is that the next phase in the development of European social policy cannot be based on the idea that social progress must go into retreat in order for economic competitiveness to recover. On the contrary, as has been stated on many occasions by the European Council, the Community is fully committed to ensuring that economic and social progress go hand in hand. *Indeed, much of Europe's influence and power has come precisely from its capacity to combine wealth creation with enhanced benefits and freedoms for its people.* (Green Paper 1993)

More recent documents underpinning Social Policy continue to grapple with difficult questions regarding the correct balance to be struck between efficiency, productivity, labour standards, social responsibility, and the role European companies play in this regard and in the context of global competition.

Transatlantic Comparisons

Unfortunately by the time of the Lisbon Summit in March 2000 continued high unemployment rates and lower productivity rates compared with the United States caused a further considered examination of the role of Europe in the global context. In addition challenges presented by further enlargement of the Union had also to be addressed. Subsequent communications from the Commission (Communications from the Commission to the Council 2000, 2001a, b) including an interesting and provocative Green Paper on Corporate Social Responsibility (2001) reiterated similar themes described in earlier documents. The Social Policy Agenda document restated 'a new strategic goal' for Europe to become the 'most competitive and dynamic knowledge-based economy capable of sustainable economic growth with more and better jobs and greater social cohesion', yet the document continually underlines the importance of Europe's 'social model' and reiterates the 'essential linkage between Europe's economic strength and its social model'. These later documents also articulate more clearly the place of Europe within the global context, almost with a new confidence despite somewhat more negative economic indicators than the US, and are more specific in criticism of other models.

In particular European social policymakers seem eager to reject what are perceived as outcomes of the policy choices made in the United States regarding the role of corporations. For example, the Communication on Employment and Social Policies notes that the 'European model is distinguished from others by its framework and design, and by the nature, focus and distribution of the policies.' The document goes on to describe the significantly different method of funding of social spending between the EU and US, the former being largely publicly funded, the latter being much more privately funded. It also notes the fact that in Europe 'benefits appear more evenly spread' than in the US where 'for example 40% of the population does not have access to primary health care, even though spending per head is actually higher as a proportion of GDP than it is in Europe'. It also notes that distribution of income is much wider in the US than in the EU, although there is evidence of some widening in several EU countries. These European countries are interestingly Ireland and the UK, the countries with corporate governance structures most similar to the US, which has the widest income distribution figures and also the lowest literacy figures.

Finally, the Green Paper on Corporate Social Responsibility (2001) clearly identifies a European understanding of the corporation as having non-legal and social responsibilities in many areas including relationships with consumers, the environment, public authorities and other investors. One of the most important stakeholders identified in the Green Paper is the corporation's 'human capital' and the paper states that 'going beyond basic legal obligations...can also have a direct impact on productivity'. At the same time the paper is quick to emphasise that corporate responsibility is not and should not be seen 'as a substitute to regulation or legislation'. Corporate responsibility is also a subject of considerable interest in the United States (Mitchell 2001a). The role of ethics in corporate life has been of interest to progressive corporate law scholars in the US for some time (Johnson 2002).

In conclusion, therefore, political and philosophical understandings of the role of the corporation are significant in relation to specific legislative outcomes particularly in relation to the role of employees as non-shareholding stakeholders. It would seem to be beyond doubt that this is the case in relation to other non-shareholding stakeholders also.

Owners and Stakeholders

The divergence between European responses to employee welfare and stakeholding and that which pertains in the United States may be explained by differences found in patterns of ownership. It may also be the case that current patterns of ownership in turn affect efforts to change responses to stakeholders other than shareholders and so the argument made by Roe and others (Roe 2002a; La Porta *etal.* 1997, 1998, 1999) that patterns of corporate governance are politically determined must be considered seriously by those who propose radical change.

In the early 1990s the US corporation, quoted on the stock exchange, represented a more diverse corporate ownership, with ownership in Europe still a lot more concentrated in the hands of founding families, with fewer shares and companies quoted on the stock exchanges of Europe. Throughout the 1990s claims were made by commentators that a pattern of convergence between different governance systems was beginning to emerge. For example, in Europe a trend towards privatisation of state enterprises added to the 'phenomenal growth' of equity markets in a number of OECD countries in Europe. This was further fuelled it was claimed by 'a growing process of disintermediation in the financial markets, shifting savings from the banking sector to equity (and bond) markets' (OECD 2002). On the other hand growth in institutional shareholding probably led to a decrease in diversity of shareownership in the US, with 2002 figures showing that 'less than 100 large non-bank financial institutions hold approximately 20% of the top 20 most liquid markets in the world'. Despite evidence of convergence, it must be emphasised, however, that figures during the late 1990s for stock exchange turnover still show a significant difference between the level of stock exchange activity in Europe overall, a mere €32 500 m. for 1998 compared with €13 bn in the US for 1998 (Iskander and Chamlou 2000; OECD 2001a).

The concentrated ownership structures of European companies seem to facilitate the extension of stakeholder rights beyond the traditional shareholder to employees. The European ownership structure utilises substantial relational monitoring mechanisms in any event and therefore including employees as a monitoring stakeholder group seems less intrusive. On the other hand the ownership structure of US companies has led to a much more private notion of ownership of corporate wealth, with shareholders as the sole and rather passive monitoring group. Paradoxically it seems that the diverse public ownership of the US Megacorp has led to an acceptance of the role of the corporation as a private legal actor rather than a public actor, in relation to 'other stakeholder' issues. It is proposed that in turn, this understanding of the role of the corporation has had a significant impact on the acceptability of legal and government regulation. The converse condition seems to pertain in the European context. These arguments find empirical support in the fact that of all the European countries it is the UK that has resisted most the further extension of the social policy of the EU (Maw 1994; Jeffrey 1995).[7] It is interesting that the US publicly held corporation and companies quoted on the London Stock Exchange seem to share a fundamental distinguishing characteristic, i.e. a wide dispersal of share ownership, the original dispersion described by Berle and Means (1932).[8] There is a consequent resistance to relational monitoring and to state or governmental regulation. European and Japanese corporations do not demonstrate this huge separation of ownership and control. This is significant in terms of how Europeans view ownership and vested interests in the company. The social corporation is in fact more of a reality than it is in the Anglo-American understanding of the corporation.

The Significance of Relational or 'Insider' Models versus Arm's-length Financing or 'Outsider' Models

More relevant than the actual spread of ownership may be the type of governance structures which have been clearly identified by corporate finance scholars. The European model of governance has been characterised as one of relational governance and the US one as being dominated by arm's-length financial monitoring. These are often now described in more simplified language as 'insider' and 'outsider' systems (Childs and Rodrigues 2003). Management of European corporations conduct their business under the watchful monitoring eye of both the holders (often family relatives) of significant blocks of shares, and also their bankers or financiers. In addition in many European countries, employee representatives are also given a place on the supervisory board of directors. In contrast management of US corporations are accountable to the board who are in turn accountable to the shareholders only, whether these are institutional shareholders or not. Accountability in large corporations to shareholders is not coherent, quite simply because of the diversity of ownership interests. The role of capital markets as a monitoring device is typically presented to fill this accountability vacuum (Fama 1988, 1991). However, in recent times and particularly since the corporate accounting scandals of 2002 the informational difficulties presented by this system have been high-lighted (Millon 2002; Mitchell 2002; *George Washington Law Review* 2002). So ownership structures are different, the role of the capital markets is significantly different and governance models are different.

Voice and Ownership

However, this discussion of ownership, which focuses simply on share-holding or governance structure, ignores a fundamental shift in our conceptual understanding of ownership which in my view has always underpinned the development of the limited liability corporation from the very beginning of its legal 'birth' during the nineteenth century and which has become even more pronounced over time as corporations grow in size and stature. It is argued here that the corporation does not simply represent a *division* between ownership and control along the lines proposed by Berle and Means in the 1930s but that current corporate structures on both sides of the Atlantic represent a 'fragmentation of ownership rights in corporate wealth and property, where rights or incidents of ownership can be distributed in different ways' (Lynch-Fannon 2004). Some of the implications of this frag-mentation are considered in previous research (Lynch-Fannon 2004).

Employees as Stakeholders: The Practical Effect of Theoretical Debate

Leaving the fragmentation of ownership aside for the moment, overall the relational governance model which predominates in all major European economies with the exception of the UK and Ireland seems to provide the key as to why the role of the state in regulating corporate affairs in relation to the inclusion of employees as stake-holders and in relation to other employee welfare matters is acceptable.

Workers are entitled to representation on boards of large corporations (differently defined) in Germany, France, Italy, Spain and the Netherlands and this has been the case since the 1940s. At EU level, legislation supporting the participation of workers on management boards has been advocated continually since the 1980s with varying degrees of success. Along with the acceptance of financiers or bankers as a constituency to which they were clearly accountable, management accepted that employees were also a key significant constituency within the corporate structure. This recognition has provided the basis for the development of future regulation of corporate activities in the achievement of employee welfare. Workers are part of the corporate structure and have been for decades. In addition the role of trade unionism is regarded as significant in the future development of social policy. However, at European level the 5th Directive on Company Law, which attempted to introduce employee directors in all similarly sized companies, failed. Since then, a number of directives have been passed and implemented by member states changing governance structures in significant ways for companies throughout the European Union. The Regulation introducing the Societas Europea (2001) is accompanied by a Directive (2001) providing for the involvement of employees on boards of management. Clause 19 of the Regulations states that the directive is 'an indissociable complement to this Regulation and must be applied concomitantly'.

The directive in its draft form provided that at least one-third and not more than one-half of a supervisory board would be made up of employees, but the final directive represents a compromise between opposing views of corporate governance structures (i.e. the UK and Irish position, informed by the Anglo-American common law tradition on the one hand and the continental European tradition on the other) and instead sets out a negotiating model for companies which is designed to lead to an agreed model for employee involvement. The European Works Council Directive (1994) provides for the establishment of procedures for the provision of information to, and consultation with, employees at a European level in large multinational companies.[9] Estimates are that over 1000 firms operating in Europe are covered by these provisions and this figure will grow with enlargement to the east. Interestingly this directive covers at least 250 US multinationals, including at least 48 Fortune 500 companies. In March 2002 the Information and Consultation Directive was passed to establish a 'general framework setting out minimum requirements for the rights to

information and consultation of employees in undertakings or establishments within the Community'. The directive required legislation
to implement information and consultation structures where there are
at least 50 employees in an undertaking, or at least 20 in an establishment or unit of business, regardless of whether the company is unionised.
Finally, the Acquired Rights Directive (1975, 1998) has been
amended to provide for the election of worker representatives for the
purposes of consultation even where there is no union or pre-existing
staff council or committee of any kind. In addition to the main purpose of
the directive, which is to protect rights of employees under contracts
of employment during the transfer of businesses and undertakings, there
are extensive information and consultation obligations imposed by the
directive. Employers must be informed at least 30 days before the date of
the transfer and must be provided with reasons for the transfer, with
information on the legal, economic and social implications of the transfer
for employees, in addition to any measures envisaged for the employees.

In contrast these kinds of structures which support management–
labour dialogue are not legislatively supported in any way in the
United States and in fact some legislative obstacles exist to their introduction. Section 8(a) of the National Labor Relations Act (1948)
prohibits the creation of management dominated employee representative structures and the current view is that most, but not necessarily
all, of the more modern management–labour structures are illegal
under this provision (Estreicher 1998). Furthermore the formal recognition of the importance of social partner input in terms of setting the
European Social Policy agenda and in terms of implementing specific
legislation[10] is non-existent in the United States. Instead two different
models are proposed to answer calls for increased employee involvement in corporate governance. These two models are identified here as
the predominant models or solutions offered by US commentators
without proposing that these are the only models offered. The first
relates to the advancement of employee share ownership schemes as a
method of increasing employee voice. Childs and Rodrigues (2003)
identify employee share ownership as a means whereby employees are
co-opted into 'ownership and participate in control'. They hypothesise
that first, employee share ownership schemes have both a financial
and symbolic value to employees and their families and second, that it
is significant for the firm that it will have 'a large number of informed
inside members of the firm' (Childs and Rodrigues 2003). They do
acknowledge, however, that these schemes have been controversial.

On further consideration it is not clear why employee shareholders should be any less or more effective in the governance of corporations than other shareholders, given the constraints which they will face in their capacity as shareholders, much documented by all of us concerned with mainstream corporate governance, nor is it clear that this will help either employees as stakeholders or firms to advance the concerns of employees or adequately respond to those interests and concerns (Lynch-Fannon, 2003).

The second model proposed and favoured by many US commentators on the role of employees in corporate governance structures is an extension of the fiduciary model. This has been considered at length in previous research (O'Connor 1991, 1993, 1995). Here it is proposed to focus exclusively on what is purportedly delivered by regulation which is dependent on fiduciary obligation and that is a legal replication of trust. For many corporate governance scholars, both lawyers and non-lawyers, trust is an important concept. Thus Childs and Rodrigues (2003) identify trust as an important component of a hierarchical structure but also state that the hierarchical organisation principle has been weakened by an erosion of trust between managers and employees. They propose that in fact this crisis of corporate governance stems in its entirety from a breach of trust and they argue that '[N]ew organizational forms are intended to promote trust in the light of the recognition that trust promotes superior performance through economising on transaction costs, through promoting collective learning and through engendering superior commitment.' This description of the role of trust does not sit well with current legal scholarship on the role of trust nor does it seem to fit with dominant economic analysis. For example, Williamson (1993) argues that trust has no place in the study of economic interactions and continues to argue that the use of the term trust by social science disciplines to explain economic transactions is misplaced.

The Meaning of Trust

Leaving the intricacies of the argument between economists and social scientists regarding the role of trust for others it is, however, apt to observe here that for lawyers a particular meaning is given to the concept of trust in our legal system which is particularly important in the area of trust law but also significant in the concept of fiduciary obligations imposed on corporate directors. As Mitchell (2001a) observes 'Fiduciary duty is famously about trust.' He goes on to negate the argument that trust is only rational when it is supported by credible commitments and argues that our lawyer's understanding of trust expressed in the law's construction of a fiduciary duty is centrally and profoundly responsive to our instinctive need to trust and be trustworthy:

> in its original design, fiduciary obligation is self-enforcing. It is one of the few instances in our law where we levy a moral injunction against an actor as such, holding the trustee legally accountable to an otherwise aspirational standard of conduct that depends for its efficacy on the good faith of the actor... we rely on the fiduciary's good faith, the fiduciary's trustworthiness, to fulfil the duty.

Thus, central to the legal enquiry on corporate governance matters is the concept of trust embodied as it is in the fiduciary obligation. Within the legal academy it is, however, acknowledged that the concept of fiduciary obligation is so developed and so specifically directed at the relationship between the director and his or her corporation as a whole, it is difficult to see how it can be effectively (in legal terms, at least) extended to encompass specific individual stakeholders, including even shareholders (Lynch-Fannon 2003). Furthermore, although resonating linguistically with those from other disciplines it is difficult to identify how the concerns of these other disciplines are given expression in the lawyer's conceptualisation of trust. In answer to this question perhaps it is apt to consider some criteria for healthy organisational structures presented to us by organisational theorists Manville and Ober (2003a) who look to the city-state of Athens in ancient Greece to identify solutions to problems of employee motivation, particularly in larger organisations and companies. Elements which they found to be valuable in the Athenian model included first, clear participatory structures provided to the 'citizens' or community, second, shared communal values with particular value placed on freedom from discrimination and freedom from censure and finally, they identify practices of engagement which they describe as 'good engagement practices' where decisions are made by those with knowledge of the issues and with the greatest at stake. It is argued here and also indicated elsewhere (Lynch-Fannon 2004) that these conditions are replicated by the European Social Model of governance which provides for participatory structures supported by legal mandate as described above. Common to both US and EU models are laws that protect participants against discrimination. However, not present in the US model but present throughout the member states of the European Union are laws which protect employees from the termination at will doctrine, thus allowing employees to act and speak freely without fear of censure of the most drastic sort. In addition in the European Social Model we find legal and extra-legal 'structural' support of the 'trade union model' (Lynch-Fannon 2003) where the social partners are encouraged to participate at local, national and policy level. These characteristics also mirror the criteria of good governance structures identified by Manville and Ober. It would seem, therefore, that law does have a place in answering the requirements of good governance structures affecting employees through the implementation of specific legislative provisions, some of which are described in this section. However, it is not the case that the legal construct of fiduciary obligation imposed on directors and owed to the corporate entity is particularly effective in answering these demands.

Conclusion

From this comparative consideration of employees as corporate stake-holders we can draw the following points.

First, different legal responses to questions of employee welfare seem to be linked to different ownership patterns and governance structures. High levels of labour market regulation are linked to concentrated ownership structures and relational monitoring models, or 'insider' models whereas less labour market regulation is linked to a more dispersed shareownership structure and the finance model of monitoring, or the 'outsider' model. Although even when comparing two very different systems such as that of continental European countries and the United States it is difficult to identify the nature of this link, whether it is simply correlative or in some way causative. In this regard the Australian governance system which is a finance model or 'outsider' governance structure with a high degree of employee protection, together with the position of Ireland and the UK, again finance or outsider models but also participants in the European Social Model would lead us to question the causative nature of this link. This question requires further research.

Second, whatever the source of its legitimacy, the European Social Model response to employee welfare involves both legal regulation of the *individual* employment relationship through the mandated granting of vacation and other rights to job tenure and security and regulation of *corporate structures* providing for the channelling of information to employees followed by consultation. In both senses the employee's position compares favourably with that of his or her US counterpart. In both areas of legislative activity the corporation is viewed as a legitimate subject of state regulation even to the extent that the corporation is regarded as a public actor regulated with a view to achieving broader social goals. These goals include, for example, the goal of increased labour market participation of women with children by providing support through maternal and other family leave rights (Directives 1989, 1996). Interestingly, this strategy seems to have failed to encourage women to combine work with family life, with predominant numbers of European women opting for paid work rather than childbearing (European Commission 2004).[11] This outcome is relevant to the final point.

Finally, the European Social Model seeks to regulate internal corporate structures in the ways discussed in this article. As described, many of the participatory structures both legal and extra-legal that are supported by the Social Policy Agenda reflect best governance practices as described by many organisational theorists. However, this kind of legal intervention is not present in the United States and is not a likely development in the near future. A final question we are thus left to consider is whether the European Social Model has over time displayed any considerable success in its attempt to marry competitiveness with the other goals of the European Social Model. Indicators of economic success are complex and not supportive of generalised statements (Lynch-Fannon 2004; Gordon 2004) but it does seem that half way through the Lisbon 10 year programme, success continues to be somewhat elusive for Europe as compared with the United States. If the European Social Model has not contributed as it should have to competitive success as compared with the United States, what impact does that have on corporate governance theory as it currently stands?

Notes

1. At that time corporate lawyers were a rare breed in academia and even now the corporate lawyer as full-time academic is surely an oddity.
2. *Salomon* v. *Salomon and Co. Ltd* [1895–9] All E.R. 33. By the mid-nineteenth century the Joint Stock Companies Act 1856 provided the legal framework which facilitated both incorporation in a separate legal entity and the ability of investors or shareholders to limit their liability for the debts of that company.
3. Columbia University President Nicholas Murray Butler stated in 1911: 'I weigh my words when I say that in my judgment the limited liability corporation is the greatest single discovery of modern times...Even steam and electricity are far less important than the limited liability corporation, and they would be reduced to comparative impotence without it.' Quoted in William M. Fletcher, 1 *Encyclopedia of the Law of Private Corporations* (1917), p. 1.
4. An interesting and topical example of this synergy is represented in the current consideration of university governance systems in Ireland. See, for example, the report of the Conference of the Heads of Irish Universities (CHIU) on University Governance which refers to all the corporate governance reports from Cadbury in the UK through to Hempel, the Threadway report in the United States and Vienot in France. *The Financial Governance of Irish Universities: Balancing Autonomy and Accountability* (Higher Education Authority, Dublin, 2001), p. 15.
5. See further Lynch-Fannon (2004) for a consideration of the meaning of efficiency in the context of the law and economics school analysis of corporate law.
6. 'Ownership also has always implied responsibility for the harms that one's property can inflict on others, but by and large, this has been a minor consideration in most people's thinking. Those who flagrantly abused or neglected their property might, at worst, lose it. In the late twentieth century, however, as a result of unprecedented growth in our technological capabilities and the scope of business activities we have entered another realm.' Green (1993).
7. 'No one should compel or exhort national change for the sake of change, or for the sake of an artificial (therefore inevitably unsuccessful) imposed uniformity. In Europe, our structures for and concepts of corporate governance vary, as has been seen, very widely indeed. It would be a lamentable example of empirical and arrogant self-satisfaction for any nation to seek to impose its own systems on its neighbors, even motivated by the best of peaceful and federal objectives.' Jeffrey (1995).
8. For an interesting commentary on this phenomenon see Werner (1981) where the notion that this dispersal of ownership and control is a perversion

of the original structure of the corporation is described as the 'erosion doctrine'. Werner disagrees with this doctrine and argues that it was not necessarily envisaged that property and control should remain under a unified possession.

9. The directive includes all groups with more than 1000 employees with at least 130 employees in establishments in at least two member states.

10. For example, see the role of the social partners regarding the implementation of Council Directive 96/34/EC [1996] OJ L145/4 on the Framework Agreement on Parental Leave concluded by UNICE, CEEP and the ETUC.

11. A 2004 European Commission Report on the Social Situation of the European Union at p. 7 observes that the 'increasing divergence in population trajectories between the USA and the EU, caused by the recovery in US fertility levels and the upward swing in immigration into the US, will persist: while the population of the EU will stagnate and begin to shrink ... These differences will have important economic and strategic implications in the medium to long term'.

7

Multilateral Regulatory Initiatives – A Legitimation-based Approach[1]

George Gilligan

Introduction

Of special interest for this chapter is the growing push for increased transparency and exchange of information in financial services from multilateral organisations such as the Organisation for Economic Cooperation and Development (OECD), the Financial Action Task Force (FATF) and the European Union (EU). It is not unsurprising perhaps that such organisations are becoming increasingly active in multilateral contexts, because although it is a recurring historical truism that whenever and wherever there is trade then also there is a strong potential for conflict, in recent decades the potential for more complex trading disputes and conflicts is increasing. There are many factors contributing to this trend, including: cumulative effects of developments in information technology, the liberalisation of capital markets since the 1970s and the broader influences of globalisation. The emergence of the World Trade Organisation (WTO) can be seen as testimony to the need under the competitive paradigm that is late-modern capitalism for forums in which the global context of trade issues, especially the potential for conflict, can be considered.

The increasing influence of multilateral regulatory organisations such as the WTO, FATF and the OECD, and the effects of their initiatives/ mechanisms to mediate conflict/promote agendas, invite a number of important questions. Should there be multilateral regulatory frameworks in, for example, the financial services sector? If so, who should construct these regulatory frameworks and how should they be policed?

These questions have massive implications, beyond the scope of a single chapter (or one suspects a single book). However, in order to evaluate some of the relevant issues and act as a window on the broader discourses surrounding not only multilateral regulation, but also corporate governance (especially in an international context), this chapter focuses on the activities in recent years of the OECD with regards to what it terms *harmful tax practices* and the ramifications of its initiatives in this area (OECDHTPI).[2] The OECD's work in this area has been carried out largely through its Forum on Harmful Tax Practices which is a subsidiary body of the OECD's Committee on Fiscal Affairs.[3] Trade conflicts will occur in most industries at some time, but the financial services sector has become a site of particular tensions and conflicts, partly as a result of it being one of the most integrated elements of the global economy. For example, in recent times in some international forums there has been growing tension regarding the levels of transparency and international cooperation provided by certain jurisdictions, and this international–local tension is an ongoing theme for this chapter.

How Should Regulatory Discourse (Especially Multilateral Regulatory Discourse) be Deconstructed? The Potential of Explanations Grounded in Legitimacy Theorising

Some of these contemporary tensions in financial services are likely to be reproduced in other areas of global trade in the future as part of ongoing trade-offs and interaction between a globalising economy, the need to counter terrorism in a post-September 11 world, the rise of networked governance and legitimate jurisdictional self-interest. Of course the interconnected realities of governance in contemporary life in general, and in trade in particular, mean that no multilateral regulatory initiative can act in isolation from the effects of other multilateral regulatory activity and reactions to such activity. Nevertheless as can be seen in the discussion below, by using the OECDHTPI as a window on current multilateral regulatory discourse in relation to financial services, a number of emerging international governance issues can be examined. For example, is erosion of national sovereignty increasingly becoming a price to be paid by at least some of those jurisdictions that want to participate in the global market for financial services? Some globalisation commentators such as Held (1999) and Ohmae (1995), who have been labelled *hyper-globalisers* or *neo-medievalists*, would view such a development as appropriate. Other writers on globalisation see state sovereignty and globalisation not as oppositional, but interactive and mutually supportive (Sassen 1996).

However, if traditional understandings of national sovereignty are being eroded as a price of market participation, then it raises interesting issues of legitimacy and how prevailing sets of power relations will manifest within both national and international regulatory infrastructures of financial services. Similar processes can be seen in the ongoing evolution of corporate governance standards that can be seen as acceptable across a number of jurisdictions, issues that are the focus of other chapters in this volume.

The key claim of this chapter is that legitimacy-based approaches have significant interpretative potential for understanding regulatory praxis. It is my view that it is essential not to assume legitimacy as a given, and instead recognise that legitimacy itself can be a complex and elastic concept. Legitimacy affects the character of power relations and can help explain systems of power, not only how power works as an ongoing process, but also how it originates. In Beetham's view, there are two types of *story* of legitimacy: one is a story of developmental stages; and the other is how self-confirming processes are at work within any settled power relations to reproduce and consolidate their legitimacy (Beetham 1991, 98–99). This power of routinisation and its capacity for self-affirmation should not be underestimated. However, this cycle is never perfect or complete, and is open to contextual influences, whether those influences reside in arenas as diverse as the domestic political sphere or the international regulatory context (Franck 1988, 1990). Legitimacy is integral to any system of regulation or body of knowledge, and it can reside in positions of authority or in institutions (Tyler 1990, 29). However, it is a complex concept involving not only beliefs, but also: legality; judicial determination; consent, both active and passive; and of course perhaps most crucially with regard to the subject matter of this chapter, the potential for differential interpretation. This chapter considers the OECDHTPI and their regulatory context from a perspective emphasising legitimacy issues, because the financial services sector is an area in which legitimacy and consent can be at times highly affected by cultural and political specifics, and therefore subject to various and sometimes competing interpretations (Gilligan 1999).

Perceptions of legitimacy can be fluid in certain contexts and on certain issues so it is helpful to think of it as a continuum of belief and evaluation. Suchman offers three models of organisational legitimacy: (1) pragmatic legitimacy – rooted in self-interested calculation, with an emphasis on notions of exchange and value; (2) moral legitimacy – normative evaluations are crucial, with an emphasis on notions of consequence, procedure, structure and personality; and (3) cognitive legitimacy – comprehensibility is crucial, with an emphasis on notions of predictability and plausibility. Although moving *up* the legitimacy scale from pragmatic to moral to cognitive is difficult, it can achieve more profound and self-sustaining levels of legitimacy (Suchman 1995). Regulatory initiatives, including of course multilateral regulatory initiatives such as the OECDHTPI, can move up and/or down this continuum of perceived legitimacy in the eyes of those interpreting them. Similarly, this approach has potential for evaluating initiatives across a broad range of corporate governance activities.

A legitimacy-based approach can be an especially useful analytical tool when considering regulation of the financial sector because the intensely competitive environment of the financial services sector informs all regulatory developments in the area. Private, corporate and state forces are continually at work in the world of financial services regulation, which functions within more flexible and ill-defined parameters than many other areas of law. There is constant interaction between state and private influences, and between the regulators and regulated. It is inevitable that regulators respond to the market forces of their industry and regulatory control is a reciprocal arrangement, shaped by negotiated and symbiotic relationships. It is not a static phenomenon, but rather a process of continuing political adaptation within a regulatory setting, in which actors can erode existing regulation, lobby for change and take advantage of competition between different regulatory regimes. There is a continuing balancing between ensuring market integrity and limiting regulatory burden, and perceptions of risk and liquidity are two of the many important factors that shape this competitive regulatory space.

A key concept in discerning and classifying the various interpretations of multilateral regulatory initiatives is legitimacy. As international organisations such as the FATF and the OECD assume a higher profile in how international regulatory financial infrastructures are constructed there is an increasing emphasis on the legitimacy of the specific processes involved. This is especially the case regarding who actually participates in the relevant decision-making and their relative levels of influence on decisions that are made. Indeed, in the cut and thrust of debates on any subject, it is by claiming legitimacy for a particular view of the world, or of specific phenomena, that a party will try to persuade others to support their position. This is very much the case regarding the OECDHTPI.

However, legitimacy can be a culturally specific matter and play a key role in struggles for ideological, political and cultural dominance. As such it may be difficult to apply standards of legitimacy regarding systems of financial regulation that may be prevalent in wealthy large jurisdictions such as France or Germany, in much poorer jurisdictions such as the Marshall Islands. It may be equally difficult to justify such standards in places such as Liechtenstein and Monaco, which are relatively wealthy small jurisdictions, but are heavily dependent upon financial services for a significant proportion of their GDP. For example, it is an economic fact of life in an increasingly competitive sector, that the levels of secrecy that a jurisdiction can offer client investors may be related to the totals of capital flows routed through that jurisdiction, and subsequently the levels of fees and other associated incoming revenues that are generated by these flows. Self-interest is sure to be a powerful influence in such scenarios.

An analysis grounded in legitimation can be helpful when examining developments in regulation, because regulatory norms and standards can be local, national or international phenomena. As regulatory space and discourse become both more congested, and more contested, increasing importance is accorded to those actors perceived as possessing specialist knowledge and/or professional legitimacy. This professional knowledge often may be employed strategically in regulatory disputes, whether they are local or multilateral in nature. For example, there has been considerable discussion in international forums about the blacklists of the FATF and OECD, whereby, for example, those juris-dictions with bank secrecy regimes that are perceived as obstructive in some quarters might be penalised by the international community in other trade contexts. Any subsequent sanctions could be extremely damaging to smaller jurisdictions and raise issues of legitimacy. The OECDHTPI are not the only set of contentious multilateral taxation strategies to emerge in recent times. For example, there has been ongoing disagreement over a period of some years between various member states of the EU, the European Commission (EC) and other European jurisdictions such as Switzerland concerning the efforts of the EU (driven by the interests of specific EU member states, in particular France and Germany), to introduce a Savings Tax Directive (hereafter referred to as the EUSTD), with regard to the provision of information regarding the assets of citizens of individual member states who may have chosen to locate such assets in different jurisdictions to their home country (Gilligan 2003).

The Regulation of Taxation Game

One should not be surprised that the political stakes associated with international taxation regulatory initiatives seem to be high, because taxation in a very real sense might be considered the lifeblood of the state, certainly taxation revenues are at the very least a key fuel source for maintaining the engine of the state's activity. Similarly taxation infrastructure is a key determinant of both micro and macro economic policy, and of the organisation of commerce itself, within both the public and private sectors, and also between them. Also, it is especially true of a highly competitive global financial sector, in which jurisdictions, financial institutions and finance centres continually strive to maintain or increase their market share that tax regimes and other systems of regulation are elements of the competition between different jurisdictions to attract capital. This economic and simultaneously political imperative is a major driver in the construction of systems of regulation that are sensitive to the requirements of investment capital and as such can act also as a major justification for promoting particular types of regulatory reform.

So, not unexpectedly, debates and decisions about taxation can be expected to touch the self-interest of actors, whether at the level of: the individual's hip pocket (after all how many people actually enjoy paying tax?); the national treasury; or a global player such as the EC or a large transnational corporation (TNC). For example, where a legal person decides to domicile its business for taxation purposes can be one of its most important business decisions and can excite strong reactions. A recent example of this phenomenon in June 2004 was the opposition in some quarters of the US Congress to the decision by the US Department of Homeland Security to award a US$10 billion contract to Accenture, because Accenture is headquartered in Bermuda:

> The House Appropriations Committee voted 35–17 last Wednesday to modify the Department of Homeland Security's $32 billion budget in order to prevent the Bermuda-based company from taking up the contract, on the grounds that it would not be paying its fair share of US taxes . . . The Bill's sponsor Rep. Rosa DeLauro, a Connecticut Democrat, argued that: 'It is simply wrong for Homeland Security to award an expatriate with the largest corporate contract to date. We have two competitors who are paying their taxes in the US,' she added. (Godfrey 2004)

However, the contract actually was won by Accenture LLP, the US entity of Accenture, which of course pays taxes on its activities in the US. Consequently, as the relevant Bill has progressed though the US Congress it has been amended to remove the language blocking the awarding of the contract to Accenture. This case illustrates two important issues. First, the overwhelming practical impact of the political context which is a subject discussed throughout this chapter. Second, the sort of resentment, confusion and ambiguity that has been reproduced on many occasions, in many jurisdictions around the world, to what may be perceived by some as avoidance or evasion of their taxation obligations by some corporate organisations and/or wealthy individuals. Unsurprisingly, alternative interpretations of issues such as these are offered by those individuals and organisations that specialise in advising others as to what strategies they might employ to reduce and/or minimise their tax obligations. The latter has become a multi-billion dollar global industry in recent years and its growth has in part prompted not only criticism in some quarters of jurisdictions that are deemed to operate with high levels of bank secrecy, but also the development of specific initiatives such as the EUSTD and the OECDHTPI.

The increasing interconnectedness of economies is especially pronounced in the finance sector. Also the increasing scale and hybridisation of financial services, financial products and market participants inevitably result in continuing formation of additional zones of risk. These outcomes are products of a sector that is moving increasingly towards market-based, rather than relationship-based, financial intermediation. Despite this trend away from the personal to the virtual, normative issues remain vitally important if somewhat less predictable. In addition, the growing numbers of finance centres mean that jurisdictions that may be very different in a whole host of ways are now interdependent players in the matrix of trust that underpins the world of finance.

The OECD Initiatives Regarding Harmful Tax Practices (OECDHTPI)

Continuing expansions of risk in the financial services sector place its networks of trust under increasing strain, as numerous forms of white-collar crime can be hidden more easily within the millions of electronic impulses that represent the complex trading of modern financial markets across a myriad of jurisdictions. It is this expansion of risk that has become an increasing concern for international organisations such as the FATF and OECD in recent years. These efforts have been given greater urgency in the aftermath of the terrorist attacks on New York and Washington DC on September 11, 2001. However, before, and since, September 11, 2001, the FATF and the OECD separately have engaged in specific listing initiatives that have become widely referred to as blacklists, highlighting what the FATF or OECD have seen as problematic, or non-cooperative, juris-dictions that currently are operating in international financial services. Of particular relevance for this chapter has been the OECDHTPI. It is important to note that the OECDHTPI really started in 1989 with the Fiscal Degradation Paper, whose four separate drafts were OECD internal discussion documents. However, the first major OECD publica-tion in the public domain on these issues was its May 1998 report, *Harmful Tax Competition* (OECD 1998). That report stated that the four key criteria for identifying harmful tax practices should be: (1) no or nominal taxes in the case of tax havens, and no or low taxation, in the case of member country preferential tax regimes; (2) lack of transparency; (3) lack of effective exchange of information;

and (4) no substantial activities, in the case of tax havens, and ringfencing, in the case of member country preferential regimes (OECD, 1998 19–35).

In May 2000, the OECD declared that the following 34 jurisdictions met the OECD's technical criteria as tax havens: Andorra, Anguilla, Antigua and Barbuda, Aruba, Bahamas, Bahrain, Barbados, Belize, British Virgin Islands, Cook Islands, Dominica, Gibraltar, Grenada, Guernsey/Sark/Alderney, Isle of Man, Jersey, Liechtenstein, Liberia, Maldives, Marshall Islands, Monaco, Montserrat, Nauru, Netherlands Antilles, Niue, Panama, Samoa, Seychelles, St Lucia, St Christopher and Nevis, St Vincent and the Grenadines, Tonga, Turks and Caicos, US Virgin Islands and Vanuatu (OECD 2000). In April 2002, the OECD published its second blacklist and classified as *Uncooperative Tax Havens*: Andorra; Liberia; Liechtenstein; Marshall Islands; Monaco; Nauru; and Vanuatu. In May 2003, the list was revised to remove Vanuatu (OECD 2003a). The list was further revised in December 2003 to remove the Republic of Nauru (OECD 2003b). In March 2004, in its Progress Report the OECD confirmed that it still considered Andorra, Liberia, the Principality of Liechtenstein, the Republic of the Marshall Islands and the Principality of Monaco as Uncooperative Tax Havens (OECD 2004b).

Since May 2000 the OECD has been making strenuous efforts to sway the original 34 to commit to the elimination of those tax practices that the OECD considers harmful. For example, in November 2001, the OECD reported success for its strategies when it listed Aruba, Bahrain, the Isle of Man, the Netherlands Antilles and the Seychelles as now being 'committed jurisdictions' to the elimination of harmful tax practices, and in addition stated that due to recent legislative and administrative changes, Tonga would 'not be considered for inclusion in any list of uncooperative jurisdictions' (OECD 2001b, 9). Since then there have been further letters or other forms of commitment from a number of jurisdictions including: Barbados; Antigua and Barbuda; Grenada and St Vincent and the Grenadines; Guernsey and Jersey; St Lucia; Dominica; Anguilla and Turks and Caicos Islands; US Virgin Islands; the Bahamas; Belize; the Cook Islands; the British Virgin Islands; Niue; Panama; and Samoa. The OECD considers the commitments by various jurisdictions to be indicators of the success of its strategies regarding harmful tax competition. However, it should be noted that not only have alternative social constructions been put forward in relation to the levels of success achieved by the OECD to date (discussed in more detail below), but also there has been substantial criticism concerning the intrinsic legitimacy of the OECDHTPI. Many of the jurisdictions named in the OECD lists have complained in the media and other public forums at various times about being categorised in such a manner. For example, the Caribbean Community (CARICOM) criticised the actions of the OECD, the FATF and the Financial Services Forum (FSF):

> Heads of Government of the Caribbean Community, meeting in Canouan, St Vincent and the Grenadines, expressed grave concern at a recent series of orchestrated activities by the G7, through three organizations of its creation. These activities, which are unilateral and inconsistent with international practice, are designed to impair the competitive capacity of Caribbean jurisdictions in the provision of global financial services . . .
>   Heads of Government took note that each of the reports was prepared by bodies in which the Caribbean has no representation and was based on incomplete information and on standards set unilaterally by these bodies. They deplored the fact that the lists were published with the objective of tainting jurisdictions in the eyes of the investment community and the international financial market. They condemned the actions of the OECD in particular as contrary to the tenets of a global market economy promoted by G7 countries. They reiterated that the proposed OECD actions have no basis in international law and are alien to the practice of inter-state relations. (CARICOM 2000a, 8–9)

Mr Owen Arthur, Prime Minister and Finance Minister of Barbados, was scathing of what he saw as the OECD's: 'institutional imperialism' and its 'use of crude threats and stigmas' (*The Tribune* 2000). The basis of the arguments of these critics is to attack the legitimacy, and therefore the credibility, of the initiatives of the OECD, the FATF and the FSF. It is a clear example of competing social constructions of legitimacy being used to explain differing perspectives and evaluations of the same social phenomena. Some critics have contended that the major motivation for the OECDHTPI is the concern of certain OECD members for revenue being lost through the tax management strategies of high net worth individuals or legal persons. For example, Sir James Mitchell, Prime Minister of St Vincent and the Grenadines:

> Let it be clear that harmful tax competition has nothing to do with drug money or money laundering. We are doing nothing that is illegal or

immoral. Tax competition is really about whose treasury gets the money. The international financial community urges competition and open markets but when we succeed they declare it unfair. (CARICOM 2000b)

It is important to note that membership of the OECD is dominated by the more powerful advanced economies and that the vast majority of those who have featured on the OECD's blacklists are not well represented within the organisations. Critics of the OECDHTPI have highlighted this relative exclusion from the evaluation and black-listing processes of the interests and *voice* of those that are most affected. For example, in February 2003, Sir Ronald Sanders, Antigua and Barbuda's Chief Negotiator on international financial services reflected on the early efforts of the OECDHTPI as 'high-handed' (Tax-news.com 2003).

The lack of support for the blacklisting processes by many of those listed is not surprising and typifies what some legitimacy theorists might refer to as *a lack of compliance pull*. Under this construct of compliance pull, the more legitimate a rule, initiative or regulatory framework is perceived to be by those who are subject to its effects, the greater the level of compliance they will be accorded. Similarly, the lower the levels of legitimacy accorded to specific rules, the lower will be the levels of compliance accorded. Interestingly the compliance pull–legitimacy relationship is an interactive one, so that increasing levels of compliance pull will strengthen the legitimacy and compli-ance levels achieved by rules/initiatives etc., and decreasing levels of compliance pull will have the opposite effect (Raustalia and Slaughter 2002, 541). The interactive compliance pull–legitimacy relationship is important with respect to the OECDHTPI and will be crucial to their ultimate success. Since 2000 the OECD has been adopting the classic *sticks and carrots approach*. The *carrots* approach is seen in their increased interaction with critics of the initiatives and the *sticks* approach is clear in the numerous signals regarding the threat of punitive measures against problem jurisdictions. Both approaches aim both to increase the levels of compliance with their preferred standards and to raise the legitimacy of the initiatives themselves among those most subject to their effects.

The commitment to the sticks approach can be seen in the fact that despite the type of fierce criticism that they have received from some quarters, the OECD seems committed to this strategy of *outing* those jurisdictions they perceive as not acting in accordance with accepted international standards. As far as the OECD is concerned their strategy is working as only seven of the original 34 jurisdictions classified as tax havens in May 2000 were blacklisted as uncooperative tax havens in April 2002. However, there are others who take a different view. For example, lobby groups such as the National Taxpayers Union (NTU), and the Center for Freedom and Prosperity (CFP), which have emerged to play a high profile role in the debates on tax competition. Both the NTU and the CFP are based, like so many other lobby groups (unsurprisingly), in Washington DC, and have argued fiercely against the overall legitimacy of the OECDHTPI. The CFP has produced a large number of strategic memoranda and other publications arguing that the OECDHTPI are inimical to notions of individual freedom, harmful to concepts of free trade and therefore against the national interest of the US (CFP 2001; Mitchell 2001). The CFP has made much of the political reality that since January 2001 there has been a Republican rather than a Democrat President in the US, and that this seems to have had a slowing and emasculating effect on the momentum and timetables of the OECDHTPI. For example, the CFP has reiterated persistently its alternative social construction regarding many of the letters of commitment that the OECD had received from a number of jurisdictions:

> almost all of the commitment letters sent to the Paris-based bureaucracy included level playing field clauses, stating that the jurisdiction would not implement bad tax policy unless all OECD member nations agreed to abide by the same misguided rules. (Mitchell, 2002, 1)

This requirement for a universal standard to apply for all affected jurisdictions, whether or not they are members of the OECD, has become known as the *Isle of Man clause*, because the Isle of Man was the first jurisdiction to insist in its commitment letter to the OECD that its commitment to the OECDHTPI was dependent on all OECD member jurisdictions adopting similar levels of commitment on issues of tax competition. Since then many of the other jurisdictions that subsequently signed letters of commitment to the OECDHTPI have inserted this Isle of Man clause as a condition of their own commitment. Now the language above employed by Mitchell to describe the so-called Isle of Man clause is more pejorative than the actual language in the relevant letters of commitment from the jurisdictions concerned, but it highlights the notion of challenge to the legitimacy of the OECD's interpretations of the progress of the OECDHTPI. Also, it should be pointed out that the OECD itself admits that even among its own membership there are sharply differing views about elements of the OECDHTPI. For example, Belgium and Portugal abstained from the 2001 Progress Report; Luxembourg recalled its sustained abstention since 1998 and reapplied that abstention in 2001; and Switzerland applied its 1998 abstention to any follow-up work undertaken since 1998 (OECD 2001b, 4). The continuing abstention of Luxembourg and Switzerland was acknowledged by the OECD in its 2004 Progress Report (OECD 2004b, 4).

So, it is manifestly clear that there is not unanimity within the OECD on its strategies in this area and inevitably this undermines to a certain extent the legitimacy and subsequent impact of its actions. For example, Lynette Eastmond, Director of the Secretariat of the International Tax and Investment Organisation (ITIO),[4] has questioned whether OECD members and other developed economies are: 'prepared explicitly to confirm their intention of abiding by the standards demanded of small and developing economies' (Tax-news.com 2001). Ms Eastmond's comments focused on the positions of Belgium, Luxembourg and Portugal in particular and were made following the release of the OECD's 2001 Progress Report (OECD 2001b). The ITIO emerged from the activities of the Joint-working Group on Cross-border Tax Matters, which itself was an initiative to mediate growing tensions between the OECD and many small and developing economies (SDEs) that operated as offshore finance centres, and which felt threatened by the increasingly interventionist activities of the OECD and certain other international organisations. The ITIO is but one of a series of strategic responses from various parties affected by the OECDHTPI and increasingly opposition is centring on notions of a level playing field for all players. The ITIO has received support from the Commonwealth Secretariat, which also has been critical of some aspects of the OECD approach. For example: 'While the OECD has called for transparent and open tax regimes from offshore finance centres, its own process for seeking international co-operation has been less than transparent and inclusive. Multilateralisation of this process would be desirable' (Commonwealth Secretariat 2000, 9). However, the ITIO continued to stress that: 'non-OECD countries, including members of the ITIO, have long objected to being asked to implement standards that OECD states themselves refuse to accept'

(ITIO 2002). The ITIO has been reported as complaining in particular about what it sees as 'a lack of a level playing field in the whole process' which has been the OECD's campaign against perceived harmful tax practices (Banks 2002). The ITIO has been active in its campaign to legitimate the activities of its members and eager to present more positive alternative constructions of how they function in the contemporary financial services sector, rather than the more negative images stimulated by the OECD blacklists. The activities of the CFP, Commonwealth Secretariat and ITIO can be seen as attempting to move the OECDHTPI down levels on any hierarchy of legitimacy. As part of this campaign of delegitimation, the ITIO in conjunction with the Society of Trust and Estate Practitioners (STEP)[5] commissioned the international law firm Stikeman Elliott to produce a critique of the review procedures engaged in by the OECD regarding the OECDHTPI (Stikeman Elliott 2000).

These efforts to promote the notion of a level playing field as a driver of the discourse on tax competition contributed to the formation of the Global Forum on Taxation. It has sought to bring together in a more cohesive way how the OECD, certain OECD members and many of those jurisdictions likely to be affected by the OECDHTPI interact on tax competition issues. The latter are described by the OECD as Non-OECD Participating Partners (NOPPs) and such terminology represents not only a softening in the approach of the OECD as it becomes more sensitised to the priorities of non-OECD members, but also is recognition of the need for a more cooperative approach to issues of tax competition. The Global Forum met in Ottawa in October 2003 and again in Berlin in June 2004, where it produced a policy document to progress efforts towards achieving a level playing field (Global Forum on Taxation 2004). The Global Forum is increasing in its strategic importance and there seems to be a growing recognition by the OECD that coordinated actions against harmful tax practices need the capacity for differential implementation. Whether a global playing field can ever be achieved remains a moot point and despite this evidence of increased cooperation, there are likely to be many more sharp exchanges, and ongoing ebbs and flows in debates on tax competition as political and economic conditions change in the future. Different actors in the debates regarding tax competition will offer alternative social constructions of the same sets of political and economic realities, in order to legitimate their actions to their separate constituencies. These processes of alternative social construction are not unusual, they are engaged in by individuals, groupings and organisations on a constant basis all around the world and in many contexts. Also, we should not be surprised by the fact that different actors have differential capacity for influence in a multilateral environment (Dagan 2002, 23). For example, there is only one contemporary superpower, so inevitably the view of the US has more impact on most multilateral contexts than the voice of another jurisdiction.

Conclusions

What conclusions might one draw from this discussion? First, it is undeniable that the OECDHTPI, in particular their blacklisting strategies, have had a significant galvanising effect. The relevant OECD Secretariat is small but has had a very big influence. The cumulative effect of greater regulatory activity by the OECD, the FATF and the IMF is accelerating a process by which hierarchies of offshore finance centres are emerging. The resentment that some jurisdictions have towards this process is heightened because some non-OECD jurisdictions are being pressured by the OECD to implement standards that OECD members themselves refuse to accept.

Second, in an era of globalisation, economic and political ties between many jurisdictions are deepening and jurisdictions increasingly are playing a mediating role regarding the interests of much business that may be conducted within their spheres of influence. The political context remains crucial and almost inevitably it is intertwined with expectations regarding vested interests. These developments are affecting the sovereignty of jurisdictions as local political priorities become more intertwined with international politics and the requirements of international business. The regulatory world reflects the realities of those domains which it purports to influence and so a major consequence of these developments is that regulatory structures and processes have become more internationalised. A variety of modes of governance are emerging that have a capacity for impacts of broad international scope. This political reality reflects an era of networked governance as regulatory relations are reconfigured, driven by trends towards hollowed-out government and hollowed-out corporate governance. The increasing importance of gatekeepers such as the OECD in the world economy is a product of these trends, and the OECDHTPI, their effects and the opposition that they have attracted from some parties are not so surprising examples of these forces at work.

Third, it is important to remember that different jurisdictions have different perceptions about what are their respective legitimate interests. It is difficult to first disentangle and then evaluate precisely how much the OECDHTPI are *offensive* towards tax havens etc., and/or *defensive* regarding the activities of natural and legal persons within OECD member states. Despite a broad trend globally towards increased transparency in business (strengthened considerably in recent times by concerns about the financing of terrorism), some jurisdictions, both certain OECD members and certain offshore finance centres, retain a commitment to stronger secrecy provisions, while some of their peers are pursuing increased transparency in their financial systems. The political, social and economic implications of this asymmetry are apparent, as is the need for compromise on how appropriate levels of transparency in financial systems might be achieved. Statutory legislation and/or political pressure will not automatically achieve this goal. It is more likely that in many cases it may be the combined effects of both the supporting regulatory infrastructures, and prevailing levels of commitment to specific standards of behaviour within both the political and the business environments that emerge as the key factors.

The above discussion shows that, if I might paraphrase George Orwell for a moment, the experience of the OECDHTPI appears to suggest that all finance centres are equal in the sense that they can access a globalising financial sector, but some are more equal than others. As we have seen, the stance and tone of the OECDHTPI have altered over the years in response to prevailing political realities that include the effectiveness of the voice of opponents and how much compliance pull the OECD has upon affected parties. However, in addition to the effects of political power one should not forget the influence of normative factors and how these help to shape perceived hierarchies of legitimacy.

Normative issues are crucial when seeking to understand issues of compliance, whether at the local, national or international level. Franck in his efforts to produce a general theory of compliance stressed that levels of compliance are shaped substantially by how legitimate the relevant rules are considered to be by those communities supposedly subject to them (Franck 1988, 706). Indeed there is growing empirical evidence of 'a linear relationship between legitimacy and compliance, as legitimacy increases, so does compliance' (Tyler 1990, 57). Most people believe that laws should be obeyed and it is this broader normative commitment to compliance as a general principle among those regulated which is perhaps the greatest asset that regulators and international organisations can access. This broader normative commitment is crucial for the development of national and international crime prevention strategies in the financial services sector, and is relevant for all finance centres, whether they be huge centres of international finance or small islands acting as offshore finance centres.

Similarly, one should not forget the powerful influence of Adam Smith's *Invisible Hand* (Smith 1884). That is to say, market forces themselves and, in particular, the decisions and choices of the consumers of financial services and products. Market participants are likely to engage in some forum shopping between jurisdictions. However, underregulation may be just as unattractive for some as overregulation. Some investors may prefer more costly finance centres, precisely because some may have a better reputation for stability, investor protection and transparent regulatory standards. Other investors may select finance centres that have less onerous regulatory regimes, lower costs or greater secrecy provisions. Under this paradigm of regulatory arbitrage, exchanges and finance centres understandably exploit what they perceive as their cost or other structural advantages, such as a particular jurisdiction's system of company law, or levels of bank secrecy, in order to gain competitive advantage.

There is an urgent and growing need for more and continuing empirically informed research on the efficacy of international regulatory initiatives such as the OECDHTPI. There have been some econometric studies in the area of tax competition. Janeba and Schjelderup found that increasing tax competition is likely to bring overall positive effects to the welfare of communities, because although the supply of public goods would decrease, so too do rents to politicians (Janeba and Schjelderup 2002). However, Sorensen when investigating the difficulties associated with international tax coordination found that approaches need to be global rather than regional to achieve any significant positive effect (Sorensen 2001). It remains hard to produce certainty in the econometric domain when trying to specify the universal benefits of multilateral regulatory initiatives such as the OECDHTPI. Nevertheless, despite this relative lack of certainty, multilateral regulatory activity in this area seems set to increase, and not only by the OECD. For example, the IMF, especially as a result of its efforts to develop more common methodologies in the evaluation of the financial services sectors of different jurisdictions, through its Financial Sector Assessment Program and its Reports on the Observance of Standards and Codes.

Returning to the central theme of this chapter, permeating specific research studies and more general debates is perhaps the key philosophical, political and economic issue for both theoretical and pragmatic decision-making on international tax competition – how far should regulatory competition go? This issue can be posed in different ways. How far should international organisations such as the OECD shape the levels of regulatory competition regarding tax or indeed any other trade-related area? Who should construct the regulatory frameworks for international financial services and how should they be policed in order to protect the legitimate interests of affected actors, such as the right to compete in open markets or the right of a jurisdiction to preserve its tax base?

The elusive holy grail of successful international regulation is at heart an issue of balance and enlightened decision-making. There is a growing body of evidence that there could be a dependent relationship between successful multilateral regulatory activity and perceptions regarding the legitimacy of that activity. The above discussion indicates that approaches grounded in notions of legitimacy can not only be useful in evaluation of how multilateral initiatives and gatekeepers emerge, operate and, in particular, adapt their strategies and structures, but also can act as a window on some of the key political determinants in contemporary governance praxis. Increased regulatory competition is not bad, but it has to be tempered with appropriate checks and balances. It is undeniable that substantial amounts of resources that are owed, or due to national tax authorities, are being lost/concealed/invested in international financial markets. Reconciling the competing claims of nation-states for tax revenues, finance centres for market access and financial institutions for freedom to operate is a substantial challenge. Issues of national sovereignty need to be factored heavily into the development of international initiatives, and the input of affected jurisdictions sought in an inclusive manner, in order that multilateral regulatory efforts may have a realistic hope of success. Similarly, numerous political and economic realities should remain in focus at all times, especially the reality that less developed economies have less regulatory capacity, indeed less capacity, in most areas. Consequently, there may be utility in pursuing demand side strategies based on incentive models that aim simultaneously not only to decrease taxation burdens in all countries, while at the same time ensuring that all countries have functional taxation systems targeting optimal levels of social capital creation, but also to foster meaningful development in less developed jurisdictions and effective integration of all jurisdictions into global and regional economies. This as they say is *a big ask*. Indeed it may be impossible to achieve in practice, but pursuing such a goal offers some potential to help mediate international-local tensions in the governance of financial markets and services.

Notes

1. This chapter draws on the conference paper: Gilligan, G.P. 2004. 'Who is in charge of my back yard anyway? International:local tensions in the governance of financial markets', presented at the International Colloquium: Governing the Corporation – Mapping the Loci of Power in Corporate Governance Design, 20–21 September 2004, Queen's University, Belfast.
2. The OECD has launched a number of initiatives on harmful tax practices which are discussed in more detail below and hereafter are referred to as the OECDHTPI.
3. For general background information regarding the structure of the Forum on Harmful Tax Practices see: http://www.oecd.org/topic/0,2686, en_2649_33745_1_1_1_1_37427,00.html.
4. Members of the ITIO are: Anguilla, Antigua and Barbuda, Bahamas, Barbados, Belize, British Virgin Islands, Cayman Islands, Cook Islands, Malaysia, St Kitts and Nevis, St Lucia, Turks and Caicos and Vanuatu. Organisations that have formal observer status with the ITIO include: the CARICOM Secretariat, the Commonwealth Secretariat and the Pacific Islands Forum Secretariat.
5. STEP has branches in 26 jurisdictions and a membership of more than 8000 who are drawn largely from the legal, accountancy, corporate trust, banking, insurance and related professions.

8

Corporate Social Responsibility as Regulation: The Argument from Democracy

Lisa Whitehouse

Introduction

In keeping with many of the themes raised within this collection, this chapter examines the nature and extent of corporate power, the regulatory responses to it within Anglo-American legal regimes and the challenge posed to the existing paradigm of corporate regulation by the concept of 'corporate social responsibility' (CSR). The failings of the current system, evidenced by the collapse of companies such as Enron and Parmalat, have helpfully been explored by other contributors to this work (see, for example, Melis and Melis; McBarnet). In seeking an effective response to those deficiencies, O'Brien offers an alternative to the current preference for ad hoc regulation and voluntary initiatives in the form of 'enforced self-regulation' while McBarnet argues for a bottom-up approach which, envisages a transformation in the attitudes of corporate managers away from 'creative compliance' with the regulatory framework and towards compliance with the spirit of the law. In an attempt to add something of value to this worthwhile debate, this chapter will contend that the likely success of proposals such as these would be enhanced greatly by the implementation of a regime of CSR which has the potential to resolve, in a holistic way, the failings of the current paradigm.

The chapter will begin with an exploration of the underlying premise of Anglo-American company law regimes which views the company as a private institution compelled to prioritise the interests of its shareholders, synonymous with 'profit maximisation' (Roach 2001; Wedderburn 1985), tempered only by ad hoc regulation designed to protect the interests of other parties such as employees and creditors. Dissatisfaction with this 'profit maximization within the law' (Parkinson 1996, 42) paradigm has manifested itself in many forms but perhaps most notably in the creation of the concept of CSR which seeks to ensure that companies do more than simply obey the law in pursuit of profit.

As the second section of this chapter will indicate, however, while academics and policymakers alike have identified corporate power as increasingly problematic, the solution they have offered has proven to be devoid of substantive content and sufficient theoretical grounding. For example, what are the goals of CSR? How are those goals justified? What standards should we use in evaluating whether those goals have been achieved? The failure by advocates of the concept to offer meaningful answers to these questions has resulted in CSR operating as an 'empty vessel', devoid of a legitimate normative framework and incapable of resisting opposing claims.

In an effort to add a degree of clarity to the debate, the third section of this chapter will seek to offer a meaningful conception of CSR by reference to fundamental democratic principles. It will contend that the priority afforded, since the 1980s, to the economic values associated with a liberal democracy coupled with a transition in the power relationship between the state, companies and the citizenry in western liberal democracies has created a relationship in which companies now rival nation-states as centres of power. This balance of power has become increasingly questionable as private companies have exhibited their capacity to exercise public power in an unaccountable and often unconstrained manner (Hertz 2002; Klein 2000; Monbiot 2001). To this extent, therefore, corporate power has exceeded the boundaries of legitimacy as established by the democratic settlement.

Despite this, regulators continue to view CSR as an aspiration which companies should be encouraged to pursue rather than an essential tool in reinstating corporate power within the terms of the democratic construct (as evidenced by a number of recent voluntary initiatives introduced by the Department of Trade and Industry 2002 and 2004, the Commission of the European Communities 2001 and 2002, and the United Nations in the form of the Global Compact). The reluctance or unwillingness on the part of legislators to view the company for what it is, namely, a source of significant public power, has resulted in CSR becoming instrumental in encouraging corporations to accept responsibilities beyond those imposed by law rather than the means by which to achieve a paradigm shift in the way the corporation is conceived.

In an attempt to reverse this situation, this chapter will return to the democratic fundamentals of CSR. The basis of the argument is that a liberal democracy will not tolerate the exercise of unaccountable public power in the hands of any individual or group, regardless of the value of their contribution to society (Stokes 1986, 178). It is essential, therefore, if corporate power is to be brought back within the confines of the democratic settlement, that corporate regulation seeks to ensure that corporate power is made accountable and that all fundamental democratic values are protected. CSR has a role to play in this respect by countering the current dominance of economic concerns and reinstating social democratic values within the regulatory framework. The means by which to achieve this may include the use of 'enforced self-regulation' and a change in managerial attitudes but what this chapter argues is that in order for these means to prove effective, academics, policymakers and legislators alike must re-evaluate the current paradigm by recognising and responding to the potential for large corporations to exercise significant public power.

Regulating Corporate Power: The Current Paradigm

Concern regarding the increased concentration of social, economic and political power within large private corporations has been evident within academic literature since the 1950s. Galbraith (1952, 29), for example, writing in 1952 noted that,

> With size goes the ultimate responsibility for the decision affecting the largest number of employees, over prices that affect the largest number of customers, over investment policies which work the greatest change in the income, livelihood or landscape of the community.

Substantial contemporary literature offering numerous examples of the adverse impact of corporate activity suggests that such concerns remain current and that the increasing power of corporations has not been matched by a corresponding increase in regulatory measures designed to make such power legitimate (Hertz 2002; Klein 2000; Monbiot 2001). While moves within Europe and the US have been made in respect of, for example, ensuring the integrity of the auditing process and financial markets (including the Public Company Accounting Reform and Investor Protection Act 2002 in the US, known more commonly as Sarbanes-Oxley), the protection of employees (for example, the Employment Rights Act 1996) and the environment (for example, the Environmental Protection Act 1990), the fundamental goal of corporate activity, as required by Anglo-American company law regimes, has remained largely unaltered since the early twentieth century. As Berle (1931, 1049) noted in 1931,

> all powers granted to a corporation or the management of a corporation, or to any group within the corporation, whether derived from statute or charter or both, are necessarily and at all times exercisable only for the ratable benefit of all the shareholders as their interest appears.

Kelly and Parkinson's (2000) attempt, in 2000, to reject 'shareholder exclusivity' in favour of the recognition of wider interests indicates the enduring quality of this fundamental duty. The justifications which underlie the primacy given to shareholder interests have been well rehearsed but it is perhaps worth noting them in summary at this point. A traditional argument derives from the concept of ownership. Although contestable on the basis that, as a separate legal personality, the company and the company alone owns its own property (see, for example, *Macaura* v. *Northern Assurance Co.* [1925] AC 619), it is generally accepted that shareholders own the company or at least its capital because 'they bear the residual financial risk on the company's capital' (Gamble and Kelly 1996, 73). The consequence of this assumption is that shareholders, as 'owners', have the right to have the company run in their interests alone, as Ireland (1999, 33) explains,

> It is a natural corollary of this assumption that the interests of share-holders should take priority, if not complete precedence, over all others; and that shareholders should, as of right, have a substantial, if not an exclusive, say in the running of companies.

This apparent link between ownership and shareholder exclusivity came into question during the 1930s when Berle and Means (1936) identified a divergence between those who owned and those who controlled the company. Their seminal work offered both an empirical and normative account of what has been termed the 'separation of ownership and control' (Ireland 1999). Having observed a transition in the management of companies from owner-managers to control placed in the hands of professional managers with a diversified share ownership, Berle and Means concluded that shareholders were either unwilling or unable to control management and that this presented an opportunity to broaden the interests capable of recognition with corporate decision-making, 'neither the claims of ownership nor those of control can stand against the paramount interests of the community' (Berle and Means 1936, 356). More significantly, Berle and Means' observation led to the fundamental implication that shareholder exclusivity could no longer be justified, as Stokes (1986, 178) explains,

> one of the traditional defences of private property which states that an optimal allocation of resources results from owners (who it is assumed control their property) pursuing their own self-interest could be invoked to justify insisting that the company was run in the interests of shareholders alone. Clearly that justification collapsed once it became clear that shareholders in large public companies no longer exercised any real control or responsibility over their property.

The link between the separation of ownership and control and the denial of shareholder priority has been challenged by Parkinson (1996) who suggests that the latter does not necessarily follow the former. While the justification from ownership remains a contested issue, however, a more fundamental question has been raised regarding whether shareholders have any ownership rights in the company at all.

Ireland, in an attempt to debunk what he terms the 'ownership myth' (Ireland 1999, 48), contends that, as a result of diversified shareholdings, passive investing and separate corporate personality, shareholders have been transformed from owners to 'rentiers', namely, investors 'who took little or no direct interest in the companies in which they held shares, other, of course, than in the dividends they paid' (Ireland 2000, 147). In consequence, shareholders are undeserving of special privileges or exclusive governance rights in respect of the company.

While Ireland's claims may dispense with the rationalisation arising from ownership, there exist other justifications for shareholder exclusivity including the contention that it is the most economically 'efficient' option. Deriving from the view of the corporation as a 'nexus of contracts', writers such as Easterbrook and Fischel (1989) and Jensen and Meckling (1976) argue that, as a web of relationships, the company is not amenable to the concept of ownership or ownership rights. Shareholders, therefore, do not obtain priority interests as a result of their ownership but rather for the reason that they are best placed to ensure that the company is run efficiently. As Kelly and Parkinson (2000, 118–121) explain, the 'transaction costs' version of the nexus of contracts theory contends that rational actors seek to contract in a way that minimises transaction costs. Shareholders, however, unlike other parties related to the company, put their entire investment at risk and cannot protect themselves contractually because of the open-ended character of their rights so, instead, they receive governance rights.

In rejecting this contention and making the case for a more pluralist approach, Kelly and Parkinson (2000, 122) claim that it is right that the bearers of residual risk should have governance rights but that shareholders are not the only bearers of such risk. Employees, for example, bear residual risk where they undertake specialised jobs because they cannot go elsewhere and the company will have to train new staff to replace them. Their risk is not fixed which places them in a similar position to shareholders (Kelly and Parkinson 2000, 124–125).

While these arguments may or may not justify the priority given to shareholders within Anglo-American company law, the practical manifestation of that objective has taken a further normative leap. It has been assumed that, 'the interests of the company' which directors are duty bound to prioritise (*Re Smith & Fawcett Ltd* [1942] Ch. 304), are equivalent to the interests of its shareholders synonymous with their financial interests and therefore equivalent to the making of profit and, in practice, 'profit maximisation'. The jump from the 'interests of the company' to 'profit maximisation' has been questioned by Carroll (1991, 41) who notes that while the profit motive was introduced in order to fuel entrepreneurship, 'at some point the idea of the profit motive got transformed into a notion of maximum profits, and this has been an enduring value ever since'.

The justification underlying the pursuit of profit maximisation, however, derives from economic theory which contends that the 'public interest' (for a detailed account of this concept see Feintuck 2004; Held 1970) is served where societal wealth is maximised, therefore companies should seek to contribute to that goal by maximising their profits. It should be noted, however, that profit maximisation does not and, according to Parkinson (1996, 41), should not operate unconstrained for two reasons. The first is that while economic considerations may form an integral part of the public interest, there are other values that we might consider of equal if not higher importance.

The second is that defects in the market may allow corporations to incur costs that are not internalised by the firm, thereby leading to the inefficient use of resources and a reduction in the overall wealth of society. While Coase (1960, 18) suggests that the individual company or the market has the potential to deal effectively with 'harmful effects', his reliance on the existence of perfect competition leads Parkinson (1996, 42) to note that market failure allows companies to 'ignore the costs that its activities impose on others'. In response, society seeks to prevent these 'negative externalities' through regulation.

The layering of these constraints upon the ultimate goal of profit maximisation has produced what Parkinson (1996, 42) terms 'profit maximization within the law'. The justification for this approach, apparent within Anglo-American company law, is that it serves the 'public interest' by ensuring the pursuit of overall wealth creation tempered by regulation that deters social costs from being incurred. Friedman's (1969, 133) phrase may be well worn but it summarises accurately the responsibility of business as required by current company law rules, which is 'to use its resources and engage in activities designed to increase its profits so long as it stays within the rules of the game'.

It has become apparent, however, that there is significant dissatisfaction with the 'profit maximisation within the law' paradigm. In particular, legal constraints designed to protect particular interests and values are limited, leaving many individuals and communities vulnerable to the harms caused by some corporate activity with little or no opportunity for redress (obvious examples are provided by incidents such as Union Carbide in Bhopal in 1984 and the *Exxon Valdez* in 1989). Second, many companies choose to ignore the rules and undertake prohibited activities or as McBarnett suggests within this collection, engage in 'creative compliance' with the law. It seems apparent, therefore, that current legal constraints and enforcement procedures are ineffective in deterring negative externalities.

Third, activities undertaken by companies may operate within the law but outwith the ethical standards expected by society. Reich (1998, 9) cites a number of examples of unethical but legal behaviour such as, the use of child labour and redundancies coupled simultaneously with pay increases for top executives. While some unethical practices become the subject of substantial media attention, including, for example, the cases of Enron and WorldCom (other examples include Shell's dumping of the *Brent Spar* in 1995 and the Nestlé baby food scandal in 1970), one must assume that many others operate unnoticed.

Dissatisfaction with the current regulatory regime has manifested itself in many forms, most recently in respect of protests against globalisation, but there is a rich heritage of debate concerning the role of corporations within society which has given rise to a number of concepts including 'corporate social performance' (Carroll 1991; Wood 1991), 'corporate citizenship' (Andriof and McIntosh 2001; McIntosh *et al.* 2003) and 'sustainability' (Andriof and McIntosh 2001; Henderson 2001). The remainder of this chapter, however, is concerned with a concept that has remained at the centre of the debate for the last 75 years, namely, CSR.

Corporate Social Responsibility

Since the initiation of the debate concerning CSR in the 1930s, the concept has given rise to extensive academic literature and has been the subject of numerous initiatives introduced at the national, European and global level (including the European Commission's Green Paper on CSR and the United Nations Global Compact). Despite its apparent familiarity and frequent use, however, it is a concept bereft of a universally accepted definition and legitimate normative framework, as Hester (1975, 25) notes, 'there has been no general agreement as to the meaning of corporate social responsibility or how it should be implemented, despite the fact that many businessmen enthusiastically have adopted the concept during the past decade'.

Despite the lack of a commonly accepted definition, it seems safe to assume that CSR is concerned with ensuring that companies go beyond the 'profit maximisation within the law' formula; that they do more than simply obey the law and make money for their shareholders. As Andriof and McIntosh (2001, 15–16) suggest, CSR arises from a deeply held vision by corporate leaders that business can and should play a role beyond just making money. It embraces an understanding that everything a company does has some flow-on effect either inside or outside the company, from customers and employees to communities and the natural environment.

Beyond this, it is difficult to be more specific but an examination of some of the relevant literature highlights a number of themes, usually played out on contested ground, that, at the very least, serve to establish the boundaries of the concept.

The Spectrum of CSR: From 'Enlightened Self-interest' to the 'Public Interest'

CSR as 'Enlightened Self-interest'

The legal duty imposed upon directors to prioritise the interests of the company has served as a focal point for the CSR debate and for some advocates of the concept, as a major stumbling block towards reform. The apparent prohibition on the consideration of interests other than those of shareholders in the decision-making processes adopted by directors appears to deny the possibility of corporate activity which is other than profit maximising. As Clarkson (1995, 112) notes,

> So long as managers could maintain that shareholders and their profits were supreme, the claims of other stakeholders could be subordinated or ignored. There was no need for the manager to be concerned with fairness, justice, or even truth. The single-minded pursuit of profit justified any necessary means, so long as they were not illegal.

The full extent of shareholder exclusivity and its impact on the consideration of other interests was highlighted by a number of cases in the UK and the US in the early part of the twentieth century which held that 'socially responsible' activity on the part of corporations was *ultra vires* or in breach of duty (Blumberg 1972). Wedderburn (1993, 235), for example, cites *Parke* v. *Daily News* ([1962] Ch. 927) in which the judge ruled that the directors' decision, to award £1 million to ex-employees who had just lost their jobs as a result of the sale of the company's assets (statutory redundancy payments were not in place at the time), while 'laudable', was not taken 'in the interests of the company' (Wedderburn 1993, 235). In a similar vein, courts in the US gave their support to the supremacy of shareholder interests. In the case of *Dodge* v. *Ford Motor Co.* (204 Mich. 459, 170 NW, 668 (1919)), for example, 'the Michigan Supreme Court repudiated Henry Ford's desire to benefit employees and consumers by sacrificing profits' (Millon 1991, 230; Nunan 1988).

This view was reversed eventually by the introduction of legislation, offering albeit limited support for the inclusion of employee interests in corporate decision-making (for example, s. 309 Companies Act 1985; see Davies 2003; and for proposals to replace this section see White Paper 2002) and within the common law by judicial decisions which recognised that activities such as charitable giving, by enhancing the company's reputation among potential customers, could be viewed as being consistent with the goal of profit maximisation (see, for example, the US case of *A.P. Smith Manufacturing Co.* v. *Barlow* 39 ALR 2d 1179 (1953)). In effect, the courts promoted a view of CSR as 'enlightened self-interest' (Barnard 1997; Eisenberg 1998; Smith 1997) a concept perhaps best described by Minow's (1999, 1004) refrain that 'Companies can do well by doing good.'

While the profit maximisation goal served initially as a hurdle to the implementation of activity such as charitable giving, for some commentators, the duty to profit maximise is not only unproblematic but equivalent to CSR. Friedman (1969, 1995), for example, despite being characterised as the most vehement and well-known critic of CSR, advocates a particular version of the concept which promotes the maintenance of 'profit maximisation within the law' with the additional layer of adherence to some ethical standards. As he suggests, corporate executives have a responsibility, owed directly to shareholders, 'to conduct the business in accordance with their desires, which generally will be to make as much money as possible while conforming to the basic rules of the society, both those embodied in law and those embodied in ethical custom' (Friedman 1995, 138). Friedman rejects outright any further constraints on the profit motive and the consideration of interests beyond those required by law or enlightened self-interest and views the imposition of other social responsibilities upon directors as fundamentally undemocratic, for the director will be 'engaging in a fundamentally governmental venture for which he has never been democratically elected or chosen' (McClaughry 1972, 8).

According to Friedman's view, the 'public interest' is served where societal wealth is maximised and that, by seeking to maximise their profits, companies are simply playing their part in the attainment of that goal. This view of CSR, with its focus strongly on economic values, has been criticised for failing to recognise that corporate performance can and should be measured by reference to a broader range of factors. As Davis (1960, 75) argues, 'the general public does not seem to want business confined only to economics. They also have human expectations of business.' Friedman is not alone, however, in promoting the maintenance of the goal of profit maximisation.

The Four Faces of CSR

Carroll (1991, 2001), one of the most prolific writers on the subject, advocates a model of CSR that, since its introduction in 1979, has served as a point of reference. In offering what he himself describes as 'a comprehensive definition of corporate social responsibility' (Carroll 1991, 40), Carroll identifies four aspects of CSR which he classifies as economic, legal, ethical and philanthropic. In order to illustrate the relative importance of each element, Carroll (1991, 42) offers a pictorial view of CSR in the form of a pyramid with economic interests at its base followed by legal, ethical and philanthropic duties. While ranking them in order of importance within the pyramid, Carroll is keen to emphasise the dynamic relationship between the four components arguing that companies should seek to view the component parts in the round and seek to fulfil each simultaneously. To this extent, therefore, a CSR firm is one which strives 'to make a profit, obey the law, be ethical, and be a good corporate citizen' (Carroll 1991, 43).

While it would seem reasonable to suggest that society would welcome companies who behave as 'good corporate citizens', it cannot be assumed that the values promoted by Carroll are necessarily justified. Wood (1991, 695), for example, contends that Carroll's account fails to establish principles, preferring instead to categorise corporate behaviour under the four headings, 'Carroll's categories...can be viewed as domains within which principles are enacted, but not as principles themselves.' She suggests, for example, that the pursuit of economic success may be undertaken for any number of motives, some of which may run counter to the interests of society but which satisfy Carroll's definition of economic responsibilities.

Despite the criticisms levelled at the work of Carroll, it has proved influential in determining the content of CSR to the extent that others have sought to move the debate on in order to determine the individuals or groups to whom corporations owe their economic, legal, ethical and philanthropic responsibilities. While the position at law is unequivocal, corporate managers must prioritise the interests of the company, the underlying aim of CSR is to extend beyond the narrow confines established by law so as to include parties both inside and outside the company.

In order to be meaningful, however, it is necessary to establish the boundaries of corporate responsibility, or to determine what Freeman (1994, 411) has described as the principle of 'Who and What Really Count', as Wolfe (1993, 1694) suggests,

> Everyone in society is a nonshareholder of any given corporation except the shareholders, which makes the term 'nonshareholder' fairly close to meaningless...If there are to be rights established against directors, we need criteria that determine which nonshareholders have such rights and why.

In an attempt to identify, with a degree of clarity, those interests worthy of such 'rights', a number of commentators have advocated the theory of 'stakeholding'.

Stakeholding

Introduced during the 1960s, it was not until the 1980s that the 'stakeholder perspective' (Andriof *et al.* 2002) became familiar within academic literature. Synonymous with the idea that 'companies *need not* and *should not* be operated solely in the interests of their shareholders' (Ireland 1996, 287) stakeholder theory attempts to take the denial of shareholder exclusivity a stage further by identifying those individuals or groups whose interests are deserving of recognition within corporate decision-making.

In offering a relatively straightforward definition, Carroll (1991, 43) suggests that stakeholding concerns those who have 'a stake, a claim, or an interest in the operations and decisions of the firm'. These persons or groups would, according to Robertson and Nicholson (1996, 1102), include, in addition to shareholders, employees, consumers, the community, and the environment. On the basis of Wolfe's observation above, however, these definitions are too broad to serve any useful purpose. Assistance is provided, however, by Clarkson (1995) who, in offering a more detailed exposition of the stakeholder approach, considers it necessary to establish a hierarchy among these groups at the top of which are 'primary stakeholders', 'a *primary* stakeholder group is one without whose continuing participation the corporation cannot survive as a going concern' (Clarkson 1995, 106). Groups within this category would include employees, customers, governments and communities.

Those individuals and groups who are capable of affecting the corporation or are affected by it but who 'are not essential for its survival' (Clarkson 1995, 107) are classified by Clarkson as 'secondary stakeholders'. This category of stakeholder would include groups such as the media and special interest groups who, although not essential to the success of the company, 'can cause significant damage to a corporation' (Clarkson 1995, 107).

The importance of the distinction between primary and secondary stakeholders is that primary stakeholders will receive priority treat-ment at the hands of the corporation. Clarkson's objective, however, in noting the existence of these two groups, is not to sideline secondary stakeholders, but to make the case for the inclusion of a broader range of interests within corporate decision-making by demonstrating that shareholders are not the only group essential to the survival of the company. For his purposes, therefore, the claims of shareholders will not automatically trump the competing claims of other primary stakeholders and profit maximisation may have to be sacrificed so as to further the claims of groups such as employees and customers.

Despite the stakeholder approach proving particularly amenable during the 1990s to New Labour and the Third Way (Ireland 1996; Giddens 1998), the popularity of the concept within academic litera-ture has waned in recent decades. The reason for this may be due to its failure to counter the prevailing preference within the law for share-holder exclusivity but it may also be argued that it has been superseded by a concern to promote a wider conception of societal interests. Rather than demanding that corporate managers consider the interests of those individuals or groups who can show evidence of a 'stake' in the company, some commentators have sought to justify the consideration of a more inclusive interest, known commonly as the 'public interest'. As will become apparent, however, reliance upon a concept as equally nebulous as CSR has failed to enlighten the debate to any significant extent.

The 'Public Interest'

The justification for the view that corporations should ultimately serve the public interest derives from what has been termed the company's 'licence to operate' (Gamble and Kelly 2000, 21). As legal creations, companies exist only for the reason that society, through its legal system, considers their continued survival to serve some worthwhile purpose. As Dahl (1972, 17–18) puts it, 'Corporations exist because we allow them to do so. Why should we allow them to exist? Surely only insofar as they benefit us in some sense.'

As Gamble and Kelly (2000, 27) note, this view of the corporate form necessarily raises questions regarding the interests to be served by their formation and continued existence, 'In every national jurisdiction the granting of a "licence to operate" to companies inevitably raises questions as to what they should give in return.' In seeking to answer these questions, Parkinson (1996, 22) argues persuasively that the potential for corporations to exercise 'social decision-making power', that is, private power which has public consequences, raises questions regarding the legitimacy of that power. His view is that 'the possession of social decision-making power by companies is legitimate... only if this state of affairs is in the "public interest"' (Parkinson 1996, 23). While conceding that consensus does not exist regarding what constitutes the 'public interest', he is willing to offer at least a general definition of the concept,

> the term is meant to refer to some defensible balancing of the interests of affected groups, be they for example employees, customers, suppliers, the local community, or the community at large on the one hand, with on the other those of the shareholders and creditors that are the more traditional concern of company law. (Parkinson 1996, 22)

Parkinson's view of the public interest is open to the criticism that it concerns the interests of particular individuals or groups as opposed to any overarching conception of the 'public interest'. It is, in effect, more akin to stakeholding but, Parkinson (1996, 22) is not concerned primarily with offering a definition of the public interest but rather with the 'appropriate mechanisms for securing it'. His objective is to demonstrate that while profit maximisation might be consistent with the public interest, 'the point is that making profits for shareholders must now be seen as a mechanism for promoting the "public interest", and not as an end in itself' (Parkinson 1996, 24).

While Parkinson relies admittedly on a somewhat vague conception of the public interest, Gamble and Kelly (2000), in examining how the company has been conceived in terms of it, offer a more detailed exposition. According to their view it 'can arise through a sustained negotiation and interaction between all groups in the society to establish the principles and institutions through which the society should be governed' (Gamble and Kelly 2000, 25). In defining it as a political concept and process, they are able to reject the view that the public interest is constituted simply by the dominant interest of those in power, what may be termed the 'majoritarian view' (Feintuck 2004; Held 1970), or the aggregate of all private interests within society. Rather, they contend that it will only arise through public discourse about 'the constitutional principles on which social order is based' (Gamble and Kelly 2000, 26).

By viewing the public interest as a continual process of deliberation, Gamble and Kelly concede that one all-encompassing definition of the concept is unobtainable and that different conceptions will arise (Gamble and Kelly 2000, 25). By defining the public interest in this way, however, Gamble and Kelly offer an insight into how the concept is determined but not the principles that should guide it. Despite noting that 'the key debate is...not over whether there is a "public interest" or not, but over what kind of first principles should be employed in defining the "public interest"' (Gamble and Kelly 2000, 26), they choose not to engage in that discussion, preferring instead to offer a historical account of how the public interest has influenced the conception of the firm. While this may serve as a worthwhile task, it offers little in the way of assistance to those seeking a definition of the 'public interest' for present or future purposes.

Ambiguity and Discord

A review of aspects of the CSR literature highlights a number of recurrent themes, the most obvious of which is that consensus regarding the meaning of CSR or the norms that should comprise its substantive content remains elusive (Whitehouse 2003a, b). The reason for this inability to reach agreement may be due to a number of factors, not least of which is that a poorly defined concept offers greater malleability to those who wish to use it in support of particular views, as Stone (1975, 72) suggests, 'bad enough that the notion is fuzzy. Even worse, it is transparently this very fuzziness that accounts for its broad consensus of support.'

While a reluctance to reach consensus on the part of some commentators might explain the ambiguity that surrounds CSR, it is perhaps more likely to derive from its status as a political concept. CSR raises questions about the values that we as a society consider to be worthy of protection and to what end. It is evident from a review of the relevant literature that focus has been given to a set of specific values such as the economic success of corporate activity, the protection of private property interests and the prevention of harm to those both inside and outside the company often with the ultimate purpose of furthering the 'public interest'.

The failure to establish with sufficient clarity and by reference to fundamental and legitimate criteria the meaning of the 'public interest' or to justify particular values as worthy of protection has resulted in the CSR debate failing to extend beyond the constant and often repetitive expression of claim and counterclaim. Henderson's (2001, 26) view of CSR as 'a radical doctrine, both in what it says and in the consequences that it is liable to bring about', is reminiscent of Friedman's view of CSR as a 'fundamentally subversive doctrine' (Friedman 1969, 133). That these two views were expressed in 2001 and 1969 respectively, indicates the lack of progress made within the debate.

What is necessary, therefore, in order to move the debate forwards is to establish the fundamental purpose of CSR and to justify the values that it seeks to protect by reference to legitimate criteria. In an attempt to extend the debate beyond its current confines and to invest the concept with both purpose and meaning, therefore, the following section will attempt to establish and justify, by reference to democratic values, CSR's credentials as an effective and legitimate tool in the regulation of corporate activity.

The Democratic Credentials of CSR

In an attempt to draw upon fundamental democratic principles in defence of a compliance model of CSR it is first necessary to establish what is meant by 'democracy' (Arblaster 2002; Goodwin 1997; Leys 2003). This could, of course, form the basis of several papers but taking the particular model of democracy adopted by the majority of western states, namely the liberal-democratic model, we can summarise its inherent aspects as:

1. Supremacy of the people;
2. Equal civil rights for all individuals;
3. The consent of the governed as the basis of legitimacy;
4. The rule of law: peaceful methods of conflict resolution;
5. The existence of a common good or public interest (see Goodwin 1997);
6. Personal freedom and individualism; and
7. Capital and markets.

The dominance of neo-liberal policies within the UK and the US since the early 1980s has ensured that the latter two elements of the liberal-democratic model have received particular support and this, in turn, has had significant implications for the status of large corporations. While the policies of the Reagan/Thatcher era have become a familiar target for those seeking to criticise the move to market liberalism and the pursuit of economic rationality, it is difficult to deny that those policies have had far reaching effects. The dual policies of privatisation and deregulation created, in particular, a new and significant role for private companies. State-owned companies, managed so as to serve a public service ethos, were replaced by private companies guided by a private profit motive, a transformation particularly apparent within the utility services.

Morgan (2003), in offering an account of the pursuit of economic rationality within the bureaucratic machine of the Australian government, highlights the impact that such policies have on citizens and in particular vulnerable citizens as end-users of essential services. In relation to the utilities sector, for example, Community Service Obligations are no longer perceived as a means of reducing social cost but as an economic cost, 'Social equity is explicitly characterised as a burden on commercial efficacy and funded on that basis' (Morgan 2003, 159).

The readjustment in the balance of power between the state and companies redefined the role of the state so that it was no longer the provider of social entitlements but rather the facilitator of open markets. In order for this transition to take place, it was also necessary to redefine the relationship between the state and the citizen. In seeking to emphasise the individual citizen's responsibility to secure their own needs, the Conservative governments, between 1979 and 1997, sought to make the private sector responsible for the provision of 'public goods' including housing and health care. In noting the impact of policies directed at the housing market and, in particular, the erosion of the public rented sector, Whitehouse (1998a, 187–188) suggests that,

> In relation to the concept of citizenship, the residualisation of the public rented sector has engendered the view that it is not the responsibility of the state to play a significant role in the provision of the social entitlement to decent housing. Instead, it is the responsibility of individual households to obtain that entitlement for themselves.

The impact of these and similar policies has resulted in the demotion of the individual from the status of citizen to consumer (Whitehouse 1998b). While this shift in status may seem uncontroversial, particularly as the term 'consumer' is often combined with concepts such as 'rights' and 'protection', it is apparent that a consumer's ability to exercise choice and power within the market depends heavily upon their financial means, access to information and power of other players within the market including companies. While the rhetoric of consumerism promises to eradicate any inequalities through regulation (Lewis 1996, 12) it is clear that market failure persists and individual citizens remain vulnerable to the demands of large companies.

The transference of many of the responsibilities once taken on by government to private companies has necessarily afforded the latter with increased influence over the welfare of individuals and communities, as Arblaster (2002, 100) notes, 'privatization of so many functions and properties which were previously in the public sector, and for which, therefore, government was ultimately responsible, represents a substantial shift of power away from government into the private sector'. A corresponding increase in measures designed to ensure that such power was undertaken in the public interest, however, has not been forthcoming, rather 'the role of nation states has become to a large extent simply that of providing the public goods and infrastructure that business needs at the lowest costs and protecting the world free trade system' (Hertz 2002, 9–10).

The transference of considerable public power to private corporations may be argued to be unproblematic. It seems that by their very size and status, companies cannot avoid taking decisions that affect the interests of individuals and communities on a grand scale. The difficulty, however, lies in the fact that these decisions are taken in private and in the interests of shareholders, as Hirst (1998, 364) notes, 'Some difficult or detrimental decisions may be economically inescapable; but even these are made by a few senior managers rather than a wider range of affected interests, and thus they lack legitimacy.'

The ability of unelected company managers to exercise significant public power in an unaccountable manner poses also a substantial threat to democracy, as Arblaster (2002, 103) suggests, 'the growth of non-accountable corporate power over public life creates a lack of popular confidence in democracy itself which can only be rectified by bringing more and more of that power into the public and accountable sector'. To this extent, therefore, corporate power has exceeded the boundaries of the democratic settlement and can no longer be justified, as Hirst (1998, 364) notes, 'power without democratic accountability is illegitimate. It is as simple as that.'

It would appear, therefore, that the 'profit maximisation within the law' regime coupled with the priority afforded to the economic values of the liberal-democratic model have created a situation antithetical to democratic expectations. As Stokes (1986, 156) explains, 'Liberalism is hostile to the existence of centres of unbridled power, believing that power unless limited and controlled may threaten the liberty and the equality of the individual which are the two fundamental tenets of liberalism itself.' It is imperative, therefore, if democracy is to prevail, that the exercise of public power by companies is 'limited and controlled'. The means by which to achieve this may include the use of voluntary initiatives but as current practice has shown, such

initiatives by themselves are simply inadequate to protect fundamental democratic rights and responsibilities. As Hertz (2002, 242)
suggests, 'the market cannot be counted upon to ensure that corporations will always act in our best interest, so we must be able to
continue to count on government's ability to play the role of regulator
of last resort'.

While the UK company law regime offers a degree of regulation in
relation to the protection of particular issues, it is apparent that the
preference for ad hoc regulation coupled with voluntary initiatives has
failed to keep pace with the increasing power afforded to large
companies and the drive for economic rationality (Whitehouse 2003a, b).
The result has been significant with individuals and communities
incurring a variety of social costs, corporate managers able to influence
the political process and nation-states reluctant to regulate these
'behemoths' (Hertz 2002, 8).

It seems clear, therefore, that a new approach to regulating
corporate power is required. Parkinson (1996, 2) contends that there
are three choices: retain profit maximisation as the goal with external
constraints designed to protect the public interest; reconfigure the
objectives of companies away from profit maximisation and towards
the consideration of all interests; and view all corporate power as
illegitimate and therefore in need of dispersal or transference to a
legitimate authority. This chapter favours the first of these options.
The reason for this is that economic success undoubtedly constitutes
one means of furthering the public interest. It is, however, only one
aspect and will, on occasion, be outweighed by other more pressing
concerns, 'while the efficient creation of wealth may be regarded as
a high social priority, we also recognize individual and collective
interests and values that ought not to be sacrificed in its pursuit'
(Parkinson 1996, 41).

It is possible to argue, therefore, that the primary concern of CSR,
should not be how corporations can be encouraged to undertake
philanthropic activities or behave ethically but how their ability to
exercise public power can be legitimated so as to ensure that all
values associated with a liberal democracy are protected. By
accepting that its role is concerned with countering the current preference for economic values and reinstating social democratic values
within corporate regulation, it should prove possible to move the
CSR debate forwards so as to discuss the form that such regulation
should take.

Conclusion

The debate concerning CSR has for too long focused on the question of profit maximisation and the private property interests of shareholders. While these aspects are important, academics and politicians alike appear to have lost sight of or have refused to acknowledge the fundamental threat to democracy posed by corporate power. In consequence, the whirlwind of debate over the last 75 years has consumed substantial energy while ultimately going around in circles.

In an effort to reignite the debate, this chapter has put forward the contention that CSR should seek to legitimate the exercise of public power by corporations through the mechanism of compulsory regulation justified by reference to fundamental democratic principles. The underlying principle is that private property rights and wealth creation are allocated and protected to serve ultimately wider interests so that where profit maximisation conflicts with wider democratic goals, such as the pursuit of the public interest, regulation is justified to protect those democratic values. As Hertz (2002, 66) argues,

> By making economic success an end rather than a means to other ends, governments and people have lost sight of the fact that economic growth was supposed to have a higher purpose – stability, increased standards of living, increased social cohesion for *all*, without exclusion.

CSR should, therefore, serve to counter the current preference for economic rationality and market liberalism by reintroducing the social values associated with a liberal democracy; only then will corporate power be legitimate.

9

The Criminological Lens: Understanding Criminal Law and Corporate Governance

Laureen Snider

Introduction

This chapter examines corporate misconduct through the lens of criminal law. It explores the potential of criminal law to bring corporations to justice and improve compliance, institute deterrence, and promote equality in law enforcement. This is done by examining, first, the history of stock market regulation in Canada; second, new initiatives in criminal and non-criminal law; third, reasons to believe such measures can be effective; and fourth, factors that continue to frustrate and weaken the establishment of legal control over business.

On 12 February 2004, the federal government in Canada passed Bill C-13, amending the Criminal Code to increase penalties for insider trading, augment the investigative resources of the Crown, and strengthen whistleblower protection. In December 2003, a high-level report told the federal government to end 100 years of decentralised provincially based stock market regulation and create a new national regulatory body and a single regulatory code (Phelps *et al.* 2003). Both initiatives were responses to high profile corporate scandals, particularly WorldCom and Enron in the United States, which followed the collapse of the technology stock market bubble. They exemplify what media and officialdom trumpet as the state's crackdown on corporate crime. Two decades of government-sponsored deregulation and downsizing, of denying the ubiquity and severity of corporate crime and forgetting the lessons of the past, have now ended.

Laissez-faire see-no-evil, speak-no-evil attitudes to business, and the deregulatory policies they inspired, are no more. Governments today are expanding corporate criminal liability, extending it to CEOs and boards of directors (Archibald *et al.* 2004). However, charges of 'overregulation' have already begun in the United States: chambers of commerce say governments have launched 'witch hunts that imperil the American dream'; conservative politicians predict that 'draconian' new regulations will destroy the New York Stock Exchange (Leonhardt, *New York Times*, 10 February 2002, 3–1; Cernetig, *Globe & Mail*, 1 June 2002, F8).[1]

The history of business regulation should make us cautious of government promises to crack down on corporate crime. More than 200 years of struggle, with many more defeats than victories, were necessary to force capitalist states to, first, recognise that corporations must be held responsible for corporate acts that cause injury, death, and financial destruction; second, to pass laws with teeth; and third, to actually resource and enforce these laws (Carson 1970, 1980; Snider 1993). State reluctance to hold capital to account in the past has produced a series of regulatory cycles, each beginning with a high-profile event – a major bridge collapse or ferry accident, a series of frauds, massive corporate bankruptcies. The event is typically followed by volumes of lofty rhetoric from various politicians and officials, and eventually by draft legislation. After a series of revisions, new laws are passed. They are usually much weaker than originally promised, and in some cases totally unenforceable (as was the case with Canada's first anti-combine laws) (Stanbury 1977, 1986–87; Snider 1978). If the laws are usable, and the issue is still politically salient, a flurry of well-publicised charges will be announced, followed by plea bargains, convictions, fines and appeals. Once the media spotlight has moved off, the regulatory body reverts to status quo ante and normal regulatory patterns, characterised as 'benign neglect' or 'capture', reappear. In the 1980s a new wrinkle in this pattern appeared, first in the United States and Britain, now globally. Under the sway of neo-liberal doctrines, the economic and political power of business increased dramatically. Instead of reverting to status quo ante, governments began aggressive campaigns to turn back the clock and dismantle regulation (a process advocates called regulatory reform). In the UK, this took the form of wholesale privatisation of publicly owned enterprises.[2] In the

United States and eventually Canada, public relations campaigns were launched depicting regulators as inefficient, empire-building bureaucrats, regulatory agency budgets were slashed, and self-regulation replaced regulation through government and criminal law (Fooks 2003; Tombs 1996; Doern and Wilks 1996, 1998).

This chapter, then, asks the following questions: Does a compliance-based culture deal with the root cause(s) of corporate misconduct? Can criminological research on crime provide a more granular understanding of corporate governance? If governments 'really mean it' at this particular historical juncture, can such fine words be translated into new surveillance and enforcement practices that will outlast the present media frenzy?

Before tackling these, it is necessary to define the terms which will be employed. Stock market fraud is a type of financial crime, which is itself a category of corporate crime. Corporate crime refers to 'illegal acts committed by legitimate formal organizations aimed at furthering the interests of the organization and the individuals involved' (Snider 1993, 14; Pearce and Tombs 1998; Coleman 1989; Braithwaite 1989; Shapiro 1984, 1990). There are two kinds of corporate crime: financial and social. Insider trading, restraint of trade, stock market fraud and fraudulent business practices are all financial crimes. They victimise investors, consumers, business competitors, and government (the latter as investor and, in many cases, as loan guarantor of last resort). Social crimes, both environmental (air and water pollution) and health and safety crimes (unsafe workplaces, dangerous working conditions), victimise different, less powerful, groups – workers, employees and citizens as a whole. This basic fact of political economy means that enforcement benefits very different interests in financial versus social crime.[3]

Social regulation adds costs and threatens bottom-line profit levels. Financial regulation creates a level playing field for business, which needs order and predictability to prosper and grow. A state which monitors and sanctions those who loot company coffers, sell fraudulent stocks and trade on inside knowledge is performing a vital function for capitalism, acting in the long-term best interests of investors and corporations as a whole. Where cowboy capitalism runs wild, where regulatory and legal systems are known to be ineffective or absent, investor resistance may develop. With advanced communications, loss of confidence can quickly escalate from local to global levels, possibly producing runs on the national currency, and economic collapse.[4] Thus there are good, structurally based reasons for nation-states to develop effective systems to control financial crime.

History of Securities Regulation in Canada

The establishment of regulatory agencies to oversee stock exchanges in Canada originated in two 'nation-building' priorities: first, the need to raise capital to promote the development of natural resources, particularly the mining industry; second, the need to control the industry's lamentable susceptibility to fraud. Mining has long been identified as central to the Canadian economy – resource development still accounts for more than 10% of Canada's GDP (*Report on Business Magazine*, TSX Advertising Supplement, June 2004, from Statistics Canada data). After the fur trade disappeared, and the easily exploitable timber resources were cut (in eastern Canada before 1900), attention turned to wealth in the ground. Raising capital to allow private entrepreneurs to develop natural resources was an important duty of the Canadian capitalist class. It was also a major objective of the Canadian state. Stock exchanges were established in regional centres such as Toronto, Montreal and Vancouver to give new mining companies a place to raise seed capital (as it was then called) to finance exploration and development.

Given the nature of the terrain (wilderness), and of exploration (a low-tech, individualistic, labour-intensive process), finding, extracting and processing wealth in the ground was a high risk venture. Prospectors competed to survey and claim every likely-looking chunk of muskeg and moose pasture. Rudimentary geology, rudimentary technologies and basic (often non-existent) systems of communication meant that, for much of the twentieth century, anyone with an elementary knowledge of science could 'salt' a likely section of land (that is, plant valuable minerals on or in it), raise a fortune by selling dreams of riches to gullible investors, and disappear. In the first half of the twentieth century, this happened frequently enough that key corporate and political actors became fearful. If too many scams became known, investment capital would disappear, and where would Canada be then? Worse, what would happen to their careers as stock promoters and bankers? At this juncture, provincial and territorial governments were forced to create regulatory bodies, designing each one to meet the capital-raising needs of resource industries in its particular region.

The history of regulation in Ontario, the economic engine of Canada and home of the largest and most influential stock exchange, illustrates the essential features. The granddaddy of Canada's regulatory agencies is the Ontario Securities Commission, established in 1945. This followed a recommendation of the 1944 Royal Commission on Mining aimed at repairing the Securities Act then in existence, which could only act once fraud was discovered. The OSC, in contrast, would be empowered to prevent as well as sanction fraud. Only companies meeting standards high enough to ensure 'the integrity of the applicant' would be allowed to sell stocks in Ontario (Condon 1998, 19), and applicants would have to file a prospectus disclosing 'all material facts'. The new rules would be backed with 'more rigorous prosecution' and possible cancellation of registration (Condon 1998, 20).

However, because promoting the mining industry was the primary purpose of regulation, sanctions were not the regulatory strategy of choice. Instead, facilitating the industry, seen as central to Canada's growth and prosperity, became the primary regulatory goal; catching crooks and promoting ethical behaviour were distinctly secondary. OSC listings shed light on the significance and centrality of resource industries at this time: in 1951, 227 of 327 shares listed on the Toronto Stock Exchange were mining and oil stocks; in 1961 this fell slightly, with 101 mining and oil stocks, 81 industrials and 19 unclassi-fied others (Condon 1998, 29). Indeed, the Toronto Stock Exchange was the largest dealer in mining stocks in the world throughout the 1950s and 1960s.

The bulk of day-to-day regulation, however, was then and is today delegated to the industry itself, through the self-regulatory organisation or SRO. The most important SRO was the Toronto Stock Exchange (TSE, now TSX). To government actors at the time, who were closely connected to key financial actors, it was 'obvious' that members of the TSE were best positioned to regulate and discipline their peers. The early OSC decision to allow mining companies registered on the TSE exemption from OSC disclosure requirements indicates both the centrality of the TSE and state reluctance to impede the mining industry's pursuit of capital. That self-regulation necessarily involved serious conflicts of interest between the TSE as promoter versus policing agent was a reality the regulators ignored.

A second self-regulatory organisation, the Broker-Dealers Associ-ation (now the Investment Dealers Association), was established in

1947. According to the OSC chair at the time, it was established at the behest of the OSC, which wanted a private sector limit on OSC powers and territorial ambitions (Condon 1998, 24–25). For the regulators themselves to be so apologetic about their role once again illustrates government reluctance to get in the way of business. Like the TSE, the BDA was charged with both promoting the industry and regulating it, with particular emphasis on those not covered by other professional or ethical codes. To strengthen the BDA, the OSC refused to register non-BDA members.[5]

In the 1960s, two highly visible public scandals, three Royal Commissions and a provincial inquiry compelled the government of Ontario to reassess this system. The first crisis was the 1964 collapse of the Windfall mining company whose CEO, Viola MacMillan, was accused of defrauding the public, hiding relevant material facts, and selling worthless shares under false pretences.[6] The second was the 1965 bankruptcy of the Atlantic Acceptance Finance Company, triggered by the illegal and unethical financial practices of its senior executives. Law reform struggles focused on the nature, meaning and extent of mandatory disclosure. The OSC wanted measures ensuring greater investor protection, depicting the investor as 'prudent' and 'risk-averse'. The TSE and business overall saw investors as responsible, knowledgeable subjects who should be free to choose high-risk stocks. Although the TSE had been weakened by a Royal Commission Report which had denounced it as 'a private gaming club', its position triumphed nonetheless. Business, it said, did not oppose the principle of mandatory disclosure, it only opposed the specific investment-discouraging measures sought by the OSC (Condon 1998). This change of tactics and language was successful, the Securities Act of 1966 did not adopt the OSC-sponsored changes.

When the United States abandoned restrictions on broker commission rates in 1975, the OSC came under heavy pressure to copy the US. Once again the debate pitted economic against legal values, with the TSE and allies arguing that rates should be set only by markets, the only trustworthy path to free, open competition. The OSC argued that government had an obligation to keep rates 'fair' and 'reasonable'. Rates remained fixed in the 1978 Act. However, the OSC reversed itself a scant decade later when it ruled that fixed rates were now prohibited under Canada's competition laws (revised in 1986).[7] Other 1970s debates involved corporate takeovers and mergers: at what stage should investors be informed that a takeover bid or merger was under negotiation, how much should they be told? The OSC argued for maximum comprehensive disclosure; once again it lost. As Condon put it: 'The attempt to require more detailed and contextual information to investors at the time of distribution of new securities largely failed' (Condon 1998, 220). However, legal change is never a zero-sum affair: through struggle and negotiation, the positions of both 'sides' were refined and sometimes rethought. The revised Securities Act of 1978 reflected this (Condon 1998, 242).

Developments since 1980

The pace of change accelerated in the 1980s and 1990s. A neo-liberal, anti-regulation revolution was launched by the election of Ronald Reagan in the US (November 1979) and Margaret Thatcher in Britain. The discourse of private enterprise, the entrepreneur and capital in all its guises were in the ascendance. Regulation and government were transformed from 'necessary evils' to 'superfluous impediments'. Chicago School economics, specifically their claims that markets must be 'freed' from government to operate efficiently, became both rhetoric and policy (Friedman 1962; Posner 1976, 1977). Two decades of privatisation, deregulation and decriminalisation began. In the United States and Britain, regulatory agencies in a range of arenas were vitiated – a favourite device was the appointment of the agency's harshest critic as its new head (as with the Occupational Safety and Health Act – OSHA – in the United States) (Calavita 1983). Regulatory agencies with business support survived; regulation opposed by business, however beneficial for families, labour or the environment, did not.

Although Canada was a late convert to neo-liberalism in many sectors (Clarkson 2002; Snider 2004), business was the exception. In 1986 the Conservative government of Brian Mulroney redefined laws on price fixing, false advertising, mergers and monopolies, replacing the draconian but ineffective Combines Investigation Act (omnibus legislation covering conspiracy, bid-rigging, predatory and discriminatory pricing, misleading advertising and marketing practices such as pyramid sales), with the 'flexible', business-oriented Competition Act (Stanbury 1986–87; Snider 1993). On 30 June 1987, the traditional 'four pillars' of economic regulation – banking, insurance, trust operations and securities – were dismantled.

The 'four pillars' were laws meant to prevent any single financial institution from becoming dominant over all types of financial transactions. Banks were not allowed to sell stocks or own brokerage houses, insurance companies could not lend money or own banks. When these restrictions were repealed, new financial services accelerated inter- and intrasector competition. In the 1990s share-selling competition went global. One result was that the number of shareowners in Canada increased, while the distribution of wealth became (even) less egalitarian (Fudge and Cossman 2002; Barlow and Clark 2002; Sharpe 1998). In 1990, 23% of all Canadian adults owned publicly listed securities, by 2003 46% did, and stockholdings accounted for 20% of total household assets per family (Phelps *et al.* 2003, 6; *Report on Business Magazine*, June 2004). Although this increased public involvement was almost entirely indirect – most of the money was in pension and mutual funds controlled by professional fund managers – public interest in the integrity of markets increased.[8]

In the last decade, new communications technologies and the allied globalisation of capital have revolutionised every aspect of financial markets. With capital virtually unrestrained by national governments following widespread deregulation, money crosses borders at lightning speed. Businesses once dependent on local banks and exchanges now list on exchanges throughout the world. Multinational security firms do business on a 24/7 basis. With nations forming increasingly large trading blocks, market volumes have increased: 'between 1980 and 2000, private capital flows...increased more than six-fold to nearly US$4 trillion annually worldwide' (Phelps *et al.* 2003, 2). Stock exchanges have become both more specialised and more international. Canada now has only four national exchanges: the Toronto Stock Exchange handles senior equities, TSX Venture handles junior equities,[9] the Bourse de Montréal is the national derivatives exchange, and the Winnipeg Commodity Exchange specialises in commodity futures and option exchange (Phelps *et al.* 2003, 4).

Capital markets have also become increasingly important as suppliers of growth capital: in 2002 88% of long-term financing for Canadian firms came from markets, up from 73% in 1990 (Phelps *et al.* 2003, 4). With the rise of the speculative economy and futures markets, investment requires no commitment to a particular nation-state, sector or business, no in-depth knowledge of the 'true' value of the company. Buying and selling, getting in and out quickly, to achieve maximum short-term profit, is all that counts. And while there are more avenues of investment, waves of takeovers and mergers throughout the 1980s and 1990s have produced greater corporate concentration. In Canada today, 777 companies, worth over $75 m, account for 98% of all market capitalisation; the largest 60 companies alone make up 51.6% of the total (Phelps *et al.* 2003, 5).

The plethora of new financial players and sharply increased competition has weakened crucially important networks of informal social control. In a city such as Toronto, key players 30 years ago were similar in class origins, ethnicity, religion and gender (Porter 1965; Clement 1975). The elites who ran the Toronto Stock Exchange typically had private school and summer camp ties from childhood, and organisational ties as adults. Female elite members were wives, not colleagues or competitors. Government regulators and politicians often came from similar backgrounds. Now this white Anglo-Saxon gentleman's club, while still there, has been weakened. The ethics, values and codes of behaviour these men promoted and enforced no longer rule the roost. Whatever the flaws of this old-boy network (sexism, racism, ethnocentrism, class prejudice and more), the rules of the game at that time were known to all the key players, and broadly respected – if only because the personal and professional consequences of deviation were so high.

Finally, three developments with important counterhegemonic potential must be noted. First is the establishment and growing strength of new oppositional stockholder rights groups. With the bursting of the technology-inspired market bubble of the 1990s, such groups have become increasingly aggressive, sometimes resisting takeovers, disputing key personnel decisions or questioning executive compensation packages. Many have begun to lobby politically, demanding more disclosure, more information on profit levels and debt loads, and even (sometimes) questioning environmental practices and labour conditions (Yaron 2002). Second, with 24 hour business news and the heightened buzz of investment chatter, a new style of investigative financial journalist has emerged. Canada's major national newspaper, the *Globe & Mail*, now publishes a regular corporate social responsibility 'report card' and features stories on insider trading or executive compensation. Third, new technologies offer unprecedented opportunities to tighten regulation. Trades can be tracked as they happen, electronic 'markers' differentiating insider trades can be purchased. Surveillance equipment is easy to acquire and install. And email has changed the nature of evidence-gathering, making it impossible to render messages permanently irretrievable to those with sufficient time, resources and computer savvy to retrieve them. These technological innovations give regulators the potential to notice and act on 'abnormal' trading patterns the minute they occur. They make evidence-gathering easier by facilitating access to high-level debates and decisions. Whether this potential will be realised, however, depends more on the relative power of the parties than the characteristics of the technologies.

Like most modern states Canada today has a sophisticated and complex regulatory system utilising Self-regulatory Organisations (SROs) and government agencies. Thirteen securities commissions, one in each province and territory,[10] oversee capital markets and assess sanctions. Securities commissions were established to facilitate resource extraction and capital raising in the (mining) industry. They have always been viewed, by government and business, as a necessary evil – sometimes more 'evil' than 'necessary', sometimes the reverse. In 2004, however, oppositional groups and media are celebrating regulation, hailing tough enforcement, passing new laws and resuscitating others.[11] The next section examines new legal initiatives designed to accomplish these ends.

The New Crackdown

On 12 February 2004, the federal government introduced a series of amendments to the Criminal Code of Canada. The Bill makes 'improper insider trading' a criminal offence, and increases maximum penalties from 10 to 14 years. Maximum penalties for 'market manipulation' were doubled from 5 to 10 years. 'Tipping', defined as 'knowingly conveying inside information to another person[12] with knowledge that it might be used to secure a trading advantage or illegal benefit', becomes an offence which can be prosecuted as indictable or summary. If indictable, a maximum prison term of five years can be imposed; if summary, fines are assessed (Mackay and Smith 2004, 5). In introducing the Bill, the Minister of Justice carefully emphasised that 'stiff criminal penalties' will only be applied to 'the most egregious cases' (Mackay and Smith 2004, 4). However, to encourage greater judicial severity, courts will be given a list of 'aggravating factors'. Bill C-13 also provides whistleblower protection to employees who report illegal activities, and empowers courts to obtain production orders to force third parties and organisations such as banks, whether under investigation or not, to provide all necessary documents.[13] Non-compliance with a production order can be met with fines up to $250000 and six months in jail.[14]

Bill C-13 is the Canadian government's most recent and visible response to Enron, WorldCom, and associated corporate scandals in the United States, and its response to charges that Canada was formerly 'too lenient'. Lenience is deemed problematic because it impairs investor confidence – not because it imperils justice, threatens the rule of law or denies victims the compensation they deserve. Imposing new criminal offences on powerful financial elites is not something the federal government does often, speedily, or easily. Attributing criminal liability to management for unsafe working conditions, for example, has been debated for 50 years (Glasbeek 2002; Bittle 2004). Constitutional issues compound the difficulties because, while the federal government has responsibility over criminal law, the provinces control stock exchanges and the securities industry. Insider trading was previously handled by provincial securities commissions as administrative proceedings or by provincial courts on a quasi-criminal basis. Bill C-13 strengthens federal authority, giving the Attorney General of Canada concurrent jurisdiction with provincial Attorneys General in all cases that 'threaten the national interest in the integrity of capital markets' (Mackay and Smith 2004, 2).

While federal–provincial jurisdictional struggles are longstanding, Bill C-13 was initiated as Canada's response to US legislation, specifically the Sarbanes-Oxley Act of 2002. Since the North American Free Trade Agreement (NAFTA) passed in 1988, the Canadian economy has become ever more tightly bound to the United States. Canada is America's largest trading partner, Canadian firms make up the largest group of non-American companies who sell shares in the US (Schrecker 2001; Snider 2004). The New York Stock Exchange is particularly important; when the American government acts, Canada must follow. Indeed Bill C-13 was legitimated in exactly those terms in House of Commons debates (Department of Finance Canada 2003).

The blueprint for a Canadian response was apparently worked out in March 2002, at a private dinner meeting attended by a 'select group of government officials, senior regulators and industry officials', including David Brown, Head of the Ontario Securities Commission, David Dodge, Governor of the Bank of Canada, and the deputy Minister of Finance. The implications of Enron for Canadian markets, strategies to restore investor confidence, and possible policy initiatives were discussed (Howlett, *Globe & Mail*, 28 June 2003, B1; Howlett and McFarland, 30 March 2004, B10). Some of these have since been adopted by provincial regulatory commissions, albeit in piecemeal fashion.

Umbrella groups such as the Canadian Securities Administrators, which represent all 13 provincial regulators, have urged their members to adopt measures to promote 'Best Practices' in business. Measures endorsed include mandatory halts in trading before major corporate announcements, real-time 'markers' differentiating insider trades from others, measures to control 'bucket shops' offshore, and the establishment of international databases (News Release, Canadian Securities Administrators, 12 November 2003). Ontario has taken the lead (Phelps *et al.* 2003, 26). The OSC has decreed that CEOs and CFOs (chief financial officers) must personally certify the accuracy of information in financial statements. Audit committees must include directors who are independent of management, and audits must be overseen by the Canadian Public Accountancy Board (the CPAB, a new regulatory body created in July 2002). To obtain OSC approval to list on the Toronto Stock Exchange, publicly owned companies must have their financial statements done by a firm recognised by the CPAB. In September 2003, Ontario and Quebec adopted another measure, this one pioneered by Manitoba a year earlier, which allows Securities Commissions to order investor repayment 'where losses were incurred by illegal acts or improper advice' (Department of Finance Canada 2003).

At the SRO level, the chartered accounting profession has been particularly active, passing new standards and oversight measures and a tighter disciplinary process. The Canadian Public Accountancy Board (CPAB) was set up to regulate audit standards. (However, firms listed in Canada can bypass the CPAB by registering with the American body – the Board of Public Companies' Accounting Oversight Board – instead (Howlett, *Globe & Mail*, 27 January 2004a, B1, B5). Actors such as 'independent' security analysts (researchers who tell investors which stocks to buy, avoid or sell) have also come under scrutiny. New rules for security analysts were passed in June 2002, following an earlier report by the Toronto Stock Exchange, the Broker Dealers Association, and the Canadian Venture Exchange (*Setting Analyst Standards*, October 2001).

Finally, a group of major institutional investors, all financial heavy-hitters, formed the Canadian Coalition for Good Governance in

June 2002.[15] This august body recently issued a series of recommendations designed, in its words, 'to provide more power, oversight and
independence to boards of directors and audit committees'.[16]
Although the TSX adopted new corporate governance guidelines in
1995, it too is discussing new rules such as requiring 'continuous
disclosure' by publicly listed firms (*Globe & Mail*, 11 March 2004).
Changes are even suggested to executive compensation, long a taboo
subject, through proposals that would require listed companies to get
shareholder approval before adopting certain executive compensation
packages (*Report on Business Magazine*, July/August 2004, 84–86).
Soaring executive compensation levels combined with plummeting
stock values and profit levels make distinctly bad optics.

Enforcement

Enforcement is now widely lamented as a weak spot. The Wise Persons
Committee asserts: 'Canada suffers weak and inconsistent enforcement
and investor protection. Wrongdoers too frequently go unpunished,
and adjudication is unduly delayed' (Phelps 2003, 25). Moreover the
system is 'costly, duplicative and inefficient' (Phelps 2003, 25). Jail
sentences for senior executives are virtually unknown,[17] and global
fraudsters, we are told, have identified Canada as the 'jurisdiction of
choice' (S. Won, *Globe & Mail*, 28 May 2004, online). Canada, opined
Steven Sibold, Chair of the Canadian Securities Administrators (CSA),
has a greater run-up of inside trades prior to major announcements
than does the US (*Toronto Star*, 13 November 2003, C7).

In response, a heavy duty task force to investigate illegal insider
trading was established in September 2002. Representatives from
Ontario, Quebec, British Columbia and Alberta Securities Commissions, and from the major SROs – the Investment Dealers Association,
the Bourse de Montréal, and Market Regulation Services – issued
a report containing 32 recommendations. The report called for
more and better RCMP investigations, increased regulation of
'offshore accounts' from regions with inadequate regulatory regimes,
and new rules governing how 'senior managers, directors, lawyers
and accountants' deal with inside information (*Toronto Star*,
13 November 2003, C1; also Phelps 2003, 26). A team approach
utilising the talents of professionals and law enforcement personnel

from a variety of agencies and all three levels of government was recommended.

The federal government acted with unusual haste: a year later, $120 million of new funding was set aside to create six dedicated Integrated Market Enforcement Teams (IMET for short), in Toronto, Montreal, Vancouver and Calgary. Each will be staffed with experts in capital markets, economics and accounting, from federal and provincial police forces and from self-regulatory bodies. Two Toronto teams are now operating, with members from the RCMP, the OSC, the Investment Dealers Association (IDA), the Mutual Fund Dealers Association (MFDA) and Market Regulatory Services (MRS Inc.), a body in the TSE which oversees and reports suspicious trading patterns (*Toronto Star*, 14 March 2004; *Globe & Mail*, 23 May 2004).

On 14 June 2004, IMET made its first arrest, when Steve McRae of 'no fixed address'(!) was charged with theft over $5000 and laundering the proceeds of crime. Between July 1998 and March 2000, McRae is accused of removing 17 securities certificates from unclaimed accounts at HSBC Canada Inc., his employer at the time, and selling them for $370 000 (RCMP News Release, 14 June 2004). IMET is presently working on a second case, described as a 'cross-border market manipulation and insider trading scheme' (S. Won, Howlett and McFarland, *Globe & Mail*, 28 May 2004, online).[18]

Even before Bill C-13 was passed, Ontario increased penalties for illegal insider trading, with provisions stipulating jail terms up to five years and fines up to $5 million per count. Alternatively, companies could face fines up to triple the profits made or losses avoided. Before 2003 maximum jail terms were two years and $1 million in fines (*Toronto Star*, 12 March 2004, C1, C3). OSC head David Brown reports that, from 2000 to 2004, the number of inside trading cases prosecuted tripled, more than 100 actions were settled, the average length of judicial proceedings dropped from 21 to 13 months, and trial time declined from 15 to 11 months. When jail sentences were sought (he does not tell us how often this was), they were received 80% of the time. Brown attributed any remaining problems to complexities and confusion caused by 'lack of coordination' between three levels of police (federal, provincial and city), three levels of government, and 13 Regulatory Commissions (*Globe & Mail*, 30 March 2004, B3; Speech by David Brown, 27 May 2004). OSC's Director of Enforcement, Michael Watson, also admitted: 'A lot of people don't . . . think there is anything wrong with it.' Rewards are high, risks of being caught and convicted are low (*Toronto Star*, 14 March 2004, C3).

However, examples of regulatory inaction and 'lenience' abound. Bre-X Minerals imploded in the spring of 1997 when it was discovered that gold assays at their mine in Indonesia (once hailed as the world's largest gold deposit) were 'salted'. Stock prices plummeted from $200 a share to zero. Only now have charges been laid – a former executive faces eight counts of insider trading, accused of selling $84 million of Bre-X stock just before stock prices collapsed (*Toronto Star*, 14 March 2004, C3). Another high profile case is Livent, a Toronto entertainment company that went bankrupt in 1998. The OSC waited several years after SEC took action, finally charging Livent's chief executives with manipulating financial records to hide losses of $100 million in 2003 (CBC News Online, web posted 26 June, 2002, accessed 23 June 2004).

Poonam Puri (2001) found historically lax enforcement patterns unchanged in her analysis of the Competition Act, the Income Tax Act and other federal legislation. Mary Condon (2003) reports that securities regulators overwhelmingly prefer administrative action to penal sanctions. When compared to Criminal Code or other penal statutes, they take less time and allow agencies to control the entire process. But such actions attach no stigma of criminality, and minimum shaming through negative publicity. Moreover, examining records from all 13 jurisdictions across Canada, and allowing for significant interprovincial variations, only 83 administrative decisions were taken from 2000 to 2003 (Condon 2003, 419, footnote 4). The remaining 213 cases were 'resolved' with settlement agreements where no guilt is admitted and sanctions are moot. Settlements were the regulatory instruments of choice in Alberta, British Columbia and Ontario, the provinces with the highest activity levels (Condon 2003, 439, footnote 22).

Nor have the self-regulatory organisations been proactive or punitive.[19] The Investment Dealers Association, like most SROs, is both lobbyist for the brokerage industry and its internal regulator. Complaints about investment firms, most centred around 'unsuitable' investments and unauthorised trading, soared 41% in 2003. Some of this increase is real, some is an artefact of new reporting rules and tracking systems. In 2003 there were 1506 complaints, 629 civil claims, 11 criminal charges and 57 internal investigations. Out of this total, the IDA opened 729 files, handing out total fines of $265 189 to firms, and $3.2 million to individuals.[20]

The mammoth mutual fund industry doubled in size in the last decade, from $131.5 billion in 1994 to $474 billion today (K. Damsell, *Globe & Mail*, 22 June 2004, B8). A task force established in 2002 by the Canadian Securities Administrators reported significant conflicts of interest and lax enforcement of the weak rules and standards then in existence. It recommended that companies be forced to establish independent governance boards able to fire managers who put company interests before those of unit holders. This idea was first floated, and endorsed by regulators, in 1969!

However, the powerful mutual funds industry launched a successful countercampaign, arguing that investor protection must be tied to market efficiency, to avoid 'burdening the industry with unnecessary and costly structures' (E. Church, *Globe & Mail*, 22 June 2004, B9). The former senior regulator for the OSC, its representative on the task force which recommended the changes, took employment with the mutual fund industry and changed her tune. 'The CSA was asking for the impossible and the unnecessary', she says in her new capacity (E. Church, *Globe & Mail*, 22 June 2004, B9). A lobby group representing the 200 largest mutual fund firms said: 'The interests of investors and the industry are the same' (K. Damsell, *Globe & Mail*, 22 June 2004, B8). As a result review committees are only empowered to 'vet' those conflicts of interests 'referred to them' by fund managers. Lacking veto power and meaningful sanctions, they can only instruct fund managers to 'publicize the committee's displeasure' (E. Church, *Globe & Mail*, 22 June 2004, B9). Mandatory requirements, in other words, have been replaced by persuasion.[21]

Thus, in the middle of the self-advertised greatest crackdown ever on financial crime, evidence that the power of business to resist, shape and defeat regulatory initiatives is everywhere.

Reasons for Optimism

The above section illustrates that there has been, thus far, more rhetoric and posturing from government and SROs than tough, zero-tolerance action. Outside a few new laws, standards and maximum penalties, what reasons are there to believe that law, particularly criminal law, will be more effective in the twenty first century than in the nineteenth and twentieth?

Several of the developments mentioned earlier have the potential to change enforcement patterns and therefore improve deterrence. Oppositional stockholder rights groups, with increased aggressiveness and willingness to lobby politically for measures to protect investors, could provide much-needed support for beleaguered regulators. The absence of such pressure groups in the past, leaving no advocates for strict enforcement to go against powerful corporate lobbies, has left regulators swinging in the political winds. However, though such groups may secure better investor protection, investors are still a privileged minority group in most countries. Private suits do little to redress the losses suffered by employees who lose jobs and pensions, or citizens whose taxes must cover corporate losses. In addition, lawsuits deliver the biggest benefits to the largest, most powerful investor groups, the so-called 'secured creditors'. They offer little to the vast majority of unsecured creditors whose life savings, pensions and nest-eggs have been destroyed. And they deliver minimal shaming of guilty parties, no collective or public remedies.

Increased public involvement and interest in share ownership combined with high profile investigative financial journalism could also increase political pressure on government to enforce laws. Stories can point out the massive inequalities in sanctions given traditional versus corporate criminals. The multinational corporation steals millions and is fined the equivalent of its profits for half a day; the welfare cheat steals hundreds, is imprisoned for five years and cut off welfare forever. Such exposés have the potential to strengthen oppositional groups and pro-regulatory forces, and this may have long-term effects on regulatory patterns.

The most publicised innovation, the most fervently promoted panacea, is the technological fix. New technologies such as 'markers' distinguishing inside trades, new surveillance capabilities and always-retrievable email records do have potential to strengthen law enforcement. They increase accountability and visibility by making it harder for government and SROs to claim ignorance when suspicious trading patterns occur. In theory, new technologies increase transparency, and make convictions more likely (but only if offences are prosecuted). However, those who see technology as an automatic corrective, putting an end to lax enforcement and lenient sanctions, should examine patterns of power within and outside corporations. CEOs and boards of directors make decisions regarding what technologies will be introduced and how they will be used. They commission new designs and decide how and against whom these tools will be deployed. Thus far the primary targets of technological surveillance, the recipients of the most intrusive, inescapable monitoring, have been low-level employees, clerical staff and factory workers, not senior management and directors (Ehrenreich 2001; Snider 2002).

Reasons for Pessimism

There are other reasons to resist optimistic scenarios. Under globalised markets (most) nation-states have less power to fashion nation-specific regulatory regimes than in the past. In Canada and throughout the world, American power has increased. The US has the most politicised regulatory system in the world; business and free enterprise are celebrated as nowhere else, and both government and regulation are vilified.[22] When pro-regulatory forces are in the ascendance, as they are today, tough-sounding measures are passed, enforcement is vigorous (relatively speaking) and American 'get tough' rhetoric blankets the developed world. However, when the boom and bust cycle of stock markets swings back to boom, when the media forget today's financial scandals, when neo-liberal forces and business resume muscle-flexing, what will prevent budget cuts and deregulation from becoming the norm once again? As O'Brien (2003, 1) notes, the contemporary American regulatory frame is 'structurally unbalanced'. As a result, 'where external controls...on profit maximization are weakened, we can expect increased incidence of illegal corporate activity' (Pearce and Tombs 2003, 18).

Business power has not diminished, indeed the adoption of neo-liberal policies and rhetoric have dramatically increased it, on a worldwide basis (Pearce and Tombs 2003; Mishra 1999; Monbiot 2000). Capital has a monopoly on information about its activities, a monopoly protected by laws on patent protection and competition. Such information is defended as essential to protect trade secrets and promote 'competitive advantage' (Fooks 2003; Tombs and Whyte 2003). At the level of values, making money is now widely accepted as the only measure of worth, the only 'fair' mechanism to distribute income across class, race and gender divides. This message, promoted through advertising, marketing and public relations campaigns, puts profit maximisation first. 'U.S. business spent 60% more on marketing in

1992 than the US as a nation spent on all private and public education' (Glasbeek 2002). The 100 largest transnational corporations in the world account for the bulk of this spending. Although lip service is paid to law obedience, transnationals are now attempting to shape definitions of 'social responsibility' and 'good corporate citizenship' (Shamir 2004). Not surprisingly, they promote individual ethics and voluntary action and decry government regulation and criminal sanctions.[23]

The celebration of profitability also affects patterns of socialisation, shaping conscience and ethical standards. If doctrines of greed dominate popular culture, value systems promoting honesty, social equality and responsibility for others will be seen as uncool or 'wimpish'. Ethics campaigns and education in corporations seeking to promote 'good corporate citizenship' are forced to work against deep-seated cultural forces and socially engrained attitudes. For social control to work, for individuals to police themselves and their peers through shaming the self and significant others (Braithwaite 1989), pro-social moral standards must be internalised. Values which tell families and religious leaders that the most important responsibility of business is to make money and produce profits every quarter, and tell executives that this is the road to riches, power and social respect, make corporate crime inevitable. Celebrating CEOs who achieve wealth and fame by risk-taking (which often means rule evasion), or promoting companies for 'dismantling the New Deal regulatory legacy' (Fooks 2003, 17) transmits messages that defeat shaming by justifying and excusing law breaking.

Conclusion

Globalisation and the resilience of anti-regulatory arguments in neo-liberal states make it simplistic to take the latest state promises at face value. However, it is equally simplistic to assume that patterns of the past necessarily predict the future. Cultures, human beings, financial forces and technological change are much more complex than such formulae recognise. The strengthening of criminal and non-criminal law will certainly have consequences. Whether these will be short or long term, deep-seated or superficial, however, remains to be seen.

Notes

1. The author would like to acknowledge the financial support of the Social Science and Humanities Council of Canada, and thank Mary Condon, Steve Bittle, and Justin O'Brien for comments and assistance.
2. And, ironically enough, required new regulations and new regulatory bodies! (Pearce and Tombs 2003).
3. There are also splits within each designation: between industrial and financial capitalism (with many claiming that the needs of the latter have eclipsed the former), and between occupational health and safety movements (typically working class) and environmental movements (typically middle class).
4. The latest examples of this phenomenon occurred in Mexico and Argentina.
5. The Prospectors and Developers Association predated the BDA, but it has never been a key player. Opposed to the establishment of the OSC in 1945, it was seen primarily as an interest group.
6. Sending Viola MacMillan to prison and cracking down on penny stock promoters in Toronto stimulated the growth of the Vancouver Stock Exchange. The VSE then became the favoured speculators' market, with lax or absent regulations and 'a flaccid internal self-regulating body that would protect the name of any broker found chiselling' (Macbeth 1985, 126).
7. This is a classic example of what Haines and Gurney (2003) call Regulatory Conflict, because the OSC argued that fixing rates would violate the Combines Investigation Act (now the Competition Act), federal legislation designed to promote competition.
8. Control of companies is still concentrated within small corporate elites, and wealth distribution is wildly – and increasingly – unequal. In 1982 the average CEO in the US earned about 45 times as much as the average employee, by 2000 he (seldom she) earned 458 times as much (Cernetig 2002).
9. The Toronto Stock Exchange now handles 95% of all equity trading in Canada, 30 million transactions a year, with 530 employees handling 1340 senior equities (*Report on Business Magazine* June 2004). These are essentially blue chip stocks from established, often transnational corporations. The TSX Venture Exchange lists stocks from smaller, less established 'emerging' companies, 2275 in 2004. It was formed by combining the small capital components of the Toronto, Vancouver, Alberta and Winnipeg exchanges, to allow entrepreneurs to raise capital quickly. Allowing 'a prospector to get a grubstake to go out and do his thing', is as important today – and probably as male-dominated – as it was when these words were written in 1945 (Advertising Supplement of the Toronto Stock Exchange, *Report on Business Magazine*, June 2004).

10. In the spring of 2003 the federal commission set up the 'Wise Persons Committee', charged with investigating the practicality and efficiency of this arrangement (www.wise-averties.ca). A report issued in September 2003 recommends that this system be abolished and replaced with one national regulatory body, controlled and administered by the federal government, with regional offices.

11. This includes self-regulatory bodies such as the Toronto Stock Exchange, which recently published a three page advertisement in Canada's premier business journal touting its capacity to monitor every trade 'in real time', and its power to reverse trades (Advertising Supplement, *Report on Business Magazine*, June 2004).

12. Michael Watson, head of enforcement at the OSC, in testimony to the Senate Banking Committee in June 2003, argued against this wording. It would make successful prosecution impossible, he pointed out, because the Crown would be required to prove first that the informant knew the information had not been disclosed to the public, and that he/she specifically sought to take advantage of this fact. He recommended that 'knowing use of inside information' be changed to 'trading with knowledge of' inside information. This recommendation was not acted upon, the original wording remains.

13. The Canadian Bankers Association argued in Committee Hearings that such penalties would be 'very unfair', and requested more time to comply with production orders. Their pleas were apparently not heard.

14. Changes in civil and administrative law are also being considered, such as measures to amend the Canada Business Corporations Act to 'strengthen corporate governance' (Department of Finance, Canada 2003).

15. The federal Ministry of Finance, however, insists corporate governance is 'already strong'. They argue that because Canada has more small public companies and closely held corporations than the US, it should place 'greater reliance on principles and voluntary guidelines' than the Americans. One would assume this means they are against greater criminalisation, a position quite different from that taken by the Ministry of Justice (Canada, Minister of Finance, www.fin.gc.ca/toce/2003, 10 September 2003, accessed 5 July 2004).

16. As Ronen Shamir (2004) notes, multinational corporations are now attempting to shape the meaning of corporate social responsibility, in ways that minimise structural oversight and maximise voluntary, individualistic, corporate-friendly initiatives.

17. This is not new, concern that this might send the 'wrong' signal to investors is. Canada has seldom imposed jail sentences in any kind of corporate crime, financial or social. Over the 100 year history of the Combines Investigation Act, passed in 1889, now the Competition Act, legislation that covers everything from price fixing to false advertising, no

executives have ever served prison time. Orders of prohibition, which allow companies to escape liability by promising not to commit the offence again, have been the dominant disposition (Snider 1978, 1993; Stanbury 1977; also Puri 2001).

18. On 2 February 2005, the IMET team staged a highly visible raid on the Bank of Nova Scotia head office. Alleging that the Bank refused to hand over internal documents, 25 officers armed with a 60-day search warrant and a trailer-length van sent a message to Toronto's financial community. Arrest(s), we are told, will follow (Globe & Mail, 2 February 2005, A1, B1, B5).

19. The most important Self-Regulatory Organizations (SROs) in Canada are the Investment Dealers Association of Canada, the Mutual Fund Dealers Association of Canada (MFDA), and the stock exchanges in Toronto and Montreal (the TSX, TSX Venture Exchange, and the Bourse de Montréal (ME)). There are also specialised private services, notably Market Regulation Services Inc. (MRS), an independent body which does market surveillance, investigation and enforcement for the Toronto Exchanges, and the Canadian Investor Protection Fund (CIPF), an industry-funded body to prevent investment dealer insolvency (Phelps et al. 2003, 18).

20. An OSC report published in 2001 recommended that the lobbying and regulatory functions of the IDA be separated, due to extreme conflicts of interest. However, the final version of the Report did not do this. As reported in the press, the investigators 'were ultimately persuaded...that such a move wasn't justified' (K. Howlett, Globe & Mail, 27 January 2004a, B5).

21. The lobby group also tells us the industry has a new Code of Ethics which prevents members from 'personal trading and receiving gifts' (K. Damsell, Globe & Mail, 22 June 2004, B8). Presumably the Code is silent on executive compensation, which rose steeply despite declining equity levels (11.3% in 2002, 2.8% in 2003) (A. Willis, Globe & Mail, 23 June 2004, B9).

22. American business history is a case in point. A series of scandals, from the railway trusts of the nineteenth century, the price fixing scandals in the 1950s and 1960s, Penn Central in the 1970s, Mike Milken and the junk bond scandal in the 1980s and the trillion dollar Savings and Loan debacle (Calavita et al. 1997; Rosoff et al. 1998) all initially produced tough rhetoric and new measures, followed by deregulation, budget cuts and regulatory neglect.

23. International legal systems are in their infancy, and at this stage none of the world's most powerful countries is willing to cede any sovereignty to them.

10

Detecting Fraud and Managing the Risk

Nicholas M. Hodson

Introduction

This chapter draws on personal experience of responding to incidents and suspicions of fraud and to fraud risk management concerns over a 17-year period. It examines briefly the pervasiveness of fraud, identifies concerns in the regulatory response to recent financial reporting fraud. It looks at two examples from practice of fraud detection strategies and discusses issues related to the management of fraud risk.

The fundamental character of fraud and what distinguishes it from theft is deception. You are not supposed to find it! That poses challenges in both detection and risk management. These challenges invite some simple but compelling responses

If you want to find fraud you have to know what it looks like.
If you want to prevent fraud you have to know what causes it.
There is always evidence of fraud when it occurs.
The real numbers always exist.

This chapter discusses these notions among other things.

Pervasiveness of Fraud

Surveys of corporations conducted by Ernst & Young globally and surveys of employees in North America have provided snapshots of the pervasiveness and character of business fraud at points in time.

Over a period of 16 years Ernst & Young has conducted surveys of corporations that indicate consistently that the most serious frauds businesses experience are those committed by employees. A tenet of investigation based on practical experience is, 'If you want to know what's going on, get someone who knows to tell you.' That implies that you know who knows. The corporate surveys told us that employees committed the most serious frauds. So in 2000 we decided to ask the people who committed these frauds what was going on. We commissioned a leading polling firm to conduct a telephone survey of Canadian employees. The key question was:

> Thinking specifically about your place of work and the types of fraud listed above as well as other forms of fraud, I would like you to tell me whether you are *personally* aware of any situations *involving yourself or people you know* where fraud occurred approximately in the last year? Please remember your answer is entirely confidential, and we are only asking about situations you have witnessed personally.

We pre-sensitised the interviewees by asking their opinions about the seriousness of different types of fraud to raise their focus beyond trivial thefts of stationery and to avoid the legal definitions of what is and isn't fraud.

In 2000, one in four Canadian employees answered 'yes' to that question. In 2002 we repeated the survey and included the US. The affirmative response to the key question in 2002 was one in five in both jurisdictions. The change from one in four to one in five may be attributable to degradation in the sampling precision as the polling firm reduced its sample size for the 2002 survey. Among other questions in the survey, we found no significant difference between the responses in Canada and in the US, dispelling any treasured Canadian myth about their intrinsic comparative honesty.

Subject to increasing imprecision as inferences are drawn from subsets of the sample, we found no compelling differences in the responses among geographies, industries, ages, or job seniority levels and, in the case of Canadian employees, over time. Importantly, it suggests that the propensity of employees to engage in fraudulent activity applies to a reasonably stable segment of all employees – junior and senior alike. As more senior employees have greater opportunity and derive the greatest benefit from fraudulent activity it is hardly surprising that managers represent a disproportion component in the values lost through fraud.

The messages that come from these surveys are that employees present the greatest threat and employers with significantly more than five employees have almost certainly been victims of fraud in the last 12 months.

The Recent Evolution of Fraud

SEC press releases are an interesting bellwether of the prevalence of fraud and where it resides on the agenda of regulators. Table 10.1 summarises press releases from 1997 to 9 September 2004.[1]

The pattern is compelling; from zero to 35% in eight years. It is also worthy of note that the reporting of fraud allegations involving financial intermediaries has outstripped allegations of fraud by issuers in every year except 2002. In the case of allegations of financial reporting fraud the overwhelming majority of incidents have involved the manipulation of core earnings and revenues by senior management who have collusively subverted financial reporting controls to overstate actual results.

Table 10.1 SEC press releases concerning fraud 1997–2004

Year	Press releases	Financial reporting fraud allegations	Securities and other fraud allegations	Fraud (%)
1997	117	0	0	0
1998	129	0	8	6
1999	177	3	19	12
2000	194	7	17	12
2001	152	4	14	12
2002	180	18	11	16
2003	184	15	44	32
2004 (9 Sep.)	126	17	27	35

Limitations in the Response

Part of the regulatory and legislative response to these incidents of significant corporate fraud has been to stiffen sanctions and require certification by senior management of financial statements and internal controls with related attestation by auditors (see McDonough and O'Brien this volume). One of the problems with the response from a fraud investigator's perspective is the seeming disconnect between the most serious risk and internal controls. The most serious risk is clearly the collusive subversion of financial reporting controls by senior management. Where then are the controls that mitigate the risk that existing controls may be subverted by senior management? Is it reasonable to contemplate the notion of controls that mitigate the risk that other controls will be subverted?

In the United States, the Public Company Accounting Oversight Board, the new regulatory authority established by Congress through Sarbanes-Oxley, has at least recognised the problem. In its second published auditing standard, the PCAOB noted:

> Internal control over financial reporting cannot provide absolute assurance of achieving financial reporting objectives because of its inherent limitations. Internal control over financial reporting is a process that involves human diligence and compliance and is subject to lapses in judgment and breakdowns resulting from human failures. *Internal control over financial reporting also can be circumvented by collusion or improper management override.* Because of such limitations, there is a risk that material misstatements may not be prevented or detected on a timely basis by internal control over financial reporting. *However, these inherent limitations are known features of the financial reporting process. Therefore, it is possible to design into the process safeguards to reduce, though not eliminate, this risk.* (PCAOB Auditing Standard No. 2, para. 16, emphasis added)

Internal controls or other safeguards designed to improve the ethics infrastructure, such as codes of conduct, are helpful when they apply to all employees, including senior management. Having a code does not necessarily mean that its values are internalised across the corporation as demonstrated by O'Brien in this volume. In virtually every reported case of significant financial reporting fraud, controls at a business process level have been subverted. When significant fraud is disclosed, after the investigation, assuming the organisation survives, the question on the lips of stewards of organisations that I have personally experienced is 'How do we stop it happening again?' I used to wonder why it was that they asked that question and not 'How do we stop it happening in the first place?'

Investigations invariably respond to the question, 'How did it happen?' or 'Why wasn't it caught sooner?', both euphemisms for 'Who is to blame?' Response to those questions implicitly identifies the owner(s) of the risk. This is the person, or the people, who ask the risk management question in the course of an investigation. Why then would these people not have asked the question, 'How do we stop it happening in the first place?' It could be that the risk had not been identified or, if identified, had been considered remote. Even at the time this was implausible. It is especially so in the current climate. More probably, the failure to ask the question is linked directly to the fact that responsibility had not been allocated. The people who are now asking the forward-looking risk management question are those who recognise that they are, perhaps by default, being identified as responsible.

Responsibility serves to concentrate the mind and is a powerful causal factor in the development of coherent risk management strategies. If you want action, make someone expressly accountable. The corollary is regrettably true. If you fail to make someone expressly accountable, no one will manage the risk. The significant frauds associated with major corporations from Enron to those alleged at Hollinger created perhaps the greatest threat to the capital markets since the Securities Exchange Act of 1934. Sarbanes-Oxley, the PCAOB and its regulatory clones elsewhere are the spawn of these events. If the current stewards at MCI/WorldCom, the entrails of Enron and all the others are asking the question 'How do we stop it happening again?', a different question is apposite for those as yet untouched by scandal: 'How do we know that what happened at Enron, WorldCom, Adelphia, Tyco etc., couldn't happen here?' And, at the risk of repeating the obvious, what happened was that senior management colluded to subvert financial reporting controls.

Progressively more senior managers and internal auditors are responsible for implementing, operating and monitoring controls to mitigate the risk of misstatement of components of financial reports and enterprise-wide risk management structures within their organisations to foster an ethical environment. But who has the responsibility for managing risks related to the senior management. Classic agency theory of management would suggest that responsibility rests with the board.

It is perhaps insightful to look at the way boards of public issuers respond to incidents of suspected financial reporting fraud that implicates senior management. In North America the incident response team is generally the audit committee. The committee typically retains its own legal counsel and, through counsel, retains agents to undertake an investigation on its behalf. If the responsibility to investigate appears to be assumed by audit committees as their responsibility, that seems to imply 'ownership' of this particular risk. The PCAOB also states in Standard No. 2,

> Although the audit committee plays an important role within the control environment and monitoring components of internal control over financial reporting, *management is responsible for maintaining effective internal control over financial reporting. This standard does not suggest that this responsibility has been transferred to the audit committee.* (Emphasis added)

The events that brought Standard No. 2 into existence were financial reporting frauds perpetrated by management. On its face, this seems to be a disconnect. The PCAOB acknowledges that the audit committee has an oversight role in management's maintenance of effective control over the financial reporting process, which suggests that, in its oversight capacity, the audit committee would need assurance that controls are in fact established and operating effectively in order to mitigate the risk of senior management subverting controls over the financial reporting process.

The ambiguity is unhelpful. At the very least governance design clarifications are required that expressly address the audit committee's responsibility for overseeing the effectiveness of controls over the risk of fraud by senior management.

Those design clarifications might include an articulation of the audit committee's responsibility relating to the risk of collusive subversion of financial reporting controls by senior management and the acknowledgement of a funding requirement to permit the audit committee to exercise its oversight. The board deals with senior management succession and compensation. It seems reasonable then to contemplate that the board (audit committee), in discharging its financial reporting responsibilities, explicitly addresses risk assessments relating to the risk of collusion. As a practical matter, who else can do it?

Detecting Fraud

Most of the major financial reporting frauds reported in the last few years have been significant in their size and serious to catastrophic in their ramifications. Anyone can detect fraud when it reaches a scale that is unsustainable. The challenge is to prevent it in the first place or to detect it in sufficient time to mitigate the consequences.

My wife asked me the other day to help her set the table for dinner. Having laid out the placemats, cutlery and basic condiments she asked if I would get some balsamic vinaigrette dressing for the salad she was making. She then said she would get it, adding, 'You won't find it because you don't know what you are looking for.' I assured her otherwise but she insisted and produced, from the recesses of the refrigerator, a glass jar in which she had made a dressing. The jar was marked 'Hellman's Mayonnaise'. It was true. I would probably have failed to find it. Fraud is like that. It is based on deception (not, I hasten to add, that my wife was actively engaged in intentional deception on the subject of the salad dressing). Had she told me it was at the back of the fridge in a mayonnaise jar, I probably would have found it. I would have known what I was looking for.

The fundamental thesis of fraud from the perspective of its perpetrators is that you're not supposed to find it; so even if you are looking for it, it can be hard to find. If you are not looking for it the likelihood of finding it is even more remote. Boards and auditors have a history of not finding fraud and until recently auditors, at least, have been limited by self-imposed standards that enshrined a tenet of reliance on the presumption of management's good faith. If you believe that you have no responsibility for a risk there can be little expectation that you will look for evidence of its existence or recognise it from its footprints when you see them.

While current auditing standards now acknowledge that a responsibility to detect material fraud by management cannot easily coexist with the presumption of management's good faith, audit processes designed to detect such fraud remain problematic, if for no other reason than not having looked for fraud for several generations there is no deployed body of knowledge among auditors, or boards for that matter, about what fraud does look like. And while the SEC press releases and secondary media reporting describe the nature of the fraud they do not generally describe the nature of the evidence that led to the conclusion that the fraud as described had in fact occurred. The reporting of this evidence would be of significant help in education about the characteristics that fraudulent activity presents.

Previous experience as an auditor is limiting in a fraud investigation context. Training and experience in auditing focus on finding and evaluating evidence to support the premise that the assertions embodied in financial statements are right. The terminology of auditing – confirmation, verification, assurance – are terms that imply corroboration rather than challenge. When suspicious circumstances exist, the initial premise changes from assertions being right to the premise that they may be wrong and that leads to a fundamentally different approach. My own experience in educating auditors in the very different methods deployed by investigators suggests that it is very hard for them to make the key conceptual switch.

When faced with the suspicion that there may be needles in the haystack, audit experience would lead to sampling the hay to support a conclusion that the hay was what it purported to be, within sampling precision and confidence levels. Investigative experience would lead to renting a metal detector. The difference is that the focus has shifted from the hay to the needles and knowing what needles look like is crucial to the effectiveness of the investigation.

A deductive methodology contemplates the development of working hypotheses and the evidentiary characteristics such hypotheses would produce if they matured to permit a search to be made for such evidence if it exists. This leads to the need to have a detailed knowledge of the relevant business processes and their related controls against which to test the hypotheses in order to develop a profile of the evidence such hypothetical activity would produce. In many cases, the hypotheses are not initially hard to construct as there may be specific allegations or well-founded suspicions but invariably investigations have to respond to the question, 'If he/she/they was/were doing this, what else was going on?' The response to this question requires a deductive analysis. And allegations and suspicions are sometimes misinformed and incomplete.

Fraud, thankfully, is still largely a minority activity. That means that the majority of the output of business processes, financial reporting being one of those, is the result of legitimate activity. Legitimate business activity involves a rich structure, both in series and in parallel, of complex interactions involving a degree of randomness and with sometimes uncertain outcomes and timing. Fraud, on the other hand, is a focused activity with a predetermined outcome involving as few interactions as possible and with a managed timeline. The deception of fraud is achieved through the simulation of legitimate activity. You don't see it because it doesn't look different from what you might have expected to see. Because of the richness and complexity of legitimate activity, it is, for all practical purposes, impossible to simulate completely. If it was it wouldn't be fraud. There are, consequently, always evidentiary characteristics that distinguish fraud from legitimate activity. These may not be evident at a high level where the simulation may be effective, but at more granular levels, the evidence exists. It may be more or less compelling but it exists.

Attempts to develop fraud detection models rely predominantly on the numeric data in financial statements. They are limited in their effectiveness by the scope of the evidence that feeds them and accordingly tend to produce problematic rates of false positives and negatives. The relationships among the financial statement data across time series are often corrupted by disjunctive events such as mergers and acquisitions. While the approach is valid, these models would benefit from more information than financial statement figures can provide. The problem academics face is access to detailed underlying financial data. Professional practitioners have an abundance of access to data – their limitations are not having the time to experiment, read, and document and share conclusions.

As the outputs of business activity become increasingly derived from electronic data, its use as an evidence source becomes increasingly important. In the current state of the art it is improbable that electronic evidence alone would be sufficient to prove to be an acceptable standard for judicial or regulatory purposes that fraud had occurred and to assign culpability. But as a tool to identify the indicia of fraud electronic data analysis is invaluable. In fact it would be inconceivable to conduct almost any investigation of significant fraud without a comprehensive range of computer-based forensic and data analytical tools. Much effort has gone into the development of technologies to assist in the process of detecting fraud and while many of these are highly sophisticated tools, they are still tools that need priming with data and rule sets. Finally, they require the professional expertise gained through active experience running investigations to interpret anomalies.

Business processes for financial reporting are largely similar in most developed countries and financial reporting requirements are becoming increasingly harmonised. The particular paradigm of financial reports when combined with the knowledge of the dominant objective of financial reporting fraud, namely to overstate core earnings, means that there is a relatively consistent body of electronic evidence and a finite number of common schemes by which financial reporting frauds can be perpetrated to realise the desired effect.

Depending on whose taxonomy you wish to adopt there are perhaps seven or 10 recognised methods by which financial statements are fraudulently misstated. Many of these methods have variants that add complexity, but the number is still finite. This implies that if the methods and their variants are known and there is a high level of similarity among financial reporting business processes, it is reasonable to contemplate methodologies with global application for the detection of the characteristics of fraudulent reporting schemes that rely on the ability to distinguish the characteristics of normal activity from those of fraudulent activity.

Fraudulent Financial Reporting Considerations

Why would senior managers engage in any fraudulent scheme to inflate results of operations? Probably because the market has set an expectation or been led to believe that the operations will produce a particular result and the reality is that operations are falling short of those expectations. This implies that the actual results are known. Otherwise it would be difficult to measure the amount by which a fraudulent manipulation was necessary. The lead-time of knowledge that a shortfall exists is relevant to the response. The longer the lead-time the more manipulation options exist.

Take, for example, the irregularities at Sunbeam, one of the earliest cases in the current manifestation of corporate scandals involving fraudulent accounting. It must have been obvious that the results, which had been eroding for some time, would not easily be turned around. The new management hired to effect a turnaround must have known or contemplated that likelihood early in its analysis of the situation. This knowledge or belief in the need for alternatives provided the time to develop a series of strategies, some more deeply embedded in the fabric of the operations than others. As often happens when operational problems prove intractable, the initial manipulations compound the problems as the shortfall between expectations and reality increases. Such was indeed the case at Sunbeam and the house of cards built by Al 'Chainsaw' Dunlap collapsed.

In other cases the prediction of actual results is more complicated. This typically means that the lead-time to react is less. The key message here is that the financial reporting fraud is generally reactive and therefore time sensitive. So the timing of the reaction is a relevant consideration in detecting fraud.

As fraud succeeds only as long as the deception holds, the more people who have to be involved in the scheme the greater the risk that the knowledge of the deception will leak and the fraud will be disclosed. It follows that the fewer the people involved the less the risk. There is, however, a counterproposition. If it is likely that someone will discover the fraud, the risk can be mitigated by involving and thereby implicating them in the fraud. This makes them less likely to blow the whistle and presents the possibility of plausible deniability defences for the principal parties engaged in the fraud.

Fraudulent Financial Reporting – An Example

The deferral of costs from operations to capital assets is a seductive scheme from a perpetrator's point of view, as it can be executed by few people, appears to produce earnings and cash from operations and does not involve many of the more complex relationships among financial statement components associated with revenue recognition schemes, which always create cash flow problems that need managing. (It is a truism within the financial investigating community that you can never turn fictitious receivables into cash.)

Consistent with the notion that the fewer people involved the better, the manipulation of the results can be achieved by capitalising operating costs through journal entry transfers at period ends involving very few people. A similar result could also be achieved by capitalising costs at the point when they are initially incurred, but this has to involve other people and there is a timing problem; it has to be done before actual period results are available. Journal entries offer a more responsive, less risky strategy.

While auditors examine capital expenditures, they typically do so, as with many auditing procedures, on a test basis, founded on an assessment of risk and materiality. Most controllers or finance directors (many are former auditors) are aware of the scope of audit processes and the thresholds that auditors employ in testing. It would be feasible to contemplate a scheme to achieve the desired result and to deceive auditors that would operate predominantly below the threshold of their testing and have plausible explanations developed for reasons why capital expenditure budgets had been exceeded. Such a fraud could escape detection by a board and auditors for some time and should operations turn around or the waters become muddied by acquisitions and divestitures, it might never surface.

An effective way to detect such a fraud would be to consider the circumstances as a working hypothesis, to postulate the evidence that it would present and search for that evidence. For such a hypothesis to mature, there would have to be evidence of journal entries that transferred costs from operations to capital assets and there would be a likelihood that these journal entries would be developed by a more senior finance official close to or after a month end when the preliminary real results were known.

An extract from the company's financial database searching for journal entries that debited capital assets and credited expenses would indicate a high volume of relatively small value entries period by period shortly after the preliminary end results came in from subsidiaries. If a search produced such findings they would be validated by focused interviews, examination of internal emails and other documents. If no such evidence was disclosed by the search, the next variant would be to consider the capitalisation of costs at the time of initial entry and to consider the transfer of expenditures among affiliated entities where they are moved from the operations of one subsidiary to the balance sheet of another – both increasingly risky strategies as they involve more people and are harder to manage.

Asset Misappropriation – An Example

One of the more prevalent schemes we see in practice is the diversion of funds through the creation of fictitious suppliers. Its objective is to divert funds directly from the organisation rather than the deception of the capital markets. Fraud in purchasing, procurement and payment processes also includes the following stratagems:

- bid rigging, where a small group of suppliers conspire to take their turn at the trough;
- phantom bidders, where it appears that competing bids have been sought but in reality a single entity is behind all of the bidders;
- skimming, where an intermediary is interposed between the buying organisation and the actual supplier;
- kickbacks, one of the more difficult abuses to prove, where the supplier pays a secret commission to the person controlling the buying decision (and usually recovers the cost plus a margin through overbilling the buying organisation);
- reprocessing paid invoices, where a copy of an invoice that has already been paid is submitted fraudulently and paid again in a way that allows the fraudster access to the cheque.

Fraudulent suppliers are attractive schemes, as they do not need to involve any party other than the fraudster him or herself and consequently present a low risk and a 100% share of the rewards for the fraudster. Analysis of the evidence that such a risk hypothesis would present illustrates the process of developing an evidence profile of the difference between a legitimate supplier and a fictitious one. Setting up a supplier is a fairly routine process in most organisations and as different types of organisations employ similar processes in managing and recording purchasing and payment transactions, there is a helpful similarity of the structure of this activity across a wide range of organisations.

The consideration of the evidence profile begins with the development of the hypothesis itself and tests that hypothesis against the business environment and related controls in which it would be executed. The test is effectively a simulation of what the risk hypothesis would have to involve if perpetrated in a particular environment and what the fraudster would have to do or be likely to do to mitigate the risk of discovery. The simulation is then compared to the profile of legitimate activity and the discriminating characteristics identified.

There is seldom only one characteristic that distinguishes fraud from reality. The fraudster's objective is to make the activity and the fictitious supplier appear legitimate. In a legitimate supplier relationship, the supplier's name will be recorded in a master file record with

address, phone and other details. While credit checks and other validation of authenticity of suppliers are sometimes conducted, they are
frequently done only for customers – not for suppliers. A fraudster
would need to know this and subvert the control if necessary and
possible. Purchase requisitions and orders will have to be processed
and approved; goods or services will have to be delivered (services are
preferred to goods among fictitious suppliers as their non-delivery is
easier to conceal). Invoices have to be issued, approved, allocated to a
cost centre, expense or asset account, and payment has to be made.
The activities from purchase requisition to payment are generally
recorded electronically. While the specific details of the fields
recorded can differ, the broad requirements for effective financial
management and the tracing of supplier transactions are similar.

A fictitious supplier has to be operated below the noise level and
escape identification by other means. There are unlikely ever to be
more than a few, if there are any. Large organisations may have thousands of suppliers. There are a number of strategies for eliminating
many of these from consideration. The supplier will not be among the
largest suppliers of the organisation – it would be too hard to conceal.
It will also not be among the dormant and unlikely to be among
extremely small or infrequently used suppliers. Dormant suppliers
would obviously provide no reward for the fraudster and the risk would
not be worth taking for trivial reward. These can be effectively eliminated from consideration. And if you are wrong the consequences are
not serious – for now. Thresholds requiring some subjective judgement
need to be set to establish these boundaries.

As the supplier is fictitious, it will not be a supplier that we know to
be real. A comparison to an external list will facilitate the removal of
suppliers like Ernst & Young or Microsoft, for example. But investigators
need to beware of suppliers with names very similar to the names of
legitimate suppliers. We have seen cases where such a name has been
deliberately selected. It can create the deception that the supplier is in
fact real and somehow related to the legitimate supplier.

It is improbable that a dispute will ever exist with a fictitious
supplier. If it did, it would, of course, have to be a fictitious dispute.
Accordingly, any suppliers with credit notes in their transaction
history can be eliminated from further consideration. As noted, it is
improbable that the fraudster would risk setting up and operating a
fictitious supplier for trivial reward so it is improbable that a fictitious
supplier will have a record of any invoices in trivial amounts. Suppliers

with trivial invoice amounts can be eliminated from consideration. This requires the setting of a triviality threshold, which requires an element of subjective judgement relevant to the specific circumstances of the case.

There is likely to be only one person in the organisation who knows that the supplier is fictitious – the fraudster who set it up. So only one person will place orders on the supplier. An interesting filter, as it also has the capacity to identify the fraudster. Suppliers with multiple ordering initiators can be eliminated from consideration. In most organisations these filters will eliminate the significant majority of what are likely to be legitimate suppliers. What remains has a higher risk profile.

Having eliminated these suppliers, probability tests can be applied to the remainder to the residue. A real business has a name, frequently one that will create an association with the primary products or services it offers. It will have a place of business, a telephone and fax number, an email address or website, employees, often a value added or other tax or regulatory registration, limited liability and other characteristics that a fictitious supplier will not share. It will have invoices numbered for reference purposes that proceed in a sequence consistent with the passage of time. It will have descriptions of the goods or services it provides on its invoices and there may be shipping and receiving documents to accompany goods or inspection reports that relate to services. The invoices will have quantities if goods are involved and prices. The invoice totals will appear on the invoice. Frequently the invoice will quote a contact person as a reference for correspondence.

The fraudster has to invent all of this. The name of the fictitious supplier, in contrast to the objective of a real supplier, will be as anonymous as possible. We have found on occasion that the imagination of the fraudster only runs to some vague service and a set of initials. In fact in some cases these have been the fraudster's own initials or those of family members. We extract suppliers with initials in their names. It is improbable that a fraudster will go to the lengths of renting premises for the fictitious supplier and will need some convenience address. This may be a PO box reference or a residential address or a 'care of' address. It may even be the address of the fraudster or a family member or accomplice. We match the addresses of suppliers against the addresses in the employee master file.

As the supplier is fictitious it will be unlikely to have a telephone number registered in its name but the lack of a telephone number on the invoices would be a risk. A reverse phone number search can reveal whom the number is registered to. A call to the number can also be revealing. Absence of a fax number, while marginally less suspicious, increases the probability that the supplier is fictitious. Absence of a website or other electronic means of contact also increases the probability as does the absence of limited liability status, tax or other registration numbers.

The fraudster has to invent the goods or services being invoiced. Goods are more troublesome than services so suppliers of services are more likely to be fictitious. The invoice details may be either vague or possibly copied from the details of another supplier's invoices. The invoice amount may require separate disclosure of sales or value added taxes as is the case in my own jurisdiction. Absence of taxes increases the probability that the supplier is fictitious. The amount itself has to be contrived. The fraudster's objective is to optimise his or her personal risk/reward equation and will generally have authorisation limits beyond which a further authorisation is required. This means that the invoice values will tend to have a low standard deviation slightly below that threshold. Invoices have reference numbers. The fraudster has to invent these as well. Sometimes the people who do these things are not too smart so we look for suppliers with invoices in sequential order. This means it only has one customer.

The fraudster's objective is to put the money in his or her pocket as soon as possible with the least risk. He or she will probably know when the cheque runs are processed. (The use of electronic funds transfers rather than cheques does not substantively affect the profile.) Fictitious documents present a risk as long as they are in current circulation so the likelihood is that he/she will submit the fake invoice for payment on or about the last date required to make the next cheque run. This minimises the time the false documents are in circulation but also shortens the time between the invoice date and the payment date. Large suppliers frequently negotiate prompt payment terms but smaller suppliers tend to have to wait longer for their funds. A small supplier with a fast payment history increases the probability of the supplier being fictitious.

While each of these criteria bring probabilities of fictitious suppliers the probabilities are uncertain. However, an accumulation of criteria increases the probability of a supplier being fictitious and generally reduces to a manageable number those suppliers worthy of either further investigation or monitoring. Most of these characteristics are detectable through using data analytics which, once set up, are efficient and inexpensive. The hard part is developing the rule set in the first place. While, as noted before, these analyses are unlikely to prove fraud has occurred they are invaluable indicators of conditions of higher risk that can be further evaluated by other evidence such as interviews and visits to the purported premises.

The purpose of setting out this detail is to illustrate the premise that evidence of fraud always exists. In some cases it is evident to a greater degree than others. The more detailed the evidence is, the more energy is required by the fraudster to identify and address personal risks and the greater likelihood of the fraudster's attempted simulation being incomplete. While these examples are illustrative of detection processes, general knowledge of their existence also acts as a preventive measure through reducing the perceived opportunity and they serve to identify opportunities to improve preventive controls such as the routine validation of suppliers through credit references. In certain environments high transaction volumes lend themselves to screening by neural networks and other pattern recognition software. While these tools are widely used in credit card portfolio management and securities trading, for example, they have a high propensity to generate false positives and are less effective in lower population volumes.

Managing the Risk

Fraud is high on the list of our more intractable social problems. Like war, poverty, along with death and taxes, it seems to have an inevitability that we are unable to escape. If its elimination would be naive to contemplate, improvement in its management is certainly realisable. There are other problems that would qualify as socially intractable. Drunk driving is one that comes to mind. It is still with us but in my North American experience, a better-managed risk than it was when I was a youth in Belfast. I believe it is an instructive analogue to the management of fraud risk.

In North America a grass roots organisation of victims and their friends, relatives and empathisers has crusaded for changes in legislation and policy, and for increased sanctions, for many years. While it will always be a work in progress their efforts have had notable effect.

What has happened? The likelihood of drunk drivers getting caught has increased through enabling legislation, increased enforcement and improved technology. The sanctions have increased significantly through increased fines, increased insurance premiums and the potential loss of the privileges of driving. The social acceptability of drunk driving has eroded. This has been achieved through an effective communications strategy that removes deaths from drunk driving from the realm of statistics to dramatic personal re-creations of children orphaned, siblings and parents grieving. In other words they made it a personal issue that was hard to ignore.

Three levers were pulled in a comprehensive strategy

- enforcement reduced the *opportunity*;
- sanctions balanced the *motivation*; and
- communications reduced the ability to *rationalise* that driving drunk was not a problem.

Like drunk driving, fraud is a crime and is also predisposed by the same three conditions. The conditions, motivation, opportunity and ration-alisation ability have become widely accepted as the predisposing conditions that have to exist for fraud to occur. The historical response by the corporate world has been to focus largely on oppor-tunity, by a system of internal controls that act to prevent and detect misstatements however caused. Less has been done to address the two other predisposing conditions.

An intractable problem requires the most comprehensive response. This problem has three dimensions and the response has focused predominantly on one. It is true that if there is no opportunity there can be no fraud but that is just not realistic. Business managers are paid to put assets at risk to make returns for a range of stakeholders. Running a business with controls that absolutely prevent fraud is probably possible but not economically feasible.

Little has been done to address motivation, perhaps the most compelling lever in the recent cases of fraud where individuals realised hundreds of millions of dollars for their fraudulent efforts. Why, for example, would a senior finance officer whose job is to produce and publish financial information have performance-based compensation tied to the company's operating result over which he or she has no influence but the overriding access to defer costs or accelerate revenues. If performance-based compensation is relevant at all it should surely be tied to a measure such as timely production of numbers, consistency of application of policies, and development of a financial reporting anti-fraud programme, which would include the management engaged in the financial reporting process.

The most apparent effort made to deal with rationalisation ability is the establishment of codes of conduct. But Enron had a code of conduct. The inescapable conclusion is that, if it is not visibly adopted, followed and 'lived' by the leadership it is useless. In fact it is worse than useless. People respond more to the behaviour of role models than what they read in policies and when it is in conflict disaffection or acceptance follows. Either is a bad result.

Before we consign codes of conduct to the shredder, perhaps we ought to ask why it is that our models of governance produce such despicable people as the leaders of the rogues' gallery of organisations that have heaped disgrace on themselves in the last three years and does it in fact run deeper than governance models to a broader level of moral decay? If one considers the factors that have influenced the direction of motivation, opportunity and rationalisation during the last two generations they are not encouraging. A linear projection of these trends into the future is no more encouraging. Compared to 40, 20, 10 years ago do people today

- have better role models in their political leaders?
- have better role models in their business leaders?
- have better role models in their religious institutions?
- have a religious institution?
- have better moral education from school, family, religious organisations?
- have more loyalty to their employer?
- have a better belief that what's good for their organisation is good for them?
- have lower expectation of a better lifestyle?
- have less likelihood of facing personal financial pressure?
- have less performance-based compensation?
- face higher social and financial sanctions for fraud?
- have less personal functionality through technology?
- have more people checking what they do?
- have managers with a deeper understanding of their business?
- have to wait longer for positions of trust?

Is there light ahead? Not if we continue to do what we have been doing. For senior management to put fraud risk management high on their agenda it has to be consistent with their own objectives. There has to be a clear value proposition aligned with their own value systems. Or the objectives and value systems have to change.

If their objectives are tied to their compensation and that compensation is tied to the company's performance their objectives are tied to the company's performance. Unless there can be a clear demonstration that the effective management or avoidance of the sanctions for ineffective management of fraud risk adds value consistent with their performance objectives, it is improbable that anything beyond perfunctory regulatory compliance will be achieved. It is also probable that increased sanctions and a focus on controls will have some positive effect but it remains to be seen how effective the regulations will be as the fundamental value propositions for fraud still exist and the responsibility for management of senior management fraud remains unclear.

Note

1. The tabulation categorises releases into only one dominant category notwithstanding some releases relate to more than one category. Some releases combine reports of several incidents of alleged fraud. These are summarised as a single reference. More than one release sometimes relates to the same incident of fraud as investigations are announced, charges are laid and settlement is reported. The distinction between financial reporting and securities fraud in some cases is subjective. The table should be seen as a broad indicator rather than a precise analysis.

11

After Enron: Corporate Governance, Creative Compliance and the Uses of Corporate Social Responsibility[1]

Doreen McBarnet

Introduction: Beyond Fraud

Enron in the late summer of 2001 was the world's largest energy trader, the seventh largest corporation in the US and darling of market analysts, who were urging investors to buy. By 2 December 2001 Enron had filed for bankruptcy, till then the largest bankruptcy in US history. In between, on 16 October, it had announced its third quarter results for 2001 would include, completely out of the blue, a charge against earnings of $585 million and previously unreported debts of $1.2 billion (Powers 2002). The regulators, the Securities and Exchange Commission (SEC), began to investigate and by November Enron had restated its accounts of the last five years. As the story unfolded over succeeding months, it emerged that Enron had 'not only wiped out $70 billion of shareholder value but also defaulted on tens of billions of dollars of debts' (Partnoy 2002, 1).

The public has been left reeling over how such a huge collapse could occur without warning, and how such huge debts and losses could have been hidden from the market. Enron has become an icon for corporate wrongdoing on a massive scale, not just for the accounting issues but for all that followed – employees losing their retirement benefits, locked into Enron shares, as the value of those shares vanished, while senior executives had been selling at still high rates and taking multi-million dollar bonuses; accountancy firm Arthur Andersen shredding masses of Enron-related documents, and its own subsequent demise; auditors and analysts in general coming under scrutiny and criticism for lack of independence; allegations of political and regulatory corruption. Civil and criminal lawsuits are in process, there has been a series of investigations by Congress, as well as the SEC and the Justice Department, and there has been a rush to new legislation and regulation.

Enron is being treated as a watershed. 'After Enron' or the 'post-Enron world' are phrases used repeatedly in the press and in academic analysis to suggest an event of enormous significance, and there may be some temptation to demonise Enron, and Arthur Andersen, in order to shore up the notion that they are rotten apples in an otherwise basically sound and honest corporate world. 'Enron's demise is not business as usual in America' said one investigating Congressman (Tauzin, Subcommittee on Oversight and Investigations 2002b, 32). This chapter focuses on the issues at the heart of the Enron case, its corporate structuring and financial reporting practices, and there the question has to be raised of what 'business as usual in America' – and the UK and elsewhere – actually is, in order to put Enron in context and draw out its wider implications for corporate governance.

There have to date been 30 indictments for fraud in relation to Enron's practices, going to the very top of the executive chain, and it would be easy to focus attention only on the clear breaches of law at the heart of those indictments – outright fraud or law-breaking in the form of lies about products being marketed, structures improperly accounted for in that they failed to comply with the rules on the treatment adopted, insider dealing, frauds against Enron and obstruction of justice. Yet to do so would be to create a disjunction between the legal charges brought by regulators in court and many of the charges made by Congress, the media and the general public. For them part of the outrage of Enron lies simply in the fact that the market was fundamentally misled on Enron's financial status by its use of off-balance sheet accounting devices, and the issues this raises for the reliability of financial reporting in general. As two congressional investigators put it:

'Off the books transactions were purposefully designed to mislead shareholders about Enron's precarious financial profits' (Greenwood, Subcommittee on Oversight and Investigations 2002b, 2), and: the 'broader issues are capital systems and transparency in accounting' (Deutsch, Subcommittee on Oversight and Investigations 2002a, 4).

These concerns take us deeper than fraudulent accounting. They necessarily raise issues about the widespread and endemic practice of creative accounting. Enron used a multitude of fraudulent and creative practices to keep profits high, liabilities low, stock prices rising and credit ratings good, but the core technique was the use of what are variously known as Special Purpose Entities (SPEs), Special Purpose Vehicles (SPVs) or 'non-subsidiary subsidiaries'. These were partnerships, constructed to fall outside the rules requiring their finances to be consolidated in Enron's group accounts, thus keeping them 'off balance sheet' (OBS). It could be argued from SEC guidelines (Partnoy 2003, 210) that if just 3% of the capital investment in the SPV came from an independent outside body and remained at risk throughout the transaction, and the independent owner exercised control of the SPV, then the vehicle could be treated as 'off balance sheet', i.e. Enron did not have to include its losses or liabilities (or, in theory, profits or assets, but unsurprisingly OBS vehicles rarely have those) in its group accounts. Complex deals largely using derivatives were then done between the SPVs and Enron itself both to formally manage risk and to further enhance reportable financial performance. Some 4300 SPVs were in play by the time of Enron's demise.

These transactions were astonishingly complex and the indictments involve clear allegations of fraud in the construction of the deals. My concern, however, is broader, and it is this. Much has been made of Enron's breach of accounting and other rules, and in relation to the core SPVs, the fact that they did not always comply with the rules which allow such entities to remain off the balance sheet. There were instances, for example, where the three per cent rule was invoked to justify an accounting treatment, but not, as later investigation demonstrated, actually adhered to (Powers 2002). Yet, even if it had not broken the rules, it seems clear that Enron would have been misleading the market just as much. If it had only engaged in off-balance sheet structuring within the rules, it could still have kept significant debts and losses out of its own accounts. Indeed it is arguable that much of Enron's off-balance sheet activity did not breach the rules. Rather it creatively exploited the rules or utilised regulatory gaps, including the 'regulatory black hole' of derivatives (Partnoy 2002, 2). Certainly, Enron's OBS vehicles were not, as has sometimes been said, 'secret' partnerships. Their existence was disclosed in the notes to the accounts as is required by the rules. They may have been disclosed in ways which were economic with the truth, or via other forms of 'non-disclosing disclosure' (McBarnet 1991a) but sufficient material was put into the public domain to be in compliance with legislative and statutory requirements.

This is not to defend Enron. On the contrary it is merely to refine the charges. It is to suggest that Enron engaged in creative accounting as well as fraudulent accounting, and to underline the fact that the creative accounting, just as much as the fraudulent accounting, was, to cite our first Congressman again, 'purposefully designed to mislead shareholders about Enron's precarious financial profits' (Greenwood, Subcommittee on Oversight and Investigations 2002b, 2). What is more, Enron has been far from alone in engaging in such creative accounting. This, in turn, raises with a vengeance the 'broader issues' concerning our second Congressman, namely 'capital systems and transparency in accounting' in general (Deutsch, Subcommittee on Oversight and Investigations 2002a, 4).

Public reaction has been raised not only by the outright fraud involved but by the capacity of both business and auditors to mislead the market and violate trust through OBS structuring – whether fraudulent or not – and indeed through creative accounting more generally. And that to me is the more fundamental issue. Indeed the second biggest collapse in history – Enron has been upstaged in size if not complexity by WorldCom – could still have happened, completely out of the blue, even if it had *not* been breaking specific rules. It has certainly happened before.

There are parallels, for example, with Polly Peck in the UK (*Re Polly Peck International plc (in administration) (No. 3)* [1996] 2 ALL ER 433 1996). Polly Peck went bust in August 1991, just weeks after the analysts had been describing it too as undervalued and a must-buy. When it collapsed what had been reported in the books as £2 billion assets was suddenly redefined as £1.5 billion in liabilities. As with Enron, there were allegations of fraud on related issues but the accounting figures themselves were largely down to creative use of the rules, or in this case of gaps in the rules. One commentator noted: 'This is the other side of the Polly Peck miracle. Stated profit margins...are perfectly correct within generally accepted accounting standards, but they tell a misleading story' (Brewerton, *The Times*, 2 October 1990).

That is why we need to contextualise Enron in the wider world of corporate legal practice. Viewed from this perspective, it was neither the material fact of market deception nor the methods deployed to achieve it – SPVs and other off-balance sheet techniques – that differentiated Enron. Rather, the corporation was a relatively rare example of malefaction precisely because it sometimes used these techniques improperly, uniquely, got caught out and had to expose the reality behind the façade, and perhaps because it was an extreme case. Creative accounting was used not so much to enhance a business but to create one. There is a lot of technically proper but still thoroughly misleading creative accounting going on out there. There may also be a lot of technically *improper* accounting that never gets exposed. Certainly large numbers of US corporations seemed to suddenly find it necessary to restate accounts after Enron and before the new Sarbanes-Oxley legislation took effect. But the important point is this: even where accounting is technically proper and can claim to be 'perfectly legal', where it creatively exploits rules and regulatory gaps rather than engages in outright fraud, it can still be highly misleading.

The creative construction of 'perfectly legal' accounting treatments raises just as significant questions for corporate governance as participation in outright fraud. In the following sections this chapter will, first, set Enron in context by looking briefly at the kind of 'perfectly legal' off-balance sheet structures which have constituted widespread, routine corporate practice. Second, it will ask what can be done through accounting law to constrain creative accounting, and assess some such attempts. Third, it will begin to explore the culture that fosters such practices. Finally, it will consider the potential for contemporary concepts of corporate social responsibility to be brought into play to help enhance corporate governance and corporate control more generally.

Enron in Context: Perfectly Legal Creative Accounting

Enron is far from alone in setting up OBS SPVs to hide liabilities and create paper profits, and this practice has a long history. My own research in the UK in the late 1980s and 1990s demonstrated the widespread use of SPVs and other OBS techniques to manipulate accounts.[2] Creative accounting more generally was indeed shown to be rife in the UK in this period (Griffiths 1986, 1995; Smith 1992). Similar practices are in use in the US.[3] Nor is creative accounting an Anglo-Saxon phenomenon. One Enron indictment concerns abuse of reserves but again our past research, this time in Germany, demonstrated use of reserves to be common practice there as a way of manipulating accounts.

OBS SPVs were commonly used in the UK in the 1980s to manipulate accounts. 'Non-subsidiary subsidiaries' were set up, companies which were in economic substance subsidiaries, but which were carefully structured in their legal form to fall outside the rules defining a subsidiary (subsidiaries' finances having to be included in group accounts). Debts or losses could then be tidied away in them, off the balance sheet of the company setting them up. Such techniques were used routinely by household name companies, such as Cadbury Schweppes, Habitat, Burtons, Storehouse, Dixons, and many more.

As company law rules defining subsidiaries stood, it was far from difficult to keep bad financial news hidden in a way which could claim to be not breaking the rules but complying with them and therefore 'perfectly legal'. True, company law also contained the overriding principle that accounts should give a true and fair view, and the accounts produced after the set-up of such SPVs, it could be, and was, argued, did not do that, but accountants and lawyers looked to the detail of the law, to specific definitions and precedents, queried the meaning of 'true and fair' and its capacity to override specific rules, and endorsed the practice. Companies could properly claim they had the approval of their advisors. Just like Enron.

Also like Enron they sometimes had to shop around to get accountants and lawyers who would say that some of their more exotic structures and accounting innovations were indeed perfectly legal. But then there was and is no requirement to disclose just how much opinion shopping had gone on until an endorsement was achieved. So long as one barrister or accountancy firm was prepared to take a 'bullish' interpretation of the law, that was all that was needed in practice to claim reporting treatments were perfectly legal.

OBS SPVs were used for all sorts of things including the manufacture of paper profits. A property development company, for example, would

set up an SPV to do its development for it. It then lent it money for
the purpose and charged interest. The SPV did not pay the interest but
since the interest was *payable*, the company could add it to its books to
enhance its profits (by many millions of pounds at a time). Meantime
the SPV used another creative accounting technique, defining the
interest as capital expenditure so the cost did not appear on its own
profit and loss account (as a loss). Magic. Profits from nowhere and
vanishing expenses. Just like Enron. Property development company
Rosehaugh, for example, had 16 SPVs. Just like Enron their existence
was disclosed in the notes to the accounts, at length indeed, seven
pages of detail, but, also just like Enron's 'impenetrable footnote
disclosure' (Partnoy 2002), or 'obtuse' provision of information
(Powers 2002, 17), disclosure was so opaque that it was later said by
one analyst that one would need to be a professor of accounting to
have any hope of deciphering their significance (Christopher Hird,
House of Cards, Radio 4, 1991; and see *Accountancy* February 1990, 32).
Such 'non-disclosing disclosure' is a recurrent theme in both creative
accounting and tax avoidance (McBarnet 1991b; McBarnet and
Whelan 1999).

Unlike Enron most companies did not collapse, but they were
still misleading the market. And keeping debts off the balance sheet
and profits up had a number of valuable consequences, indeed
purposes. Performance-related pay and bonuses for senior executives
could boom. Just like Enron. Huge debts could be taken out that
would not have been possible if they had to go on the balance
sheet − or at least would not have been possible without upsetting
the debt/equity ratio. This ratio is key in corporate finance and
corporate governance. It is used most obviously for assessing good/
bad buys in the stock market. But it is also used as a trigger in loan
covenants for calling in loans if banks think the company's debt is
getting out of hand, and is also frequently used in a company's
'constitution', its memorandum and articles of association, as a trigger
requiring shareholder consultation before, for example, directors
may make a highly leveraged acquisition. Artificially protecting the
debt/equity ratio, then, meant basic corporate governance controls
could be bypassed.

This was exemplified in the case of Beazer, a UK housebuilding
company. It acquired, through an SPV, the US corporation Koppers,
worth twice Beazer's own value, in a deal described as 'impossible'
and 'sheer magic' (Angus Phaure, County NatWest, *Accountancy*,

April 1988, 9). Just as in Enron, derivatives formally shifted the risk, which, however, ultimately fell on Beazer, not the SPV, and indeed came back to haunt it within a few years (McBarnet and Whelan 1997; *The Times*, 26 June 1991).

And some companies did collapse. When property development company Rush and Tomkins went bust in 1991, an estimated £700 million pounds worth of hitherto unreported debts suddenly emerged from associated but OBS joint ventures (*The Times*, 30 April 1990). Sometimes the scope to take on more debt than could really be sustained itself led to collapse – or fraud to try to hide it. Again just like Enron. Maxwell Corporation is best remembered for raiding pensions, but one of the reasons it did so was because it had overextended itself by buying Macmillan via huge debts (Bower 1992). The purchase was made via an OBS SPV. It could not have been done without it, there being too much debt already. But, in practice, as is often ultimately the case, the risk came back to Maxwell.

There are many other direct parallels with Enron. One Enron SPV was set up to take advantage of the beneficial regulatory treatment available for windfarms it owned (*SEC* v. *Andrew Fastow*, US District Court Southern District of Texas, Houston Division, 2 October 2002). If the windfarms were more than 50% owned by an electric utility or electric utility holding company they would not be eligible for the benefits, and since Enron was about to acquire Portland General Electric it would lose out. It therefore used an SPV to buy the windfarms. There is a close parallel to this in the UK in the context of broadcasting. A broadcasting company, EMAP, wanted to take over another broadcasting company but if it did so it would hold eight licences. Since the statutory limit for one company's holding was six, the takeover would be disallowed. It therefore set up an OBS SPV to formally make the takeover. This was contested as mere form but upheld in court (*R.* v. *Radio Authority, ex parte Guardian Media Group* [1995] 2 ALL ER 865).

In short, Enron's manipulation of its accounts – and other regulations – needs to be understood in this wider context of normal business practice, normal, and arguably 'perfectly legal', legal practice – 'creative' rather than fraudulent accounting – yet nonetheless routinely frustrating the whole idea of true and fair accounts, routinely distorting market information, and undermining corporate governance.

What is to be Done? Strategies for Legal Control and their Limits

The immediate reaction to a scandal such as Enron is a demand for legal change, and the US has already produced the Sarbanes-Oxley Act. But law is not always the panacea hoped for. Such problems as compromises built into new law, inadequate sanctions, inadequate resources for policing, can all be listed as potential factors in law's failure to offer effective control. It is also increasingly recognised that new rules, even if they are fully resourced and uncompromised, can themselves prove inadequate simply because of the ability of the regulated to adapt to them. A new rule may stop today's objectionable creative accounting device, but leave the way open for the new device ingeniously constructed tomorrow to thwart the new rule. The more specific and prescriptive the rule is, the clearer the criteria the new structure has to meet or circumvent.

In post-Enron USA proposals have therefore been put forward not just for a tightening of regulations and strengthening of sanctions but for a change of regulatory style. The suggestion is that there should be less emphasis on specific rules and more on principles.[4] Harvey Pitt, for example, SEC chairman at the time, argued to the House of Representatives: 'Present day accounting standards are cumbersome and offer far too detailed prescriptive requirements for companies and their accountants to follow. We seek to move toward a principles-based set of accounting standards, where mere compliance with technical prescriptions is neither sufficient nor the objective' (Pitt 2002; and see Bratton 2004). This is exactly the strategy adopted by the UK in the 1990s in a bid to constrain creative accounting and specifically off-balance sheet financing.

Enron's SPVs were built on rules and guidelines which determined whether or not an entity should be consolidated into a group's accounts partly on the basis of specific thresholds of equity ownership. This was also the case in 1980s company law in the UK. The rules on consolidation (the requirement for a holding company to include all its subsidiaries in its group accounts) at that time involved two questions for determining whether company B was a subsidiary of company A, and therefore had to have its financial accounts included in A's. First, does A own more than 50% in nominal value of B's equity share capital? Second, is A a member of B and does it control the composition of B's board of directors?

There were simple and complicated ways to ensure B fell outside these criteria and therefore could stay off A's balance sheet. It would be a 'non-subsidiary subsidiary',[5] a subsidiary in substance but not in form. One way was to set up a 'diamond structure', in which A set up two subsidiaries B and C, owning 100% of B and 50% of C. B and C then owned 50% each of D. A in effect owned 75% of D but D fell outside the definitions of a subsidiary. Another route was for A to get a friendly bank, B, to hold 50% of the SPV, C, in the form of preference shares. C had a board of four directors, two from A and two from the bank, but A's directors had more voting rights and A therefore controlled the vote of the board without controlling, as the statute phrased it, its composition. Though such practices might have been constrained by concerns over challenge under the purportedly 'overriding' principle that accounts give 'a true and fair view', the *Argyll* case (Ashton 1986; McBarnet and Whelan 1999, 90), and wider legal discussions of the exact nature and status of the 'override' provided ammunition to counter any such challenge and indeed, encouraged the spread of the practice.

Creative accounting using OBS techniques was rife, but there also followed scandals, collapses, review committees, a campaign to clean up accounting (spearheaded by David Tweedie, then chair of the UK's Accounting Standards Board, now chair of the International Accounting Standards Committee, the IASC) and significant changes in law and in accounting regulation. The story, and the changes made, are complex and are detailed elsewhere (McBarnet and Whelan 1999), but for the purposes of this chapter the point is that radical changes in the law were made, with the express purpose of controlling creative accounting, and specifically the abuse of OBS financing and SPVs. What were these changes and how has the new regime fared?

At the core of the new regime was the view that law was failing to control creative accounting because of weak enforcement, inadequate regulation, and too much emphasis on rules. Precise rules and thresholds were too easy to circumvent; creative accounting thrived on repackaging transactions and structures to fall just outside them. They provided too clear a recipe for avoidance. Changing from one precise rule to another to catch the latest device simply stimulated the creation of yet another new device designed to escape the latest legal criteria. A new approach had to be adopted. Lord Strathclyde, for example, in the House of Lords, stated: 'Our intention is to curb the use of off balance sheet financing schemes through controlled non-subsidiary undertakings.

Any definition of the term will encourage attempts to avoid the provision by artificial constructions with the intention of escaping from the letter of the definition' (Strathclyde, HL Deb, vol. 03, col. 1018).

In essence, therefore, the new regime adopted a philosophy of shifting regulatory style from detailed prescriptive rules to broader purposive principles, from narrow criteria to broader catch-all ones in the drafting of definitions, and from an emphasis on legal form as the criterion for deciding on appropriate accounting treatments to an emphasis on economic substance. There was also a revision of the law on the 'true and fair override' to make it more accessible. The stated mission was that there be a shift of focus in financial reporting, and by implication in auditing, from the letter of the law to its spirit (e.g. Dearing, *The Times*, 24 January 1991). A new standard-setting body was set up under creative accounting's arch enemy David Tweedie, and a new agency, the Financial Reporting Review Panel, was set up to investigate accounts, policing no longer being left entirely to auditors. New sanctions were introduced for directors found in breach of regulations.

The off-balance sheet SPVs of the 1980s, and the rules which were interpreted as permitting them, were clearly targeted. So in the 1989 Companies Act (itself implementing European company law's Seventh Directive), the definitions of a subsidiary included a 'catch-all' definition which avoided mention of 50% thresholds or precise forms of control and instead required consolidation in broader terms. B would have to be included in A's consolidated accounts, in the event of A having 'a participating interest' in B (which might take forms other than equity ownership), and 'exercising an actual dominant influence' ('actual' rather than in any particular legal form). A lynchpin of the new regime was Financial Reporting Standard 5 (FRS5, ASB 1994). This stated categorically that transactions should be reported according to their economic substance, putting economic reality before formal legal structuring. It also specifically tackled 'quasi-subsidiaries', entities which fulfilled the functions of a subsidiary despite falling outside the statutory definitions of one, and required their inclusion in the 'quasi-holding company's' accounts.

Great hope has been attached by opponents of creative accounting to the potential of a principle-based regime for avoiding the limitations of rule-based regulation and providing a more effective means of controlling creative accounting. Tweedie noted, for example: 'We believe this is the surest means of forming standards that will remain relevant to innovations in business and finance and which are most likely to discourage ingenious standards avoidance practices' (FRC 1991, para. 5.5). Close analysis of the new regime, however, and of other jurisdictions following similar strategies,[6] suggests even a shift to principles poses problems for effective legal control. Again this is detailed elsewhere (McBarnet and Whelan 1991, 1999; McBarnet 2003) and I will simply note some of the main problem areas.

First, there is a problem with sustaining principles as principles. There are too many factors which can produce a drift from principles to rules, clarifying and narrowing the ambit of their control, and providing more recipes for creative accountants to work on. Lobbying, demand for guidelines, court cases and just the build-up of informal precedents on what is allowed in practice and what is not, are examples of the factors that eat away at principles and can convert them in effect back to rules.

Second, our empirical research suggests enforcers face problems in putting principles and indeed stronger powers in general into practice. There is too much room for contestability over what is true and fair, what is substance. There is concern about losing in court. Indeed, there is concern about winning in court if the win would nonetheless lead to tighter definitions of what is not allowable and by implication what is. There is concern about losing control to the judges.

The strength of a principle-based regime as a means of control also lies in the uncertainty it generates. Hence David Tweedie's response, when asked early in the new regime how it would fare: 'We're like the cross-eyed javelin thrower at the Olympic Games. We may not win but we'll keep the crowd on the edge of its seats...' Not knowing where the regulatory javelin will fall may make for greater caution among would-be creative accountants. It also encourages settling with enforcers rather than contesting them; there is reluctance to be the company that puts its head on the block to test the legal interpretation of the new regime. On the other hand if uncertainty is strength, the last thing the regime wants is to have its limits clarified, and regulators also may be too wary of a court case to flex their muscles too much. Yet there is a paradox here, because if the javelin is never wielded it will cease to deter.

What is more, the strength provided by uncertainty is also a potential weakness in terms of issues of legitimacy. Principle-based regimes can be readily open to criticism as too uncertain, as open to retrospectivity, as giving regulators too much power, as opening the way to arbitrary decision-making. The strategic response to creative accounting is itself susceptible to critique as 'creative control', and as an unacceptable violation of the rule of law. One empirical consequence of this is a tendency on the part of enforcers to limit themselves in how they use their powers. In turn the consequence of that is to limit in practice the theoretical scope of the principle-based regime for control.

What is more, even principle-based systems can fall prey to creative accounting. Regulations, even regulations based on principles, have to be based on words, and even abstract words can be scrutinised for creative interpretations or uses. Alternatively coexisting rules or even other principles can be brought in to limit the reach of the principles in question.

The 1989 Companies Act, we saw, introduced the 'catch-all' phrase 'actual dominant influence' in an effort to stop novel methods of control slipping through the net of more specific definitions. Yet that phrase then spawned 'deadlocked joint ventures' where A and B set up a partnership, C, in which the equity was held 50–50 and the power of each was 'deadlocked': neither A nor B exercised 'actual control' and C remained off the balance sheets of both. Rush and Tomkins' partnerships, unheard of until its bankruptcy as noted above, were deadlocked joint ventures of this kind. Though further regulations, especially FRS5, might be thought to catch this now, accountancy firms have suggested there could still be ways of constructing entities to keep them, arguably, off balance sheet, for example by making C a corporate joint venture, and using an exemption in the Companies Act to avoid consolidation. Another suggested route was to use 'revolving chairs', with A and B appointing a chairman for C with a casting vote each alternate year. Other sections of company law, and GAAP principles on consistency, could then be invoked to keep C out of the accounts of both (Ernst & Young 1997). Even the idea of 'substance over form' itself has been used creatively and counterpurposively.[7]

Whether rule based or principle based, there are then problems in controlling creative accounting through law. Yet one could argue that ultimately creative accounting is only a problem because of another issue, and that is not just the law itself but the attitude taken toward law by those allegedly subject to it, and the culture that fosters it.

The Culture of Creative Compliance

Whatever law, and whatever kind of law, is put in place as a mechanism for controlling business, it is mined for opportunities for circumvention. That is the reality of business regulation in action. And it is the reality of business regulation in action in any legal arena. Tax avoidance, a close cousin of creative accounting, is another obvious example, but legal creativity is to be found in any area where there are attempts to control corporate activity[8] through law, be it in the context of employee protection, environmental issues, health and safety, food and drugs or tenancy controls (McBarnet 1988). The concept 'creative accounting' captures the practice in financial reporting but we need a broader concept to capture the pervasiveness of the practice. I've dubbed it 'creative compliance' (e.g. McBarnet and Whelan 1997).

Routine techniques of creative compliance are to search out gaps in the law – 'where does it say I can't?'; to scrutinise the 'ex-files' of exemptions, exclusions, exceptions to see whether transactions or structures can be repackaged to fit within them, whether they naturally do or not; to find or press for specific definitions and thresholds as guidance then 'work to rule'; to construct completely innovative techniques which the law has not yet regulated and avoid control that way.

Creative compliance is in fact the product of two factors. Limitations inherent in the nature, substance and enforcement of law provide the opportunity, but that opportunity also has to be actively taken up by those subject to the law, in this case corporate management, as well as their advisors and auditors. It is not just how law is constructed and enforced that determines its impact but how it is received. If change is to come it is, therefore, not just the law we need to address but the attitude towards law assumed by those subject to it, and the pervasive culture that fosters it.

The culture of creative compliance is essentially negative. It is based on an attitude of 'why not?' If a practice is not expressly and specifically defined as illegal why should it not be used and claimed as legal? If a particular type of transaction is expressly outlawed why should it not be refashioned in form if not in substance and claimed to be different?

It is a culture which defines compliance in a minimalist way, focusing on compliance with the letter of the law rather than its spirit, and which sees it as the responsibility of legislators and regulators to get the letter of the law right. If the way the law is drafted allows loopholes to be teased out, then it is deemed perfectly legitimate to utilise them, regardless of the intentions of the lawmakers.

It is a culture which treats law not as an authoritative and legitimate policy to be complied with, but as an obstacle to be circumvented, indeed as a 'material to be worked on' (McBarnet 1984), and, regardless of the policy behind it, tailored to one's own interests.

It is a culture which is highly attentive to law, but which looks to law not to ask: 'is what I want to do allowed by law?' but: 'how can I find a way to justify it regardless?'

It is a culture in which law is a game, a game in which it is legitimate to come up with any interpretation one can, any argument one can dream up, however, in one's own view, 'spurious', 'bullish' or 'sailing close to the wind' that argument may be.[9]

And as long as that culture persists, so will attempts to thwart law through creative compliance, in the arena of corporate governance and beyond. So again, we need to ask: what is to be done?

Corporate Governance, Creative Compliance and Corporate Social Responsibility

And this is where one might begin to explore, as one part of a much wider agenda,[10] the potential role for the contemporary movement and contemporary ideology of Corporate Social Responsibility (CSR). CSR is the concept of the moment not only among forces such as non-governmental organisations (NGOs) seeking to control business, especially multinational corporations, but also within business itself, where 'the business case' for CSR policies is now established jargon, focusing on such issues as 'reputation risk management'. Companies are pressed or volunteer (for a variety of 'business case' reasons) to adopt CSR policies, often set out in codes of conduct and reported on in social reports on the 'triple bottom line' of social and environmental as well as financial performance (Elkington 1997). The business world now features socially responsible investment (SRI), 'ethical banks', and a whole industry of CSR consultants, conferences, and newsletters (McBarnet 2004a; Zadek 1998). CSR has entered popular culture, with films such as The Corporation (2004), and a range of books on the subject geared to audiences beyond either academe or business (Klein 2000; Bakan 2004).

CSR is usually presented as companies going the extra mile, over and above their legal obligations, which are assumed as basic. As Chris Tuppen, social and environmental programmes manager at British Telecom, put it in the company's first social report: 'The key issue is really what companies are going to do beyond mere compliance with the law' (cited in Perrin 1999). That perspective on CSR, however, assumes a baseline of compliance with the law that is in fact problematic. This is so not only because there is significant *non-compliance* with law in business practice, but also because of the routine use of *creative compliance*. Enron has demonstrated both. The whole point about creative compliance of course is that it can claim to be, in strict legal terms, compliance. But the question can be asked: should creative compliance be seen as satisfying CSR's assumed standard of compliance with the law? Is compliance with the letter of the law enough if it flagrantly thwarts the spirit of the law? Is it enough for companies proclaiming themselves to be *socially responsible* to comply in form but not in substance with the law?

Companies use creative compliance techniques in relation to all aspects of regulation, social and environmental as well as the more esoteric areas of corporate finance. But even in the strict context of law on financial reporting, there are significant issues for social responsibility. The market is part of society and, when Enron collapsed, it was not just shareholders who were affected, but employees at Enron, and, through pension funds, a multitude of employees elsewhere. Tax law, which Enron also circumvented on a grand scale and which is a routine target of corporate creative compliance, is a social issue. Indeed it is paradoxical that companies present it as good CSR practice to engage in charitable giving to hospitals, schools and universities,[11] but at the same time carefully avoid taxes, so reducing the public purse and making it less easy for government to make such public provision itself (except of course by turning to creative means which happen to reduce the liabilities on its own balance sheet, for example Private Finance Initiatives or PFIs).

And this is where the contemporary ideology of CSR and the movement behind it might just possibly be brought to bear in relation to the issues of financial reporting, corporate governance and creative compliance more generally raised in this chapter. The CSR movement is a topic in its own right with significant limitations and even dangers, but also with its own strengths (McBarnet 2004a). And given the limitations of law in relation to creative compliance it may be worth exploring the potential for a role for the extra-state forces of civil society and the market that are so often seen as the 'drivers' of the CSR movement.

NGOs, ethical investment funds, activist shareholders, the purse power of aware consumers, internet campaigns and the like currently put pressure on companies to commit, or be seen to commit, to a different way of doing things. These pressures tend currently to be focused on issues such as human rights and the environment, but they could as readily be brought to bear in calling for a different attitude to legal responsibility on the part of business. Corporate social responsibility is generally seen as encouraging companies to go beyond legal obligations to a wider social responsibility. But business might best demonstrate a new attitude of corporate social responsibility not so much by *surpassing* law's requirements, but by meeting those requirements in spirit at least. Expanding the agenda of Corporate Social Responsibility in this way could be one more means of putting pressure on business to enhance the quality of corporate compliance, supplementing the forces of law with the forces of market and moral pressure.[12]

Enron, ironically, could only help. A significant tool of the CSR movement has been publicity. One positive thing to come out of Enron is the massive publicity it has generated and the exposure to a wide public of what has normally been the esoteric world of corporate financial structuring and manipulation of the law. It matters little whether everyone understands the detail or not. The fact of both complex fraud and complex manipulation through 'perfectly legal' creative accounting has been brought out into the open. After Enron there is potential for more scrutiny, more active public distrust and more pressure on companies to clean up their acts. Enron could indeed be seen as priming the canvas for any campaign to make companies claiming to be *socially* responsible, *legally* responsible. By such means might the very flagrancy and scale of the Enron case prove, ironically, to have a positive legacy for corporate governance.

Notes

1. This chapter draws on research on 'Regulation, responsibility and the rule of law' funded by the ESRC under its Professorial Fellowship Scheme.

A version of this paper was presented at the CAPPE workshop on Auditing and Ethics, ANU, Canberra, and at the colloquium of the International Society of Business, Economics and Ethics, Melbourne, July 2004.

2. I will draw on this research, much of which was carried out with Chris Whelan, in this section and the next (see, e.g. McBarnet 1991b, 2003; McBarnet and Whelan 1991, 1997, 1999). Key parts of this body of work are also brought together in a recent volume of collected essays: McBarnet 2004b. The final two sections rely on new research being conducted under the ESRC professorial fellowship scheme.

3. Partnoy notes too that 'accounting subterfuge using derivatives is widespread' (Partnoy 2002: 5).

4. And the Sarbanes-Oxley Act has charged the SEC with producing a more principle-based regime (Sarbanes-Oxley Act 2002, s.108(d)).

5. There were various other terms for this kind of structure, e.g. a 'controlled non-subsidiary' or an 'orphan subsidiary'.

6. For example, in relation to tax avoidance in the UK, Germany and Australia.

7. For example, via 'in-substance defeasance'. See McBarnet and Whelan (1999), Chapter 11, Rosenblatt (1984), FASB (1996).

8. This also applies beyond the corporate arena to 'high net worth' or other 'well-advised' individuals.

9. To cite from interviews with senior lawyers, accountants and business executives.

10. This wider agenda is being explored in the ESRC research programme.

11. Enron was a significant donor to the University of Texas, for example.

12. Indeed, there are currently indications that tax avoidance at least, if not yet creative compliance more generally, is beginning to be recognised as a CSR issue in the business press. A recent special report on 'Responsible Business' in the *Financial Times* included an article headed 'The range of issues: tax avoidance is rising up the ethical agenda', citing the campaigning of the Tax Justice Network (*Financial Times*, 29 November 2004). Or again: 'Corporate Social Responsibility: The tax avoidance story as a morality tale' (*Financial Times*, 22 November 2004).

12

The Role of Lawyers: Hired Guns or Public Servants?

Jeremy P. Carver

Lawyers today are involved in every aspect of any financial transaction of significance. This is true to an extent far greater than a generation ago. No doubt the primary cause of this is the size and, in particular, the complexity of modern transactions. The risks involved in any transaction spanning several different countries and jurisdictions are inevitably greater. Today's financial markets are more sophisticated than those of yesterday. We are more 'risk-conscious' than we were: not least because the funds invested today incorporate the savings of many with little understanding of the markets, as opposed to the few who were quite knowledgeable as to what they were doing.

But does the greater involvement of lawyers in the negotiation and conclusion of transactions, and in the everyday workings of corporations, provide any guarantee that these dealings are more reliable? The answer is an equivocal 'perhaps'. For some, the participation of a first rate lawyer provides more than mere *comfort* that the risks involved have been analysed and covered. The experience of the lawyer ensures that past mistakes are avoided, and that the relevant laws and rules have been identified and applied or accommodated. But no lawyer can be better than the instructions he or she receives, or the information provided in order to enable him to do the work. And not all lawyers are good, or are selected on the basis of their established excellence. Economics and other factors will play a part in the selection.

Moreover, this book and the conference from which it originated are not addressing the situation of an ideal corporate client, well managed and perfectly compliant with all applicable laws and regulations. They are concentrating on the normal, mixed set of actors, conducting themselves in ordinary circumstances where corners can – and often are – cut in order to conclude the deal or launch the product. The issue I have to address is what is the role of the lawyer in that situation? Can he or she make a difference? Will his conduct affect the soundness of the transaction, the reliability of the investment?

The short and obvious answer is 'yes' – for better or worse. The lawyer's participation is not mere window-dressing, to enable the deal-maker to apply some 'kite mark' of quality assurance to the transaction. The lawyer is well paid, and presumably gives value. The long hours of negotiation and due diligence have a purpose; and they usually follow a period of research and creativity in acting as midwife to the deal within the competing dynamics of commercial realities and regulatory pitfalls. Thus, if we accept the significance of the lawyer's role, the way in which he performs that role will have an impact; and it is that on which this brief chapter concentrates.

I postulate four possible scenarios for today's financial law specialist, although these roles and the dilemmas inherent in them are common to most lawyers. The first role is as *hired gun*. This role draws its content from the cowboy of the classical Wild West. Hollywood's imagery produced many idealised heroes, played by James Stewart, Gary Cooper and the like. Hollywood and Sergio Leone's 'spaghetti westerns' also turned out cowboys of a more enigmatic character. But the essential element of the 'hired gun' was that he and his artillery were available for hire, and, when hired, did the job for which he was hired, however dangerous or dirty. The risk and effort involved were reflected in the price. If the price was right, the man would do what he had to do, i.e. what he was hired to do. He could be Shane – quintessentially noble and decent; or he could be Jesse James – a cool and ruthless killer; or a range of characters in between.

I do not want to overglamorise the role of lawyer as hired gun. Most will recognise the phenomenon, and will see that the defining characteristic is the relationship between lawyer and client. The lawyer recognises no master other than the one that has hired him; and that client's interests are – at least within the instructions given, and perhaps increasingly wider – paramount. The lawyer will fight for the sole best interests of the client, whether as negotiator, as advisor, or as gladiator in a dispute settlement forum.

There are many such lawyers. In practice at least, the majority of lawyers involved in financial law practice are seen often in such a light. It reflects the commercial reality of the relationship. Not only will a satisfied client pay more readily the fees earned on the transaction; but it is more likely to return for the next one, thus cementing an ever-closer relationship of mutual dependence. As the scale of collaboration increases, the importance of the client to the lawyer intrudes into other areas of that lawyer's practice. He must give priority to the most important client, i.e. the client who makes the largest contribution to gross fees and profit. Other clients must take their turn, even at the risk of them going elsewhere – thus increasing further the economic tie, potential subservience and risk of capture.

Such a lawyer will argue, with some force, that there is nothing in such a relationship that implicates the lawyer in a breach of ethics or legal rules. But there must be a valid question mark as to whether the lawyer can still act with the same degree of objectivity for a client who is less important for the lawyer. The factors that have created the relationship – the mutual knowledge and understanding of the respective skills – militate against objectivity. The lawyer becomes easily caught up in the commercial imperatives that drive the client, particularly when these feature in the economic relationship between them.

Let me take an example from a training scenario that we developed in Clifford Chance several years ago in conjunction with a leading international banking group with whom we had a long-standing relationship of considerable importance to both. We ran these schemes for our younger qualified associates, meeting under intense conditions with groups of bankers. They were put under the type of stress that arises on a frequent basis in real life. A scenario was provided in which a team of lawyers is advising a team of bankers, each with a specified role to play. A sequence of events unfolds: major financing is needed, the deal is assembled and negotiated with the customer, an offering has to be prepared, due diligence performed, different sets of market rules have to be identified and addressed. The deal is important, and difficult. It has been won after keen competition. The fee structure is such that the bank will be paid only if the offering succeeds. It involves an emerging market, so that extensive research must be conducted. Delays recur. More resources are poured in; but the progress is barely perceptible. A breakthrough is made; and it is now only days from closing. A new fact emerges, which, if disclosed, would be catastrophic for the deal. The banking team knows about it; so do the lawyers. The bankers are quite clear: they want to bury it. What do the lawyers do?

Painted thus, and as a hypothetical question, most would answer in one sense only. In the cut and thrust of realistic game play, the answers were interesting. We found that, often, under pressure from the client, lawyers did buckle. What was even more interesting was when we introduced two groups of lawyers into the scenario: one the same team of transaction lawyers, and the other a team of financial litigators. Invariably, the litigators took a firm and uncompromising stand: the new fact *had* to be disclosed irrespective of the consequences. This led almost inevitably to a situation in which the team of transaction lawyers fell out with the litigators. Indeed, it was clear that the non-trial lawyers would take the side and perspective of the bankers, to oppose the puritanical – and uncommercial – stand of the litigators, who were ridiculed as failing to appreciate the market and as being impractical and naive.

This useful training scenario provides a simple illustration of the differences between my first and second legal roles: the first is that of the hired gun. The second is that of *public servant*.

At first sight, the description of the lawyer in private practice as 'public servant' seems anomalous, even perverse. But it is not. On qualification, every lawyer finds himself designated as suddenly acquiring standing to address a court – sometimes even the highest court in the land. Deontological rules vary from country to country, and even between jurisdictions within a single state. But it is virtually inevitable that every set of rules regulating the legal profession will contain obligations governing the relationship between a lawyer and the court he may be called upon to address when representing a client. Among those rules there will be an obligation not to mislead the court. Some may impose a higher standard of candour, for example requiring the lawyer to present a full and frank reflection of the facts known to the lawyer and of the applicable law, even the parts favouring the other side's case. The reason for this is simple, at least in the English common law tradition: the system of justice depends on it. Unless a judge can be confident that counsel appearing before him has presented all the salient facts and all the relevant case law, he must conduct his own far more thorough investigation into the facts and law, with inevitable effects on delay. The adversarial system of legal process depends critically on the duty of counsel not to mislead the court. It is a cornerstone of the ability of the English Commercial Court to render speedy and predictable decisions to markets far beyond the United Kingdom.

The lawyer's duty to the court is *higher* than the duty he owes to his client. Of course, he must represent the interests of the client to the maximum extent; but this does not extend to doing or saying something that is untrue, nor – even more important – to failing to disclose something of which he is aware that is relevant for the case, but which damages the client's case. This comes back to the training scenario just described. It also helps to explain why the trial lawyers understood more clearly the obligation to disclose despite the damage that would be thereby done to the client's business interests.

The origins of this are found in some of the beginnings of the legal profession in England. The story of King Henry and Thomas a-Becket is well known. How Thomas, a close friend of the king, was made Archbishop of Canterbury, precipitating a bitter fight between the two, resolved only by Thomas's martyr's death. Tension between monarch and church grew worse, with the church retaining a full and active role in the legal process. Secular lawyers participated; but the king's plans were frustrated by the ability of the church to control any lawyer who failed to heed its political pressure. This continued until a brilliant advisor to the king persuaded him to establish the legal profession as self-disciplining. Thus, any lawyer that transgressed would be held to account by the profession as a whole, and could thereby be freed from the external control of the church – or indeed of any other third party, including the king.

The right to self-discipline is one of the most cherished attributes of the legal profession; and it is frequently cited as a cornerstone of a free and democratic community, where the law can be applied to all without fear of consequences. Much of this is, frankly, overblown. The right to self-discipline arose for very pragmatic and special circumstances of seven centuries ago that do not pertain today. Today, this – like all other inherited privileges – needs to be scrutinised more critically. Like other rights, the beneficiaries of those rights have commensurate duties. The right cannot be justified other than on the basis that it continues to be justly earned. In other words, it is essential that the legal profession insist upon, and enforce, the highest standards of ethical conduct. I would argue that this extends across the range of professional conduct: both in court and outside across the negotiating table or assembling a complex transaction.

This leads directly to my third role of the lawyer, namely **neither** hired gun, **nor** public servant. I mention this because the truth is that, today, there is much that a lawyer is often called upon to do that requires no professional skill whatsoever.

When I joined Clifford Chance (under its then name) in 1969, one of the senior partners of the time had a persistent habit of trying to drive home forcefully to the young lawyers that they must constantly guard against becoming *stationers*. This was not a joke; he meant it with great sincerity. He understood that lawyers of his time were even then under pressure to provide their clients with better and better-looking documents. 'Time' was frequently 'of the essence'. The lawyer's relationship with the printers (for a substantial offering) helped deliver this. The arrival of word processors widened the scope of the lawyer's role, without calling on his professional skills at all.

In similar vein, today's lawyer may do much to manage his client's interests without a legal qualification or background. He may be called on to create companies, and set up elaborate corporate vehicles to maximise the return for investors (for example, with Enron). It has nothing to do with lawyers save that a lawyer may be devising a complex tax structure and is familiar with working with company registrars and lawyers from other jurisdictions.

An even starker contrast with the lawyer's role and that of non-legal experts arises over that modern habit of regulating markets, namely the 'tick-box' form-filling that many find themselves committed to, in particular in the US markets. The accurate return on a particular questionnaire may well call for judgement; and that judgement might be based – in part – on legal experience. Nevertheless, it is frequently a very dull way of earning a living. Even more important is the fact that such form-filling seems to be a peculiarly futile manner of imparting information critical to the market's understanding of a transaction. Form-filling certainly occupies lawyers' time; but it seems to have played no role in prosecuting the major corporate actors whose cases are now being heard in the USA and elsewhere. Would Enron and WorldCom have survived if the host of lawyers involved had done a better job in ticking SEC forms? Of course not.

One corollary of the lawyer working as neither hired gun nor public servant is that he is probably working only for himself. Like a printer, his sole concern is to meet his own business expectations. Those may include the delivery of an excellent service and the need to keep his costs competitive in order to attract new business. Today's global law firms are very substantial business; and the demands of meeting billion dollar revenue expectations are sufficiently daunting to turn the heads of most private lawyers. But it becomes a fatal distraction. The work of being a good lawyer does not change its essential character in line with the number of noughts involved in the transaction. Thirty years ago, the lawyer who concentrated on delivering the best service to his client, irrespective of his own interests, found that he was properly remunerated by satisfied clients, almost as night follows day. The work may have become more demanding, and more competitive. 'Job satisfaction' may seem harder when there are no weekends and few hours' sleep. But the lawyer who turns to meeting his, rather than his client's, needs will quickly find that he has broken that link between work and proper remuneration.

So, what is the fourth and final characteristic of the modern commercial lawyer? What role is there for a lawyer who is just a hired gun, or just a public servant, or merely working for himself? The answer is that he can be all three. The lawyer cannot escape the commitments inherent in the lawyer–client relationship. It is a contractual one, placing mutual obligations and expectations on both. But the obligation to serve the interests of the client is not unqualified. It is conditioned by a set of public duties, including the duty not to misinform.

This specific duty has come into sharp contrast recently in the context of suspicious transactions. When money-laundering regulations were introduced, there were demands that certain professionals – specifically lawyers and accountants – should be excluded on the basis that they already owed duties that were tightly defined. The public duty a lawyer owes to the court was already in place alongside the duty of confidentiality owed to the client. Money-laundering regulations were inappropriate for such people. I and others in London argued against the restrictive view. This was in part because the logic of the alternative case was flawed; but mainly because there was a growing number of lawyers in the third category: not really working as lawyers, but using the skills and experience to assist clients to salt away ill-gotten proceeds of corruption or crime in discreet tax shelters. It was nearly 10 years ago that New York's Deputy District Attorney John Moscow pointed the finger at London as the single largest money-laundering centre in the world. The accusation was, and probably remains, true. In the largest financial marketplace, even a tiny percentage of laundered funds constitutes a significant total. It is no good being complacent, and accepting that such a small proportion of total funds is acceptable. One of the responsibilities of being the largest financial centre for many types of financial instruments is the heightened duty to police it in every way. It is a duty owed by every practitioner in that market, including the lawyers and accountants.

To their credit, the Law Society, representing solicitors of England and Wales, argued in the joint European body, the CCBE, that lawyers should not be exempted from having to report suspicious transactions. They were met with bitter opposition from almost all other bar associations, including the English Bar Council whose knowledge and understanding of the issues can be negligible because of the extent to which solicitors shield them from direct involvement in their client's financial affairs. The Law Society has made progress, supported by the European Commission, which has a decidedly less reverential attitude to lawyers and accountants than their own professional bodies.

Case studies can help to illuminate broad propositions; and I conclude with a specific, and true, account of a case which brought all these strands together in a marked way. The case took place in Singapore just over 20 years ago. It was startling – even shocking – for those involved.

Singapore was in the throes of its inexorable economic success: led as usual by its shrewd and determined government, with significant business opportunities for hard-nosed entrepreneurs. The handful of traditional leisure clubs to serve the increasingly prosperous local and foreign businessmen and their families had become very successful businesses in their own right, and there was a rush to meet demand by creating new clubs. A group of four businessmen found the right site and decided to rush it to market on the crest of this wave. They hired as a lawyer a leading partner in what was widely thought of as the best law firm in Singapore. Their idea was simple: after assembling the necessary ingredients, and while the premises were under construction, they wanted to invite 250 'founder members' to come in as lead investors, who would then make their return by selling membership of a running club at a presumed significant profit. Clubs are generally membership associations, which create their own rules; and the vital issue for these businessmen was whether the deal could be structured so that it was outside the scope of the public offering rules requiring onerous and time-consuming prospectus obligations. If it did, it saved both time and significant stamp duty.

So briefed, the lawyer went to see the Deputy Registrar of Companies and described to him the proposed transaction and why, in the lawyer's view, it was outside the prospectus rules. The Deputy

Registrar was impressed; but reluctant to give the green light on his own authority. He suggested that that the lawyer obtained a formal opinion from a London commercial QC (a frequent practice in Singapore). In due course, he returned to the Deputy Registrar with such an opinion, and the green light was given. The offering to the 250 founder members went ahead; and the authorities were concerned. It looked very much like a public offering for which the prospectus rules applied. They prosecuted the four directors, and added to the indictment their lawyer, one of Singapore's very best. A high profile trial was fixed, and five leading English QCs arrived to represent the defendants. Intense negotiations took place on the eve of the trial; and prosecution and defence arrived at plea bargains, which were announced to the judge as the trial commenced. The first four were accepted, and the agreed fines and punishments announced. But when it came to the lawyer's turn, the judge refused the agreed plea, and said that it was far too lenient. The astounded defence team had to face an immediate trial of their client alone. The facts, as they emerged publicly, were not good: the lawyer had sought a legal opinion in London; but it had been clear that the proposed transaction was caught by the rules. This was not what the clients wanted, so their lawyer had instructed a completely fresh QC, given distinctly less relevant information, who had come up with the 'clean' opinion. The 'bad' opinion was buried, and the other used to secure the Deputy Registrar's consent. Having seized the lawyer's files, all this had become evident, including the extent to which the lawyer and his clients had deliberately set out to evade the rules. The judge threw the book at the lawyer: with a hefty fine, a term of imprisonment and a recommendation for disciplinary proceedings by the Singapore Law Society. He was duly struck off.

The result was indeed shocking to all those practising as lawyers in Singapore at the time; but despite my own professional involvement in the case, it was impossible on an objective basis to fault the government in its ruthless determination to impress upon the profession and entire business community the need for higher standards of ethics and probity to maintain Singapore's success. Needless to say, it worked!

13

Financial Reporting, Corporate Governance and Parmalat: Was it a Financial Reporting Failure?

Giovanni Melis and Andrea Melis

Introduction[1]

The Parmalat group, a world leader in the dairy food business, collapsed and entered bankruptcy protection in December 2003 after acknowledging that billions of euros were missing from its accounts. Its collapse has been labelled as 'European Enron' and has led to a profound questioning of the soundness of accounting and financial reporting standards as well as of the Italian corporate governance system. The main purpose of this chapter is to attempt to understand why the financial reporting system and the corporate governance system failed in the Parmalat case.

Senior management (or, at least, part of it) and the controlling shareholder are clearly at fault in the Parmalat case. This prompts a series of questions. How was it possible? In particular, this chapter will attempt to provide an answer to the following questions: Was the corporate misreporting due to a gap in accounting standards? Was it only due to a failure of the gatekeepers?[2] Was it a financial reporting failure or were demand-side information agents such as financial analysts at fault too? Could or should a sophisticated external analyst have been suspicious of Parmalat's reported economic and financial results?

It has been argued (e.g. Rusconi 1986; Yin 1989; Hamel *et al.* 1993) that a case study needs to rely on a wide variety of sources of evidence in order to be successful. However, access to corporate data is difficult when the case study concerns a bankrupted company such as Parmalat in which prosecutors are still investigating and some of the key corporate actors are accused of fraud. Despite these obvious difficulties to access data, this case study relies on a good variety of sources, such as corporate financial statements (including board of statutory auditors' report, external auditors' report, etc.), corporate ownership and control data, corporate governance reports, board of directors' minutes, shareholders' annual meetings' minutes, corporate conference presentations to institutional investors, financial analysts' reports, reports of the public authority responsible for regulating and controlling the Italian securities markets and, last but not least, testimonies of key actors in front of Italian parliamentary committees.

This chapter is structured as follows. The first section examines the ownership and control structure at Parmalat, with special attention to the role of the Tanzi family as ultimate controlling shareholder. The second section discusses the role of accounting standards to understand to what extent the Parmalat scandal is also due to a failure of the generally accepted accounting principles. The third examines the role of information supply-side agents (i.e. internal governance agents and external auditors) to describe how the internal monitoring structure failed. The fourth section analyses the role of demand-side information agents, with a particular focus on financial analysts. The final section concludes.

Parmalat's Ownership and Control: The Role of the Tanzi Family

An analysis of the ownership and control structure of the Parmalat group shows a complex group of companies controlled by a strong blockholder (the Tanzi family) through a pyramidal device.[3] Despite ownership disclosure rules, the structure of the group is not easy to trace, especially at the international level outside the companies included in the consolidated financial statements.

Parmalat Finanziaria was first listed at the Milan stock exchange in 1990 and belonged to the MIB30[4] from 1994 until 1999 and again since January 2003 until its collapse. Its main shareholders (as per 30 June 2003) were represented by Coloniale SpA, which owned 50.02% of the company voting share capital,[5] and two institutional investors (see Figure 13.1).

Figure 13.2 shows a simplified structure of the Parmalat group, putting in evidence only the links that are most relevant to understand the case study. In fact, the whole group structure includes over 200 companies operating in approximately 50 countries worldwide.

Coloniale SpA, the holding company of the group, was under the control of the Tanzi family, through some Luxembourg-based unlisted companies. Therefore, the Tanzi family was the ultimate controlling shareholder of the Parmalat group.

Large shareholders have the incentive to exercise monitoring (Shleifer and Vishny 1986). Previous empirical studies of Italian listed companies (e.g. Bianchi *et al.* 1997; Molteni 1997; Melis 1999) confirm that the blockholder is a shareholder who is willing and able to monitor the senior management effectively. The presence of a blockholder reduces the agency problem between senior management and the controlling shareholder(s), but it creates a new one between the controlling shareholder(s) and minority shareholders (La Porta *et al.* 2000; Melis 2000). In fact, the controlling shareholder may wield its power to pursue its interests even at the expenses of the minority shareholders.

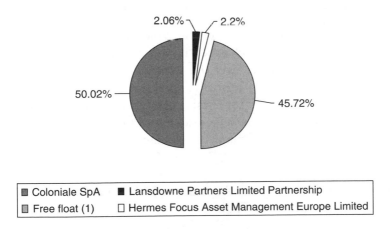

Figure 13.1   Parmalat Finanziaria's ownership structure

Source: Elaborated with data based on CONSOB database updated at 30 June 2003. (1) Free float includes all shareholdings with less than 2% of the voting capital at the end of June 2003.

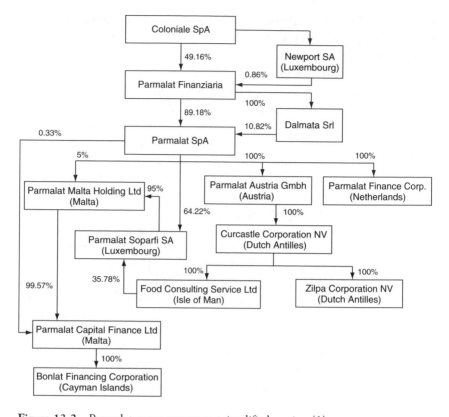

Figure 13.2   Parmalat group structure: a simplified version (1)

(1) All companies are based in Italy, unless a different country is expressly mentioned.

Tanzi, the founder of the company, acting as controlling share-holder, chairman and chief executive officer, was both willing and able to exercise his power over the whole Parmalat corporate group. He is accused of having funnelled billions of euros to companies privately owned by the Tanzi family. His role is clearly central to the scandal; however it cannot be considered in isolation when analysing the fundamental causes of the Parmalat case.

Fundamental Causes of the Accounting Debacle at Parmalat: Were Accounting Standards at Fault?

The first question that the Parmalat case raises is whether senior management used various accounting tricks to avoid disclosing relevant losses or the financial misreporting was simply due to false accounting. If it were the first, senior managers would have exploited gaps in generally accepted accounting standards in order to manage corporate earnings, assets and liabilities. There is an important caveat, however. The use of generally accepted accounting principles cannot eliminate one basic limitation of the financial reporting system: the possibility of different accounting treatments being applied to essentially the same facts. There is still room for flexibility (and consequent subjectivity) when differences of opinion (which may or may not derive from diversity of interests) about a certain phenomenon lead to significant variations in reported economic and financial results. Thus, different results may be reported, each formally (but not substantially) complying with the overriding requirement to show a true and fair view of the company as a going concern. Such flexibility gives rise to the so-called 'creative accounting' phenomenon (e.g. Griffiths 1986; Naser 1993; McBarnet this volume).

The introduction into the equation of more detailed, less flexible generally accepted accounting principles is not able to eliminate this discretion, because the valuation process of corporate activities (e.g. the period of depreciation of an asset) is intrinsically subjective (Melis 1995). This arises from an inherent contradiction between the going concern and the periodicity principles: the former assumes the operations to be a continuous flow, while the latter requires a break of flow into comparable time segments. It is then essentially the 'spirit' of the assessment that characterises the choice between different alternatives. When the choice is made not to pursue the spirit of the 'true and fair view' overriding accounting principle, financial statements tend to present a corporate image which is functional to the interest of the most powerful stakeholder, and this is likely to happen at the expense of the weaker stakeholders.

Although it cannot eliminate discretion, the institution of specific accounting rules for specific transactions does lead to more uniform reporting of the covered transactions. Nevertheless, as Weil (2002) points out with regard to Andersen's treatment of Enron's accounts, uniformity has a cost: the so-called 'show me where it says I can't' problem, i.e. aggressive corporate management's claim that if an accounting standard does not prohibit something, then it is to be considered as allowed.

Mechanical and inflexible accounting standards increase the external auditor's dependence on specific rules (and eventually weaken its position). More seriously, they create a dynamic that provides incentives to financial engineering specifically designed to get around these rules (Palepu and Healy 2003). As a result, the Financial Accounting Standards Board itself has proposed changes designed to create a more 'principles-based' approach to standard setting (FASB 2002).

If this might have been the case for Enron, it was not for Parmalat. The latter adopted Italian accounting standards (CNDC-CNRC 2002) and, in order to fill the gaps of the former, international financial reporting standards (IASB 2003) in its financial statements. The former and, especially, the latter are considered more 'principles-based' accounting standards, i.e. broadly applicable accounting rules that derive from basic accounting principles, in comparison to US GAAP, relatively more detailed accounting standards.

The problem becomes one of enforcing generally accepted accounting principles in the face of determined opposition from a dominant corporate insider that has the incentive to make the financial reporting system pursue his/her own interests, rather than pursuing the overriding 'true and fair view' goal. The presence of a dominant stakeholder has been found to be associated with poor disclosure (Forker 1992) and an overall inadequate quality of corporate communication.[6] It is a task of a sound corporate governance system to solve this problem, improving the quality of the information provided by the financial reporting system by making corporate insiders accountable (Melis 2004a).

In the Enron case, not only did senior management take advantage of US accounting standards' limitations to manage its earnings and balance sheet (Palepu and Healy 2003), but also its financial statements did not conform to existing US GAAP (Catanach and Rhoades, 2003). This does differentiate the Parmalat case from its American counterpart. Few accounting issues were found at Parmalat. There is little evidence that Parmalat's financial statements violated the letter of the adopted accounting standards, although they clearly violated the overall 'spirit', since the overriding 'true and fair view' objective was not pursued.

The major issue within Parmalat was the falsification of accounts, rather than an exploitation of a gap in the accounting standards that allowed it to conceal the 'true' corporate financial results. The Enron case was about sophisticated earnings management (Palepu and Healy 2003). Parmalat does not involve complex accounting techniques, rather senior management (or part of it) simply falsified company accounts to manage earnings, assets and liabilities that could not be managed otherwise. Parmalat's former chief finance officer (CFO) acknowledged that systematic falsification dated back over 15 years. The question that immediately springs to mind is how was it possible for each conduct to remain undetected for so long? Where were the monitors?

The Failure of the Gatekeepers: Where were the Monitors?

As with Enron (see Coffee 2002), the Parmalat case demonstrates a clear case of gatekeeper failure. Within the Parmalat group the most important reputational intermediaries that acted as gatekeepers were the board of statutory auditors, the external auditing firm, and the internal control committee. In the next sections their respective roles will be examined and discussed.

Role of the Board of Statutory Auditors

Until 2003, Italian law required listed (and unlisted) companies to set up a board of statutory auditors.[7] Its main duties and responsibilities included (Draghi reform 1998, Art. 149): (a) to check that the actions and decisions of the board of directors are in compliance with the law, specific corporate by-laws germane to the corporation and that the executive management and board were in observance of the so-called 'principles of correct administration'; (b) to review the adequacy of the corporate organisational structure, including the internal control system, the administrative and accounting system as well as ensuring the reliability of the latter in correctly representing any company transactions; (c) to ensure that the instructions given by the company to its subsidiaries concerning the provision of all corporate information necessary to comply with the disclosure requirements established by the law are adequate.

Among other requirements, corporate by-laws are required to provide the number of auditors (not less than three) and ensure that one statutory auditor (or two, when the board is composed of more than three auditors) is appointed by the minority shareholders (Draghi reform 1998, Art. 148).

Parmalat Finanziaria's board of statutory auditors met the legal minimum requirement. This is rather common among Italian listed companies: approximately 92% of the boards of statutory auditors are composed of three members (CONSOB 2002). Even among the largest companies listed in the MIB30, only approximately 31% have set up a larger board of statutory auditors (see Figure 13.3).

The size of the board of statutory auditors has a direct influence over the level of protection on minority shareholders because some powers (e.g. to seek the cooperation of the company's employees in performing its tasks or the right to convene a shareholders' meeting to discuss contested directorial decision-making) may only be exercised if at least two statutory auditors agree.[8] As already noted, minority shareholders are only given the right to appoint two auditors when the board of statutory auditors exceeds three members.

Previous research (e.g. Melis 2004b) highlights that in a corporate governance system characterised by the presence of an active controlling shareholder, like the Tanzi family at Parmalat, the board of statutory auditors serves primarily as a legitimating device, rather than a substantive monitoring mechanism. Its inefficiency as a monitor has been attributed both to its inability to effectively access information related to shareholders' activities, as well as to its lack of independence from the controlling shareholder. Empirical evidence from the Parmalat case seems to confirm the failure of the board of statutory auditors as an effective gatekeeper. There is no record of the Parmalat Finanziaria board of statutory auditors highlighting any concerns in public

69%

31%

☑ Board of statutory auditors composed of five members
☐ Board of statutory auditors composed of three members

Figure 13.3 Size of the board of statutory directors among Italian MIB30 listed companies (1)

Source: Elaborated with data based on CONSOB database. Data updated at December 2003.
(1) One company listed on MIB30 has not set up a board of statutory auditors. Being based in the Netherlands it has chosen a two-tier board structure, with a supervisory council.

documents nor in disclosures to either the courts or to CONSOB[9] (Cardia 2004). Its capability as an effective controlling force is further underscored by the fact that in December 2002 it was called by an institutional investor (which owned approximately 2% of the company shares) to investigate related party transactions between Parmalat Finanziaria and a Tanzi owned company that operated in the tourism sector (HIT SpA). Its answer was that no irregularity, either de facto or de jure, was found.

Role of the External Auditors

Grant Thornton SpA served as auditors for Parmalat Finanziaria from 1990 to 1998. However, Pecca and Bianchi, respectively President of Grant Thornton in Italy and senior partner, had a long association with Parmalat. Both were involved with auditing Parmalat in the 1980s as auditors of Hodgson Landau Brands.

Due to the mandatory auditor rotation,[10] Grant Thornton was taken over by Deloitte & Touche SpA as chief auditors in 1999. However, Parmalat found a loophole in the law that allowed its favoured advisors to remain as a 'subcontractor'. Contrary to the spirit of the law (see McBarnet this volume) they continued as auditors of Parmalat SpA as well as some offshore subsidiaries. Of particular importance here is that in this subcontracting role, Grant Thornton, through Pecca and Bianchi, audited the Cayman Islands-based Bonlat Financing Corporation, which held the now well-known fictitious Bank of America account.

This non-existent bank account raises key issues concerning the role of the external auditor. It seems reasonable to argue that Grant Thornton auditors could have discovered the fraud if they had acted in accordance with general auditing standards and exhibited the proper degree of professional 'scepticism' in executing standard audit procedures.

Even if the letter that confirmed that the Bank of America account existed was forged (and we now know it was), auditors are still at fault: cash deposits are not complicated to evaluate as they can be easily matched to a bank statement as part of a company's reconciliation procedures. The aim of such procedure is to ensure that bank statements received directly by the client and used in the reconciliation process have not been altered. Prosecutors pointed out that instead of getting in contact with Bank of America directly, the auditors relied on Parmalat's mail system. The breach of fiduciary duty included allegations of sins of commission as well as omission. According to evidence provided to Italian prosecutors by the former CFO of Parmalat (Tonna), it was the Grant Thornton auditors who proposed the idea of the setting up of Bonlat Financing Corporation. This had the effect of ensuring that the true extent of the crisis facing the group was effectively concealed from the incoming chief auditor, Deloitte & Touche.

In the Enron case, as Palepu and Healy (2003) point out, the auditing firm (Arthur Andersen) first failed to exercise sound business judgement in reviewing transactions that were only designed for financial reporting engineering rather than for business purpose, then 'succumbed' to pressures from Enron's management (see Walker, O'Brien and McBarnet, this volume). Likewise in the Parmalat scandal, Grant Thornton auditors were either grossly incompetent or (more likely) not 'independent' from their client.

The mandatory auditor rotation provision in Italian law proved ineffective. In part this can be blamed on the deception involving the establishment of the offshore subsidiaries. But given the wider systemic problems within the organisation, it is difficult to reconcile the fact that it took Deloitte & Touche four years from its first appointment to announce in the interim review of the financial accounts that it could not verify the carrying value in one of Parmalat's chief investments, the Epicurum Fund. Cardia (2004) notes that the decision to publicly question Parmalat originated not within Deloitte & Touche but emerged as a direct consequence of CONSOB's pressure on the auditor. More alarmingly, it appears that Deloitte & Touche had failed to alert the CONSOB privately of any underlying problem in the corporate health of its client.

In their reports Deloitte & Touche auditors only underlined that up to 49% of total assets of the group and 30% of the consolidated revenues came from subsidiaries, which were audited by other auditors. It was stated that their opinion concerning those assets and revenues was basely solely upon other auditors' reports. That is to say that Deloitte & Touche had been relying on Grant Thornton's work to give their opinion about Parmalat Finanziaria consolidated financial statements. Apart from the role of a single external auditor, a more general policy question arises from the Parmalat case: what is the point of setting up a mandatory rotation of the chief auditor if the latter may rely on the report of an auditor that has, through the exploitation of loopholes, not been forced to rotate?

Role of the Internal Control Committee

Parmalat Finanziaria set up an internal control committee in 2001 in order to comply with the Italian code of corporate governance best practice. The Preda Code (1999, 2002, para. 10.2) recommends that such a committee serve four interrelated functions. They should assess the adequacy of the internal control system, monitor the work of the corporate internal auditing staff, report to the board of directors on its activity at least every six months, and hold separate discussions with the external auditing firm. While the committee is appointed by the board, under the terms of Italian code of best practice it should be composed of non-executive directors in order to ensure both autonomy and independence. The Preda Code (2002, para. 10.1) further recommends that the majority of the members should be independent directors.[11]

The role of the audit committee is central to effective control systems (see McDonough and Walker this volume). In many of the US companies involved in financial reporting fraud, the audit committee was either non-existent or dysfunctional (COSO 1999). Moreover most audit committees did not appear to be composed of members literate in financial and accounting matters. A recent survey of UK audit committees' chairmen (Windram and Song 2004) reports that independence is ranked as the most important attribute of an audit committee member, even above director's financial literacy. The Preda Code (1999, 2002, para. 3.2) also acknowledges that when a company is controlled by a group of shareholders, the need for some directors to be independent from the controlling shareholders is crucial. Audit committee meeting frequency and director financial literacy were not a problem in the Parmalat case: the majority of the members of the internal control committee had an accounting background and the committee used to meet bimonthly. The problem was its independence, or rather the lack of it.

At Parmalat Finanziaria, the internal control committee was composed of three members, two of whom were also members of the executive committee. The only non-executive member of the internal control committee was the chairman, who was allegedly an independent director. However, further investigation (based on data which was publicly available, but not provided by the company) reveals that the alleged independent director (Silingardi) was in fact the Tanzi family's chartered public accountant. It seems reasonable to believe that his relationship with the controlling shareholder represented a clear and material conflict of interest capable of undermining his capacity to exercise autonomous judgement.

The independence of the committee was further weakened by the fact that one of its other members was the CFO, who had held the position from 1987 until March 2003. To complicate matters Tonna also held the position of chairman at Coloniale SpA, the Tanzi family holding company which was also the major shareholder of Parmalat Finanziaria. None of the members of the internal control committee could have been considered as truly independent. By allowing its CFO to sit on the committee, Parmalat was breaking best practice guidelines which implies that the corporation saw its function as 'self-monitoring' practice. It also raises the question, explored in detail by Hodson in this volume, of the organisational difficulties involved in combating deliberate fraud perpetrated by senior management.

Parmalat: The Role of Financial Analysts

One might argue that if financial statements are falsified as occurred in the Parmalat case, external financial analysts cannot be held accountable. Because of the information asymmetry that exists between corporate insiders and outsiders, they have to rely on the honesty and integrity of the internal governance agents. The case clearly demonstrates that the process of financial statement analysis is intrinsically flawed in the Parmalat case. But is that the limit of responsibility? Were there any signals that a sophisticated investor or financial analyst could (or should) have noticed? Did financial analysts actually report any concerns prior to the catastrophic collapse of the group? And if not, should they have?

Financial analysts received considerable criticism for failing to provide an earlier warning of problems at Enron and other major corporations in the United States (see O'Brien this volume). Palepu and Healy (2003) report that just eight weeks before the fall of Enron, the mean rating for its stock was 1.9 in a five point scale, which translates into a 'buy'.[12] Even after the accounting problems had been announced, reputable institutions continued to issue 'strong buy' or 'buy' recommendations for Enron. In the next section we investigate the role played by the financial analysts in the Parmalat case.

Role of Financial Analysts: Empirical Evidence

What happened was not very different. Financial analysts did not detect any of the structural deficiencies within Parmalat until the very penultimate moment (see Table 13.1).

The London office of Merrill Lynch was the first to alert the market publicly in its 5 December 2002 research report (Merrill Lynch 2002), in which Parmalat was downgraded to a 'sell' rating and the volatility risk was raised from 'medium' to 'high'. The rationale governing the decision can be traced back to the following concerns: (a) the rising cost of capital; (b) 'inefficient balance sheet management'; (c) Parmalat's 'regular tapping of the debt market', and related questions about the underlying cash generation capabilities of the group. Merrill Lynch issued seven further public reports reinforcing its 'sell' recommendation. This was an outlier. The rest of the financial community seems either

Table 13.1 Financial analysts' recommendations for Parmalat Finanziaria SpA

Period	Buy(%)	Hold(%)	Sell(%)	Non-rated (%)	Mean
November 2002–December 2003	53	30	11	6	2.1
November 2002–December 2003 (1)	59	33	2	6	1.8
November 2002–November 2003	57	31	11	1	2.1
November 2002–November 2003 (1)	63	35	1	1	1.8
November 2002–October 2003 (1)	69	31	0	0	1.6
November 2003–December 2003	30	37	15	18	2.6
17 November–December 2003	30	30	15	25	2.6

Source: Elaborated with data available at Borsaitalia Stock Exchange. 'Buy' includes 'strong buy', 'buy', 'accumulate', 'add' and 'outperform' recommendations; 'Hold' includes 'hold', 'neutral' and 'market perform' recommendations; 'Sell' includes 'sell' and 'reduce' recommendations. The sum of the three recommendations does not equal to 100% because of the presence of 'non-rated' reports. Mean is calculated taking 'strong buy' into account as 1, 'Hold' as 3 and 'Sell' as 5. (1) These values exclude the 'sell' recommendation reports by Merrill Lynch.

to have not been aware of what was going on at Parmalat or, if it did, to have failed to disclose any concern.

If we exclude Merrill Lynch's reports from the sample, in the period from November 2002 (one year before the crisis) to October 2003 (two months before the company collapsed), the mean analyst recommendation listed for Parmalat Finanziaria was 1.6 out of 5, with no 'sell' recommendations (see Table 13.1).

The next to break this herd mentality, Caboto IntesaBCI, issued a public report on 17 November 2003 with a 'sell' recommendation. Three days later, Mediobanca Research Industry (2003) issued a 'non-rated' report claiming not to have the adequate information required to make a reliable valuation. This, it claimed, was the result of Parmalat's 'opaque' financial structure and concern over core business profitability. Even after the announcement that Parmalat had failed to liquidate its stake in the offshore Epicurum fund, a reputable institution such as Citigroup issued a 'buy' (medium risk) recommendation for Parmalat Finanziaria. This was just two weeks before the company filed for bankruptcy. How was it possible?

The Treadway Commission (1987) underlined three primary criteria for assessing the risk of fraudulent financial reporting: oversight issues, performance pressures and changing structural conditions. Catanach and Rhoades (2003) assert that the Enron case met all the three above-mentioned criteria. Parmalat showed troubling symptoms in, at least, two of the above-mentioned criteria: oversight issues and performance pressures.

With respect to the former, Parmalat employed complex ownership and financial structures to execute its business strategy which set hurdles for analysts (and auditors) to effectively monitor its operations. With regard to the latter, while in the Enron case performance pressures derived from relevant contractual incentives (e.g. debt and stock options) that put pressures on senior management to sustain and improve operating performance (Catanach and Rhoades 2003), at Parmalat performance pressures were due to the very high level of debts that characterised its financial structure which, without a reported 'rosy' performance, would have led to insurmountable costs in the raising of capital and curtailed the controlling shareholder's interest in empire building.

It could be argued that qualitative factors such as those proposed by the Treadway Commission may be difficult to apply in single cases. In such cases, qualitative arguments need to be supplemented by analysis based on quantitative data. Therefore, we use the data in the public domain about the Parmalat group and its own company statements (that have since been shown to be misleading), to assess the extent to which a sophisticated financial analyst could (or should) have been suspicious of Parmalat's reported financial results and the business model that underpinned them.

Parmalat's Consolidated Financial Statements Analysis

When financial statements are falsified as in the Parmalat case, traditional analysis techniques are intrinsically flawed. Calculating financial ratios on false accounting numbers may not make great sense. Parmalat's numbers were forged adequately to ensure the reporting of a 'rosy' picture. Taking this significant limitation into account, the analysis of Parmalat Finanziaria's consolidated financial statements is still of some interest. It shows that a sophisticated financial analyst could have had some doubts about Parmalat's performance. Some evidence was found with regard to: (a) the nature of the business; (b) the liquidity management profitability; (c) the nature of the reported liquidity.

The first doubt is self-evident. As late as April 2003, during a conference with investors and financial analysts, Parmalat's senior management clearly stated that 'Parmalat is a food group with a focus on milk, dairy products and beverages' (Parmalat Finanziaria 2003). Financial statements analysis shows that in the period from 1998 to 2002 cash, equivalents and other short-term securities represented approximately over 25% of total assets. In 2002 these flows represented 32.7% of business activity (see Table 13.2).

Was Parmalat still a food group or had it turned into a financial group? Empirical evidence seems to suggest the latter. There would have been nothing wrong if Parmalat had changed its core business, but minority shareholders should have been informed about the size and nature of the risk undertaken by the firm. Financial analysts should have clearly stated in their reports that the growing dominance of securities trading necessitated a change in risk assessment since the analysis of a food company differs significantly from that of a financial company – but very few of them did.

Table 13.2 Elaborated with data based on Parmalat Finanziaria consolidated financial statements (amounts expressed in million of euros)

	Balance Sheet									
	1998	%	1999	%	2000	%	2001	%	2002	%
Non-current assets										
Intangible assets	1414.8	19.3	2205.3	23.4	2394.1	23.6	2376.8	22.6	2163.0	21.0
Property, plant and equipment	1944.9	26.6	2202.4	23.4	2269.0	22.3	2243.1	21.3	1817.5	17.7
Long-term financial assets	249.0	3.4	385.2	4.1	522.2	5.1	508.4	4.8	723.4	7.0
	3608.7	49.3	4792.9	50.9	5185.3	51.0	5128.3	48.7	4703.9	45.8
Current assets										
Inventories	506.2	6.9	566.9	6.0	587.0	5.8	719.1	6.8	547.9	5.3
Receivables and prepayments	1370.3	18.7	1791.0	19.0	1689.2	16.6	1768.1	16.8	1666.4	16.2
Other securities	708.5	9.7	937.2	10.0	782.2	7.7	1459.7	13.8	2412.9	23.5
Cash on hand and at banks	1131.0	15.4	1326.0	14,1	1920.4	18.9	1464.8	13.9	950.6	9.2
	3716.0	50.7	4621.1	49.1	4978.8	49.0	5411.7	51.3	5577.8	54.2
Total assets	7324.8	100	9414.0	100	10 164.1	100	10 540.0	100	10 281.7	100
Equity and reserves										
Attributable to the group	1276.9	17.4	1551.6	16.5	1714.4	16.9	1873.8	17.8	1541.0	15.0
Attributable to minority interests	694.6	9.5	936.0	9.9	928.9	9.1	961.3	9.1	708.6	6.9
	1971.5	26.9	2487.6	26.4	2643.3	26.0	2835.1	26.9	2249.6	21.9
Non-current liabilities										
Provision for risks and charges	43.7	0.6	277.0	2.9	326.8	3.2	418.8	4.0	410.5	4.0
Retirement benefit obligations	43.8	0.6	67.7	0.7	68.0	0.7	68.9	0.7	66.8	0.6
Borrowings	2915.3	39.8	3873.2	41.1	4448.8	43.8	4389.8	41.6	4538.3	44.1
Current liabilities										
Trade payables	729.0	10.0	986.7	10.5	1085.8	10.7	1259.4	11.9	1113.9	10.8
Borrowings	1209.1	16.5	1154.6	12.3	1075.9	10.6	985.2	9.3	1287.2	12.5

	1998	%	1999	%	2000	%	2001	%	2002	%
Other payables	412.2	5.6	567.2	6.0	515.4	5.1	582.8	5.5	615.4	6.0
	2350.4	32.1	2708.5	28.8	2677.1	26.3	2827.4	26.8	3016.5	29.3
Total equity and liabilities	7324.8	100	9414.0	100	10 164.0	100	10 540.0	100	10 281.7	100

Profit and Loss

	1998	%	1999	%	2000	%	2001	%	2002	%
Operating income										
Sales	5078.1	100	6357.4	100	7349.3	100	7801.6	100	7590.0	100
Other operating income	85.0	1.7	69.3	1.1	85.7	1.2	106.5	1.4	113.3	1.5
Total	5163.1	101.7	6426.7	101.1	7435.0	101.2	7908.1	101.4	7703.3	101.5
Operating expenses										
Cost of sales	2874.2	56.6	3534.5	55.6	4020.7	54.7	4434.3	56.8	4255.8	56.1
Services, leases and rentals	1066.9	21.0	1311.0	20.6	1534.6	20.9	1538.0	19.7	1600.1	21.1
Personnel	624.5	12.3	776.4	12.2	914.8	12.4	932.6	12.0	864.0	11.4
Other operating expenses	49.5		53.6		55.9		49.7		55.5	
Capitalised costs and expenses	−14.7		−13.1		−9.1		−30.9		−37.1	
Depreciation and amortisation	211.1	4.2	319.5	5.0	390.9	5.3	405.7	5.2	375.8	5.0
Total	4811.5		5981.9		6907.8		7329.4		7114.1	
Operating profit	351.6	6.9	444.8	7.0	527.2	7.2	578.7	7.4	589.2	
Financial incomes	173.9	3.4	212.3		235.1		250.7		245.4	
Finance costs	−274.8	−5.4	−308.1	−4.8	−348.4	−4.7	−373.1	−4.8	−402.7	−5.3
Extraordinary items	21.8	0.4	−17.1	−0.3	−35.2	−0.5	−42.2	−0.5	−58.5	−0.8
Income tax	−106.1	−2.1	−135.9	−2.1	−143.4	−2.0	−152.1	−1.9	−104.1	−1.4
Group profit	166.4	3.3	196.0	3.1	235.3	3.2	262.0	3.4	269.3	3.5
Minority interest	31.1	0.6	22.2	0.3	40.6	0.6	43.6	0.6	17.3	0.2
Net profit	135.3	2.7	173.8	2.7	194.7	2.6	218.4	2.8	252.0	3.3

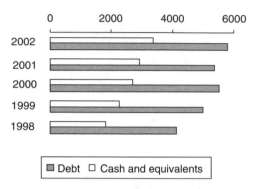

Figure 13.4 Progression of Parmalat Finanziaria's total debt and cash and equivalents
Source: Elaborated with data based on Parmalat Finanziaria consolidated financial statements, period 1998–2002. Amounts expressed in millions of euros.

The second doubt concerns the volume of Parmalat's liquidity. Parmalat continued to tap the market for relatively small (yet rather complex) debt issues, while its liquidity continued to rise. In fact, although Parmalat's net debt position improved since 1999, this was not due to debt repayments, rather to the rising amount of cash and equivalents (see Figure 13.4).

We now know that in fact such liquidity did not exist. But if we assume that financial statements were true and fair as financial analysts did, a critical question was not posed in the reports. Why did Parmalat not use its liquidity to pay off its debts?

Parmalat senior management first claimed that the financial structure served tax considerations: the income on cash and equivalents (based in 'offshore' countries) was not liable to tax, while the debt interests were tax deductible. Then they admitted a 'slight opportunity cost' of 0.15% for 'financial flexibility' (Parmalat Finanziaria 2003). Even taking all the reported liquidity as minimising the risk of default, the considerations used by Parmalat's senior management to explain the choice of having such a high total cash and total debt position could have been questioned more thoroughly. Although in theory maintaining a high level of cash might be fiscally profitable, the relatively small amount of the reported interest earned does not seem to justify such an aggressive financial structure. Moreover, an analysis of the reported interests earned/paid on the respective cash and debt balances would have shown that such financial structure could have hardly been profitable. The group claimed to invest in, at least, A rated investments, while its Standard and Poors' credit rate was BBB–. A more in-depth analysis seems to confirm this argument (see Table 13.3).

Table 13.3 Reconciliation of Parmalat Finanziaria's interest paid and received

Long-term financial assets	2000	2001	2002
Income on long-term receivables	38.9	29.9	32.8
Year-end balance	381.6	379.7	409.4
Implied interest rate	*10.2%*	*7.9%*	*8.0%*
Income from Non-current investments	3.1	3.0	3.8
Year-end balance	38.4	44.3	210.1
Implied interest rate	*8.1%*	*6.8%*	*1.8%*
Income from long-term financial assets**	2.1	5.3	3.4
Year-end balance	102.3	84.3	103.8
Implied interest rate	*2.1%*	*6.3%*	*3.3%*
Current financial assets			
Income from current investments	44.9	52.8	66.7
Year-end balance	782.2	1459.7	2412.9
Implied interest rate	*5.7%*	*3.6%*	*2.8%*
Other financial income (cash)	108.8	70.3	84.8
Year-end balance	1920.5	1464.8	950.6
Implied interest rate	*5.7%*	*4.8%*	*8.9%*
Total financial income	197.8	161.3	191.5
Currency gains	37.5	89.4	53.9
**Income from associates and subsidiaries	−2.1	−5.3	−3.4
Total	233.2	245.4	242.0
Total financial assets	3225.0	3432.8	4086.8
Investments in associates and subsidiaries	−102.3	−84.3	−103.8
Total	3122.7	3348.5	3983.0
Implied interest rate	*7.5%*	*7.3%*	*6.1%*
Financial liabilities	**2000**	**2001**	**2002**
Interest expenses on bond	36.4	46.9	55.7
Year-end balance	642.7	992.7	1545.9
Implied interest rate	*5.7%*	*4.7%*	*3.6%*
Interest relating to associates	2.2	3.8	4.4
Year-end balance	29.4	51.8	31.6
Implied interest rate	*7.5%*	*7.3%*	*13.9%*
Interest expenses on other debt	247.0	247.5	246.5
Year-end balance	4369.7	3932.4	3889.9
Implied interest rate	*5.7%*	*6.3%*	*6.3%*
Total financial charges	285.6	298.2	306.6
Currency losses	62.8	74.8	96.0

Table 13.3   (Continued)

Interest relating to associates	−2.2	−3.8	−4.4
Total	346.2	369.2	398.2
Total financial liabilities	5684.5	5969.6	7013.3
Liabilities relating to associates	−29.4	−51.8	−31.6
Total	5665.1	5917.8	6981.7
Implied interest rate	6.1%	6.2%	5.7%

Source: Elaborated with data based on Parmalat Finanziaria consolidated financial statements 2000–2002 according to the methodology used by Merril Lynch (2002). Amounts expressed in millions of euros.

The nature of the reported liquidity should also have raised some doubts. Parmalat senior management argued that their choice to have such a financial structure represented efficient liquidity management. Operating in what it termed a 'difficult market environment', Parmalat promised to use its liquidity to reduce its debt position by approximately €900 million within 2005. Such an amount represented approximately 25% of the overall reported liquidity. When taken together with a basically unchanged net debt position, this promise could have made financial analysts deduce that despite having over three billion of reported liquidity, only approximately 25% was, in fact, liquid and available in a short time. Therefore, the remaining 75% should have been included in the non-current assets, thus increasing significantly Parmalat's net debts' position.

Conclusions

Given its scope and limited length, this chapter has not analysed some potentially important aspects of the case. Further research about the Parmalat case could address issues related to the role of the banks, which as lenders had a relevant stake in the Parmalat group, as well as CONSOB, whose supervisory role has been questioned by the media. Nevertheless, some important conclusions emerge.

The role of the controlling shareholder is clearly central to the Parmalat scandal; however, it cannot be considered in isolation in analysing the fundamental causes of the Parmalat case. This chapter has attempted to understand why the financial reporting system and the corporate governance system failed in the Parmalat case. First, the role of accounting standards has been briefly discussed to understand to what extent the Parmalat scandal was due to a failure of Italian generally accepted accounting principles. While financial misreporting is probably the most evident issue, it was due to false accounting, rather than to the use of creative accounting techniques.

This chapter has examined the role of the information supply agents (board of statutory auditors, internal control committee, senior management and external auditing firm) in the Parmalat case. The role of the controlling shareholder and the failure of the gatekeepers seem to explain at least the Parmalat story.

Failures in the supply of information, attributable to the external auditors, the internal control committee and the board of statutory auditors, are important, but they too should not be considered in isolation. On the demand side of information, financial analysts seem to have not detected Parmalat's collapse until the penultimate moment. However, using company data publicly available at that time, we argued that some evidence existed that might have led a sophisticated analyst to have some doubts on Parmalat's reported performance. The Parmalat case, therefore, demonstrates that the failures that allowed it to happen were systemic and rooted in a deeply flawed corporate governance regime, both in Italy and in the governance of the international financial markets in which it operated.

Notes

1. This paper is the result of a joint effort of the two authors. In particular, Giovanni Melis wrote the section 'Parmalat's consolidated financial statements,' while Andrea Melis wrote the other sections.
2. Gatekeepers have been defined as reputational intermediaries who provide verification and certification services to investors (Coffee 2002). For an in-depth, more theoretical definition see the work of Kraakman (1986).
3. Pyramidal groups are widespread in Italy, and have been defined as 'organisations where legally independent firms are controlled by the same entrepreneur (the head of the group) through a chain of ownership relations' (Bianco and Casavola 1999, 1059). For an in-depth analysis of how such groups work in Italy see Onida (1968) and Saraceno (1972).

4. MIB30 is the Italian equity share market segment that includes companies with a capitalisation above €800 million.
5. Coloniale SpA held 49.16% directly, and another 0.86% indirectly through the Luxembourg based Newport SA.
6. See Oricchio (1997) and Melis (2004a) for a review.
7. Since January 2004 the new company law allows companies to choose between a unitary board structure (with an audit committee within the board of directors), a two-tier board structure (with a management committee and a supervisory council), and the traditional board structure with the board of statutory auditors.
8. See Melis (2004b) for further analysis on the relationship between the composition of the board of statutory auditors and the level of minority shareholders' protection.
9. CONSOB (Commissione Nazionale per le Società e la Borsa) is the public authority that is responsible for regulating and controlling the Italian securities markets.
10. The Italian law (Draghi reform 1998, Art. 159) makes lead auditor rotation compulsory after three appointments (each lasts three years), leading to a maximum of nine years for audit engagement. The external auditing firm is appointed by the shareholders' meeting, although the board of statutory auditors has a voice on the choice of the auditing firm.
11. According to the Preda Code (2002, para. 3) an independent director is defined as a director who meets the following criteria:

   - s/he does not entertain, directly, indirectly or on behalf of third parties, nor has s/he recently entertained, with the company, its subsidiaries, the executive directors or the shareholder or group of shareholders who control the company, business relationships of a significance able to influence their autonomous judgement;
   - s/he does not own, directly or indirectly, or on behalf of third parties, a quantity of shares enabling them to control or notably influence the company or participate in shareholders' agreements to control the company;
   - s/he is not close family of executive directors of the company or of any person who is in the situations referred to in the above paragraphs.

12. Palepu and Healy (2003) weight a 'strong buy' recommendation as 1 and a 'sell' recommendation as 5.

14

Corporate Regulation in Ireland

Paul Appleby

Introduction

There have been some fundamental changes to the structure of company law regulation in Ireland since 2001. I propose in this chapter to introduce you, first of all, to the framework of regulation in Ireland which prevailed for several earlier decades and to proceed to discuss the events which led to a fundamental reappraisal and reconstitution of that framework. I conclude with some personal observations of the initial impact of the new regime.

Corporate Regulation in Ireland up to 2001

The basic legislation to which all companies are subject in Ireland comprises the Companies Acts. It is important at the outset to be aware that Irish company law has traditionally been heavily influenced by the equivalent code in the UK. The Irish Companies Act of 1963 (as enacted) had many features of the UK Companies Act of 1948. Our originally enacted Companies Act of 1990 similarly borrowed and refined elements from the UK Companies Act 1985, the Insolvency Act 1986 and the Company Directors Disqualification Act 1986 in particular.

Our domestic company law has also of course been increasingly influenced by the European Union, since we joined it in 1973. We have, like other member states, transposed significant EU legislation into our domestic law. While these have been and continue to be the two primary sources of influence on the shape of Irish companies legislation, there has more recently been a distinct domestic response to the problems of corporate misconduct which emerged particularly in the late 1990s.

Before outlining what these problems were, I will briefly outline the main actors in the corporate regulation arena towards the close of the twentieth century:

- the Minister for Enterprise Trade and Employment and her department was and is responsible for the preparation of Irish companies legislation. The Minister was also responsible for the enforcement of such legislation, but the resources (legal powers, staffing, etc.) available to it for doing so over an extended period were totally inadequate;
- the Registrar of Companies which is attached to the Department of Enterprise, Trade and Employment was and is responsible for the incorporation of companies and for ensuring that company-related information which is required by the Companies Acts to be filed and made available to the public is done so promptly. Again, the required investment in resources (IT, staffing and general infrastructure) had not been made at an appropriate level for some time to enable the Registrar's Office to perform its functions effectively;
- there were five professional accountancy bodies which were recognised by the Minister for Enterprise Trade and Employment for the purpose of awarding practising certificates to auditors and regulating their auditing members. The Minister was also responsible for supervising the adequacy of the accounting bodies' regulatory practices. Again, the credibility of these bodies' regulatory role came under scrutiny as the 1990s drew to a close;
- other relevant actors in the corporate arena at this time were the Central Bank of Ireland which was responsible not only for Irish monetary policy but also for the regulation of banks and certain other financial service entities, the Revenue Commissioners which were responsible for the collection of tax revenue from individuals and corporate entities and the Irish Stock Exchange which regulated, among other things, Irish listed companies.

The Emerging Scandals and their Influence on Legal Change

What occurred in Ireland since 1996 in particular gave rise to much reflection on the manner in which the company law regime in Ireland had been operating. And this period of evaluation has produced a number of innovative approaches to the regime of corporate regulation.

The Tribunal of Inquiry (Dunnes Payments) and its Consequences

The cause of the changes in Ireland can be traced unsurprisingly to business scandals, and from 1996 on, they began to emerge regularly into the public domain. While there were many individual events of concern, there were several distinct strands, the first of which arose from a bitter family dispute for control of the Dunnes Stores group, a large grocery and retail business in Ireland. A consequence of the recriminations in that dispute was that it became public knowledge that one of the principals of the group had provided financial support over a number of years:

- to a person who was a then serving government Minister and who, prior to his appointment, had been directly involved in a refrigeration business which serviced shops in the Dunnes Stores group; and
- to a former Taoiseach (Prime Minister), who had been a partner in an accounting practice in Dublin before entering politics full time in the 1960s. There was also a commercial relationship between a son of the Prime Minister and the Dunnes Stores principal in that the latter availed of the services provided by the son's helicopter business.

Because of concerns that these payments and relationships might have involved the Ministers in question exercising their public duties in a corrupt manner, the government eventually established a Tribunal of Inquiry to investigate these payments by or on behalf of Dunnes Stores. The formal proceedings of this Tribunal of Inquiry were held in public.

The remarkable outcome of this Tribunal of Inquiry is that it discovered that the former Prime Minister and others (some of whom turned out subsequently to be quite prominent business people) had been customers of a secret offshore banking operation linked with the

Cayman Islands. This had been run for 25 years by a deceased former co-partner of the former Prime Minister in their accounting practice. For much of this period, the individual in question was prominent in a small merchant bank based in Dublin and subsequently became chairman of one of Ireland's largest listed companies where he continued to run the secret operation from his private office in the company. None of the relevant regulatory authorities knew of the existence of the operation or detected its activity.

This Tribunal of Inquiry Report[1] (which became known as the McCracken Report) resulted in the progressive undertaking by the Tánaiste (Deputy Prime Minister) and Minister for Enterprise Trade and Employment of a series of confidential company investigations using the powers of inquiry available to her in the Companies Act 1990. These included two Dunnes Stores companies, the refrigeration business of the then Minister, the helicopter business of the Prime Minister's son, four offshore entities and two licensed banks in Ireland which had facilitated the offshore activity. One of these investigations was subsequently transformed to an inquiry undertaken by Inspectors appointed by the High Court into one of the offshore entities, namely Ansbacher (Cayman) Ltd.[2]

The McCracken Report also led to the establishment by the relevant recognised accountancy body of a formal Committee of Inquiry to investigate the conduct of certain of its members related to the events discussed in the Report. This Inquiry related to two accountancy practices (one large and one small) and several individual members of the body. Because its proceedings were to be held in private, the Minister for Enterprise Trade and Employment, in her capacity as the body's regulator, used her legal power to insist on observer status for her department at these proceedings.

Planning Tribunal of Inquiry

But business misconduct began to emerge openly in other areas. A separate Tribunal of Inquiry was set up in 1997 to examine the area of payments made by development interests to secure favourable planning decisions from local authorities. The public proceedings of this Inquiry[3] quickly attracted significant public interest due to the regular revelations of questionable corporate conduct.

National Irish Bank Ltd Inquiry

Separately in late 1997/early 1998, RTÉ, the national radio and television station, broadcast allegations suggesting that National Irish Bank Ltd, a licensed retail bank, and a subsidiary company, National Irish Bank Financial Services Ltd, had been:

- overcharging some of its customers by levying unwarranted fees and interest charges on their accounts; and
- assisting some of them in evading their taxation obligations by selling them offshore insurance products which did not have the required legal authorisation.

These allegations also resulted in the establishment at the Minister's request of an inquiry by Inspectors appointed by the High Court into both companies. The Inspectors' Report[4] into these matters was published in July 2004.

The kindest representation that could be placed on these unfolding events was that there was a 'disconnect' between the law which was supposed to define the parameters of acceptable business and personal conduct and the real situation in the marketplace. However, it was also clear that some business interests used and abused the law and ignored ethical considerations when it suited.

Review of Company Law Compliance and Enforcement

This developing situation in 1997 and 1998 led the Minister for Enterprise Trade and Employment to establish a Working Group to review the whole area of company law compliance and enforcement. The Group's conclusions were stark and uncompromising:

- 'Irish Company Law has been characterised by a culture of non-compliance...'[5];
- 'Enforcement of the law in relation to non-registration type offences is very rare and wholly unpredictable'[6];
- 'Those who are tempted to make serious breaches of company law have little reason to fear detection or prosecution. As far as enforcement is concerned, the sound of the enforcer's footsteps on the beat is simply never heard.'[7]

In their recommendations, the Working Group recommended:

- strengthening the law relating to company law enforcement,
- establishing an independent multidisciplinary entity which would be dedicated to improving company law compliance and enforcement and which would be headed by a Director of Corporate Enforcement; and
- the setting up of a Company Law Review Group (CLRG) which would consolidate, modernise and keep Irish companies legislation under continuing review in the light of market developments.

In early 1999, the Irish government endorsed the Report's recommendations which were subsequently implemented in the Company Law Enforcement Act 2001. Both my Office (the Office of the Director of Corporate Enforcement (ODCE)) and the CLRG were established in 2001.

The Inquiries into Deposit Interest Retention Tax

While these decisions were being made, evidence of business misconduct kept emerging. A review in 1999 by the Comptroller and Auditor General,[8] the state auditor, suggested that many licensed financial institutions had facilitated to a greater or lesser extent evasion by their customers of deposit interest retention tax (otherwise known as DIRT). In a series of public hearings subsequently conducted by the Committee of Public Accounts in the Oireachtas (Irish Parliament), past and present directors and senior management of the country's financial institutions and representatives of their auditors were interrogated on their performance and on their compliance with respect to the legal obligations in this area. Senior officials of the relevant state authorities were also closely questioned. The Committee's Report heavily criticised the banks, their auditors and the relevant state authorities for their actions and omissions in the DIRT saga. Most of the institutions concerned subsequently made tax settlements with the Revenue Commissioners arising from the practices that were disclosed.

The Review Group on Auditing

Following a recommendation of the Committee of Public Accounts in their Report,[9] the government set up a Review Group on Auditing to examine among other things:

- whether self-regulation in the auditing profession was working effectively and consistently;
- whether any new or revised structures and arrangements were necessary to improve public confidence, and if so, what form they should take; and
- various other matters associated with the auditor/client relationship.

The Group's extensive Report[10] recommended the establishment of an Irish Auditing and Accounting Supervisory Authority (IAASA) to regulate the accounting and auditing profession, to examine the financial statements of public limited companies and to promote quality professional standards. Many of the Group's recommendations were implemented in the Companies (Auditing and Accounting) Act 2003.

Preparations are now under way to bring many of the Act's provisions into effect. The Interim Board of IAASA has recently appointed a chief executive, and the Board is expected to assume many of its functions in a few months' time once the recruitment of its staff is well under way.

Directors' Compliance Statements

Arising from a specific recommendation of the Review Group on Auditing, the 2003 Act also requires that the directors of major companies make public statements of compliance with respect to their tax, company law and any other relevant enactments that could materially affect the company's financial statements. The auditors of those companies must also publicly state if, in their opinion, the directors' compliance statements are fair and reasonable. It should be noted that this recommendation pre-dated Enron and many of the other international financial scandals which have come to light in recent years. This requirement has been characterised as a moderate version of the US Sarbanes-Oxley Act.

In conjunction with other interested parties, my Office published in July 2004 a Consultation Paper and Draft Guidance on these obligations with respect to Directors' Compliance Statements.[11] In parallel, the Auditing Practices Board has recently published a Draft Bulletin[12] on the duties of auditors in evaluating the compliance statements of directors. Both documents are generating considerable business and professional interest at present.

Other Developments

As well as these specific changes in the core company law area, both the Revenue Commissioners and the Central Bank of Ireland have undergone substantial restructuring. In the latter context, an Irish Financial Services Regulatory Authority was established last year with a wider remit, a greater consumer focus and an ability to levy substantial fines on licensed entities for breaches of their regulatory obligations. And the relevant legislation now provides for greater information sharing between the company, tax and financial services regulatory authorities by way of an exemption from their general statutory duty to keep confidential information coming to their attention.

Mission and Goals of the ODCE

Having outlined the events which have stimulated the establishment of the Office of the Director of Corporate Enforcement and other changes, it is appropriate that I now turn to discuss the Office's role and activity. The mission of the Office is:

- to encourage compliance by companies and individuals with relevant requirements of the Companies Acts 1963 to 2003; and
- to bring to account those who disregard the law.

Consistent with this mission, the ODCE's Strategy Statement for 2003 to 2005[13] identifies its five principal goals as:

- encouraging improved compliance with the Companies Acts;
- uncovering suspected breaches of company law;

- prosecuting detected breaches of the Companies Acts;
- sanctioning improper conduct with respect to insolvent companies; and
- providing quality services to internal and external customers.

Encouraging Improved Compliance

The ODCE's remit extends to all companies operating in Ireland which are subject to the Companies Acts. This typically ranges from small family businesses to listed public companies and from multi-national enterprises to companies formed for local community purposes. Many of the individuals involved in smaller companies in particular have little understanding of the Companies Acts and the related obligations, and these rely to some extent on their professional advisors to keep them compliant.

In order to bridge this information deficit and assist compliance, we have reached out to individual directors and stakeholders in the company law arena by producing basic guidance material. We have, for instance, published seven booklets on the key duties and obligations of each of the primary stakeholders (namely companies, company directors, company secretaries, members/shareholders, auditors, creditors and liquidators/examiners/receivers).[14] A number of these guides have been issued to the registered office of every Irish-registered company.

Second, we have produced, often in cooperation with professional interests, specific guidance on some of the new obligations which have been introduced to improve corporate compliance standards. Examples include:

- the new obligations on auditors to report to the Director of Corporate Enforcement suspected indictable offences under the Companies Acts;[15]
- the new obligations on liquidators to report to the Director on the conduct of the directors of insolvent companies in liquidation;[16] and
- the forthcoming obligations on company directors to prepare and publish compliance statements as part of their annual report to shareholders.

My staff and I also regularly attend meetings, seminars and conferences to deal directly with issues of concern to stakeholders and produce information materials on the ongoing work of the Office. Presentations made to professional interests, our Annual Reports and other guidance and information are all accessible on the ODCE website at www.odce.ie/.

Uncovering Suspected Breaches of Company Law

The main sources of information for suspected corporate misconduct and the associated incidence of reports are as follows:

- auditors and their professional bodies via their new mandatory reporting obligation with respect to indictable company law offences;
- the general public who have concerns about corporate misconduct;
- state authorities via the new information-sharing arrangements; and
- the media and other public information sources, such as that available in the Register of Companies.

While a wide range of potential offences is coming to attention, the following matters constitute some of the main issues which are being detected by the Office:

- the failure to keep proper books of account and/or fraudulent trading;
- persons acting as company directors while restricted, disqualified or an undischarged bankrupt;
- persons acting as auditors or liquidators while not qualified or while disqualified by virtue of their being or having acted as a director of the company in question;
- the provision of loans from company assets to directors or other connected persons in excess of the permitted levels;
- the failure to arrange to make a timely and accurate disclosure of information to company shareholders at general meetings or to the Registrar of Companies;
- the provision of falsified or inaccurate information pursuant to company law obligations;
- the failure of auditors and liquidators to comply on time with their reporting obligations.

Enforcement Actions

Since its establishment in late 2001, the ODCE has secured to date over 100 convictions against companies, company directors and others, and we have also obtained High Court Orders requiring individuals to remedy their non-compliance.

While much of the ODCE's investigative work is pursued by discussion, correspondence and formal cautioned interview with the relevant parties, the Office has exercised certain of its legal powers on about 50 occasions to investigate suspected non-compliance. These powers include:

- requiring the production of stipulated books and documents from companies, company directors, auditors and liquidators;
- the execution of search warrants on business premises and, on occasion, private residences;
- the serving of orders for the production of banking documentation;
- the arrest and on occasion the detention of suspects.

Several hundred cases remain under criminal or civil investigation at the present time.

Sanctioning Improper Conduct relating to Insolvent Companies

The liquidators of insolvent companies must now report to the ODCE and must also apply to the High Court for the restriction[17] of each of the directors of those companies unless they are relieved of that obligation by the Director. Restriction will be imposed if the Court is satisfied that a director has not acted honestly or responsibly in the discharge of his or her duties. Over 200 company directors now stand restricted, most of whom have recently been restricted as a consequence of the operation of these new measures in the Company Law Enforcement Act.

The ODCE is also examining a number of unliquidated insolvent companies and dissolved companies, where unscrupulous directors may have acted in breach of their statutory or common law duties and depleted company assets to the disadvantage of other interests. Legal action will be initiated in a number of these cases shortly.

Providing Quality Customer Services

The ODCE's staffing complement averages 37 full-time staff, and it comprises accounting, administrative, legal and police expertise. Most work together in teams to achieve their detection and enforcement results. Our budget in 2004 is €4.25 million.

The ODCE continues to provide quality customer services to its clients. Our website, for instance, has continued to attract favourable comment for the quality and quantity of available company law materials.

Impact of the ODCE on the Company Law Compliance Environment

While it is still early days in the life of the Office, I believe that there has been a substantial improvement in the overall compliance environment. This has been independently confirmed by TNS/mrbi in the qualitative phase of a market research study by the ODCE undertaken in late 2003, namely:

- Awareness of the ODCE. 'The ODCE was deemed most prominent amongst accountants/auditors and company secretaries...' 'In general, levels of awareness of the ODCE...are lower amongst company directors and shareholders.'
- Knowledge of ODCE Information Materials. 'The majority of respondents were positive about the impact that the ODCE's educational initiatives have had on the compliance environment in general, with most feeling that company directors, in particular, are more aware of the regulations surrounding their position.'
- Perception of Improved Compliance Environment. 'Widespread recognition that compliance levels have increased over the last 5 years.'
- Awareness of ODCE Enforcement Actions. 'Respondents agreed that while the ODCE's enforcement activities have played a part in improving the compliance environment, they have not yet done so to their full potential.'

Some Personal Observations

Prior to the events which I have described earlier, the state did not exercise its public interest role to any appreciable extent in regulating company affairs. It was a 'laissez faire' environment in the worst sense, where those who had the 'inside track' could, if they wished, use and on occasion abuse the applicable legislation without fear of effective challenge or sanction. Only those with the financial and professional resources to do so could defend their interests against wrongdoing perpetrated against them in the courts, while more vulnerable interests found it difficult to assert and uphold their rights.

Accountants and other professionals were often demoralised by a regime which did not encourage and reward proper professional conduct. The tendering of correct advice might often be met by the client asking: 'And what happens if I don't do that?' To which the usual answer would have been: 'Nothing' which left the conscientious advisor feeling rather pious and foolish. In summary, the framework gave little incentive or support to compliant behaviour in the company law area. Essentially, the framework of accountability which had been constructed so carefully in the legislation to create a proper theoretical balance of rights and duties between the various stakeholders (directors, shareholders, creditors, the relevant professionals and the state acting in the wider public interest) was in practice skewed totally in favour of those directors in charge of company assets.

We are making progress, I believe, in the task of developing a more balanced framework of accountability. Directors can no longer easily ignore the requirement to file company information on a timely basis with the Registrar of Companies, because of the heavy penalties and the risk of dissolution of the company which now obtain. Some directors are already the subject of civil or criminal investigation by the ODCE, and others will be aware that non-compliance now carries a significant risk to personal reputation if non-compliance should result in a future court conviction or other sanction.

The relationship between auditors and directors has also changed. The mandatory requirement on auditors to report suspected indictable offences to my Office means that auditors ignore this legal obligation at their peril. When auditors advise directors that they will be reporting suspected breaches of company law to my Office, many directors make genuine efforts to remedy their non-compliance and correspond directly with us to this effect. The effect of this provision has been to support the independent oversight role which auditors are supposed to discharge in the interests of shareholders in particular and to improve the overall standard of compliance with the requirements of the Companies Acts.

The directors of companies in financial difficulty also know that if a company goes into insolvent liquidation, they will have to account to the liquidator for their actions and omissions in the 12-month period prior to the demise of the company. If they act in a manner which has, for instance, unfairly disadvantaged the interests of creditors, they may find themselves having to justify their behaviour before the High Court. Creditor interests have reported that these provisions have deterred directors from acting unscrupulously in the final stages of a company's demise and that this has improved the return to creditors in company failures.

And the forthcoming compliance statement obligations for certain large companies should raise the profile of compliance on directors' radar screens still further.

Improving company law regulation is enhancing market information which enables creditors to better evaluate market risks. We are aware that financial institutions are now taking cognisance of the identities of the newly restricted directors in their lending policies. Other creditors now have more timely information available in the Register of Companies to examine the solvency of particular companies. In essence, commercial risk is being reduced for those market participants who use the available information to assess credit risk.

In the important area of listed companies, the obligation on the Irish Stock Exchange to report to my Office, for instance, non-compliance with the time limits for disclosure of director share dealing transactions has, I understand, resulted in greater attention now being given by companies to their obligations in this area. Again, transparency in the market benefits from this result.

The benefits of course go beyond the discrete company law area. We are aware of one particular case where a 'voluntary disclosure' of unpaid tax was made within days of our having undertaken a search of a company's premises and seizing relevant company documents. The tax authorities are also generally benefiting from our determination to proceed against companies which are failing to keep proper books of account, often by suppressing the true income of the company's business. In short, more effective company law regulation is supporting other authorities in discharging their duties in the overall public interest.

The process in which we have been and are engaged is one of behavioural change, moving from a culture of non-compliance to one of compliance. In doing so, we have adopted the 'carrot and stick' approach. We try to encourage and support compliant behaviours by producing accessible and accurate guidance materials and by supporting efforts remedying previous defaults where it is possible to do so. For those who choose not to comply or who fail on proper notice to correct non-compliant behaviours, we closely investigate the circumstances in question and consider if some form of sanction is warranted. Effective enforcement action is of course also serving to reinforce the overall compliance message.

I believe that our approach is fully consistent with that advocated by the Report of the Working Group on Company Law Compliance and Enforcement in their vision for the Office. A balanced framework of company law exists to facilitate enterprise, not to impede it. Moreover, non-compliance with company law *by some* also undermines the economic opportunities *for others*. In that context, I fully endorse the following comments made in the Working Group Report:

> Quite apart from the general desirability of compliance with, and enforcement of, the law, there are particular reasons why company law should be complied with and enforced. These include:
>
> - protection of the public from fraud and commercial irresponsibility
> - protection of employees' interests in the viability of their employers
> - protection of traders and suppliers
> - protection of the State's revenues and of the tax-payer
> - protection of investors and credit institutions
> - protection of legitimate business from fraud-based competition
> - protection of Ireland's trading and financial reputation.
>
> A compliant corporate sector should yield substantial returns in business efficiency, solvency, revenue yield, social solidarity and in terms of the public and private time saved in dealing with the consequences of non-compliance.[18]

I believe that the new regulatory arrangements which have been and are being put in place will deliver a quality regulatory environment in Ireland, where the conditions for enterprise growth and development are positive and where the threats to enterprise risk from unscrupulous conduct are minimised. I am confident that we will continue to receive the assistance of government in fulfilling our role and contributing to national progress, and I look forward to their continuing support in improving the climate for corporate development in the years ahead.

Notes

1. Report of the Tribunal of Inquiry (Dunnes Payments), August 1997.
2. Report of the Inspectors appointed to enquire into the affairs of Ansbacher (Cayman) Ltd, June 2002.
3. Second Interim Report of the Tribunal of Inquiry into Certain Planning Matters and Payments, September 2002.
4. Report of the Inspectors appointed to investigate the affairs of National Irish Bank Ltd and National Irish Bank Financial Services Ltd, July 2004.
5. Report of the Working Group on Company Law Compliance and Enforcement, 30 November 1998, para. 2.4.
6. Report of the Working Group on Company Law Compliance and Enforcement, 30 November 1998, para. 2.5.
7. Report of the Working Group on Company Law Compliance and Enforcement, 30 November 1998, para. 2.5.
8. Report of the Investigation into the administration of Deposit Interest Retention Tax and Related Matters during the period 1 January 1986 to 1 December 1998, July 1999.
9. Parliamentary Inquiry into DIRT First Report, December 1999.
10. Report of the Review Group on Auditing, July 2000.
11. ODCE Consultation Paper C/2004/1 – Guidance on the Obligation of Company Directors to Prepare Compliance Policy and Annual Compliance Statements, July 2004. A copy is accessible from the ODCE website at www.odce.ie/.
12. Auditing Practices Board Draft Bulletin 2004/3 on Directors' Compliance Statements: Reports by Auditors under Company Law in the Republic of Ireland (August 2004). This is available at www.frc.org.uk/apb/.
13. ODCE Strategy Statement, 2003–2005, January 2003. A copy is accessible from the ODCE website at www.odce.ie/.
14. ODCE Decision Notice D/2002/1 – The Principal Duties and Powers of Company Stakeholders. This guidance is in the form of seven Information Books, all of which are available from the ODCE website at www.odce.ie/.
15. ODCE Decision Notice D/2002/2 – The Duty of Auditors to Report to the Director of Corporate Enforcement, July 2002. A copy is accessible from the ODCE website at www.odce.ie/.

16. ODCE Decision Notices D/2002/3 and D/2003/1 – The Liquidation-related Functions of the Director of Corporate Enforcement, November 2002 and July 2003. Copies are available at www.odce.ie/.

17. The effect of restriction is that persons are precluded for five years from acting as a company director unless the company is adequately capitalised. In the case of a private company, the capital requirement is €63 487, and in the case of a public company, €317 435. In both cases, the allotted share capital must be fully paid up in cash.

18. Report of the Working Group on Company Law Compliance and Enforcement, 30 November 1998, paras 1.19 and 1.20.

15

Corporate Governance – More than a State of Mind?

Neill Buck

Introduction

This chapter discusses some aspects of the management of corporate governance in Australia, some background and the regulatory and organisational response to pressures to change practices. It draws on experience in consulting to companies, several case studies of recent governance issues and the responses of governments, non-government regulators and standard-setting bodies. I have found that governance needs to be at least a state of mind first among the Board and high officials and before the systems procedures, culture and behaviours necessary to sustain it can follow. Without the appropriate state of mind or, as James Reason[1] says, 'mindfulness', all of the best systems and controls for governance will not enable an organisation to match its appetite for risk with the reality of governing the organisation. Without working systems the state of mind is unlikely to help.

The author draws on his 20 years in regulation. In particular he draws upon his work over the past nine years as independent advisor, reviewer and governance, compliance and risk management auditor of over 200 companies, government agencies, associations internationally and in Australia and New Zealand. The chapter describes two high profile incidents which were the result of published review reports. It also draws on unpublished research to establish some critical control points that may be useful in assessing the risk of governance systems failing.

On 31 January 2003 at approximately 7.14 am a tragedy occurred on Sydney's outskirts near a place called Waterfall. A New South Wales State Rail Authority train overturned at high speed, killing the driver and six passengers.

In January 2004 the National Australia Bank, one of the four largest banks in Australia, made three public announcements. On 13 January it announced losses from unauthorised foreign currency trading activities. On 18 January the amount was updated to $185 m and the bank stated the amount was not expected to exceed $600 m. On 27 January it was announced that the losses were not expected to exceed $360 m. In addition to identifying inappropriate conduct in the bank, the high profile Australian *Company Director* magazine stated: 'What started as the actions of Rogue forex traders operating outside risk management guidelines escalated into one of Australia's nastiest Boardroom brawls.'[2] What makes these two events unique for governance, risk and compliance advisors is that both events were analysed independently and reported quite quickly and publicly. Two reports were published into the National Bank matters, one by the Australian Prudential Regulator Authority[3] and the other commissioned by the bank by auditors PricewaterhouseCoopers.[4] In the case of the railway accident the New South Wales government, the owner and operator of the system under the auspices of the New South Wales State Rail Authority, on the day of the accident, appointed a Royal Commissioner to conduct an investigation. His final report has yet to appear. But in addition, the New South Wales Department of Transport in association with the rail safety regulator conducted its own enquiry with a view to assisting the Royal Commissioner. They published their findings on the Ministers for Transport's website.[5]

While one may be critical of the conduct that gave rise to the events and, possibly, of the systems and structures allowing it, the organisations must be credited for allowing their internal reviews to be published so that others may learn from the events. No doubt political pressure and reputational considerations also informed the decision to publish but this level of transparency has been helpful. One of the frustrations in communicating in this area as a practitioner is that you are involved. Secrecy is mandated. Both organisations are to be commended for the open and public way in which they have exposed the issues associated with these matters.

But this chapter is not about railways and technical issues associated with trains or forex trading. It is about showing that there are common issues associated with governance incidents in all sectors and that there is something to learn from such incidents regardless of the sector – including lessons for the regulators. In other industry sectors the train wrecks may take less physical and emotional forms but they will play out in similar ways.

What the chapter concludes is that the effects on the business and the community as a whole of the failure to identify, address and manage relatively straightforward compliance, risk management and governance issues can be catastrophic. Potential crash sites can be found in all organisations and there are common indicators and treatments that can be learned from other events. Traditionally this approach has been applied to industrial accidents or plane crashes. In my view there are common principles and critical control points in all governance and corporate train wrecks.

This chapter discusses some aspects of the management of corporate governance in Australia, some background and the regulatory and organisational response to pressures to change practices. It draws on experience in consulting to companies, several case studies of recent governance issues and the responses of governments, non-government regulators and standard-setting bodies. I have found that governance needs to be at least a state of mind first among the Board and high officials and before the systems procedures, culture and behaviours necessary to sustain it can follow. Without the appropriate state of mind or, as James Reason[6] says, 'mindfulness', all of the best systems and controls for governance will not enable an organisation to match its appetite for risk with the reality of governing the organisation. Without working systems the state of mind is unlikely to help.

Finding the balance between behaviours, systems and risk provides one of the challenges facing directors, managers and their companies, regulators, the public and those involved in public policy.

Background

In Australia there have been a series of high profile incidents involving company failure, malfeasance or a major crisis or system failure of significant infrastructure. In many cases this has led to judicial or regulator enquiries, substantial reputational damage for the organisation and a variety of losses for individual, corporate and government stakeholders.

Those organisations considered in this chapter and involved in these events or incidents tend to be high profile respectable organisations in business or government. Most, but not all, would argue that at the time the directors and senior managers believed that they had competent systems of governance, risk management and compliance in place. The public aspiration for these organisations was best practice governance. The reality with the wisdom of hindsight may not have been the same.

Examples of such events are:

- The Longford Gas explosion – where the city of Melbourne (Australia's second city of some 3 million people) was without its primary energy supply for several weeks (as well as the deaths associated with the explosion). The subsequent Royal Commission was critical of government and the company involved and I understand litigation is continuing.
- The Glenbrook and Waterfall rail accidents – significant railway accidents on commuter trains travelling to and from Sydney (Australia's largest city). The Government of New South Wales, who owned the infrastructure, was criticised for allowing the rail infrastructure and systems to fall into poor repair resulting in two major crashes in five years and associated loss of life. A judicial enquiry into the first accident, the Glenbrook accident, was completed in 2002. The judicial enquiry into the second is ongoing. The Department of Transport in NSW who had portfolio responsibility for the railway system has produced a safety report on the second accident which is used as a basis for this case study.
- The collapse of Australia's second largest general insurance company HIH – the collapse was followed by a Royal Commission and there are ongoing investigations by the corporation's regulators as well as a restructure of the prudential regulator.
- The collapse of a significant telecommunications company, One Tel, an emerging and apparently successful company with substantial support from prominent businesses. Elements of this matter remain the subject of investigation and litigation by the Australian Securities Commission – the corporations and securities regulator.
- Allegations of malfeasance by some employees and failure by systems and directors in Australia's largest bank, the National Australia Bank, leading to public reports on the conduct by independent auditors and a public report by the Australian Prudential Regulator

Authority (APRA). This was followed by a six-month very public board room conflict leading to the resignation of one director and a move by others to shorten their terms.

For this chapter I have used the Waterfall train crash and the National Australia Bank trading issues to illustrate the common elements in governance system failure. It is helpful for a public discussion that each is analysed by independent reports on the public record.

My company has developed some indicators of higher risk areas for governance failure. These indicators are based on our analysis of court cases and the experiences of our clients. As many of the matters from which we draw our indicators are confidential it is sometimes difficult to substantiate the basis of the indicators with reference to publicly available information. We continue to test them using illustrations such as those contained in this chapter. We also use those indicators as guides to critical control points for risk where a governance intervention is required to manage the risk.

In response to the events outlined above and some similar recent events the Australian government, some regulators and standard-setting bodies have introduced new laws, regulations and standards.

These include:

- The Australian Standards, 3806 Compliance Programs, 4269 Risk Management and 8000 Corporate Governance series, including separate standards on Corporate Governance, Whistle Blowing and Corporate Social Responsibility.[7]
- The Corporation Law Economic Reform Program (CLERP). Under this programme the Australian Government has rewritten and reformed corporations. In a numbered series the government has changed many structures and operations in the markets, companies and business operations generally. Number 9 in the series is before the Parliament and focuses in particular on board-level governance of corporations, the role of directors and the role and independence of auditors.[8]
- The Financial Services Reform Act. Under this legislation the Commonwealth Government required all companies involved in the financial services sector, banks, insurance companies brokers and related entities, to apply for new licences including meeting mandated training standards for all customer-facing and decision-making staff, standards of pre-contractual disclosure, standards of

risk management including compliance with Australian Standards on Risk Management, Compliance Programs and Complaints Handling as well as mandated organisational capacity indicators and governance framework.[9]

- The Australian Stock Exchange (ASX) Corporate Governance Guidelines. The ASX is the stock market regulator. A listed company, it has responsibility delegated to it by the Australian Securities and Investments Commission to regulate the markets. Under the ASX Corporate Governance guidelines listed companies are required to comply or explain why not. The guidelines take the form of a voluntary code of practice.[10]

The effect of this regulation has been to change the practice of companies and organisations. Many company directors have used the press to proclaim that this is overload and perhaps it may be seen this way in the future. Those who also operate in the jurisdiction subject to the Sarbanes-Oxley Act may have another view.

To understand the issues for comparison it is necessary to draw a picture of the two case study incidents. Both discussions draw on the references cited above.

Case Studies

The Waterfall Rail Accident

Introduction

On 31 January 2003 at approximately 7.14 am, a tragedy occurred on Sydney's outskirts near a place called Waterfall. A train overturned at high speed and the driver and six passengers were killed. The accident was the second of its kind in a short number of years. The accident pointed up a number of deficiencies and issues which ranged from problems with the 000 (911) emergency call system, initially being unable to find the train and when rescuers did arrive having difficulty entering the train to rescue injured through to suggestions that workarounds for fundamental safety systems were routinely being practised.

The Final Report of a Rail Safety Investigation into the Waterfall disaster published by the NSW Department of Transport in January 2004 is an assessment of aspects of what happened in the Waterfall disaster. This case study is based on that Report.

Because the Report was prepared with a view to informing others and assisting in the improvement of safety, the findings do not, on my reading, seek to disguise some of the shortcomings in the organisation.

Risk management

The Report says that 'the investigation did not find any evidence of the existence of a combined risk and hazard register, contrary to the [State Rail Authority Safety Management System's] statement that such a register was being periodically reviewed to ensure that risks to safety were identified and managed.'[11]

This lack of effective compliance systems was seen as critical in the Report.

Unachievable returns on investments

The Report indicates that the timetable for driving a train of the type involved in the accident over the section of the railway track where the accident occurred allowed 19 minutes for the train to cover the distance between two train stations. The Report concludes that 20 minutes were actually required for a train of that type to cover that distance.

Systems for Safety and Compliance

One of the key compliance and risk management controls on trains such as that involved in the Waterfall disaster is a deadman's foot control. This is a safety device that requires constant foot pressure by train drivers – otherwise the train stops. Evidence by those who wrote the report indicated that staff had created strategies to work around this control by use of homemade devices to neutralise its effectiveness. The Report says that

> During discussions with drivers regarding the ways they used the deadman's system, some displayed direct or indirect knowledge that some drivers wedged one of the red flags from the cabin between the driver's desk and the deadman's foot pedal....Marks indicating such use were found on an examination of a random sample of 29 cars from Tangara trains of the type involved in the accident.[12]

The Report did not find this conduct as causally related to the particular accident.

Reporting Issues

The report says that 'there were remnants of a blame culture, which discouraged employees from being open about near-misses and other hazardous conditions.'[13]

Distance from Head Office

The train involved in the accident was only a few kilometres south of Waterfall (an outer Sydney suburb) on its way further south to Wollongong (a city within commuting distance from Sydney) but could not be contacted directly by Waterfall station staff. The Report says that 'as a consequence when the signaller at Waterfall became concerned about [the train] he was required to telephone Wollongong signal box and ask for a radio call to be placed to [the train] and the result reported back to him'.[14] The Waterfall station could only contact trains to the north – not those to the south, that is, further away from the head office or central station.

Accidents and Incidents do Happen

Passengers trapped on the train and those attempting to rescue them had difficulty entering and leaving the wrecked train. The report says that the train doors were locked and initially no one present could open them. The report indicates that this was not the first time that such a train had fallen on its side and the same issues of access and egress had been noted in NSW and in other countries. The report says that no central set of maps identifying road access points to the area of the accident could be quickly found. The electricity powering the train was cut off as a result of the accident and the power lines fell on or about the train. The report says that those responsible for the electricity made several attempts to restart the power using automatic and manual procedures after the accident had occurred and passengers and possibly rescuers were near the downed power lines.

The Report says 'The Rail Safety Regulator was not prepared or resourced for an investigation on the scale of the Waterfall accident. There were no investigation procedures and no critical incident response team.'[15]

Training and Procedures

The Report identifies that training did not take account of known barriers to effective teamwork and communication and whistleblowing. In this situation it was between the train drivers and train guards. (In the earlier Glenbrook accident discussed above, the barriers were between the train driver and the signal man and the overall line controller.) The Report says that the consequence was that even at the time of a serious incident the guard might be reluctant to take action which could be seen to undermine the apparent authority of the more senior crew member, the driver.

It Cannot Happen Here

The Report also says that 'There was a perception by some that railways were inherently safe, and that Waterfall was an unforeseeable accident.'[16]

A Royal Commission into the accident is continuing. The rail organisation has changed some staff and had substantial structural changes. The initial report on which this chapter is based will be followed over the next 12 months by the Royal Commissioner's Report.

National Australia Bank

Introduction

In January 2004 the National Australia Bank, one of the four largest banks, announced losses from unauthorised foreign currency trading activities. By 27 January these had risen from an initial $185m on 18 January to $360m on 27 January.

The Australian media and public watched as this saga unfolded. The regulator and the company conducted enquiries into what happened. The reports of the company enquiry, conducted by a major accounting firm and that of the regulator were made public. In this section I have drawn on the reports by the regulator, APRA, and by Pricewater-houseCoopers (PWC).

The reports indicate that losses in the National Australia Bank (NAB) were apparently caused by the conduct of four currency traders who positioned the NAB's foreign currency options portfolio in the expectation that the US dollar would stabilise and become less volatile. The reports on the events by the regulator and the independent experts found that when the market moved against them they concealed their true positions. As their positions deteriorated unchecked it took three months before they were discovered.

At the board level several directors argued about accountability and over a number of months the matter was played out in the media. In the end several directors and senior staff have left with more to follow.

The business and tabloid press reported on 12 June 2004:

A survey by Neilsen Media Research shows the NAB foreign exchange debacle and the related Boardroom purge has left it with little credibility with Bank customers.

Just 2.6% of those considering a change of banks in the March quarter would choose the NAB down from 5.6% three months earlier. This equates to some 28 000 customers.[17]

The APRA Report says:

That this were possible was first and foremost due to the collusive behaviour of the traders themselves. However it can also be attributed to an operating environment characterised by lax and unquestioning oversight by line management; poor adherence to risk management systems and controls and weaknesses in internal governance procedures.[18]

The conduct was uncovered by a relatively junior currency options desk employee who came forward and questioned the conduct.

The PWC report says that what went wrong was the integrity of the people, the risk and control framework and the governance and culture.

The reports identify that in similar large organisations there are many layers of internal controls as in the NAB.

The APRA Report notes that:

> While the collusive behaviour of the traders involved succeeded in suppressing many of the bank's early warning signals, NAB's internal control systems failed to detect and shut down the irregular currency options trading activity. NAB's internal governance model, which should have enabled timely identification and effective and quick escalation of serious risk issues . . . simply did not function.

That this could occur is symptomatic of an organisational culture lacking sufficient regard to the risks attendant with these products. In particular:[19]

- *Line Management* turned a blind eye to known risk management concerns. Despite some worrying signals of irregular trading practices on the currency options desk, these were ignored. 'Profit is king' was an expression frequently heard in our interviews with Corporate and Institutional Banking (CIB) staff. As long as the business unit turned a profit, other shortcomings could be overlooked.
- *Operations (the back office)* verification procedures contained significant gaps, raising questions about the adequacy of its resourcing and skills, and whether its mandate had been weakened by pressure to reduce costs and its growing subservience to the front office.
- *Market Risk (the middle office)*, while noting a number of irregularities, failed to engage the trading desk effectively to resolve them and failed to attract the attention of higher management or otherwise escalate its concerns.
- *Executive Risk Committees* were particularly ineffective, missing or dismissing risk information pertinent to the problems that emerged and failing to escalate warnings. If the members of the CIB Risk Management Committee had acted on the warning signs before them – for example, by commissioning a targeted review of known

control weaknesses by Internal Audit – the irregular trading would surely have been discovered.

- *The Principal Board (the Board)* was not sufficiently proactive on risk issues. Despite often asserting that risk issues were of such importance that they should be dealt with by the full board, the Board paid insufficient attention to risk issues and, until the establishment of a separate risk committee, appeared content to leave the elevation of risk issues to its Audit Committee.

The PWC report makes similar points:
In regard to the Risk and Control Framework it said:

Lack of adequate supervision – the Traders took large, complex and risky positions, while supervision was limited to headline profit and loss monitoring. Through concealment of the losses, CIB management derived misplaced confidence that risks were tolerable. Multiple risk limit breaches and other warnings were not treated seriously, and no effective steps were taken to restrain the Traders.

Warnings from the market about large or unusual currency transactions drew an aggressive response from representatives of the National and the concerns were passed off without proper investigation. In January 2003 letters from APRA received by the Chairman and the EGM Risk Management, did not prompt an adequate response from the National.

Risk management failed – there were flaws in the design, implementation and execution of risk management. Market Risk & Prudential Control (MR&PC) knew about and reported but failed to escalate persistent risk limit breaches effectively.

Absence of financial controls – our investigation identified insufficient procedures to identify, investigate and explain unusual or suspicious transactions. Normal month end processes lacked adequate cut-off procedures and did not restate results to adjust for cancelled or amended transactions.

Gaps in back office procedures – the back office failed to detect false transactions. This failure was caused in part by the one-hour window between close of day for reporting purposes and back office checking, which enabled the Traders to falsify the true position of the desk. From October 2003, junior back office staff discontinued checking internal currency option transactions. As a result, the Traders were able to process false one-sided internal options transactions without being detected.[20]

In regard to governance and culture the report said:

Board oversight – the Principal Board received risk management information that was incorrect, incomplete or insufficiently detailed to alert them to limit breaches or other matters related to the currency options desk's operations.

Principal Board Audit Committee (PBAC) – reviewed a number of reports from a range of internal and external parties that did not alert them directly to any issues in respect of currency options. After reading the supporting papers, probing of management may have revealed the seriousness of some of the control breakdowns.

Principal Board Risk Committee (PBRC) – the first meeting of the PBRC in November 2003 was not informed of the currency options desk's risk limit breaches, but was reassured that the Markets Division as a whole was well within VaR limits.

Group Executive Forum, Group Risk Forum and Central Risk Management Committee – there was no evidence of escalation of issues relating to the currency options desk to these groups.

CIB management – was aware of significant limit breaches and failed to investigate and take action. CIB management had little confidence in the VaR numbers due to systems and data issues, and effectively ignored VaR and other limit breaches. There was no sense of urgency in resolving the VaR calculation issues which had been a problem for a period of two or more years.

Risk management – MR&PC raised warnings about the currency options desk's limit breaches and other exceptions. These warnings were not escalated to the CEO or the Board.

Internal Audit – reported on significant currency options issues, but failed to follow up and ensure that appropriate controls and procedure changes had been implemented.

The National's culture – there was an excessive focus on process, documentation and procedure manuals rather than on understanding the substance of issues, taking responsibility and resolving matters. In addition, there was an arrogance in dealing with warning signs (i.e. APRA letters, market comments, etc). Our investigation revealed that management had a tendency to 'pass on', rather than assume, responsibility. Similarly, issues were not escalated to the Board and its committees and bad news was suppressed. Our investigations indicate that the culture fostered the environment that provided the opportunity for the Traders to incur losses, conceal them and escape detection despite ample warning signs. This enabled them to operate unchecked and flout the rules and standards of the National. Ultimately, the Board and the CEO must accept responsibility.[21]

Culture

The three reports quoted in this chapter indicate that despite the best systems and procedures all systems will fail to operate without the correct culture.

In the rail accident context many of the matters which were identified in the report had been identified in a previous Royal Commission into a previous accident some three years previously.

In the case of the NAB, the reports suggest that the company systems recognised the possibility of these events occurring but they suggest they were at the time unable to either prevent or initially manage the situation as well as they would have hoped when it occurred.

In both cases, had a different culture of compliance existed in some parts of the organisation it appears likely that it may have permeated the organisation making the events significantly less likely to occur.

Common features where compliance has failed

The following section takes some common features of governance and compliance failures I use in my work and applies them to the two case studies. These features may not be applicable in every situation but have helped to guide me in identifying points of weakness in governance and compliance systems in organisations in all sectors. They have also assisted in designing new systems of governance or revising or reinvigorating existing systems.

- *Lack of a strong system; evidenced by an absence of clear systems, commitment and risk assessment*

In both case studies the systems were identified as having shortcomings in this area.

- *Failure by people who can create a liability for the company but who may not have been included in the system such as through missing training or induction or a lack of inclusiveness in system design*

The APRA report on the NAB indicated that:

> The JHFX circumvented the formal recruitment processes (for example, we understand that no external reference checks were conducted) in engaging the currency options team in 1998 and 1999. Also, although a performance appraisal for one of the dealers identified excessive risk-taking as a concern, no action was taken. The other measures proved ineffective in controlling the operating environment in the dealing room and the domineering and bullying behaviours of front office staff.[22]

- *Communications difficulties either between the company and its employees or with customers or other critical stakeholders*

The Waterfall incident highlighted this lack of communication at the time of the critical event and also the communication dysfunctions between the train driver and the train guard.

It is clear from the reports on the National Australia Bank that at board level there were also communication problems. APRA notes that at least one critical document appears not to have been passed to the board.

- *Supervision or reporting dysfunctions enabling individuals or profit centres to operate outside ethical principles or the company system*

In the NAB case this appears to have been a significant contributing factor.

In the Waterfall case study the issue of the deadman's pedal (see above) and the subsequent investigation revealed what was apparently common knowledge that the system of safety control was routinely circumvented.

One feature of the Waterfall case which also illustrates this challenge involves the attempt by a number of passengers to call the triple 0 emergency line used for such emergencies. The staff at the call centre did not believe the callers that an accident had occurred and considered several of the initial calls nuisance calls.

- *The distance of the operation from the head office*

I understand that some of the forex traders were operating off shore in the NAB case study. The trading room culture is well known to those who operate in that environment but to other members of the banking community such conduct may not have been seen as the norm.

At the time of the critical incident in the Waterfall case study distance from head office was a significant factor. For example, no one could initially locate the place where the accident had occurred. Because the accident occurred in quite steep topography the conventional radio system would not work and the staff at the nearby station had to call another railway station some distance to the south to endeavour to make contact. In the end contact was made by mobile phone.

- *Creation of unachievable return on investment demands or expectations of company profits and linking such expectations to payment to individuals or the individual or business consumer's economic survival*

In the Waterfall case study this was characterised by an obsessive focus on timetable and 'on-time' running above other issues.

The NAB reports indicated that the culture which rewarded return on investment created some of the climate in which the incident could arise.

- *Start-up period of new ventures particularly where limited capital or operating funds are available and strong standards and procedures are not in place*

In both cases they were not at start-up situations. This remains one of the more effective indicators we use in governance reviews.

In the Waterfall case the safety regulator had no experience in such a devastating event and did not have appropriate plans or systems to manage the event.

- *Companies operating in a market with a small number of competitors and long-term relationships*

The railway company is a government monopoly and at the time there was no independent safety regulator.

In Australia the government has a policy which limits the number of banks to four major banks.

- *Situations where the board or senior management do not insist upon knowing about compliance systems, complaints handling and alternate dispute resolution systems*

In the NAB case study the reports indicate this appears to have been an issue.

In the railway case study the report suggests that it is difficult to believe that several of the critical issues which are described in the safety report would not have been known to senior managers if not the board. The same Royal Commissioner is hearing this matter as heard the most recent similar accident in NSW and he has commented on this matter in a preliminary report.

- *When new laws are put in place*

This does not appear to have been an issue in this case but is a common indicia.

- *Where individuals or corporations within the system may see themselves as economically captured by the company or the system*

In both case studies the individuals concerned were under significant pressure to perform.

- *Where the company internal and external complaint handling system does not meet the Australian Standard*

In each case it is difficult to believe that complaints about both sets of conduct would not have prevented the problem or at least reduced the impact, even if they had been made by staff internally.

In the NAB case study the matter was apparently exposed by a whistleblower.

In the Waterfall case study the report talks about a culture which was not conducive to reporting.

- *Where learning, training, education and general skills acquisition are not designed, developed and delivered to meet both the company's and learners' needs*

In the Waterfall case study the train guard did not have the appropriate training or confidence to take action when he might have realised that the train was going too fast. In fairness it is likely, however, that even if he had had such skills and confidence he would not have had time.

I have commented on the NAB case study and training dysfunctions above.

- *Where the corporate cultural links within the company are not apparent to all parties*

In both cases the reports point to some dysfunctions in the corporate culture links between the various areas of the organisation.

- *Where companies are either too risk averse or unaware of their business risks generally and particularly in terms of the critical control points for managing risks*

Risk management features in both case studies. In the Waterfall case study the lack of effective risk management plans was seen as a critical issue. The investigators reviewed the State Rail Authority's (the government railway company) Safety Management System (SMS). They found the following statement in the risk registers: 'the hazard and risk register is periodically reviewed to ensure it is kept up to date'.[23]

The report says that 'the investigation found no evidence of individual registers or of a combined risk and hazard register'.[24]

> Formal and informal interviews of SRA employees in less senior positions provided investigators with the following impressions of their views of the safety management system. They ranged from no knowledge, to cynicism about the intention of its introduction to a feeling that it was just another fad to a recognition by some of the importance of such a system . . .
>
> Evidence indicated that it was not uncommon for those administering and applying the system to be appointed to their positions without safety management experience or qualification.
>
> - *Where companies may suffer from corporate blindness regarding the potential for system or people failure*

In both cases it appears that some of the executive and perhaps some on the boards did not believe that the event could happen to them.

- *Where one person becomes the gatekeeper and the programme is not embedded into the company sufficiently well to survive if they leave the company*

The challenge in developing governance systems is to ensure that one or more people do not take control and become gatekeepers.

Conclusion

Governance has to be more than a state of mind.

Both these case studies illustrate the need for a robust system and procedures.

This can only occur if the culture is strong, well articulated, regularly supported and reinforced and more than just a state of mind.

Behind the systems and procedures must be a culture which encourages compliance with the governance system and allows information to pass through to the board.

At the board level members need to have the ability to receive and process both the good news and the bad news.

It is likely that I could have chosen any one of the many incidents and events which have troubled those of us involved in governance on boards or advising boards and come away with similar conclusions.

My company's experience in conducting these types of investigation or reviewing the work of others, as in this case, is that there are critical control points where a governance, risk management or compliance intervention, properly applied, may prevent the incident or event.

Therefore in designing governance systems the same issues become the guides for developing procedures, controls, reporting and accountability and training systems. Behind all this the leaders and key influencers in the organisation must set the tone so that a culture of compliance and good governance is strong enough to resist the obvious temptations of bad business and expediency.

In both case studies some of the critical elements were not addressed and governance as simply a state of mind proved in one case to be fatal and in the other provided a major short-term challenge.

Notes

1. J. Reason, *Managing the Risks in Organisational Accidents*. Aldershot Ashgate, 1997.
2. Australian Institute of Company Directors, Sydney, Australia 2004. *Company Director* 20/5, June. p. 3.
3. Australian Prudential Regulatory Authority: *Report into Irregular Currency Options Trading at the National Australia Bank*, 23 March 2004: www.apra.gov.au
4. PricewaterhouseCoopers: *Investigation into Foreign Exchange losses at the National Australia Bank*: www.national.com.au
5. NSW Ministry of Transport: *Waterfall 31 January 2003 Railway Safety Investigation: Final Report*: downloaded from www.transport.nsw.gov.au
6. J. Reason, *Managing the Risks in Organisational Accidents*. Aldershot Ashgate, 1997.
7. See www.standards.org.au
8. For a copy of CLERP 9 and further information, see www.asic.gov.au
9. See www.asic.gov.au
10. See www.asx.com.au
11. NSW Ministry of Transport: *Waterfall 31 January 2003 Railway Safety Investigation*: Final Report: downloaded from www.transport.nsw.gov.au, p. 52.
12. NSW Ministry of Transport: *Waterfall 31 January 2003 Railway Safety Investigation*: Final Report: downloaded from www.transport.nsw.gov.au, p. 49.
13. NSW Ministry of Transport: *Waterfall 31 January 2003 Railway Safety Investigation*: Final Report: downloaded from www.transport.nsw.gov.au, p. 52.
14. NSW Ministry of Transport: *Waterfall 31 January 2003 Railway Safety Investigation*: Final Report: downloaded from www.transport.nsw.gov.au, p. 47.
15. NSW Ministry of Transport: *Waterfall 31 January 2003 Railway Safety Investigation*: Final Report: downloaded from www.transport.nsw.gov.au, p. 49.
16. NSW Ministry of Transport: *Waterfall 31 January 2003 Railway Safety Investigation*: Final Report: downloaded from www.transport.nsw.gov.au, p. 49.
17. *Sydney Daily Telegraph*, Saturday 12 June 2004, p. 79 (the Business section headline).
18. Australian Prudential Regulatory Authority: *Report into Irregular Currency Options Trading at the National Australia Bank*, 23 March 2004: www.apra.gov.au, p. 5.

19. Australian Prudential Regulatory Authority: *Report into Irregular Currency Options Trading at the National Australia Bank*, 23 March 2004: www.apra.gov.au, pp. 5–6.
20. PricewaterhouseCoopers, Investigation into Foreign Exchange losses at the National Australia Bank: www.national.com.au, p. 3.
21. PricewaterhouseCoopers, Investigation into Foreign Exchange losses at the National Australia Bank: www.national.com.au, p. 4.
22. Australian Prudential Regulatory Authority: *Report into Irregular Currency Options Trading at the National Australia Bank*, 23 March 2004: www.apra.gov.au, p. 76.
23. NSW Ministry of Transport: *Waterfall 31 January 2003 Railway Safety Investigation: Final Report*: downloaded from www.transport.nsw.gov.au, p. 55, italics in original.
24. NSW Ministry of Transport: *Waterfall 31 January 2003 Railway Safety Investigation: Final Report*: downloaded from www.transport.nsw.gov.au, pp. 55 and 54.

16

Redesigning Financial Regulation: Eliot Spitzer, State–Federal Relations and the Battle for Corporate Control

Justin O'Brien

Introduction

The relationship between regulator and regulated on Wall Street has been transformed by the actions of the New York State Attorney General, Eliot Spitzer. A combative lawyer, he has fused the legal and political aspects of his office to force structural changes on the governance of key intermediating forces operating within United States capital markets. Critics claim he is a populist cast in the mould of Robespierre, who has unleashed chaos and contributed to a dangerous 'Balkanisation' of financial control mechanisms in the pursuit of political ambition. Defenders point out that without his intervention the structural defects in Wall Street analyst research, shortfalls in the governance of the New York Stock Exchange and corruption in the insurance industry because of contingent commissions and other hidden payments to steer underwriting business would remain undetected by an overarching regulatory system that has demonstrably and repeatedly failed.

This chapter traces Spitzer's rise to national prominence and the implications of his strategic application of state law to force systemic changes. Located at the intersection of economic and political governance in the pre-eminent global financial capital, it reflects themes central to this volume state–federal relations: greed, corruption, hubris and the need for enhanced accountability mechanisms to counter the deleterious impact of these problems. The focus is less on what Spitzer has uncovered, which has been dealt with elsewhere (O'Brien 2003, 2004a; Lowenstein 2004; Galbraith 2004). Rather it centres on what his concurrent investigations tell us about how the contested, contingent and interdependent nature of the national self-regulatory regime in the United States impacts on the battle for political control over the corporate form.

Explicating how the New York State Attorney General has maximised the leverage provided by the innovative application of overlapping jurisdictional power has application far beyond the confines of the geographical boundaries of the state. It provides important evidence of how ambitious policy entrepreneurs within a federal system can exploit structural vulnerabilities to challenge the dominance of corporate power over regulatory design at national and international levels. The capacity of the national government and its agencies to enforce their writ over the governance of the markets is examined therefore with direct reference to how the competing dynamics of federalism offers a counterweight to the hegemonic conception of neo-liberalism and the emergent power within it of corporate actors to distort the deliberative agenda.

While relative power in that relationship is fluid, American federalism still operates primarily on the basis of state sovereignty in the regulatory realm. As Gerber and Teske (2000, 851) have pointed out, in the context of US regulatory politics the 'venue of primary policy execution itself becomes a central feature in explaining the logic of political influence on policymaking'. It is the exploitation of this reality that gives Spitzer's intervention such crucial significance. The resulting traction is linked directly to the serendipitous confluence of the strategic importance of New York in world economic markets, the application of latent jurisdictional advantage provided to the state under the federal system of government and political ambition.

Based on an extensive interview conducted with Spitzer in New York (10 December 2004), the chapter provides crucial insights into what drives one of the most pivotal regulatory actors in the United States. The following sections situate the institutional position of the New York Attorney General within the matrix of political and economic power. First, the constellation of forces that gives Spitzer unique leverage as a policy entrepreneur is traced. The power of the markets to frame and emasculate policy responses at the national level is then examined with reference to the literature of regulatory change. The final sections examine the implications of Spitzer's capacity to exploit the gaps in the regulatory framework both in terms of capturing and reconfiguring the reform agenda.

Location, Location, Location

Spitzer maintains that any suggestion that he is hostile to the operation of free markets misses the point. He argues that his intervention is predicated on a belief that effective markets cannot be sustained without robust regulatory oversight of existing standards. 'I say repeatedly to Chief Executive Officers that you would have been better served to have adopted the gradual process of reform. It would have saved you from the gross excesses or the pain that you are going through right now' (Interview, 10 December 2004).

The early and sustained emphasis on creative proactive enforcement differentiates his office from other state and federal bodies charged with market oversight. It underpinned the 'enforced self-regulation' (Ayres and Braithwaite 1992) component of a settlement with Merrill Lynch over conflicts of interest in the provision of research reports that catapulted Spitzer onto the national and international media stage. Demonstrating that the research departments of premier securities houses manipulated corporate coverage for investment banking purposes was always problematic until Spitzer's investigators discovered just how useful email records could be. Buried deep in the hard drives, the elusive proof of systemic abuse was revealed in the dyslexic boasting of research analysts who maintained 'buy' ratings while privately describing stock as 'junk' or 'POS [Piece of Shit]' (O'Brien 2003, 155–157). Taking a case against Merrill Lynch on the basis of New York State law that predated the Securities Acts of 1933–34, Spitzer alleged that research analysts were employed as 'quasi-investment bankers for the companies at issue, often initiating, continuing and/or manipulating research coverage for the purpose of attracting and keeping investment banking clients' (O'Brien 2003, 155).

Merrill's acceptance of forced internal changes to the governance of its research department in exchange for abeyance of charges, which, if prosecuted to a conclusion, would have caused catastrophic reputational damage, created a template for wider systemic change (O'Brien 2004a). Once Merrill caved in, it was inevitable that a global settlement with other merchant banking institutions would have to be reached. For Gary Lynch, Vice Chairman of Credit Suisse First Boston and a former Director of Enforcement at the Securities and Exchange Commission, Spitzer simply outmanoeuvred the federal regulators and forced them into action:

> At that point everyone [in the investment banking community] was saying 'tell us what you want us to do'. What people hoped to avoid, which we didn't avoid, was them saying: 'No, we're not going to do that we don't want to do that. What we want to do is to have an investigation and fine you a whole lot of money'. (O'Brien 2003, 167)

The eventual penalties in a global settlement, which encompassed the major regulators and a consortium of State Attorney Generals, led by Spitzer, went far beyond financial recompense to cash-strapped state chanceries. The forced publication of the results of that joint investigation, under Spitzer's direct instruction, provided ammunition for class-action tort lawyers, whose capacity to have their case heard in either state or federal court was increased dramatically by their ability to prove just cause. An indication of the eventual cost to Wall Street of malfeasance is the fact that Citigroup alone, the largest financial services conglomerate, has set aside $4.95 billion to cover its exposure (Bloomberg 2004). By bringing the initial Merrill case and setting the agenda in relation to subsequent investigations into corporate abuse, Spitzer not only highlighted profound structural problems in the governance of the markets but also placed into play the contested limits of state and federal sovereignty.

The importance of this strategic intervention cannot be overestimated. Through his actions Spitzer has transcended a political and industry response predicated primarily on the challenge of how to limit the discretion of morally challenged executives. The capacity to alter the debate is linked to the specific circumstances of his powerbase. A senior compliance officer for a major investment bank, interviewed by the author in 2003 as Spitzer was negotiating a settlement with Merrill Lynch over tainted analyst research, encapsulates both the anger and grudging respect which the New York Attorney General generates in equal measure.

To be candid about it while the states have been bringing actions for 60 years the presence and amount of publicity they got was always somewhat contained. They were viewed as having a useful purpose but they never had celebrity status. Spitzer's case has brought glory and publicity and all this attention to state regulators, not to mention a whole lot of money to state treasuries. I think state regulators are sitting across all of the United States now saying 'Wow! We have real power, we have real authority. We have a way to be very profitable. We need to flex our muscles even more in the future.' This tension is going to grow. At some stage something is going to give. (O'Brien 2003, 144)

The tension is given tangible expression because of the rhetorical framing of 'New Federalism', which reconfigures in ideational terms the relationship between Washington and state capitals in much social and economic regulation (Rose-Ackerman 1992). This delegation of regulatory authority in response to what amounted to 'a crisis of legalism and command' (Moran 2003, 16) and overreach in the federal regulatory environment (Sparrow 2000) changed the power balance of state–federal relations in profound ways.

As the national government gradually withdrew from the regulatory playing field space opened for policy entrepreneurs to play pivotal roles in the regulation of social and economic markets. Their relative power depended on the level of interstate competition and degree of residual federal power (Lowry 1992). The institutionalisation of deregulation created a cross-cutting ideological dynamic at national level which reduced the capacity of the federal government to exercise its privileged use of concurrent powers. The changes in the national regulatory regime were not accompanied by a revisiting of the intergovernmental settlement. In part this can be traced to the difficulty in pushing through complex and potentially destabilising constitutional changes; in part to the fact that national policymakers did not factor into ideological imperatives how expanding state oversight could facilitate, in the case of New York, the serendipitous confluence of ambition, powerbase and platform.

Writing just as the bear market reared its head, Spitzer gave an early indication of how deregulation impacted on his legal philosophy.

Despite my initial skepticism, the day I awoke as Attorney General of New York, I had an epiphany – I suddenly recognized that the devolution of decision making from Washington to the States about how to enforce statutes or non statutory rights did not determine the substantive conclusion of those making decisions of the state level. Indeed, I now see this change as a tremendous opportunity for legal ingenuity and innovation on the part of state actors. (Spitzer 2000)

Given the traditional concentration of the securities and wider financial services industries in New York, its state officials have always held the potential to exert extraordinary influence over the terms of the national debate on the control of capital markets. The use of this latent power had been honoured more in breach than observance until Spitzer began his assault on the governance of the markets in the wake of the technology crash. History, however, wrote the political economist Susan Strange, is a necessary corrective to hubris. As Spitzer acknowledges with a glint of satisfaction, the myopic fixation with the present in contemporary American politics gave him the flexibility to build 'a coherent rationale under the political radar' (Interview, 10 December 2004).

Neither the securities industry nor state and national legislators gave due cognisance to how an assertive lawyer with political ambitions could use the latent power of New Federalism to revisit ground once trampled by Theodore Roosevelt and his cousin Franklin Delano, the towering figures of twentieth century New York politics who also used state-initiated campaigns against patronage and cartels to forge national careers (Black 2003; Seligman 2003). Through the utilisation of pre-emptive investigative techniques, focused on high-profile targets, a compelling narrative has been recreated. It captures populist revulsion at the rash of corporate scandals and positions Spitzer as the custodian of the reform tradition articulated in earlier battles to exert political control over corporate and vested political interests.

During an address to the National Press Club on 31 January 2004, Spitzer revelled in his notoriety. Recounting how a lawyer representing an investment bank told him 'Eliot, be careful we have powerful friends', Spitzer scathingly commented: 'I had no choice but to file the lawsuit. I mean what was I going to do at that point? Should I back down and say: "Oh, I didn't know you had powerful friends. Now you tell me. If you only had told me that last week we wouldn't be here"' (Spitzer 2005, 5).

While Spitzer claims modesty prevents overt comparison with his political icons, he maintains that, like them, his intention is not to destroy the markets but protect them from the most egregious examples of abuse: 'I operate only in the world of malfeasance and the capacity of my office to intervene involves a predicate of illegality. There has been so much misfeasance that I haven't worried about it. I think if we ever get to the point where we only had to deal with misfeasance we would have done quite well' (Interview, 10 December 2004).

Despite the fact that the Attorney General has yet to prosecute a case involving Wall Street malfeasance to judicial closure, a cult of personality has developed which business and political opponents alike have failed to deflate. Spitzer's ability to drive the media discourse on corporate excess is further consolidated by the fact that New York plays host to some of the country's most influential print publications. *The New York Times, The Wall Street Journal* and *The New Yorker* each has provided copious amounts of largely positive copy in their news pages, a process which is facilitated by an adroit media management operation conducted out of the Attorney General's Manhattan headquarters just off Wall Street on Broadway.

Spitzer has also featured on the front cover of *Time* and *Newsweek*. In 2004 he picked up the 'Person of the Year' accolade from the *Financial Times*. His capacity to capture the public Zeitgeist was verified by a flattering *Vanity Fair* profile (Seliger 2005) in which the Attorney General posed for the highly stylised portrait most commonly reserved in the magazine for Hollywood icons. Set against a backdrop of a darkened rain-soaked Broadway, Spitzer appears bathed in light, a gold American flag lapel badge glinting in reflected tungsten, one hand resting nonchalantly on the highly polished stem of an upturned umbrella. The framing reflected the Attorney General's own self-perception as a harbinger of light amid the gloom of a system that has lost moral authority.

The portrait evokes explicit comparison with the late American jurist Louis Brandeis, whose reputation was also built on confronting the danger of untrammelled corporate power. Whether Spitzer merits comparison with Brandeis, the 'progressive idealist' (Strum 1992) or Brandeis the propagandist with an unerring capacity to tack towards winning ground (McGraw 1984) is very much an open question. What is unmistakable, however, is their common determination to use the application of the law as a political weapon to force change far beyond the narrow remits of individual cases.

More problematic for state–federal relations is the fact that in the process Spitzer has not only launched a direct challenge to the authority of the SEC and self-regulatory organisations. He has played a central role in the advocacy of a fundamental redesign in national policy. This takes us to the root of Spitzer's reform agenda. For Spitzer, the central problem is how to ensure that adequate controls are placed on the operation of financial intermediaries, whose capacity to game the regulatory system is based on rational decision-making processes that calculate the net benefit of non-compliance.

According to Spitzer, the malfeasance progressively uncovered demonstrates intractable and insurmountable problems associated with the policy preferences of the national regulatory regime to privilege self-regulation. He argues that an 'insidious form of industry capture', linked to the cultural denigration of the regulatory profession, represents the most important causal mechanism driving control failures. 'The whole idea of self-regulation should be put in a box labeled "great idea that never worked" because the role of these industry associations became primarily the role of rolling back reform ideas. The excesses have demonstrated serious flaws in the paradigm. I am not convinced that it can ever work' (Interview, 10 December 2004).

This activism has led to profound disagreements with leading congressional legislators. The irony of Michael Oxley's name appearing as co-sponsor of the most stringent corporate liability legislation introduced by Congress since the 1930s was underscored by his public spat with the New York Attorney General. 'Grandstanding by ambitious and publicity-hungry political officials will not lead to healthy and responsible securities markets' was his considered estimation of the Merrill Lynch deal. Spitzer retorted in evidence to the Senate Banking Committee: 'I believe that Congress and the federal government cannot have it both ways. If Congress and the Executive Branch decide to curtail federal oversight of areas such as securities, they must recognize it is the responsibility of state securities regulators such as myself to step in and protect the investing public' (O'Brien 2003, 171).

The government's role in regulating and defining the parameters of appropriate business standards remains a critical unresolved issue (Donaldson 2004; Romano 2004). Noting that regulators are witnessing the beginning of a sustained counteroffensive by business to delineate the range and extent of internal and external control mechanisms, Spitzer has complained that 'there has been a catastrophic failure to adhere to even basic conceptions of honest dealings and fiduciary duty in every sector my Office has looked at' (Interview, 10 December 2004). The problem is not a new one but rather the contemporary manifestation of a perennial question: can the market instil credible ethical restraint or can transparency and integrity, which are integral to confidence, be achieved only through the intervention of government. If it is the latter, can this be achieved by the federal government acting alone? Does Spitzer's activism help or hinder that process? To answer these questions it is necessary to delineate the dynamics of financial regulation within the unique context of a federal system.

Mapping the Terrain

A regulatory system can be usefully mapped as a regime. Using the navigational aid developed by Hood et al. (2004, 8), a regime denotes 'the complex of institutional [physical and social] geography, rules, practice and animating ideas that are associated with the regulation of a particular risk or hazard'. While Hood et al. limit their analysis to risk, the tripartite meso-theoretical framework developed has applicability to wider questions of regulatory governance. The model's descriptive, explanatory and prescriptive power lies in its 'cybernetic' conception of regulation: an interconnected but bounded system characterised by a degree of continuity. The authors argue that in order to adequately explain regulatory dynamics, it is necessary first to differentiate context, including degree of media and public salience, from content, which is defined as 'the policy settings, the configuration of state and other organizations directly engaged in regulating the risk and the attitudes, beliefs and operating intentions of the regulators' (Hood et al. 2004, 21). Change within this system is determined by a confluence of 'sudden climacterics as well as their incremental adjustments and steady trends' (Hood et al. 2004, 9). Although the framework is designed primarily for use within a unitary system of government, by adapting it with reference to the 'regulatory space' argument adopted by Hancher and Moran (1989) we can begin the process of accurately mapping a bounded system in which both regulatory authority and form are dispersed and varied across state jurisdictions.

In contrast to a unitary state structure, within a federal system the sources of pressure on institutional capacity increase exponentially and potentially nowhere more so than in the United States. It has one of the most codified regulatory systems in the world, with a plethora of interlocking centralised bureaucratic and enfranchised self-regulating agencies operating at both federal and state level (Gerber and Teske 2000). The manoeuvrability of institutions within this structure to create, maintain, transfer or lose power depends, crucially, on relational authority relative to the degree to which other actors in the governance equation are prepared to acquiesce to real or merely symbolic oversight.

This is particularly problematic within the context of contested federalism. While the federal government facilitates, inhibits and initiates regulatory capacity (Zimmerman 2001), the exact form is dependent on the degree of cooperation forthcoming from the states. The mid-range option of 'partial pre-emption' (Zimmerman 2001), designed to foster minimum national standards, in practice can limit the federal role to the provision of technical assistance. It transfers by default enforcement responsibilities to states (Hedge and Scicchitano 1994, 134). This can have both positive and negative normative implications. Depending on the level of interstate competition, political power of interest or consumer groups and political contestation, states can engage in regulatory arbitrage. States may lack either the resources or resolve to exercise their mandate while simultaneously retain the capacity to stymie central agency resolve. Precisely because of the budgetary implications of possible industry flight, states face acute pressure to create or sustain regulatory advantage thus making uniform enforcement an impossible ideal (Teske 2004; Hedge and Scicchitano 1994, 150). Equally, the degree of industry concentration or demographic power in a particular state can create *de facto* national standards. Examples of this dominant capacity to include Delaware's pre-eminence as a destination of choice for incorporation (Murphy 2004; Strine 2002). On the other hand despite the stringent nature of emission controls in California, the critical importance of its market has forced the industry to raise standards beyond the federal threshold.

The notoriety and traction Spitzer has achieved is linked directly, therefore, to the paradox of a collection of unitary states operating within a contested federal structure. The particularity of the New York State constitution gives its Attorney General the institutional capacity to take pre-emptive action to protect what the incumbent perceives to be the public interest (Spill *et al.* 2001, 606). In contrast to New Jersey, where executive power resides in the hands of the Governor alone, there are limited gubernatorial or legislative restraints on Spitzer's capacity to initiate litigation irrespective of the will of other policy actors at state or national level.

What differentiates Spitzer as a policy entrepreneur has been his determination to demonstrate the deleterious consequences for the integrity of the market caused by the federal regulatory regime resiling from the exercise of concurrent power. Add to this mix Manhattan's geo-economic importance as a global financial and media centre, political ambition, the capacity to engineer punitive damages and headlines by setting the price for legal settlement, and public receptiveness to a socially constructed narrative based on defenestrating executive excess because of prior hubris and the inordinate power held by Spitzer to influence the future trajectory of national financial regulatory policy comes into clear focus.

In evidence to Congress in November 2004 in relation to fraud and anti-trust violations in the insurance industry, Spitzer declared unambiguously:

> It is clear that the federal government's hands-off policy with regard to insurance combined with uneven State-regulation has not entirely worked. There are too many gaps in regulation across the 50 states and many state regulators have not been sufficiently aggressive in terms of supervising this industry... At a minimum, federal involvement may be necessary to assure some basic standards of accountability on the part of insurance professionals. (Spitzer 2004, 13)

Spitzer was careful not to suggest that federal pre-emption was the answer. Rather his focus was on the lack of regulatory resolve, a discourse mechanism that neatly ensures the continued centrality of his investigative methods, ideological predispositions and wider political ambitions. In this there are significant further throwbacks to the juridical canon of Louis Brandeis. As early as 1926, Brandeis proclaimed that 'a single courageous state may, if its citizens choose, serve as a laboratory, and try social and economic experiments without risk to the rest of the country' (Teske 2004, 7). Nowhere is this resolve to provide a laboratory for economic engineering more apparent than in the strategic prosecutions of corporations as entities as well as senior executives and the concomitant defenestration of the hubris that governed the administration of the New York Stock Exchange under the tenure of Dick Grasso (Demirag and O'Brien 2004). Whether the risk of contagion can be confined to New York itself given the global importance of Manhattan as the pre-eminent financial services centre is another matter entirely. In order to test the efficacy of Spitzer's argument that radical redesign is both necessary and viable, it is first essential to trace why the Securities and Exchange Commission failed to prevent the emergence of the contemporary manifestation of market failure.

Regulating the Market: Differentiating Relative and Ideational Power

In examining the reality of American finance, the striking image of 'casino capitalism' developed by Susan Strange (1986) retains its potency. So too does the gastronomic metaphor deployed by one former market participant, who likens the markets to 'a Swiss cheese, with the holes – the unregulated places – getting bigger every year, as parties transacting around legal rules eat away at the regulatory system from within' (Partnoy 2003, 394). For Partnoy (2003, 2) 'any appearance of control in today's financial markets is only an illusion, not a grounded reality'. Perhaps the most appropriate metaphor dates back to Galbraith's (1992) seminal investigation into the causes of the Great Crash. 'Wall Street', remarked the economist, 'is like a lovely and accomplished woman who must wear black cotton stockings, heavy woollen underwear, and parade her knowledge as a cook, because, unhappily, her supreme accomplishment is as a harlot' (Galbraith 1992, 46).

By the end of century the financial devices deployed by the tease merchants of Lower Manhattan to lure the greedy and the incautious had become more sophisticated than trading on margin but the basic premise remained substantially unchanged (as did the reliance of the political establishment on vociferous, but empty, exhortations to the brothel providers to deny themselves and their customers). Galbraith returned to the fray with the publication of *The Economics of Innocent Fraud* (2004), an elegant and deeply subversive book, the central argument of which is that corporate power has become uncontrollable. For Galbraith, the 'market system' is a deliberate misnomer. 'Sensitive friends and beneficiaries of the system do not wish to assign definitive authority to the corporation. Better the benign reference to the market' (Galbraith 2004, 21).

As such, the financial services industry has amassed enormous power to inform the terms of political discourse over questions of accountability and control. The trading of stock and financial services has displaced product as the primal generator of wealth in the United States (Philips 2002). The proportion of equity *vis-à-vis* commercial lending to industrial enterprises is among the highest in the world (Hollingsworth 1997, 137–138). While increased securitisation is a global reality, the centrality of liquid equity markets as the source of capital defines American capitalism. In the process it has reinforced the short-term nature of its business model and led to a privileging of values over value (Greenspan 2004).

The necessity to meet quarterly share price targets elevated short-term tactics in preference to long-term strategy, a move mirrored in the *de facto* if not *de jure* downgrading of corporate legal and compliance programmes. Corporate policy was defined by deference to Wall Street metrics evaluating core value, a policy that in the most egregious circumstances turned legal departments into profit centres rather than gatekeepers of reputational integrity. The result was an institutionalised propensity among those in whom fiduciary trust was placed to engage in a deliberate 'gaming of the system' (O'Brien 2003, 49).

The complex and largely technical nature of financial regulation means that in the absence of crisis it attracts little overt controversy. This privileges by default the disproportionate influence of business, industry and intergovernmental lobbying. Overarching responsibility for the operation of the capital markets ostensibly lies with the Securities and Exchange Commission. Its capacity is limited by the, at times, conflicting interests of other national regulators including the Federal Reserve (the integrity of the currency and wider economic policy) and the Office of the Comptroller of the Currency. A division of the Treasury that regulates banks, the OCC is alleged by Spitzer (2005, 11) to be actively engaged in a policy to persuade major institutions to move towards federal-charter status in order to pre-empt state oversight. The New York Stock Exchange and NASDAQ (at once market makers and, in the case of the NYSE, market regulator), the National Association of Securities Dealers (the private interests of those involved in providing financial intermediation), the American Bar Association (representing the private interest demands of the legal profession), the Investment Company Institute, the American Chamber of Commerce, and diverse accounting forums are further examples of institutional actors with significant economic and political resources to shape both the context and the content of the SEC's response to critical questions of regulatory design and enforcement.

Throughout the long years of the bull market and in its immediate aftermath, the SEC lacked the political muscle or enforcement resources to deal with a confluence of internal and external flaws. In the mania that accompanied what Stiglitz (2003) terms 'the roaring nineties', no credible restraint was placed on the operation of the market, certainly not by the self-regulating associational bodies, nor by an emasculated commission, whose capacities were severely limited by Congressional figures who transferred the oversight function into a client list service available to the highest bidder (Levitt 2002).

Attempts by the SEC in 1998 to limit the provision of auditing and consultancy by accountants to whom self-regulatory authority had been delegated, were rebuffed following a concerted campaign led by Harvey Pitt. When Pitt was made chairman of the SEC in 2000, he made it a policy priority to achieve *rapprochement* with the organisations he was charged to regulate.

While the strategy may have made sense if the underlying model was sustainable, in the context of a dangerous bull market it amounted to a gross error of judgement. While critics, including Spitzer, accept that Pitt undoubtedly had the qualifications for the job, his tenure was nothing short of an unmitigated disaster: 'It is true that you cannot legislate for ethics but federal regulators, particularly Pitt, had so internalized the defences of industry that they lacked the intellectual capacity to understand what their job entailed: to ensure that the markets are governed by the tripartite principles of transparency, accountability and integrity' (Interview, 10 December 2004). Spitzer's assertion that 'an insidious form of industry capture' is at the root of the crisis represents a mirror image of the standard argument in the economics literature. There is, however, within a growing recognition that maladroit deregulation can reduce effectiveness by cultivating inertia (Kaufmann 2003).

A similar rationale pervaded relationships between regulators and the Wall Street investment banking system. The collapse of the dot.com market in 2000 and the implosion of confidence it engendered were dismissed merely as greed. This impoverished account of the structural dysfunctionality was indicative of the growing power of the securities industry that any official probe into the workings of Wall Street focused on actors, not systems. Congressional hearings were scheduled at which politicians and regulators alike collectively wrung their hands at the reality of conflicts of interest over analyst research and their inability to do anything about it. This was an intellectual deceit not supported by the facts, as demonstrated by the proactive imaginative use of new technology to capture dyslexic hubris (O'Brien 2003).

It is not coincidental that the major industries involved in corporate malfeasance – banking and financial services, energy and telecommunications – were those who simultaneously became the most important donors to the political system and were the greatest recipients of ill-thought-out deregulatory strategy. The media itself lost perspective. As the media analyst, Howard Kurtz, commented, 'what CNBC did, along with the rest of the business press, was buy into an interlocking system – now widely viewed as flawed and in some cases corrupt – in which all the key players had an incentive to push stock' (Kurtz 2002). Further analysis which incorporated the academic press found a similar dynamic at work (Dyck and Zingales 2003). As a result of the inaction at federal regulatory level and the aversion of the Democrats at national level to make political capital because of their own susceptibility to charges of equal subservience to the major benefactors, the gap between rhetoric and reality widened. This opened an ideological space to challenge hegemonic conceptions. In Gramscian terms, following the collapse of Enron and the revelations of the structural involvement of financial intermediaries, the arena moved from a tactical war of manoeuvrability to a strategic war of position (Gramsci 1998, 238–239). The media, realising a shift in public perceptions of iconic value, itself largely shifted ground towards a narrative based on defenestrating previous icons.

Political entrepreneurs, most notably the New York Attorney General, exploited the inherent conflicts of interest to the full, forcing onto the agenda a realignment in regulatory policy heretofore denied and creating a national platform for his own wider political ambitions (O'Brien 2003, 148–155). The destabilisation to the status quo posed by Spitzer's activism has become even more apparent as his department shifted its attention from well-publicised conflicts of interest within investment banking research to critical questions concerning the governance of the NYSE and the unregulated operation of the lucrative mutual fund industry.

Spitzer argues that his innovative use of New York General Business Law No. 352 – the Martin Act 1921 – demonstrates not only the efficacy of the statute but evidence that what is required is not 'designing a new standard but brushing off the accumulated dust of an old standard that has fallen out of favour'. The Act gives the Attorney General the right to investigate any business operating in the state, with the additional power to subpoena witnesses and publish the results. The power of Spitzer's mantra for structural change has been authenticated by the publication of highly embarrassing emails, which appear to show a pathological contempt among Wall Street professionals towards ordinary investors. What is also clear is that by daring to use legislation that traditionally was applied only to those trading at the margins of the financial markets, Spitzer has once exposed and transcended the politics of symbolic reassurance. The methods deployed and the consequences have amassed considerable opposition. Typical was the blistering attack launched by Thomas Donohue, the President of the US Chamber of Commerce.

In a New Year press conference highlighting priorities for the coming 12 months, Donohue accused Spitzer of spectacular abuse of office.

> He's the investigator, the prosecutor, the judge, the jury and the executioner. Spitzer's approach is to walk in and say, 'Well, we're going to make a deal, and you're going to pay $600 million to the state and you're going to get rid of this person and that person and if you don't do it by tonight then I'm going to indict the company.' What does indict the company mean? It means they're going to put you out of business. It's the most egregious and unacceptable form of intimidation that we have seen in this country in modern time. (Associated Press 2005)

The Attorney General professes that his relationship with Wall Street financiers is one of mutual fascination and incomprehension. He is perplexed by what he sees as their moral relativism; they, in contrast, fail to understand what drives the Attorney General is more than ambition. Spitzer, of course, is too canny not to accept that ambition plays a part, answering this author's question of what drives him with the retort that 'the same thing that drives a writer to win a Pulitzer' (Interview, 10 December 2004). Behind the jocularity, Spitzer made a very serious point:

> I went to dinner recently with a group of Wall Street Chief Executives. I explained to them that Merrill Lynch alone has a compliance department bigger than my entire operation. I advised them that unless there were profound changes, they would be better advised to shut it down, invest the money in a contingency fund where at least it could earn interest and use it to pay the fines for non-compliance. (Interview, 10 December 2004)

This, suggests Spitzer, is the major untreated cancer destroying the vitality of American capitalism and against which neither the corporations, the self-regulatory industries nor the federal architecture have provided an antidote. 'One of the things that I enjoy about going to Washington is the opportunity of testifying, chapter after chapter, that self-regulation has failed. What is it to be replaced with? I'm not sure' (Interview, 10 December 2004). The overarching regime, in Spitzer's view, fails to address in a systemic manner the paradigmatic power of market professionals. 'The investment banks are at the vortex of all of this', he claims, arguing that 'the risk-reward calculus was so clearly out of kilter with ethical behaviour. Yet no-one thought the paradigm needed to change. The solution is not more regulation but more innovative application of existing enforcement strategies' (Interview, 10 December 2004).

The Politics of Symbolism: Sarbanes-Oxley in Context

Following the scandal of recent years a stream of executives have faced trial and in some cases prison, although not generally for substantive charges (O'Brien 2004a). This has been accompanied by legislative reform to partially end the self-regulatory paradigm. The remit of the Public Company Accounting Oversight Board, for example, is explicitly designed to recalibrate the influence of what Braithwaite and Drahos (2000, 159) term the 'model mercenaries in the globalization of US regulatory and corporate governance practice'. There are sound structural reasons for this partial privileging. For capital markets to function effectively it is imperative that they are underpinned by a sound legal and accounting foundation (Spencer 2000). As Steve Cutler, Director of the Enforcement at the SEC, explained in a recent interview, 'we have so many breakdowns: corporate governance, the gatekeepers, the auditors, the lawyers, and the research analysts. So many corners of the market seem to have been affected. In that way it is different from prior scandals, which were focused on one kind of conduct or one set of actors' (Demirag and O'Brien 2004, 118).

Spitzer maintains that the corporate governance reforms advanced in response to that crisis serve a palliative purpose, treating the symptoms but not the cause. He is supportive of the Public Company Accounting Oversight and Investor Protection Act 2002 (Sarbanes-Oxley), but suggests its primary emphasis on only one part of the associational matrix – the audit profession and corporate boards – merely displaces the risk. For the New York State Attorney General insufficient attention has been placed on the governance of other key intermediating forces. In this he is following the lead by two of the most senior judges in the Delaware Chancery Court, who have commented that many of the provisions in the act 'appear to have been taken off the shelf and put into the mix, not so much because they would have helped to prevent the scandals, but because they filled the perceived need for far-reaching reform and were less controversial than other measures more clearly aimed at preventing similar scandals' (Chandler and Strine 2002, 6). For Spitzer the primary problem with the legislation is its roots in 'a culture of compliance and certification. There is increased individual liability but the focus is on form rather than substance' (Interview, 10 December 2004).

In the United States, this is a critical issue. The capacity to critically determine juridical norms is based on the degree of clarity and political salience underpinning the legal framework. If laws and regulations are vague, or the detail left to regulatory bodies to negotiate with institutional actors given equal voice by the 'heterarchy' of governance (Jessop 2003) particular intractable problems emerge. The dichotomy between appearance and reality in regulatory politics and the wider symbolic nature of law as a rhetorical device that is capable of manipulation through creative interpretation is particularly problematic (Edelman 1960; Stryker 1994).

Evidence of its effectiveness in instilling ethical restraint is already in question because of high profile corporate governance failures within Citigroup, Hollinger and Health South (O'Brien 2005b, c). The debate on how internal controls should be viewed by regulators further demonstrates the inordinate endogenous pressures at the national level to construct a hollow shell that provides symbolic reassurance. There is a profound risk of reduced legal liability because of judicial or agency deference to an organisational response based on the institutionalisation of 'rational myth' (Edelman et al. 1999, 447–448) that, in turn, subverts stated policy imperatives.

Hood et al. argue that viable control mechanisms are predicated on the critical interaction between how a regulatory agency gathers information; its degree of emphasis on the setting of minimum standards and its propensity or reluctance to advance strategies based on modifying behaviour. They conclude that 'regulatory assessment that focuses exclusively on standards but not [on how information is gathered or] on the effect of enforcement or behaviour-modification activity may be easier to do against tight deadlines but will fail to capture how the regime works' (Hood *et al.* 2004, 180). This tripartite emphasis on how regulations are politically developed and culturally enforced allows for consideration of what Edelman *et al.* (1999, 407) term the 'social construction' of law: 'that organizations are both responding to and constructing the law that regulates them renders law 'endogenous'; the content and meaning of law is determined within the social field that it is designed to regulate'. The countervailing pressure from New York State Attorney General serves to simultaneously add to the squeeze on SEC capability and offer a mechanism to deliver effective enforcement. And his capacity to act is rooted precisely in the structural changes in the national regulatory regime, a failure to update the intergovernmental constitutional architecture and the abeyance of concurrent powers.

Conclusion: Dining for Albany

There can be no doubt that Spitzer is an exceptionally adroit political animal. With a talent for public relations and backing from establishment figures within the New York Democrats, Spitzer launched a gubernatorial campaign at the Sheraton Hotel and Towers in Manhattan on 9 December 2004. In one stroke, Spitzer raised $3 million and positioned himself as heir apparent for the Democratic nomination. Basing his campaign strategy on a revitalisation of Clintonian triangulation, Spitzer averred that he would 'take what's best from liberalism and conservatism to solve problems in practical ways' (Slackman 2004). The similarities with Clinton's early career trajectory are striking. Like the two-term President, Spitzer has skilfully used the office of Attorney General as a platform for the pursuit of higher political office. They are by no means unique. Since 1980, more than 40% of those holding the position of State Attorney General (SAG) have run for higher office (Chen 2003). Nor is the method deployed by Spitzer to force change, through the application of state law, particularly innovative. As noted above, the increased regulatory activism of SAGs can be traced back to the scaling back of federal regulation, initiated by the Carter presidency and facilitated, or openly canvassed, by successive administrations ever since (Teske 2004). The process had three possible interlinked political advantages. For the incumbents, it provided a platform for personal political ambition; for the state it offered a financial resource through the expropriation of punitive damages to replenish coffers diminished by budget cuts; and for ideological policy entrepreneurs it filled a gap occasioned by the ideational retreat from federal oversight. Various industries have been targeted, most notably tobacco (Schmeling 2003; Mather 1998). From a policy perspective, it is the later formulation, the increased regulatory activism by SAGs, acting individually or in concert, that raises the most profound questions about the efficacy of regulatory governance in the United States.

The traditional privileging of state jurisdiction over the governance of corporations creates a competing and at times contradictory dynamic to the ambitions of federal regulation (Strine 2002; Murphy 2004, 37–39). It is precisely this dynamic that many in the securities industry are now attempting to redress by curtailing the capacity of the State Attorney Generals to intervene even if it means accepting the remit of a reinforced, federal regulator (O'Brien 2003). A similar strategy applies to the passage of the Class Action Fairness Act 2005, a tort-reform measure that is designed to limit the capacity of states to hear class-action suits with an aggregate value of over $5 million. The passage of the Act is a victory for the business lobby which, while presenting the argument in terms of ensuring federal oversight over interstate commerce, sees the removal of major tort cases from the state arena as a mechanism to reduce the kind of punitive damages seen in recent tobacco litigation (Rogers and Langley 2005; Labaton 2005).

The initial target of industry ire over the politicisation of the SAG office, Michael Moore, the Mississippi SAG and prime instigator of the multi-billion dollar attack on tobacco, has now been supplanted by Spitzer, whose assaults on demonstrable cases of industry, state and federal regulatory failure are underpinned by a coherent, if contested, policy imperative to challenge the efficacy of the existing regulatory regime.

By highlighting structural failings, his campaign has proved instrumental in prompting the most radical reassessment of the role that regulators should play in the policing of the markets since the securities legislation introduced by the New Deal reforms in the 1930s. While debate has been subsumed occasionally by discussion of the political ambitions of the messenger, the central argument advanced here is that differentiating the strategic pursuit of change from the tactical quest for office offers opportunities to understand not only the causes of the malaise but why effective corporate control has been so elusive.

17

Public Trusteeship: The Responsibilities of Transparency and Legacy

J. Patrick Dobel

Introduction

In a perfect storm environmental forces converge to generate powerful and destructive forces beyond predictable scales. The process may take years to gather, such as the cooling of oceans or changing currents and wind patterns. The widespread meltdown of large western corporations in the early twenty-first century represents the explosive result of political and economic forces. The failures can be traced to irregularities in internal auditing and public reporting.

A straightforward instrumental analysis would see the problems as ineffective governance and regulatory oversight of corporations, auditors and the auditing profession. The traditional independence of the auditors was further impaired by confusion within the auditing profession over whom they worked for and where their profits originated. Finally 'individual and institutional greed' served as a 'catch-all' excuse (Walker 2004).

The triumph of neo-liberalism coupled with aggressive United States pressure to open and deregulate markets resulted in simultaneous dilemmas and pressures. In this context, neo-liberalism represents a broad international ideological movement based on a compact which suggests the expansion of free markets will maximise socio-economic wealth. A corollary has been an aggressive focus upon minimising the role of government. This is justified on the argument that imperfect regulation can result in both the distortion of capital allocation and facilitate corruption. Differential growth rates between neo-liberal economies and more traditional mercantilist or social democratic economies gave greater momentum to the movement. At the same time a relatively low interest rate environment provided the incentive for capital to search for higher rates of return in the primary exchanges, where advances in information technology allowed for integrated 24-hour trading. Add to this the pressure from international organisations such as the World Bank and IMF to force neo-liberal change through attaching conditionality to support loans, and the primary forces governing the perfect storm begin to appear on the meteorological radar.

For the purposes of this book and chapter, this convergence had a strong cumulative impact upon western corporations. First, corporate valuations became dependent upon an ability to produce high rates of return relative to the market. Increasingly stock became the mechanism for acquisition and expansion. In a world where stock options became a normal means of compensation, the compensation incentives of chief executives were linked to high valuations, which in turn required consistently high returns. As valuations ranged higher, the need to maintain the high returns cycled upward. Second, a mythology of heroic managers was created and sustained by the mainstream and business media, which treated corporate leaders like celebrities.

The rise of 24-hour business channels like MSN privileged an analysis that saw CEOs as corporate saviours, a process that received implicit academic collaboration. Schools of business churned out case studies of saviours, displacing analysis with a perverse form of hero worship. This created an important feedback loop that reinforced the propensity towards short-term manipulation. The heroic mode gave way to the imperial CEO as top management developed an entitlement mentality toward their companies and the perks associated with such unquestioned power. The excesses of Tyco International's Dennis Kozlowski with his million dollar parties and corporate subsidised celebrity lifestyle epitomised this trend. Third, as share price lost a concrete link with earnings the market itself demonstrated greater instability. Failure to deliver high returns on a quarterly basis would be immediately punished by significant declines. Fourth, at the same time many brokerage firms consolidated or found themselves enmeshed in the conflicting roles of evaluating stocks, selling stocks and managing new stock offerings for clients. Finally, many nations, but especially the United States, the United Kingdom and Oceania, deregulated many industries and softened further their approach to market regulation. The combinations of stock brokers and market offerings, banking and investment, and auditing and consultancy, which occurred in so many business, created moral hazard, but were now permitted by hollowed out regulators.

The result of this new global economic order shifted 'regulation' of the market in three directions. First, the market came to be seen as a self-regulating mechanism. Second, because of the increased competition and brutal pressure on profit margins that China and other developing countries imposed on corporations, companies were forced into seemingly increased internal discipline. Risk assessment offices and financial reporting as well as constant scrutiny by analysts and mutual funds should have led to better financial discipline and internal efficiency in corporate governance. Third, with less intense government regulation over acquisitions and looser oversight of markets and trading, the global finance sector and markets increasingly relied upon what Christopher Hood called enforced 'self-regulation' (Hood 1998, 239).

This new financial order relied overwhelmingly upon transparency to make it work. After the financial meltdown in Asia in the late 1990s, western analysts postulated that such sudden massive losses of wealth and credibility could not occur in western markets. The key defence against such erosion lay in transparency in the auditing process. The serious problems arose when western regulators and policymakers ignored the fragility and moral hazard that encumbered the system of profession-based transparency.

Stock buyers, especially institutional managers, depend upon accurate, honest and timely reporting. Rating organisations depend upon good reporting as do analysts. Potential partners, acquirers and bankers depend upon honest accurate reporting to assess assets correctly. This accurate reporting requires strong internal financial controls, risk management and unimpeachable auditing processes.

In the global marketplace with weakened regulating and strong short-term pressures to perform and maximise short-term growth, the system, by default, came to rely upon auditors as the surrogates and guardians of public trust. As a public profession, auditors possessed their own self-regulatory structure and general accounting standards and international standards. The auditing professionals became the de facto regulators that investors, analysts, raters and banks depended upon for transparency. Auditors and the auditing profession became the gatekeepers for the most important information in the marketplace including the filings with SEC and various market regulators. This is a classic case where a private profession becomes a public profession with very strong public trust obligations magnified by the abdication of government under prevailing ideologies and policies.

The other issue ignored in the system was how trust held the global financial system together. This trust required a level of predictable behaviour and reliance upon the information being proffered in public documents. As government regulation and internal investigation receded, corporations became more and more black boxes except for the public reports certified by auditors. This certification became the guarantor of accuracy and truthfulness. Investors, raters, bankers and other actors relied upon this information and the entire system of mutual acceptance provided the pledge that permitted people to exchange money with true assessment of risk and return.

The perfect storm problem arose because of the under-recognition of the almost monopolistic role of guarantors that auditors had taken on by default and the type of institutional and economic pressure upon them that subverted their judgement. Professions are defined by their commitment to standards and to public fiduciary obligations as well as the discretion ingrained in these actions. The community pressure, standards, certification and autonomy create a wide set of soft law to govern the accounting and auditing professions. This law and the privileged role of the financial auditors depend upon the assumption that the judgement of auditors and accountants would not be compromised. In theory, the market incentives of maintaining reputation and probity should reinforce these pressures.

The role of leadership, trust and transparency is even more important because pure deterrence will not deter major white collar crime or corporate financial malfeasance. To sustain reasonable trust boundaries need to be set and inspected on a regular basis. This periodic inspection process is designed to ensure two key objectives: first, to guard against institutional defection from agreed standards, and second, to reinforce good leadership and integrity. If the probability of serious enforcement or getting caught drops, it does not necessarily increase crime per se. It does, however, lessen one set of offset pressures in organisations that may face powerful incentives to distort financial reporting or leadership cadres and cultures whose reputation and wealth depend upon meeting high but unrealistic expectations (Hodson, this volume).

The other side of the coin of trust and transparency is that the organisation must maintain an internal professional capacity to audit itself and manage risk. This internal independence can be subverted by direct pressure related to career advancement and getting caught in the trap of starting with small subversions that grow into larger ones. When the chief financial officer of WorldCom balked at continuing to inflate earnings, Bernard Ebbers, the charismatic and imperial CEO of WorldCom, ordered him 'just meet the numbers'. Ebber's own reputation as well as considerable stock options depended upon the continuous meeting of 'growth' targets and the continuous inflation of numbers. When told 'this isn't right...', Ebbers just stared at it, looked up and said, 'We have to hit our numbers' (McClam 2005).

Similarly the Tanzi's family's pilfering of Parmalat depended upon the auditors continuing to hide costs and liabilities in offline corporations (Melis and Melis, this volume). Leadership sets the tone and pressure at the top can be aggravated if the culture itself is distorted either by the personality and power of the CEO as with Ebbers or a more pervasive culture where the entire orientation of all senior management is to beat numbers and evade regulation. At Enron, the management culture enshrined strong anti-regulatory ideals and an ideological commitment to free market competition. At the same time the company found itself needing to hide its own debt structure by creating offline entities to park debt and elicit false profit. Its highly publicised and richly financed risk management office was marginalised and ignored in major decisions. This corporate reality stood in marked contrast to its public pronouncements to the wider financial community, which suggested that risk management was fundamental to project integrity (McLean and Elkind 2004).

Enron, Parmalat and other cases disclosed another problem where auditing firms become significantly dependent upon a single firm for revenues. The Houston and Chicago Partners of Arthur Andersen were not only regularly hired by Enron as senior executives but perceived Enron as their major client needing to be protected and abetted in its cutting edge financial practices. They could not afford to lose Enron. The common auditing practices became stretched to breaking point and the internal audit committees either ignored or permitted this to take place after cursory questions. The Tanzi family's relationship with the firm Grant Thornton had the same problem. Even when Parmalat rotated official auditors as required by Italian law, the new auditor accepted the records from other Parmalat companies who still used the compromised auditing firm. In addition Arthur Andersen and other firms increasingly relied upon management consulting as their major source of profit. Auditing became less valued in the profit area, and firms found themselves auditing systems that their own company had designed. The moral hazard remained high, but largely unnoticed by the regulators.

This meant that even as the market depended more and more upon neutral accurate reporting, the pressures in organisations and the leadership philosophies eroded the internal professional structures. At the same time the external profit pressures and restructuring of auditing firms slowly eroded their independence and made them more susceptible to management manipulation. Once core corporate values and incentives become distorted, it is very easy for the entire culture to co-opt individuals into the value systems even to the extent they no longer recognise the moral problems (Jackall 1988).

Trusteeship and Public Responsibility

These have not been comfortable times for the United States or the world. The level of uncertainty and violence will continue. Even as the self-reflection induced by 9/11 in the United States fades or merges into a reflexive fear, these are times 'of a worldwide heightened sense of vulnerability' that provides people with a chance to 'take stock of their lives and reassess their values and priorities' (Walker 2003). Certainly the continuing trail of corporate wreckage and misconduct highlights how important it is to reflect upon and imbed the values of stewardship and trusteeship in corporate and political governance. Stewardship as a moral stance provides an active policy and leadership perspective, not a retrospective point of view. It reminds every leader that they are not imperial CEOs responsible to no one but their own vision and interest, but carriers of a trust that others rely upon daily for livelihood and safety and that future people depend upon when it is handed on or destroyed. This chapter suggests that one way to operationalise stewardship and trusteeship is for managerial leaders to think of the legacy dimensions of their leadership.

There is a long moral tradition conceiving of public office and public professions as a trusteeship, with public officials exercising power and responsibility for wider societal good. The United Nations enshrines this view in its *International Code for Public Officials* which states that 'public office' is 'a position of trust' (United Nations 1996). In essence this means that leaders should have strong obligations to privilege the long-term welfare and to factor in the consequences of their actions on the equity and dignity of persons. It also means they have obligations to attend to the institutional legitimacy, trust and social capital of the organisation they work for not just short term gain. Trusteeship or stewardship presumes a range of discretion for public officials who serve as leaders and managers (Terry 2003; Greenleaf 1977, 1991; Cooper 1991, 1998; Bloch 1996).

The challenge of the trust conception and its wide range of discretion is always to articulate the nature of judgements permitted and the mechanisms of accountability to counteract pressures toward abuse of power and corruption (Adams and Balfour 2004; Huber and Shipan 2002; Dobel 1999). Theories of public trusteeship range from insistence upon strict adherence to law and procedure to an emphasis on the importance of principles to inform judgements to the contention that only virtue and character address the unpredictability of life and sustain persons through the tribulations and temptations of public life (Burke 1986; Denhardt 1988; Cooper and Wright 1992).

Accepting the inevitable and desirable role of discretionary judgement by public officials or public professionals, a good theory of public trust should unite personal integrity, moral commitments, legal authority and accountability and effectiveness (Burke 1986; Rohr 2002; Cooper 1998; Huber and Shipan 2002; Dobel 1999). Ideally a model of trust should integrate regime values and legal and process commitments. Possessing a trust entails a commitment to address the long-term and externality dimensions, institutional legitimacy and capacity, public equity, and character that sustain legacy-based deliberation and action. An approach to public trust should avoid what John Rawls calls 'the strain of commitment' and be livable by individuals to act with integrity and effectiveness (Rawls 1971).

This discretion links with leadership. The leadership element – changing the world and people through self-initiated action and interaction – remains inextricable with discretion. Persons should be able to use this model to judge and live in a way that sustains their emotional and moral commitments, technical expertise, accountability and effectiveness. These become extremely important. As David Walker, the Comptroller General of the United States, emphasises in this volume any effective governance system in financial markets must depend upon 'Leadership, Integrity and Innovation'. It also requires ensuring transparency and incentives aligned with legal obligations in government and in auditing institutions and ideally in corporate governance (Walker, this volume).

This chapter presents 'leaving a legacy' as an approach to organising leadership decisions and action. It argues that an individual's legacy tracks their obligations and that it unfolds daily through cumulative judgements and actions. This method reveals how people make a difference in the world and emphasises personal responsibility and significance. Legacy's relation to meaning indicates its advantages as a frame for effective leadership. First, it unites within a business context the personal search for meaning with an organisational focus on mission (Pattakos 2004). Second, it connects the individual's preoccupation with self-worth and significance with organisational results (Denhardt 1989, 1993, 2000). Third, it embeds leaders in a historical setting linking their inheritance from the past and their obligations to the future. Fourth, legacy can guide individuals to a less egocentric and imperial leadership style. Finally, a legacy orientation links individual actions to wider stewardship of institutions (Terry 2003). While legacy does not capture all aspects of managerial decision-making, it maps a broad and rich understanding of leadership and individuality linked to trusteeship.

The Concept of Legacy

When people finish or depart, the consequences of their actions upon people and the physical or social world endure as their legacy. While focusing upon legacy highlights those impacts, this type of focus can seem egotistical, as one head of a state social service agency remarked, 'If I thought of this as my legacy, I'd start putting myself before the public.'[1] Yet legacy matters precisely because the idea joins responsibility and consequences with a person's search for meaning. It becomes even more interesting in the private sector because it can link to the often strong driven egos of private sector leaders. Hard but fundamental questions such as 'Why am I here?' or 'What difference does it make that I have lived?' remind people that finding meaning in life remains of elemental importance for human moral and social life (Baumeister 1991; Wolf 1990). Human mortality adds urgency to these questions with the blunt question of what remains after physical death. People usually only ask the questions as they approach the 'end': 'Has my life had any meaning?', 'Is the world a better place because I have lived?' More than a few prominent leaders spend their later years writing memoirs or trying to influence popular understanding of their legacy after the fact.

Having meaning provides psychological and moral resources to order commitments and make decisions about what fits or does not fit within one's integrity (Dobel 1999; Carter 1996; Petrick and Quinn 1997; Denhardt, 1989, 1993, 2000; Csikszentmihalyi 2003). Leaving a legacy connects to meaning by insisting that the consequences of what people do matter and should be taken seriously. When individuals cease to exist physically, their actions still continue to impact people, institutions and the environment – the world differs for good or bad because of a human's presence. Recognising all individuals contribute and leave a legacy buttresses both responsibility and dignity.

The word legacy derives from the word *legate* – one to whom is delegated responsibility. The words derive from the Latin root for laws (*leges*) and attending to the public dimensions of life. The concept fits naturally with the tradition of leadership as a trust where leaders hold office as a temporary legate or steward for the good of others (Kass 1990). The ideal of legacy bridges with the trustee model when individual leaders make promises. Their moral legitimacy depends upon their promise to obey the law, frame their judgements by statutory intent and principle, be accountable to authority, and be competent and efficient in performance. The promise has an implicit requirement that the leaders attend to the institutions and hand them on in better shape. The vulnerability of people and colleagues who depend upon organisations heightens leaders' obligations (Rohr 1996; Cooper 1991; Huber and Shipan 2002; Dobel 1999; Terry 2003).

Realising that he or she leaves a legacy leads a person to realise that he or she inherits a world and has responsibilities towards that inheritance. Any person who claims credit for the good of a life or institution must also take responsibility for harm that can be traced back to their action or inaction. Too often trustees and legatees focus only upon the good they want remembered, but the historical responsibility of a legacy orientation entails acknowledgement and responsibility *for the good and the bad*.

The idea of a legacy scales to a context. A legacy orientation helps organise a leader's reflection because leaders experience life as a series of enterings and leavings or beginnings and endings. Attending to legacy as a managerial leader helps individuals to bridge these intellectually and morally. For an individual leaves a legacy with each interaction. Legacy leaves its imprint in a multitude of manners. It can be as casual as a piece of advice, a comment which impacts on a person's worth or performance, a slight or recognition or an act as powerful as firing a person, changing a number or cutting a programme. The scale extends from individuals to groups, meetings, projects, teams or organisations. The impact of a single intervention can ripple out through other groups, family, interactions within and outside the organisation. A person can always ask of him or herself 'What do I wish or what have I left behind?' in each interaction, precedent, meeting, rule or policy. The cumulative impact or aggregated impact of actions adds a strategic scale to legacy. Institutions and people change not with one inadvertent or swift interaction but due to the accrual of modelling, educating, and feedback.

Just as a building does not run down at once and an office does not turn into a dump without slow, persistent neglect, cultural norms of interaction or styles of disagreement change over time, seldom suddenly. Returning to the metaphor of the perfect storm deployed at the beginning of this chapter, legacy is amplified when a group or organisation reaches a tipping point. Then individual actions help transform norms or patterns (Kelling 1999; Gladwell 2000).

The concept of leaving a legacy exists in the shadow of the counterfactual of what would have happened if 'I' had not been there. The job may still get done, the directions may still get set, but the nuance and style of the doing of the job, the exact wording or implementation of the policy, the cumulative impact of outcomes on people and interactions on those can be immense. The focus upon legacy underlines moral responsibility and emphasises the consequences of 'being there'.

At an abstract level legacy extends in several institutional dimensions. The first covers the range of a person's contribution. This includes the magnitude of contributions to specific actions, but also the temporal proximity to the consequences. Many of the most interesting or compelling consequences occur down the line from the actual contribution made by the individual. An example would be a report read later that influences people or a changed financial statement that becomes the basis for future reports and expectations. It is possible, but not predictable, that the farther away from an individual's contribution to results, the less responsible a person becomes. Yet the culpability increases if the action or report becomes the basis upon which others rely in making subsequent risk-management decisions. This is often the case in financial reporting and auditing because of how important transparency is for the web of relations in the market system. What an individual did thoughtlessly might seem trivial at the moment of execution but may grow in importance for a person or system over time such as the first time an individual made a minor 'adjustment' to meet numbers as happened with the financial staff at WorldCom (Nuzum and Pulliam 2005).

Second, there is the issue of the temporal durability and traceability of the consequences following from the contribution. Some consequences can evanesce. Some consequences are immediately apparent and endure; others may seem to have no impact but turn out to have significance later. The parade of major corporate earnings restatements coupled with stock losses and managerial change over the last several years demonstrate these time delayed impacts and responsibility.

Third, the meaning of the actions and consequences is mutable. Actions and consequences possess no one stable meaning. Individuals may have one intention and they may battle to ensure that their interpretation of their actions' meanings dominates memory and deliberation; other people, however, may have very different interpretations of those actions (Lynn 1987; Wolf 2004). Even if everyone agrees on the meaning of an act at one time, this meaning can still mutate over time as individuals or society change. The reassessment of lionised imperial CEOs compared to more steady and institution building CEOs that is presently occurring represents a classic case of reinterpreting the meaning and success of leaders (Collins 2001; Collins and Porras 1997).

Finally, a legacy is often linked to a person who seeks or receives credit or blame for the results, and this can affect individuals both when they live and their reputation after their death. This is especially important if persons are motivated by the desire for fame and renown as a solution to meaning and mortality (Braudy 1986). Even if recognised and memorialised, over time the memory and meaning may fade. As with monuments, the original intent may be forgotten, ignored or reappropriated (Goodsell 1988; Gallagher 2004). The Enron building in Houston stood as a symbol of all that was good of late 1990s entrepreneurship and growth: now it serves as a reminder of betrayal and unbridled greed (McLean and Elkind 2004).

Modes of Legacy

Everyone leaves a legacy whether they want to or not. I believe legacies can helpfully be understood as metaphors that depict the ways people influence the world. The ones I discuss were developed in an iterative process using case studies and a series of interviews with senior public and non-profit officials. Interestingly many of the metaphors have long historical antecedents in past stories of leaders. Obviously other metaphors could be used, and these metaphors, while distinct, can overlap and reinforce understanding. The response of senior officials was particularly powerful to these metaphors and often laced their language. The metaphors integrate the abstract aspects of legacy and create heightened awareness of how individuals make a difference.

Monuments

All cultures create monuments. Pyramids, tombstones or buildings come to mind as enduring reminders of the success and failures of society. A monument focuses upon the physical presence left after a person leaves, and physical reminders leap to mind when people think of legacies. Yet few managers spoke of monuments per se, but often mentioned building 'monuments to ideals or good people'. Monuments can serve functional purposes or can reflect attempts to memorialise something or someone for history. Many government buildings try to do so by both memorialising a person or event and creating a public space that permits debates over conceptions of governance and legitimacy (Goodsell 1986; Wolf 2004; Gallagher 2004). A monument can reflect a collective attempt by a society to enshrine memories or recover aspects of identity. On the other hand, more than a few of the imperial corporate leaders subverted the culture and solvency of corporations like Tyco, WorldCom or Global Crossing by making huge expenditures on monuments for their imperial CEO ambitions.

Foundations

Buildings cannot survive without strong foundations. In fact buildings can be torn down and rebuilt on the same foundations. Individual character becomes the foundation of good judgement and supports sustained action in face of obstacles (Norton 1976; Sherman 1989). With skill or character as foundations, people can act with independent deliberation. The most interesting paradox about foundations as a metaphor for legacy is action. People can thrive in the structures created that may not have been anticipated or controlled by the person laying the foundations. Foundations of character and knowledge become a source of freedom and empowering, but can also be a socialised means of control and limitation. Creating healthy or distorted institutional cultures can be one of the most liberating or deleterious impacts of leadership in organisations.

Wombs and Incubators

Special environments permit new life to gestate, grow and be born into the world. Individuals, organisations, or groups can all engender interactions among individuals, place and time to gestate new possibilities and give birth in people and institutions to fresh lives, ideas or creations. More than one manager described him or herself as a 'midwife' as they thought about their impacts on others. Institutions like Social Security Administration, Wells Fargo Bank, Proctor and Gamble or the United States Marine Corps are noted as organisations that give birth to strong leaders who leave and influence other organisations. Strong leadership provides the social space and institutional protection and resources where people, ideas and practices can develop. Too often, however, an imperial CEO leadership style stultifies individuals, drives out future leaders and leaves organisations unprepared for succession (Collins 2001).

Coral Reefs

Quotidian life accumulates minute by minute, day by day, imperceptible in its impact on people and places much like a coral reef. In a healthy reef, after an individual dies or moves on, the place they occupied becomes a possible home for other persons or a new anchorage where others can add to the life of the reef. The reef life generates interdependence and nurtures a system where other individuals and organisations thrive in relation to the vitality of the reef as a whole. In high performing and successful organisations built to last, managers and leaders see themselves as contributing to a project of lasting duration (Collins and Porras 1988; Collins 2001). The reef building metaphor reminds persons that even if one's accomplishments seem insignificant, they are not. The reef grows and contributes because of individual's help, and the shell of what one accomplished whether building an office, a record, or a space becomes a potential building block for another.

Webs

Management and leadership occur through relations (Lynn 1987; Bloch 1996; Bryson 1992). Actions create or impact networks of relationships. Webs can be woven in complex ways that create elaborate hierarchies, convoluted spheres or webs of webs with horizontal threads. Webs can unite people in new and unique ways and from these relations different lives and consequences flow. These relationships generate new patterns of action and communication. The web reveals or creates interdependency. The web metaphor matches the reality of modern managerial life where the creation or managing of complex networks has become the norm (Wise 2002; Keast et al 1994). It can have positive and negative consequences. The modern webs of communication have transformed the speed and vulnerability of financial markets to speculation and manipulation as the Asian financial crisis demonstrated. Webs also suggest how entwined and vulnerable systems of moral hazard can become where relations are so interwoven that impacts in one area reverberate and amplify across others.

Sowing Seeds/Cultivating Soil

Ancient Thebes believed its people grew from the dragon's teeth planted by the hero Perseus. Ancient agricultural civilisations treat the rite and metaphor of planting and harvest as sacred. Planting and cultivation provide another way to think of patient influence that recognises successful change needs to grow roots in the community, organisation or person. This understanding sees change as occurring over time and identifies responsibility with initiating. Good leaders spend time planting seeds of knowledge and possibility and nurture them for the right moment when the window of opportunity emerges for action. One senior social services manager described her day as 'spreading seeds of possibility among stakeholders'. She discussed the need to 'fertilize and make people and places receptive to ideas'. Sometimes with 'patience you can harvest ideas, and sometimes others harvest the results, it doesn't really matter'. On the other hand most top initiated imperial change fails because the initiatives never take at the lower levels of the organisation and wither when the leaders leave (Collins and Porras 1998; Kotter 1996).

Ripples

Actions reverberate like stones dropped in a pond. The ripples move out in concentric circles and touch, disturb, or change the direction of things around them. Sometimes they barely rustle the world. At other times the ripples collide, intersect and overlap growing arithmetically into waves. The ripples move out far beyond the person who tossed the stone and often the effects are hidden from the original person. An executive director of a humanitarian relief organisation commented, 'I think it's the ones who simply stand up and say "no" or "yes". They disturb the order and others see it can be done and they move also.' These are exactly the type of individuals that imperial CEO organisations tend to discourage or drive out (Jackall 1988).

Lenses and Dreams

People's quality of mind and imagination can change under the tutelage of individuals and experience. Plato portrayed leadership as a form of getting new sight by moving from the cave of shadow to the light. Cognitively individuals focus attention and organise the world with frames of reference that order perception and provide context and meaning (Morgan 1997; Senge 1990; Bolman and Deal 1997). Imagination expands when individuals learn to see the world in new ways or picture other possibilities for themselves. Old frames are replaced or supplemented by new frames of reference. Individuals discover aspects of reality they had missed. Their perception can be sharpened or their imaginations become more supple, and they learn to see situations in different ways rather than being trapped in one comfortable internalised frame (Daloz 1996; Morgan 1997). The aspirations of individuals can be changed by leaders who believe in them and manage them in ways that the persons see new possibilities in their lives for growth and change. As one senior utilities manager said, 'the most important leader can be the one who sees possibilities for you that you do not see in yourself'. This legacy gives corporate culture such strength because a culture, whether corrupt or good, imbeds people in a way of seeing the world where actions that cross bounds of legality or professional standards are seen as normal (Jackall 1988; Schein 1985).

Each metaphor highlights a range of influence individuals can have upon the people and world – good and bad. They expand the ways of seeing how persons lead. Acknowledging them deepens a leader's array of strategies and sense of responsibility. The legacy approach to leadership reminds individuals about the connections among people and the world around them. The connections mean each action can contribute to wombs and incubation, foundations, ripples, reef coral, lenses or seeds that influence how people act. This viewpoint reinforces the relationship between present and future.

Time and History

Managerial leaders inherit people, institutions, relationships and expectations, and culture. People in organisations and environments possess memories and a sense of purpose and legacy. The inherited personnel are the guardians of what exists and what has been accomplished. The mission, history and culture remain alive in the personnel (Schein 1985; Denhardt 1993, 2000). Every leader who attends to his or her legacy should attend to the inherited legacy – for good or bad.

This approach asks for more humility about the creation of goals and missions without the sustaining support of people. It asks for more diffidence about univocal definitions of success. It asks for reticence about ego involvement while demanding energy and commitment. It requires attending carefully to the history and culture of an organisation. Creating an institutional legacy begins with understanding inherited meanings, accomplishments and stories. This understanding enables leaders to anticipate how staff will interpret actions or respond to initiatives. More than a few corporations have been destroyed in mangled mergers where antithetical cultures never mesh. An institutional legacy needs to become 'our' legacy with the members of the institution and stakeholders co-creating the meaning and mission. Whether a leader wishes it or not, personnel and clients will create their own meanings for their actions (Schein 1985).

Legacy-oriented leadership requires a continuity strategy that addresses mission and organisational practices and norms. This builds upon the foundation that exists with care, moving internally from within the meanings available. If it means significant changes, so be it, but leaders need to be aware of the levels of resistance and changes emerging from the existing matrix of meaning and commitment. It also attends to building succession and long-term legitimacy for changes rather than changes solely dependent upon a particular leader's strength and will.

Any realistic interpretation of legacy should incorporate cumulative and time dimensions. This refocuses leadership upon the present, the daily interactions and performance, not just the enticing game of high-level strategic change. The emperor Marcus Aurelius in his *Meditations* reflected 'Even if you're going to live three thousand more years, or ten times that, remember: you cannot lose another life than the one you're living now, or live another one than the one you're losing... The present is the same for everyone.' Later he reminds himself to stay attuned to the present and 'stop drifting' (Aurelius 2002, I-14, III-14). He could be speaking to all managerial leaders when he tells himself, 'Life is short. That's all there is to say. Get what you can from the present – thoughtfully, justly' (Aurelius 2002, IV-26).

The small stuff matters for a legacy. Leaders manage the quality of relations with people and organisations, the competence and performance of persons, the technology, political support, and structure to sustain the organisation's effectiveness. These emphases keep leaders and personnel coupled and emphasise that the most durable legacy left will be the quality of people led and served. Impacts upon people, environments and policy remain largely cumulative. Windows of opportunity can permit sudden changes to occur. These significant changes, however, depend upon the webs, seeds, cultivation, changed lenses and dreams that laid the foundation for movement.

An experienced state and local executive remarked, 'Leaders tend to underemphasize management because they want the big score, the notch on their belt and then after the policy victory, they move on.' This focus also reinforces the importance of professional commitment to accurate and truthful accounting since too often the short-term pressures from market and imperial managers will be monument or ego focused rather than attending to the truth of the present and how it becomes the best foundation for future growth. An honest legacy encourages leaders to ensure that people see the connection between competent daily work and the legacy for citizens and colleagues who benefit or suffer from it. Leaders need to help all their colleagues see their own legacy by seeing the worth and impact of their work. Enabling a connection with the meanings fights the cynicism, boredom and exhaustion that erode performance and self-worth (Petrick and Quinn 1997; Csikszentmihalyi 2003).

Focusing leadership on legacy naturally leads to a performance emphasis which underlines the reality that people are creating their legacy on a daily basis. Performance focus demands that leaders and workers ask what they are seeking to accomplish and connect their actual work with the legacy impact they seek. It engages the realities of accomplishments, failure and improvement and gives more reality to the belief that people are better off because individuals perform their jobs. Performance over time means building an institution's capacity with strong support structures, but also training and competence. Most important performance should challenge but be realistic; most of the corruption in reporting and financial manoeuvres occurred to meet unrealistic performance challenges rather than those tied to truthful accountability and long-term sustainability.

Legacy links so profoundly with the meaning of action that it converges on culture building. The question for leadership becomes what type of culture helps individuals to achieve a legacy. People who work in institutions will construct their own meaning of actions. This insight invites leaders to engage meaning as part of managing and leading (Schein 1985, 1999). A managerial legacy that focuses upon the quality of persons as well as performance devotes time and effort to build the meanings, practices, stories, myths and symbols for persons (Doig and Hargrove 1987).

Culture links with the concern to create something that endures. Concentrating upon durability means working on culture where the commitments are imbedded in organisational practices and passed on. It means learning, training and persuading so personnel continue to commit to goals and competencies. If the individuals who come later are not committed to the same issues and beliefs, all the institutional stability and resources will not make much difference. The legacy will end differently than intended. A supple legacy should leave a freedom and creativity to people to adapt to new changes in the environment. Foundations, webs, roots, corals, soil and seeds, dreams and lenses provide the means and ends of this approach to legacy.

The future holds little but uncertainty: environments change; policy changes; people change; evaluations change; and unanticipated consequences emerge. Organisations that cannot adapt to changed demands will not flourish. The mission itself will permute as people learn about the full implications of what their goals are and adjust to mistakes or credible changes of emphasis and direction. Any achievement is tenuous and open to future interpretations. Performance measures simply provide baselines for learning and growing, not permanent answers. The battles over the meaning of accomplishment and failure launch their own momentum to address or rectify actions. True leadership legacies generate wombs, webs, foundations and soil and seeds that become the source for others to grow, adapt and achieve autonomy without one's sustaining will.

The writer of the *Bhagavad Gita* wrote 3000 years ago, 'You have a right to your actions, but never to your actions' fruits. Act for the action's sake... The wise man let's go of all results, whether good or bad, and is focused on the action alone' (*Bhagavad Gita* 2000, 2: 45–49). The reality of legacy is that once an individual leaves, he or she should leave and let people and institutions change or even die on their own. Anything humans build will change, die, be destroyed or rebuilt over time. Yet individuals will be lured by the indispensable person temptation where they believe only they can lead the institution. Consequently, leadership demands a strong sense of humility in leaving legacies. To build a legacy in a liberal democracy or open market means to be humble and willing not only to learn but to accept that learning will change the shape or meaning of one's legacies. In this light, one of the most enduring legacies will be the quality of people helped. They will move on to live or continue a leader's work in new and unpredictable ways, even as the leader moves on. As a teacher, a leader sows seeds of skills, ideas, commitment, and these grow in new and different ways.

Conclusions

I have several ideas about how to think about leaving a legacy as leaders and managers. These guidelines focus on individual decisions but ripple out into institutional consequences. They flow from watching individuals serve as stewards of a trust given by those who came before and handed on to those who remain.

Beware of Pigeons on your Monuments

Monuments and foundations matter as social memorials, achievements, foci of action and touchstones for the future. However, focusing mainly on the monumental or physical and insisting on credit invites disappointment and distortion of personal energy and aspirations.

Begin Sooner Rather than Later

A person's legacy unfolds every day from the beginning. An individual's cumulative actions, relations, precedents and attention contribute to create a slow and almost imperceptible influence that reaches into organisations and people. People can think they are 'going along' and 'staying low' as they wait to get power and position, *then* they will *really* make a difference. This misreads the slowly accreting influence of actions and people's ability to control the meaning of actions. At the end when individuals feel freer, they often possess less leverage. To think persons can make a legacy late and fast, ignores that people have already engendered much of it. Much of what a person actually does builds upon the wombs, foundations, seeding, monuments, webs, and corals they helped earlier.

Accept the Inheritance as a Prelude to Legacy

Individuals do not manage or lead alone, and leaders build upon or are trapped by what came before. Leaders have obligations to learn the history, the true good and the true harm done by an institution and people. The true history should be integrated into strategies for action and respecting, truth seeking and sometimes destroying are central to legacy creation.

Scale Actions

Every job carries with it a reasonable scope of action. The temptation to 'go big' and 'permanent' when thinking of a legacy overlooks the present work to look beyond to what 'really' matters. This is a fundamental mistake especially of imperial leaders. Communication and relations sustain the quotidian legacy and enable other people to link their commitment and meaning to their service. The scaling of action and aspiration from person to group to institution; from purpose to institution; from immediate to long term permits legacy to unfold as an organisationally enduring phenomenon, not an imposition of will. It aligns with the need to build foundations, weave webs, change lenses and dreams, build reefs, start ripples or prepare soil or plant seeds.

Link the Small and Large

Insist upon the connection and meaning from the smallest acts of the present to the deepest aspirations of the future. Enable colleagues and workers to appreciate the meaning and legacy of their actions and communicate this endlessly. This is especially true in financial and accounting areas where the numbers seem all too disconnected from the concrete realities of accomplishment. Legacies depend upon the linkages and feedback loops between broader goals and daily interactions. Each modelled behaviour or interaction trains and directs in this way. When leaders hand on knowledge and inculcate behavioural expectations and norms, they connect real action with purpose. Every person touched in these interactions can become different, for good or bad. Every person served by competent performance or product benefits in their life for good or bad.

Not Controlling the Final Meaning

While influencing meanings is a necessary aspect of strategic and tactical leadership, in the end, the meanings of a legacy will emerge from dialogue, accountability and impacts. Memory and history will exact their own cost as memories will change or forget the original intent. Too much time spent controlling after one leaves, distorts not only one's own efforts, but also the truth of the legacy.

Leading and Letting Go

The paradox of leading for a legacy resides in learning to let go. *The Tao Te Ching* agreeing with the *Baghavad Gita* comments, 'He who clings to his work will create nothing that endures...just do your job, then let go' (*Tao Te Ching* 1988, 24). The old wisdom argues that the capacity for accomplishments to endure and continue to help the public good resides in the ability of the individuals and institutions to adapt and recreate their meaning and performance in changed circumstances. One of the true bequests of leadership is that webs, foundations, corals, lenses, dreams and wombs enable other persons to grow, move on and build their lives and successes from an individual's contribution. This means understanding that what endures must do so without the will and ego of the 'I' to sustain it or control it. This humility should not sap the drive to do good or the strategic need to fight for agendas and educate public. Individuals should take work seriously but hold it lightly.

Everyone leaves a legacy, whether they want to or not. Remembering individual impacts endure helps organise ethical reflection around it and offsets the tendency to emphasise ends over means and stresses their inherent connections. Understanding this links ethics, responsibility, position and action. The self-understanding permitted by legacy-oriented leadership asks persons to understand the full range of impact they can have on life, institutions and people. The reality of legacy reminds people that they are stewards with significance and power.

Note

1. Legacy presents a normative framework to explain the range of ways people meet the obligations of trusteeship. It also builds heavily upon three separate sources of information to support the ideas. First, it draws upon over 50 semi-structured interviews with middle to senior managers from 10 countries. Second, it draws upon both philosophical and ancient literature that provides some insight into how individuals throughout history have thought of legacy. Third, it utilises historical cases to illustrate the complex nature of legacy.

Bibliography

Accounting Standards Board (ASB) 1994. *FRS5 Reporting the substance of transactions*. ASB: London.

Adams, G. and D.L. Balfour 2004. *Unmasking Administrative Evil*. Armonk, NY: M.E. Sharpe.

Alchian, A. and H. Demsetz 1972. Production, information, costs and economic organisation, *American Economic Review*, 62, 777–783.

Allen, W.T. 1993. *Contracts and Communities in Corporation Law*, 50 Washington and Lee Law Review 1395.

American Assembly 2003. The future of the accounting profession. The American Assembly, Columbia University. American Assembly Report, 103rd American Assembly.

Andriof, J. and M. McIntosh 2001. Introduction. In Andriof, J. and M. McIntosh (eds) *Perspectives on Corporate Citizenship*, pp. 13–24. Sheffield: Greenleaf Publishing.

Andriof, J., S. Waddock, B. Husted and S. Sutherland Rahman (eds) 2002. *Unfolding Stakeholder Thinking: Theory, Responsibility and Engagement*. Sheffield: Greenleaf Publishing.

Arblaster, A. 2002. *Democracy*. Buckingham: Open University Press.

Archibald, T., K. Jull and K. Roach 2004. The changed face of corporate criminal liability, *Criminal Law Quarterly*, 48, 367–396.

Armour, J., S. Deakin and S.J. Konzelmann 2003. Shareholder and the trajectory of UK corporate governance, *British Journal of Industrial Relations*, 41/3, 531–555.

Ashton, R.K. 1986. The Argyll Foods case: a legal analysis, *Accounting and Business Research*, 17/65, 3–12.

Associated Press 2005. Chamber chief attacks Spitzer, *Los Angeles Times*, 6 January.

Aurelius, M. 2002. *Meditations*. Translated by Gregory Hays. New York: Modern Library.

Ayres, I. and J. Braithwaite 1992. *Responsive Regulation, Transcending the Deregulation Debate*. Oxford: Oxford University Press.

Bakan, J. 2004. *The Corporation*. London: Constable.

Banks, A. 2002. ITIO accuses OECD of double standards, *Tax-News.com*, 15 February 2002, http://www.tax-news.com/asp/story/story_print.asp?storyname=7327

Barlow, M. and T. Clark 2002. *Global Showdown: How the New Activists are Fighting Corporate Rule*. Toronto: Stoddart.

Barnard, J.W. 1997. Corporate philanthropy, executives' pet charities and the agency problem, *New York Law School Law Review*, 41/3, 1147.

Baumeister, R.F. 1991. *Meanings of Life*. New York: Guilford Press.

Beetham, D. 1991. *The Legitimation of Power*. London: Macmillan.

Berle, A. 1931. Corporate powers as powers in trust, *Harvard Law Review*, 44/7, 1049–1074.

Berle, A. and G. Means 1932. *The Modern Corporation and Private Property*. New York: Commerce Clearing House Inc.

Berle, A.A. and C.G. Means 1936. *The Modern Corporation and Private Property*. New York: Macmillan.

Beyer, J. and M. Hoepner 2003. The disintegration of organised capitalism: German corporate governance in the 1990s, *West European Politics*, 26/4, 179–198.

Bhagavad Gita 2000. Translated by Stephen Mitchell. New York: Harmony Books.

Bianco, M. and P. Casavola 1999. Italian corporate governance: effects on financial structure and firm performance, *European Economic Review*, 43, 1057–1069.

Bianchi, M., M. Bianco and L. Enriques 1997. Ownership, pyramidal groups and separation between ownership and control in Italy. In European Corporate Governance Network, The Separation of Ownership and Control: A Survey of 7 European Countries. Preliminary Report to the European Commission. Brussels: ECGN.

Bittle, S. 2004. Constituting the corporate criminal: corporate criminal liability in post-Westray Canada. Unpublished Paper, Department of Sociology, Queen's University.

Black, C. 2003. *Franklin Delano Roosevelt, Champion of Freedom*. London: Phoenix Books.

Bloch, P. 1996. *Stewardship: Choosing Service over Self Interest*. San Francisco: Berrett-Koehler Publications.

Bloomberg 2004. Citigroup to set aside $4.95 billion for litigation, www.bloomberg.com, 10 May.

Blumberg, P.I. 1972. *Corporate Responsibility in a Changing Society*. Boston: Boston University.

Bolman, L.G. and T.E. Deal 1997. *Reframing Organizations: Artistry, Choice and Leadership*. San Francisco: Jossey-Bass Publishers.

Bower, T. 1992. *Maxwell: The Outsider*. London: BCA.

Braithwaite, J. 1989. *Crime, Shame and Reintegration*. Cambridge: Cambridge University Press.

Braithwaite, J. and P. Drahos 2000. *Global Business Regulation*. Cambridge: Cambridge University Press.

Bratton, W.W. 2004. Rules, principles and the accounting crisis in the United States, *European Business Organization Law Review*, 5/1.

Braudy, L. 1986. *The Frenzy of Renown: Fame and Its History*. New York: Oxford University Press.

Bryson, J.M. 1992. *Leadership for the Common Good: Tackling Public Problems in a Shared-power World*. San Francisco, Ca: Jossey-Bass.

Burke, J.P. 1986. *Bureaucratic Responsibility*. Baltimore: Johns Hopkins University Press.

Calavita, K. 1983. The demise of the Occupational Safety and Health Administration: a case study in symbolic action, *Social Problems* 30/4, 437–448.

Calavita, K., H. Pontell and R. Tillman 1997. *Big Money Crime: Fraud and Politics in the Savings and Loan Crisis*. Berkeley: University of California Press.

Cardia, L. 2004. I rapporti tra il sistema delle imprese, i mercati finanziari e la tutela del risparmio, Testimony of the C.O.N.S.O.B. President at Parliament Committees VI 'Finanze' and X 'Attività produttive, commercio e turismo' della Camera and 6° 'Finanze e Tesoro' and 10° 'Industria, commercio e turismo' del Senato, 20 January.

CARICOM 2000a. Press release 91/2000, *Communique Issued on the Conclusion of the 21st Meeting of the Conference of Heads of Government of the Caribbean Community (CARICOM)*, Canouan, St Vincent and the Grenadines, 2–5 July 2000, http://www.caricom.org/pres91_00.htm

CARICOM 2000b. Press release 87/2000, *Address delivered by Sir James Mitchell, Prime Minister of St Vincent and the Grenadines, at the Opening Ceremony of the 21st Meeting of the Conference of Heads of Government of the Caribbean Community (CARICOM)*, Canouan, St Vincent and the Grenadines, 2 July 2000, http://www.caricom.org/pres87_00.htm

Carroll, A.B. 1991. The pyramid of corporate social responsibility: toward the moral management of organizational stakeholders, *Business Horizons*, 34/4, 39–48.

Carroll, A.B. 2001. The moral leader: essential for successful corporate citizenship. In Andriof, J. and M. McIntosh (eds) *Perspectives on Corporate Citizenship*, pp. 139–151. Sheffield: Greenleaf Publishing.

Carson, W. 1970. White collar crime and the enforcement of factory legislation, *British Journal of Criminology*, 10, 383–398.

Carson, W. 1980. The institutionalization of ambiguity: early British Factory Acts. In Geis, G. and E. Stotland (eds) *White-collar Theory and Research*. Beverly Hills, Ca: Sage.

Carter, S.L. 1996. *Integrity*. New York: Basic Books.

Catanach, A. and S. Rhoades 2003. Enron: a financial reporting failure?, *Villanova Law Review*, 48/4, 1057–1076.

Center for Freedom and Prosperity 2001. *CFP Halls of Fame and Shame, May 23 Edition*, Washington DC, http://www.freedomandprosperity.org/hall/hall.shtml

Cernetig, M. 2002. Witch hunt on Wall Street?, *Globe & Mail*, 1 June, F8.

Cerny, P. 2002. Webs of governance and the privatisation of transnational regulation. In Andrews, D., C. Randall Henning and L. Pauly (eds) *Governing the World's Money*. Ithaca: Cornell University Press.

Chandler, W. and L. Strine 2002. The New Federalism of the American corporate governance system: preliminary reflections of two residents of one small state. New York University Center for Law and Business, Working Paper No. CLB 03-01. Available online at http://papers.ssrn.com/abstract=367720

Cheffins, B.R. 2000. Current trends in corporate governance: going from London to Milan via Toronto, *Duke Journal of Comparative and International Law*, 10/5, 5–42.

Chen, P. 2003. The institutional sources of state success in federal litigation before the Supreme Court, *Law and Policy*, 55/4, October, 455–472.

Childs, J. and S. Rodrigues 2003. Corporate governance and new organizational forms: issues of double and multiple agency, *Journal of Management and Governance*, 7, 337–360.

Church, E. 2004. Who's standing up for the investor?, *Globe & Mail*, 22 June, B9.

Cioffi, J.W. 2000. Governing globalisation? The state, law, and structural change in corporate governance, *Law and Governance*, 27.

Cioffi, J.W. 2002. Restructuring 'Germany Inc.': the politics of company and takeover law reform in Germany and the European Union, Working Paper PEIF-1.

Citigroup 2004. Code of ethics. www.citigroup.com

Clarkson, M.B.E. 1995. A stakeholder framework for analyzing and evaluating corporate social performance, *Academy of Management Review*, 20/1, 92–117.

Clarkson, S. 2002. *Uncle Sam and Us: Globalization, Neoconservativisms and the Canadian State*. Toronto: University of Toronto Press.

Clement, W. 1975. *The Canadian Corporate Elite*. Toronto: McClelland and Stewart.

CNDC-CNRC 2002. *Principi contabili*. Milan: Giuffré.

Coase, R.H. 1937. The nature of the firm, *Economica* (NS), 4, 386.

Coase, R.H. 1960. The problem of social cost, *Journal of Law and Economics*, 3, 1–44.

Coffee, J. 2002. Understanding Enron: it's about the gatekeepers, stupid, Columbia Law School Center of Law and Economic Studies Working Paper No. 207.

Coffee, J. 2003. What caused Enron. In Cornelius, P. and B. Kogut (eds) *Corporate Governance and Capital Flows in a Global Economy*. New York: Oxford University Press.

Coleman, J. 1989. *The Criminal Elite*. New York: St. Martin's.

Collins, J.C. 2001. *Good to Great*. New York: Harper Business.

Collins, J.C. and J.I. Porras 1997. *Built to Last: Successful Habits of Visionary Companies*. New York: Harper Business.

Commonwealth Secretariat 2000. *The Implications of the OECD Harmful Tax Competition Initiative for Offshore Finance Centres*, London.

Condon, M. 1998. *Making Disclosure: Ideas and Interests in Ontario Securities Regulation*. Toronto: University of Toronto Press.

Condon, M. 2003. The use of public interest enforcement orders by securities regulators in Canada, *Research Study Prepared for the Wise Persons' Committee*, October. Online at www.wise-averties.ca.

CONSOB 2002. *Relazione annuale 2001*. Rome: CONSOB.

Cooper, T. 1991. *An Ethics of Citizenship for Public Administration*. Englewood Cliffs, NJ. Prentice Hall.

Cooper, T. 1998. *The Responsible Administrator: An Approach to Ethics for the Administrative Role*, 4th edn. San Francisco, Ca: Jossey-Bass Publishers.

Cooper, T. and D.N. Wright 1992. *Exemplary Public Administrators: Character and Leadership in Government*. San Francisco: Jossey-Bass Publishers.

COSO Report 1987. Report of the National Commission on Fraudulent Financial Reporting.

COSO Report 1999. Fraudulent financial reporting: 1987–1997 – an analysis of U.S. public companies.

Csikszentmihalyi, M. 2003. *Good Business: Leadership, Flow, and the Making of Meaning*. New York: Viking.

Dagan, T. 2002. The costs of international tax competition, University of Michigan Law, Public Law Research Paper No. 13, http://papers.ssrn.com/sol3/papers.cfm?abstract_id=315373

Dahl, R.A. 1972. A prelude to corporate reform, *Business and Society Review*, Spring, 17–23.

Daloz, L.A., C.H. Parks, J.P. Keen and S.D. Parks 1996. *Common Fire: Leading Lives of Commitment in a Complex World*. Boston: Beacon Press.

Damsell, K. 2004. IFIC lobbies for grants, critics charge, *Globe & Mail*, 22 June, B.

Davis, K. 1960. Can business afford to ignore social responsibilities?, *California Management Review*, 2/3, 70–76.

Davies, P.L. 2003. *Gower and Davies: Principles of Modern Company Law*. London: Sweet & Maxwell.

Demirag, I. and J. O'Brien 2004. Conflicting and conflating interests in the regulation and governance of the financial markets in the United States, *Journal of Corporate Citizenship*, 15, Autumn, 111–119.

Denhardt, K.G. 1988. *The Ethics of Public Service: Resolving Moral Dilemmas in Public Organizations*. New York: Greenwood Press.

Denhardt, R.B. 1989. *In the Shadow of Organization*. Lawrence, Kan.: University of Kansas Press.

Denhardt, R.B. 1993, 2000. *The Pursuit of Significance: Strategies for Managerial Success in Public Organizations*. Prospect Heights, Ill.: Waveland Press.

Department of Finance Canada 2003. Fostering confidence in Canada's capital markets. Online at www.fin.gc.ca/activty/pubs/fostering_e.html

Department of Justice Canada 2003. Backgrounder: federal strategy to deter serious capital market fraud. Online at www.canada.justice.gc.ca

Dobel, J.P. 1999. *Public Integrity*. Baltimore: Johns Hopkins Press.

Doern, B. and S. Wilks 1996. Conclusions: international convergence and national contrasts. In Doern, B. and S. Wilks (eds) *Comparative Competition Policy: National Institutions in a Global Market*, pp. 327–359. Oxford: Clarendon Press.

Doern, B. and S. Wilks 1998. Introduction. In Doern, B. and S. Wilks (eds) *Changing Regulatory Institutions in Britain and North America*, pp. 3–25. Toronto: University of Toronto Press.

Doig, J.W. and E. Hargrove (eds) 1986. *Leadership and Innovation: A Biographical Perspective on Entrepreneurs in Government*. Baltimore: Johns Hopkins University Press.

Donaldson, W. 2004. Chairman of the Securities and Exchange Commission speech to Business Roundtable, Washington DC, 14 October 2004. Full text available at www.sec.gov/new/speech/spch101404whd.htm

Donaldson, W. 2005. Chairman of the Securities and Exchange Commission speech to London School of Economics, London, 25 January 2005. Full text available at www.sec.gov/new/speech/spch012505whd.htm

Draghi reform 1998. Testo unico delle disposizioni in materia di intermediazione finanziaria, Legislative decree No. 58/1998.

Dyck, A. and L. Zingales 2003. The bubble and the media. In Cornelius, P. and B. Kogut (eds) *Corporate Governance and Capital Flows in a Global Economy*. New York: Oxford University Press.

Easterbrook, F.H. and D.R. Fischel 1989. The corporate contract, *Columbia Law Review*, 89, 1416–1448.

Eccles, R.G. and S. DiPiazza, Jr 2002. *Building Public Trust: The Future of Corporate Reporting*. Chichester: John Wiley & Sons.

Edelman, L., C. Uggen and H. Erlanger 1999. The endogeneity of legal regulation: grievance procedures as rational myth, *The American Journal of Sociology*, 105/2, 404–454.

Edelman, M. 1960. Symbols and political quiescence, *The American Political Science Review*, 54/3 (September), 695–704.

Edelman, M. 1964. *The Symbolic Uses of Politics*. Urbana: University of Illinois Press.

Ehrenreich, B. 2000. *Nickel and Dimed: On (Not) Getting By in America*. New York: Metropolitan Books.

Eisenberg, M.A. 1998. Corporate conduct that does not maximize shareholder gain: legal conduct, ethical conduct, the penumbra effect, reciprocity, the prisoner's dilemma, sheep's clothing, social conduct, and disclosure, *Stetson Law Review*, 28, 1.

Elkington, J. 1997. *Cannibals with Forks: The Triple Bottom Line of 21st Century Business*. Oxford: Capstone.

Ernst & Young 1997. *UK GAAP*. Basingstoke: Macmillan.

Estreicher, S. 1998. Employee representation in the emerging workplace: alternative/supplements to collective bargaining, *Proceedings of New York University 50th Annual Conference on Labor*.

European Commission Report on the Social Situation of the European Union 2004.

Fama, E. 1988. Agency problems and the theory of the firm, *Journal of Political Economy*, 88, 288.

Fama, E. 1991. Efficient capital markets, *Journal of Finance*, 46, 1575.

FASB 1996. Statement of Financial Accounting Standards (SFAS) 125 'Accounting for transfers and servicing of financial assets and extinguishment of liabilities'.

FASB 2002. Proposal: principles-based approach to U.S. standard setting. File reference No. 1125-001, Norwalk, CT: FASB.

Feintuck, M. 2004. *The Public Interest in Regulation*. Oxford: Oxford University Press.

Financial Reporting Council (FRC) 1991. *The State of Financial Reporting: A Review*. London: FRC.

Fletcher, W.M. 1917. *Encyclopedia of the Law of Private Corporations*, New York: Thomson West.

Fooks, G. 2003. Auditors and the permissive society: market failure, globalization and financial regulation in the United States, *Risk Management: An International Journal*, 5/2, 17–26.

Forker, J. 1992. Corporate governance and disclosure quality, *Accounting and Business Research*, 22/86, 111–124.

Franck, T.M. 1988. Legitimacy in the international system, *American Journal of International Law*, 82/4, 705–759.

Franck, T.M. 1990. *The Power of Legitimacy Among Nations*. New York: Oxford University Press.

Freeman, R.E. 1994. The politics of stakeholder theory: some future directions, *Business Ethics Quarterly*, 4/4, 409–421.

Frieden, J. and R. Rogowski 1996. The impact of the international economy on national policies: an analytical overview. In Keohane, R. and H. Milner (eds) *Internationalization and Domestic Politics*. Cambridge University Press.

Friedman, M. 1962. *Capitalism and Freedom*. Chicago: University of Chicago Press.

Friedman, M. 1969. *Capitalism and Freedom*. Chicago: University of Chicago Press.

Friedman, M. 1995. The social responsibility of business is to increase its profits. In Hoffman, W.M. and R.E. Frederick (eds) *Business Ethics: Readings and Cases in Corporate Morality*, pp. 137–141. New York: McGraw Hill.

Fudge, J. and B. Cossman 2002. Introduction: privatization, law and the challenge to feminism. In Cossman, B. and J. Fudge (eds) *Privatization, Law and the Challenge to Feminism*. Toronto: University of Toronto Press.

Galbraith, J.K. 1952. *American Capitalism – The Concept of Countervailing Power*. Massachusetts: Riverside Press.

Galbraith, J.K. 1992. *The Great Crash*. London: Penguin.

Galbraith, J.K. 2004. *The Economics of Innocent Fraud*. London: Penguin.

Gallagher, V.J. 2004. Memory as social action: cultural projections and generic form in civil rights monuments. In Sullivan, P.A. and S.R. Goldzwig (eds) *New Approaches to Rhetoric*. Thousand Oaks, Ca: Sage.

Gamble, A. and G. Kelly 1996. The new politics of ownership, *New Left Review*, 62–97.

Gamble, A. and G. Kelly 2000. The politics of the company. In Parkinson, J., A. Gamble and G. Kelly (eds) *The Political Economy of the Company*, pp. 21–49. Oxford: Hart Publishing.

Garrett, G. and P. Lange 1996. Internationalization, institutions and political change. In Keohane, R. and H. Milner (eds) *Internationalization and Domestic Politics*, pp. 48–78. Cambridge University Press.

Gerber, B. and P. Teske 2000. Regulatory policymaking in the American states: a review of theories and evidence, *Political Research Quarterly*, 53/4, 849–886.

Giddens, A. 1998. *The Third Way*. Cambridge: Polity Press.

Gilligan, G.P. 1999. *Regulating the Financial Services Sector*. London: Kluwer Law International.

Gilligan, G.P. 2003. Whither or wither the European Union Savings Tax Directive? A case study in the political economy of taxation, *Journal of Financial Crime*, 11/1, 56–72.

Gladwell, M. 2002. *The Tipping Point: How Little Things Can Make a Big Difference*. New York: Little Brown and Company.

Glasbeek, H. 2002. *Wealth by Stealth. Corporate Crime, Corporate Law and the Perversion of Democracy*. Toronto: Between the Lines.

Global Forum on Taxation 2004. A process for achieving a global level playing field, http://www.oecd.org/dataoecd/13/0/31967501.pdf

Godfrey, M. 2004. Accenture may lose out in US offshore tax debate, *Tax news.com*, http://www.tax-news.com/asp/story/story.asp?storyname=16311

Goodsell, C. 1988. *The Social Meaning of Civic Space: Studying Political Authority through Architecture*. Lawrence, Kan.: University Press of Kansas.

Goodwin, B. 1997. *Using Political Ideas*. Chichester: John Wiley & Sons.

Gordan, J.N. 2002. An international relations perspective on the convergence of corporate governance: German shareholder capitalism and the European Union, 1990–2000. Johann Wolfgang Goethe-University: Frankfurt am Main, Working Paper No. 108.

Gordon, R. 2004. Why Europe was left at the station when America's productivity locomotive departed?, *NBER Working Paper Series w10661*, August 2004.

Gormley, W. 1986. Regulatory issue networks in a federal system, *Polity*, 18, 595–620.

Gourevitch, P. 2003a. Corporate governance: global markets, national politics. In Kahler, M. and D. Lake (eds) *Governance in a Global Economy*, pp. 305–331. Princeton.

Gourevitch, P. 2003b. The politics of corporate governance regulation, *The Yale Law Journal*, May, 112/7, 1829–1880.

Gramsci, A. 1998. *Selections from the Prison Notebooks*. London: Lawrence and Wishart.

Green, R. 1993. Shareholders as stakeholders: changing metaphors of corporate governance, *Washington and Lee Law Review*, 50, 1415.

Greenleaf, R.K. 1977, 1998. *Servant Leadership: A Journey into the Nature of Legitimate Power and Greatness*. New York: Paulist Press.

Greenspan, A. 2004. 'Capitalizing reputation', remarks to Financial Markets Conference of Federal Reserve Board of Georgia, 16 April. Available online at http://www.federalreserve.gov/boarddocs/speeches/2004/

Griffiths, I. 1986. *Creative Accounting*. London: Sidgwick & Jackson.

Griffiths, I. 1995. *New Creative Accounting*. London: Macmillan.

Haines, F. and D. Gurney 2003. The shadows of the law: contemporary approaches to regulation and the problem of regulatory conflict, *Law and Policy* 25/4, 353–379.

Hall, P. and D. Soskice (eds) 2001. *Varieties of Capitalism: The Institutional Foundation of Comparative Advantage*. Oxford: Oxford University Press.

Hamel, J., S. Dufour and D. Fortin 1993. *Case Study Methods*. Newbury Park, CA: Sage Publications.

Hancher, L. and M. Moran 1989. Organizing regulatory space. In Hancher, L. and M. Moran (eds) *Capitalism, Culture and Regulation*. Oxford: Oxford University Press.

Hansmann, H. and R. Kraakman 2002. Towards a single model of corporate law? In McCahery, P., P. Moreland, T. Raajimakers and L. Renneboog (eds) *Corporate Governance Regimes: Convergence and Diversity*, pp. 56–82. Oxford: Oxford University Press.

Hedge, D. and M. Scicchitano 1994. Regulating in space and time: the case of regulatory federalism, *The Journal of Politics*, 56/1, 134–153.

Held, D. 1999. *Democracy and the Global Order*. Cambridge: Polity Press.

Held, V. 1970. *The Public Interest and Individual Interests*. New York: Basic Books.

Henderson, D. 2001. *Misguided Virtue: False Notions of Corporate Social Responsibility*. London: Institute of Economic Affairs.

Hertz, N. 2002. *The Silent Takeover: Global Capitalism and the Death of Democracy*. London: Arrow Books.

Hester, J.M. 1975. Social responsibility of organisations in a free society. In Backman, J. (ed.) *Social Responsibility and Accountability*. New York: New York University Press.

Hirst, P. 1998. Ownership and democracy, *The Political Quarterly*, 69/4, 354–364.

Hodge, P. 2003. *A Labour Economy: Are We Nearly There Yet?* IPPR.

Hoepner, M. 2003. European corporate governance reform and the German party paradox, MPIfG Discussion Paper 3/4.

Hollingsworth, J.R. and R. Boyer 1997. *Contemporary Capitalism, The Embeddedness of Institutions*. Cambridge: Cambridge University Press.

Hood, C. 1998. The Art of the State: Culture, Rhetoric and Public Management. Oxford: Clarendon Press.

Hood, C., H. Rothstein and R. Baldwin 2004. *The Government of Risk*. Oxford: Oxford University Press.

Howlett, K. 2003. Culture encouraged secrecy, *Globe & Mail*, 28 June: B1.

Howlett, K. 2004a. IDA says complaints soared 41% last year, *Globe & Mail*, 27 January: B1, B5.

Howlett, K. 2004b. OSC urges Securities Bill change, *Globe & Mail*, 11 March, B7.

Howlett, K. and J. McFarland 2004. OSC says enforcement a priority, *Globe & Mail*, 30 March, B10.

Huber, J.D. and C.R. Shipan 2002. *Deliberate Discretion: The Institutional Foundations of Bureaucratic Autonomy*. Cambridge, UK: Cambridge University Press.

IASB 2003. *International Financial Reporting Standards*. London: IASCF.

IE Staff 2004. OSC chairman urges cooperative approach to fighting economic crime, *Investment Executive*, May 27, online.

Ireland, P. 1996. Corporate governance, stakeholding, and the company: towards a less degenerate capitalism?, *Journal of Law and Society*, 23/3, 287–320.

Ireland, P. 1999. Company law and the myth of shareholder ownership, *Modern Law Review*, 62/1, 32–57.

Ireland, P. 2000. Defending the rentier: corporate theory and the reprivatisation of the public company. In Parkinson, J., A. Gamble and G. Kelly (eds) *The Political Economy of the Company*, pp. 140–173. Oxford: Hart Publishing.

ITIO 2002. ITIO seeks OECD commitment to level playing field, 12 February 2002, http://www.itio.org/news.htm#

Jackall, R. 1988. *Moral Mazes: The World of Corporate Managers*. New York: Oxford University Press.

Jackson, G. 2001. The origins of nonliberal corporate governance in Germany and Japan. In Streeck, W. and K. Yamanura (eds) *The Origins of Non-liberal Capitalism*, pp. 121–170. Ithaca: Cornell University Press.

Janeba, E. and G. Schjelderup 2002. Why Europe should love tax competition – and the U.S. even more so, NBER Working Paper No. 9334, Cambridge, Mass.

Jeffrey, M. 1995. The Commission proposals on 'atypical work': back to the drawing board…again, *Industrial Law Journal*, 24, 296.

Jensen, M.C. and M. Meckling 1976. Theory of the firm: managerial behaviour, agency costs and ownership structure, *Journal of Financial Economics*, 3, 305.

Jessop, B. 2003. *The Future of the Capitalist State*. Oxford: Blackwell Publishing.

Johnson, L. 2002. Reclaiming an ethic of corporate responsibility, *George Washington Law Review*, 70, 957.

Jones, I. and M.G. Pollitt 2002. Who influences debates in business ethics? An investigation into the development of corporate governance in the UK since 1990. In Jones, I. and M.G. Pollitt (eds) *Understanding Business Ethics Development*. Basingstoke: Palgrave.

Kass, H. 1990. Stewardship as fundamental element in image of public administration. In Kass, H. and B. Catron (eds) *Images and Identities in Public Administration*, pp. 113–130. Newbury Park, Ca: Sage Publications.

Kaufmann, D. 2003. Rethinking governance, empirical lessons challenge orthodoxy. Online at: http://www.worldbank.org/wbi/governance/

Keast, R., M.P. Mandell, K. Brown and G. Woolcock 1994. Network structures working differently and changing expectations, *Public Administration Review*, May/June, 64/3, 363–371.

Kelling, G.L. 1999. *Broken Windows and Police Discretion*. Washington DC: US Department of Justice, Office of Justice Programs, National Institute of Justice.

Kelly, G. and J. Parkinson 2000. The conceptual foundations of the company: a pluralist approach. In Parkinson, J., A. Gamble and G. Kelly (eds) *The Political Economy of the Company*, pp. 113–139. Oxford: Hart Publishing.

Kelman, M. 1979. Consumption theory, production theory and ideology in the Coase theorem, *Southern California Law Review*, 52, 669.

Kettl, D.F. 2000. *The Global Public Management Revolution: A Report on the Transformation of Governance*. Washington DC: Brookings Institution Press.

Kidder, T. 1997. *The Soul of a New Machine*. New York: Modern Library.

Klein, N. 2000 *No Logo: Taking Aim at the Brand Bullies*. New York: Picador.

Kotter, J.P. 1996. *Leading Change*. Cambridge, Mass.: Harvard Business School Press.

Kraakman, R. 1986. Gatekeepers: the anatomy of a third-party enforcement strategy, *Journal of Law, Economics and Organisations*, 2/1, 53–104.

Kurtz, H. 2002. On CNBC, boosters for the boom, *Washington Post*, 12 November.

Labaton, S. 2005. Quick, early gains embolden business lobby, *New York Times*, 18 February.

Lannoo, K. 1999. A European perspective on corporate governance, *Journal of Common Market Studies*, 37/2, 269–294.

La Porta, R., F. Lopez-de-Silanes, A. Schleifer and R.W. Vishny 1997. Legal determinants of external finance, *Journal of Finance*, 52, 1131.

La Porta, R., F. Lopez-de-Silanes, A. Schleifer and R.W. Vishny 1998. Law and finance, *Journal of Political Economy*, 106, 1113.

La Porta, R., F. Lopez-de-Silanes, A. Schleifer and R.W. Vishny 1999. Corporate ownership around the world, *Journal of Finance*, 54, 471.

La Porta, R., F. Lopez-de-Silanes, A. Schleifer and R.W. Vishny 2000. Investor protection and corporate governance, *Journal of Financial Economics*, 58/1, 3–27.

Leonhardt, D. 2002. How will Washington read the signs?, *New York Times*, 10 February, Money & Business, 1.

Levitt, A. 2003. *Take on the Street*. New York: Pantheon Books.

Lewis, N. 1996. *Choice and the Legal Order*. London: Butterworths.

Leys, C. 2003. *Market-driven Politics: Neoliberal Democracy and the Public Interest*. London: Verso.

Lindblom, C. 2001. The Market System. New Haven: Yale University Press.

Lowestein, R. 2004. *Origins of the Crash*. New York: The Penguin Press.

Lowry, W. 1992. *The Dimensions of Federalism*. Durham, NC: Duke University Press.

Lynch-Fannon, I. 2003. *Working Within Two Kinds of Capitalism*. Oxford: Hart Publications.

Lynch-Fannon, I. 2004. Employees as corporate stakeholders: theory and reality in a transatlantic context, *Journal of Corporate Law Studies*, 4, 155.

Lynn, L.E. 1987. *Managing Public Policy*. Boston: Little Brown.

Macbeth, M. 1985. Reining in the cowboys, *Canadian Business*, May.

Mackay R. and M. Smith 2004. Bill C-13: an Act to amend the Criminal Code (Capital Markets Fraud and Evidence-Gathering). Ottawa: Parliamentary Research Branch, Legislative summary, LS-468E.

Manville, B. and J. Ober 2003a. Beyond empowerment: building a company of citizens, *Harvard Business Review*, 8, 48–53.

Manville, B. and J. Ober 2003b. *A Company of Citizens: What the World's First Democracy Teaches Leaders about Creating Great Organisations*. Boston, Mass.: Harvard Business School Press.

Mather, L. 1998. Theorizing about trial courts: lawyers, policymaking and tobacco litigation, *Law and Social Inquiry*, 23, 897–940.

Maw, N.G. 1994. *Corporate Governance*. Aldershot: Dartmouth.

McBarnet, D. 1984. Law and capital: the role of legal form and legal actors. In McBarnet, D. (ed.) *Law and Capital*, special issue of *International Journal of the Sociology of Law*, 12, Academic Press, pp. 231–238.

McBarnet, D. 1988. Law, policy and legal avoidance, *Journal of Law and Society*, Spring 1988, 113–121.

McBarnet, D. 1991a. Whiter than white collar crime: tax, fraud insurance and the management of stigma, *British Journal of Sociology*, 42, 323–344.

McBarnet, D. 1991b. It's not what you do but the way that you do it: tax evasion, tax avoidance and the boundaries of deviance. In Downes, D. (ed.) *Unravelling Criminal Justice*, pp. 247–268, London: Macmillan.

McBarnet, D. 2003. When compliance is not the solution but the problem: from changes in law to changes in attitude. In Braithwaite, V. (ed) *Taxing Democracy*. Aldershot: Ashgate.

McBarnet, D. 2004a. The new corporate accountability. In Cragg, W. and C. Koggel (eds) *Contemporary Moral Issues* (new to 5th edn). Toronto: McGraw Hill Ryerson.

McBarnet, D. 2004b. *Crime, Compliance and Control*. Aldershot: Ashgate/Dartmouth.

McBarnet, D. and C. Whelan 1991. The elusive spirit of the law: formalism and the struggle for legal control, *Modern Law Review*, November, 848–873.

McBarnet, D. and C. Whelan 1997. Creative compliance and the defeat of legal control: the magic of the orphan subsidiary. In Hawkins, K. (ed.) *The Human Face of Law*. Oxford: Oxford University Press.

McBarnet, D. and C. Whelan 1999. *Creative Accounting and the Cross-eyed Javelin Thrower*. Chichester: John Wiley & Sons.

McClam, E. 2005. Ex-CFO: earnings fell short for Ebbers, *Seattle Times*, E1, 6, 9 February.

McClaughry, J. 1972. Milton Friedman responds, *Business and Society Review*, 5.

McGraw, T. 1984. *Prophets of Regulation*. Harvard: Harvard University Press.

McIntosh, M., R. Thomas, D. Leipziger and G. Coleman 2003. *Living Corporate Citizenship: Strategic Routes to Socially Responsible Business*. London: Prentice Hall.

McLean, B. and P. Elkind 2004. *The Smartest Guys in the Room: The Amazing Rise and Scandalous Fall of Enron*. New York: Portfolio.

Mediobanca Research Industry 2003. Parmalat: too many uncertanties, 20 November.

Melis, A. 1999. *Corporate Governance. Un'analisi empirica della realtà italiana in un'ottica europea*. Torino: Giappichelli.

Melis, A. 2000. Corporate governance in Italy, *Corporate Governance – An International Review*, 8/4, 347–355.

Melis, A. 2004a. Financial reporting, corporate communication and governance, *Corporate Ownership and Control*, 1/2, Winter, 31–37.

Melis, A. 2004b. On the role of the Board of Statutory Auditors in Italian listed companies, *Corporate Governance – An International Review*, 12/1, 74–84.

Melis, G. 1995. Sulla natura economica dei valori iscritti nel nuovo bilancio europeo, *Annali della Facoltà di Economia di Cagliari*, XI, Milan: Angeli.

Merrill Lynch 2002. Parmalat: The Straws that Break the Camel's Back, In-depth Report, 5th December.

Millon, D. 1991. Redefining corporate law, *Indiana Law Review*, 24/2, 223–277.

Millon, D. 1993. *New Directions in Corporate Law*, 50 Washington and Lee Law Review 1373.

Millon, D. 2002. Why is corporate management obsessed with quarterly earnings and what should be done about it?, *George Washington Law Review*, 70, 890.

Minow, N. 1999. Corporate charity an oxymoron?, *The Business Lawyer*, 54/3, 997.

Mishra, R. 1999. *Globalization and the Welfare State*. Cheltenham: Edward Elgar.

Mitchell, D.J. 2001. CFP strategic memo, 16 June 2001, to: Leaders of Low-tax Jurisdictions and Supporters of Tax Competition, Financial Privacy, and Fiscal Sovereignty, Washington DC, http://www.freedomandprosperity. org/Papers/m06-16-01/m06-16-01.shtml

Mitchell, D.J. 2002. Death of the EU Savings Tax Directive, Center for Freedom and Prosperity Strategic Memorandum, 26 August 2002, Washington DC, http://www.freedomandprosperity.org/memos/m08-26-02/ m08-26-02.shtml

Mitchell, L. 1993. *Groundwork of the Metaphysics of Corporate Law*, 50 Washington and Lee Law Review 1477.

Mitchell, L. 1995. *Trust, Contract, Process*. In Mitchell, L. (ed.) *Progressive Corporate Law 185*. Boulder, CO: Westview Press.

Mitchell, L.E. 2001a. *Corporate Irresponsibility: America's Newest Export*. New Haven, London: Yale University Press.

Mitchell, L.E. 2001b. The importance of being trusted, *Boston University Law Review*, 81, 591.

Molteni, M. 1997. *I sistemi di corporate governance nelle grandi imprese italiane*. Milan: EGEA.

Monbiot, G. 2000. *The Captive State. The Corporate Takeover of Britain*. London: Macmillan.

Monbiot, G. 2001. *Captive State: The Corporate Takeover of Britain*. London: Pan Books.

Moran, M. 2003. *The British Regulatory State*. Oxford: Oxford University Press.

Morgan, B. 2003. *Social Citizenship in the Shadow of Competition: The Bureaucratic Politics of Regulatory Justification*. Aldershot: Ashgate.

Morgan, G. 1997. *Images of Organizations*. Thousand Oaks, Ca: Sage Publications.

Murphy, D. 2004. *The Structure of Regulatory Competition*. Oxford: Oxford University Press.

Naser, K. 1993. *Creative Financial Accounting. Its Nature and Use*. London: Prentice Hall.

New York Times 2005. Did the buck stop anywhere at WorldCom?, 4 March.

Norton, D. 1976. *Individual Destinies: A Philosophy of Ethical Individualism*. Princeton, NJ: Princeton University Press.

Nunan, R. 1988. The libertarian conception of corporate property: a critique of Milton Friedman's views on the social responsibility of business, *Journal of Business Ethics*, 7, 891–906.

Nuzum, C. and S. Pulliam 2005. WorldCom's ex-controller deals blow to Ebber's defense, *Wall Street Journal*, C-1, 28 January.

O'Brien, J. 2003. *Wall Street on Trial*. Chichester: John Wiley & Sons.

O'Brien, J. 2004a. Ethics, probity and the changing governance of Wall Street, cure or remission, *Public Integrity*, 7, Winter, 43–54.

O'Brien, J. 2004b. Beyond compliance, testing the limits of reforming the governance of Wall Street, *International Journal of Business Governance and Ethics*, 1:2/3, 162–174.

O'Brien, J. 2005. Ethics and corporate governance: banking on scandal, *International Journal of Business Governance and Ethics*, forthcoming.

O'Connor, M.A. 1991. Restructuring the corporation's nexus of contracts: recognizing a fiduciary duty to protect displaced workers, *Northern California Law Review*, 69, 1189.

O'Connor, M.A. 1993. How should we talk about fiduciary duty? Directors' conflict of interest transactions and the ALI's principles of corporate governance, *George Washington Law Review*, 61, 954.

O'Connor, M.A. 1995. Promoting justice in plant closings: explaining the fiduciary/contract law distinction to enforce implicit employment agreements. In Mitchell, L.E. 1995 (ed.) *Progressive Corporate Law*. Boulder, CO, Westview Press.

Ohmae, K. 1995. *The End of the Nation State: The Rise of Regional Economies*. London: Harper Collins.

Onida, P. 1968. *Economia d'azienda*. Turin: UTET.

Oricchio, G. 1997. Valenza informativa dei bilanci ordinari e teorie motivazionali e comportamentali degli amministratori: alcune riflessioni, *Rivista Italiana di Ragioneria e di Economia Aziendale*, 97, July–August.

Palepu, K. and P. Healy 2003. The fall of Enron, *Journal of Economic Perspectives*, 17/2, 3–26.

Parkinson, J. 2003. Preface to *Working Within Two Kinds of Capitalism*. Oxford: Hart Publications.

Parkinson, J., A. Gamble and G. Kelly 2000. *The Political Economy of the Company*. Oxford: Hart Publications.

Parkinson, J.E. 1996. *Corporate Power and Responsibility*. Oxford: Clarendon Press.

Parmalat Finanziaria SpA 1998, 1999, 2000, 2001, 2002. Annual reports.

Parmalat Finanziaria SpA 2001, 2002, 2003. Informativa sul sistema di Corporate Governance ai sensi della sezione IA.2.12 delle istruzioni al Regolamento di Borsa Italiana spa. (Report on corporate governance.)

Parmalat Finanziaria SpA 2003a. Interim reports.

Parmalat Finanziaria SpA 2003b. Investors' presentation, 10 April, available at www.parmalat.net.

Partnoy, F. 2002. The unregulated status of derivatives & Enron, testimony at hearings before the United States Senate Committee on Governmental affairs, 24 January 2002.

Partnoy, F. 2003. *Infectious Greed*. London: Profile Books.

Pattakos, A.N. 2004. The search for meaning in government service, *Public Administration Review*, 64/1, January/February, 106–113.

Pearce, F. and S. Tombs 1998. *Toxic Capitalism: Corporate Crime and the Chemical Industry*. Aldershot: Ashgate/Dartmouth.

Pearce, F. and S. Tombs 2003. 'Dance your anger and your joys': multinational corporations, power, 'crime'. In Sumner, C. (ed.) *Blackwell Companion to Criminology*. Oxford: Blackwell.

Perrin, S. 1999. Show how much you care, *Accountancy*, September, 44–45.

Perrow, C. 1993. *Complex Organizations A Critical Essay*, 23rd edn New York: McGraw-Hill.

Petrick, J.A. and J.F. Quinn 1997. *Management Ethics: Integrity at Work*. Thousand Oaks, Ca: Sage.

Phelps, M., H. McKay, T. Allen, P. Brunet, W. Dobson, E. Harris, M. Tims 2003. *It's Time: Report of the Committee to Review the Structure of Securities Regulation in Canada*. Canada: Department of Finance, 17 December (online at www.wise-averties.ca).

Philips, K. 2002. *Wealth and Democracy, A Political History of the American Rich*. New York: Broadway Books.

Pitt, H.L. 2002. Testimony concerning the Corporate and Auditing Accountability, Responsibility, and Transparence Act. Before the Committee of Financial Services United States House of Representatives, Washington DC, 20 March 2002.

Polanyi, K. 1944. *The Great Transformation*. New York: Rinehart.

Porter, J. 1965. *The Vertical Mosaic*. Toronto: University of Toronto Press.

Posner, R. 1976. *Antitrust Law*. Chicago: University of Chicago Press.

Posner, R. 1977. *Economic Analysis of Law*. 2nd edn. New York: Little Brown.

Powers, W.C. Jr 2002. Special Investigative Committee of the Board of Directors of Enron Corp, 'Report of Investigation', William C. Powers Jr, Chair, Raymond S. Troubh, Herbert S. Winokur, Jr, 1 February.

Preda Code 1999, 2002. *Codice di Autodisciplina*. Milan: Borsa Italiana.

Public Company Accounting Reform and Investor Protection Act of 2002, HR 3763. Washington DC.

Puri, P. 2001. Sentencing the criminal corporation, *Osgoode Hall Law Journal*, Summer/Fall, 39, 2/3, 612–653.

Raustalia, K. and A.M. Slaughter 2002. International law. International relations and compliance. In Carlsnaes, W., T. Risse, B. Simmons and T. Risse-Kappen (eds) *Handbook of International Relations*, pp. 538–558. Thousand Oaks, Ca: Sage Publications.

Rawls, J. 1971. *A Theory of Justice*. Cambridge, Mass.: Belknap Press, Harvard University Press.

Reich, R.B. 1998. The new meaning of corporate social responsibility, *California Management Review*, 40/2, 8–17.

Report on Business Magazine 2004. Advertising Supplement to *Report on Business*, June.

Report on Business Magazine 2004. *Report on Business*, July/August.

Roach, L. 2001. The paradox of the traditional justifications for exclusive shareholder governance protection: expanding the pluralist approach, *The Company Lawyer*, 22/1, 9–15.

Robertson, D.C. and N. Nicholson 1996. Expressions of corporate social responsibility in UK firms, *Journal of Business Ethics*, 15/10, 1095

Roe, M.J. 2002a. Can culture constrain the economic model of corporate law?, *University of Chicago Law Review*, 69, 1251.

Rogers, D. and M. Langley 2005. Bush set to sign landmark Bill on class actions, *Wall Street Journal*, 18 February, A1.

Rohr, J.A. 1998. *Public Service, Ethics and Constitutional Practice*. Lawrence, Kan.: University Press of Kansas.

Rohr, J.A. 2002. *Civil Servants and Their Constitutions*. Lawrence, Kan.: University Press of Kansas.

Romano, R. 2004. The Sarbanes-Oxley Act and the making of quack corporate governance, *European Corporate Governance Institute Finance Working Paper*, No. 52/2004.

Rose-Ackerman, S. 1992. *Rethinking the Progressive Agenda: The Reform of the American Regulatory State*. New York: Free Press.

Rosenblatt, M. 1984. In-substance defeasance removes long-term debt from balance sheet, *Corporate Finance* (Euromoney).

Rosoff, S., H. Pontell and R. Tillman 1998. *Profit Without Honor. White-collar Crime and the Looting of America*. New Jersey: Prentice Hall.

Rusconi, G.F. 1986. Induzione e deduzione nelle ricerche di econ- omia aziendale, *Rivista Italiana di Ragioneria e di Economia Aziendale*, May–June.

Saraceno, P. 1972. *Il governo delle aziende*. Venice: LUE.

Sassen, S. 1996. *Losing Control: Sovereignty in an Age of Globalization*. New York: Columbia University Press.

Schein, E.H. 1985. *Organizational Culture and Leadership*. San Francisco: Jossey Bass.

Schein, E.H. 1999. *The Corporate Culture Survival Guide*. San Francisco: Jossey-Bass Publishers.

Schmeling, T. 2003. Stag hunting with the State AG: anti-tobacco litigation and the emergence of cooperation among State Attorneys General, *Law and Policy*, 25/4, 429–454.

Schrecker, E. 2001. From the welfare state to the no-second-chances state. In Boyd, S., D. Chunn and R. Menzies (eds) *[Ab]using Power: The Canadian Experience*. Halifax: Fernwood.

Schwartz, M. 2002. A code of ethics for corporate codes of ethics, *Journal of Business Ethics*, 41:1/2.

Seliger, M. 2005. Spitzer's justice, *Vanity Fair*, January.

Seligman, J. 2003. *The Transformation of Wall Street, A History of the Securities and Exchange Commission and Modern Corporate Finance*. New York: Aspen.

Senge, P. 1990. *The Fifth Discipline: The Art and Practice of the Learning Organization*. Garden City, NJ: Prentice Hall.

Sennett, R. 1999. *The Corrosion of Character*. London: Norton.

Setting Analyst Standards: Recommendations for the Supervision and Practice of Canadian Securities Industry Analysts (October 2001). Toronto: Toronto Stock Exchange, Investment Dealers Association, Canadian Venture Exchange.

Shamir, R. 2004. Between self-regulation and the Alien Tort Claims Act: on the contested concept of corporate social responsibility, *Law & Society Review*, forthcoming.

Shapiro, I. 2003. *The State of Democratic Theory*. Princeton: Princeton University Press.

Shapiro, S. 1984. *Wayward Capitalists: Target of the Securities and Exchange Commission*. New Haven: Yale University Press.

Shapiro, S. 1990. Collaring the crime, not the criminal: reconsidering the concept of white-collar crime, *American Sociological Review*, 55, 123–140.

Sharpe, A. 1998. Income distribution in Canada in the 1990s: the offsetting impact of government on growing market inequality, *Canada Watch*, 6, June.

Sherman, N. 1989. *The Fabric of Character: Aristotle's Theory of Virtue*. Oxford: Clarendon Press.

Shinn, J. 2001. Private profit or public purpose? Shallow convergence on the shareholder model, Discussion Paper.

Shleifer, A. and R. Vishny 1986. Large shareholders and corporate control, *Journal of Political Economy*, Part 1, June, 461–489.

Slackman, M. 2004. Fund-raiser provides $3 million for Spitzer campaign, *New York Times*, 10 December.

Smith, A. 1884. *The Wealth of Nations*. London: T. Nelson and Sons.

Smith, H.W. 1997. If not corporate philanthropy, then what?, *New York Law School Law Review*, 41/3, 757.

Smith, T. 1992. *Accounting for Growth*. London: Century Business.

Snider, L. 1978. Corporate crime in Canada: a preliminary report, *Canadian Journal of Criminology*, 20/2, 178–202.

Snider, L. 1993. *Bad Business: Corporate Crime in Canada*. Scarborough, Ontario: Nelson.

Snider, L. 1996. Options for public accountability. In Mehta, M. (ed.) *Regulatory Efficiency and the Role of Risk Assessment*. Kingston, Ont.: School of Policy Studies, Queen's University.

Snider, L. 2000. The sociology of corporate crime: an obituary, *Theoretical Criminology*, 4/2, 169–205.

Snider, L. 2002. Theft of time: disciplining through science and law, *Osgoode Hall Law Journal*, 40/4, 1, 89–113.

Snider, L. 2004. Resisting neo-liberalism: the poisoned water disaster in Walkerton, Ontario, *Social and Legal Studies*, forthcoming.

Soloman, J. and I. Soloman 2004. *Corporate Governance and Accountability*. Chichester: John Wiley & Sons.

Sorensen, P.B. 2001. International tax coordination: regionalism versus globalism, CESifo Working Paper No.483, Munich.

Sparrow, M. 2000. *The Regulatory Craft*. Washington: Brookings Institution.

Spencer, P. 2000. *The Structure and Regulation of Financial Markets*. Oxford: Oxford University Press.

Spill, R., M. Licari and L. Ray 2001. Taking on tobacco: policy entrepreneurship and tobacco litigation, *Political Research Quarterly*, 54/3, 605–622.

Spitzer, E. 2000. The challenge of the New Federalism, 1 May 2000. Full text at www.oag.state.ny.us/press/statements

Spitzer, E. 2002. The crisis of accountability, 1 May 2002. Full text at www.oag.state.ny.us/press/statements

Spitzer, E. 2004. *Statement to Senate Committee on Governmental Affairs Subcommittee on Financial Management, the Budget and International Security*, Washington DC, 16 November. Full text at www.oag.state.ny.us/press/statements

Spitzer, E. 2005. Business ethics, regulation and the 'ownership society', *Remarks to National Press Club*, Washington DC, 31 January. Full text at www.oag.state.ny.us/press/statements

Stanbury, W. 1977. *Business Interests and the Reform of Canadian Competition Policy 1971–75*. Toronto: Carswell/Methuen.

Stanbury, W. 1986–87. The New Competition Act and Competition Tribunal Act: not with a bang but a whimper?, *Canadian Business Law Journal*, 12, 2–42.

Stanbury, W. 1995. Public policy towards individuals involved in competition-law offences in Canada. In Pearce, F. and L. Snider (eds) *Corporate Crime: Contemporary Debates*, pp. 214–244. Toronto: University of Toronto Press.

Stiglitz, J. 2003. *The Roaring Nineties*. New York: Norton.

Stikeman Elliott 2000. *Towards a Level Playing Field – Regulating Corporate Vehicles in Cross-Border Transactions*. London: Stikeman Elliott.

Stokes, M. 1986. Company law and legal theory. In Twining, W. (ed.) *Legal Theory and the Common Law*, pp. 155–183. Oxford: Oxford University Press.

Stone, C.D. 1975. *Where the Law Ends: The Social Control of Corporate Behaviour.* New York: Harper & Row.

Strange, S. 1986. *Casino Capitalism.* Manchester: Manchester University Press.

Streeck, W. and P. Schmitter 1985. Community, market, state and associations? The prospective contribution of interest governance to social order. In Streeck, W. and P. Schmitter (eds) *Private Interest Government.* London: Sage.

Strine, L. 2002. Derivative impact: some early reflections on the corporation law implications of the Enron debacle, *The Business Lawyer,* 57/4, 1371–1402.

Strum, P. 1992. *Brandeis. Beyond Progressivism.* Kansas: University Press of Kansas.

Stryker, R. 1994. Rules, resources, and legitimacy processes: some implications for social conflict, order and change, *The American Journal of Sociology,* 99/4, 847–910.

Subcommittee on Oversight and Investigations Hearing 2002a. The financial collapse of Enron – Part 3, Committee on Energy and Commerce, House of Representatives (107th Congress: 14 February 2002), Serial No. 107–89.

Subcommittee on Oversight and Investigations Hearing 2002b. The financial collapse of Enron – Part 4, Committee on Energy and Commerce, House of Representatives (107th Congress: 14 March 2002), Serial No. 107–90.

Suchman, M.C. 1995. Managing legitimacy: strategic and institutional approaches, *Academy of Management Review,* 20/3, 571–610.

Symposium 2002. *Corporate Irresponsibility: America's Newest Export,* 70, *George Washington Law Review.* Washington DC: George Washington University Law School.

Tao te Ching 1988. Translated by Stephen Mitchell. New York: Harper Perennial.

Tax-news.com 2001. Offshore jurisdictions give guarded welcome to OECD report, *Tax-News.com,* 16 November 2001, http://www.tax-news.com/

Tax-news.com 2003. Antigua queries IMF anti-money laundering methodology, *Tax-News.com,* http://www.tax-news.com/asp/story/story.asp?storyname=10711

Terry, L.D. 2003. *Leadership of Public Bureaucracies: The Administrator as Conservator.* Armonk, NY: M.E. Sharpe.

Teske, P. 2004. *Regulating the States.* Washington: Brookings Institution.

The Tribune 2000. 6 June.

Tombs, S. 1996. Injury, death and the deregulation fetish: the politics of occupational safety regulation in United Kingdom manufacturing industries, *International Journal of Health Services,* 26/2, 309–329.

Tombs, S. and D. Whyte 2003. Scrutinizing the powerful. In Tombs, S. and D. Whyte (eds) *Unmasking the Crimes of the Powerful,* pp. 3–48. New York: Peter Lang.

Tyler, T.R. 1990. *Why People Obey the Law.* New Haven: Yale University Press.

United Nations 1996. Resolution 51/59, 82nd Plenary Meeting, 12 December, Action Against Corruption & Annex International Code of Conduct for Public Officials; http://www.un.org/documents/ga/51/a51r059.htm (5/5/2003)

US General Accountability Office, February 26, 2004. Mandatory Audit Firm Rotation Study: Study Questionnaires, Responses, and Summary of Respondents' Comments. GAO-04-217. Washington DC.

US General Accountability Office, November 21, 2003. Public Accounting Firms: Required Study on the Potential Effects of Mandatory Audit Firm Rotation. GAO-04–216. Washington DC.

US General Accountability Office, July 30, 2003. Public Accounting Firms: Mandated Study on Consolidation and Competition. GAO-03-864. Washington DC.

US General Accountability Office, June 2003. Government Auditing Standards (2003 Revision). GAO-03-673G. Washington DC.

US General Accountability Office, January 2003. GAO Forum on Governance and Accountability: Challenges to Restore Public Confidence in US Corporate Governance and Accountability Systems. GAO-03-419SP. Washington DC.

US General Accountability Office, March 2002. Highlights of GAO's Corporate Governance, Transparency and Accountability Forum. GAO-02-494SP. Washington DC.

Vogel, D. 1986. National Styles of Regulation. Ithaca: Cornell University Press.

Vogel, S.K. 2002. The crisis of German and Japanese capitalism: stalled on the road to the liberal market model, Comparative Political Studies, 34/10.

Walker, D.M. November 2002. Integrity: restoring trust in American business and the accounting profession. Article based on a speech to the American Institute of Certified Public Accountants' leadership conference. Washington DC.

Walker, D.M. 2003. Challenges, character, and core values. Commencement Address, University of Pittsburgh Graduate School of Public and International Affairs, 26 April. www.gao.gov/cghome/pittsburgh.pdf (1/23/05).

Walker, D.M. 21 September 2004. Restoring trust after recent accountability failures. Conference on Governing the Corporation, Institute of Governing, Public Policy, and Social Research, Queen's University, Belfast, Northern Ireland.

Warren, R. 2002. The Purpose Driven Life. Grand Rapids: Zondervan.

Wedderburn, K.W. 1985. The legal development of corporate responsibility; for whom will corporate managers be trustees? In Hopt, K.J. and G. Teubner (eds) Corporate Governance and Directors' Liabilities. Berlin: Walter De Gruyter.

Wedderburn. K.W. 1993. Companies and employees: common law or social dimension?, Law Quarterly Review, 109, 220–262.

Weil, R. 2002. Fundamental causes of the accounting debacle at Enron: show me where it says I can't. Summary of Testimony for Presentation, 6 February 2002, the Committee on Energy and Commerce 10.

Werner, W. 1981. Corporation law in search of its future, Columbia Law Review, 81, 1611.

Whitehouse, L. 1998a. The home owner: citizen or consumer? In Bright, S. and J. Dewar (eds) *Land Law: Themes and Perspectives*, pp. 183–205. Oxford: Oxford University Press.

Whitehouse, L. 1998b. The current trend in consumerism and its impact on the rights of home owners. In Cowan, D. (ed.) *Housing: Participation and Exclusion*. Aldershot: Ashgate.

Whitehouse, L. 2003a. Corporate social responsibility as citizenship and compliance: initiatives on the domestic, European and global level, *Journal of Corporate Citizenship*, 11, 85–98.

Whitehouse, L. 2003b. Corporate social responsibility, corporate citizenship and the global compact: a new approach to regulating corporate social power, *Global Social Policy*, 3, 299–318.

Williamson, J. 2003. A Trade Union Congress perspective on the Company Law Review and Corporate Governance Reform since 1997, *British Journal of Industrial Relations*, 41/3, 511–530.

Williamson, O. 1993. Calculativeness, trust and economic organization, *Journal of Law and Economics*, 36, 453.

Willis, A. 2004. Even in a bear market, some fund managers saw a bonanza, *Globe & Mail*, 23 June, B9.

Wilson, G. 2000. Business, state, and community: 'responsible risk takers', New Labour, and the governance of corporate business, *Journal of Law and Society*, 27/1, 151–177.

Windram, B. and J. Song 2004. Non-executive directors and the changing nature of audit committees: evidence from UK audit committee chairmen, *Corporate Ownership and Control*, 1/3, 108–115.

Wise, C. 2002. Organizing for homeland security, *Public Administration Review*, 62/2, March/April, 131–144.

Wolf, J.B. 2004. *Harnessing the Holocaust: The Politics of Memory in France*. Stanford, Ca: Stanford University Press.

Wolf, S.R. 1990. *Freedom within Reason*. New York: Oxford University Press.

Wolfe, A. 1993. The modern corporation: private agent or public actor?, *Washington and Lee Law Review*, 50/4, 1673.

Won, S. 2004 OSC chairman urges cooperative approach to fighting economic crime, *Globe & Mail*, May 28, online.

Wood, D.J. 1991. Corporate social performance revisited, *Academy of Management Review*, 16/4, 691–718.

Wood, S. 2001. Business, government, and patterns of Labour policy in Britain and the Federal Republic of Germany. In Hall, P. and D. Soskice (eds) *Varieties of Capitalism: The Institutional Foundation of Comparative Advantage*, pp. 247–274. Oxford: Oxford University Press.

Wren, D.A. 1994. *The Evolution of Management Thought*, 4th edn. New York: John Wiley & Sons.

Yaron, G. 2002. *Canadian Shareholder Activism in an Era of Global Deregulation.* Vancouver: Shareholder Association for Research and Education, at www. share.ca.

Yew, M. 2003. Tough talk on insider trading, *Toronto Star*, 13 November: C1.

Yew, M. 2003. The insider trading story, *Toronto Star*, 14 November: C1, 3.

Yin, R.K. 1989. *Case Study Research. Design and Methods.* Newbury Park, Ca: Sage Publications.

Zadek, S. 1998. Balancing performance, ethics and accountability, *Journal of Business Ethics*, 17/13, 1421–1441.

Ziegler, J.N. 2001. Corporate governance in Germany: towards a new translational politics? In Weber, S. (ed.) *Globalisation and the European Political Economy*, pp. 197–228. New York: Columbia University Press.

Zimmerman, J. 2001. National–state relations: cooperative federalism in the twentieth century, *Publius: The Journal of Federalism*, 31/2, Spring, 15–30.

Reports

Communication from the Commission to the Council, the European Parliament, the Economic and Social Committee and the Committee of the Regions on the Social Policy Agenda. COM (2000) 379 [28.6.2000].

Communication from the Commission to the Council, the European Parliament, the Economic and Social Committee and the Committee of the Regions on Employment and Social Policies: a framework for investing in quality. COM (2001a) 313 [20.6.2001].

Communication from the Commission to the Council, the European Parliament, the Economic and Social Committee and the Committee of the Regions on Promoting Core Labour Standards and Improving Social Governance in the Context of Globalisation. COM (2001b) 416 [18.7.2001].

European Commission Report on the Social Situation of the European Union 2004.

Iskander, M.R. and N. Chamlou 2000. *Corporate Governance: A Framework for Implementation.* Washington DC: The World Bank.

OECD 1998. *Harmful Tax Competition – An Emerging Global Issue.* Paris: OECD.

OECD 2000. *Towards Global Tax Co-operation, Report to the 2000 Ministerial Council Meeting and Recommendations by the Committee on Fiscal Affairs, Progress in Identifying and Eliminating Harmful Tax Practices.* Paris: OECD.

OECD Steering Group on Corporate Governance 2001a. *Corporate Governance in OECD Member Countries: Recent Developments and Trends.* Paris: OECD.

OECD 2001b. *The OECD's Project on Harmful Tax Practices: The 2001 Progress Report.* Paris: OECD.

OECD 2002. *The OECD Issues. The List of Uncooperative Tax Havens*. Paris: OECD.

OECD 2003a. *Vanuatu Makes Commitment and is Removed from List of Uncooperative Tax Havens*. Paris: OECD.

OECD 2003b. *Nauru is Removed from List of Uncooperative Tax Havens*. Paris: OECD.

OECD 2004a. *Principles of Corporate Governance*. Paris: OECD.

OECD 2004b. *The OECD's Project on Harmful Tax Practices: The 2004 Progress Report*. Paris: OECD.

White Paper (2002) *Modernising Company Law* (Cmnd 5553).

Statutes, Regulations and Directives

Directive 2001/86/EC on Worker Participation on Boards of the European Company.

Directive 94/95 EC [1994] OJ L 254/64 as amended Directive 97/74 EC OJ L010/22 on European Works Councils.

Directive 96/34/EC [1996] OJ L145/4 on the Framework Agreement on Parental Leave.

Directive 89/391/EC (as amended) on Maternity Leave and Directive 96/34/EC on Parental Leave.

Directive 75/129 EC [1975] OJ L48/29 and Directive 98/59 EC [1998] OJ L225/16 on Acquired Rights of Employees on the Transfer of Undertakings.

National Labor Relations Act (1948) 29 USC 151-69, 1948.

Regulation 2157/2001 EC [2001] L294/I on the *Societas Europea*.

Index

Index compiled by Terry Halliday